DATE DUE

Social Psychology
in Life

Social Psychology in Life

Richard I. Evans
and
Richard M. Rozelle

University of Houston

Allyn and Bacon
Boston

Third printing . . . January, 1971

© Copyright 1970 by Allyn and Bacon, Inc. 470 Atlantic Avenue, Boston. All rights reserved. No part of this book may be reproduced in any form, or by any means, without permission in writing from the publisher.

Library of Congress Catalog Card Number: 79–97002.

Printed in the United States of America.

Contents

v

Acknowledgments

In the last analysis, the problem of compiling a book of readings reduces itself for the editors to successive approximations— selecting the largest possible number of appropriate reports, published and unpublished; reducing this to a somewhat smaller number; and then engaging in the difficult task of making a final judgment concerning those which might most profitably be included.

In this task, the editors wish to express their appreciation to Rice University Behavioral Science graduate student Charles Kasdorf. Mr. Kasdorf took on the task of serving as an assistant in helping us in the crucial, early approximation stages of this book. His interest and involvement went far beyond the time for which his services were contracted.

Also our thanks to Miss Miriam Thompson, who assisted us in a variety of chores connected with this venture (aside from her normal secretarial duties), including the final compiling and typing of the manuscript.

Our thanks are also accorded to all of the authors of the individual reports we included. Finally, we wish to thank the various publications and publishers who gave us permission to use these various reports, including Aldine Publishing Company, Doubleday, McGraw-Hill, Holt, Rinehart and Winston, *Journal of Social Issues, Journal of Abnormal and Social Psychology, Social Problems, Psychological Reports, American Psychologist, American Journal of Sociology, American Behavioral Scientist, Journal of Personality and Social Psychology, Journal of Psychology, and NAEB Journal.*

Introduction

At no period in the history of psychology has a challenge to one area of psychology been greater than is the present challenge to social psychology. The vast strides in the civil rights movement, the focus on the poverty problem, the problem of violence in our culture, and the assassinations of a number of significant political and social leaders in the recent past—all these present a tremendous challenge to the social psychologist in the university setting to at least provide perspective for his students on such developments. We feel strongly that this challenge should be met in introductory psychology courses in general, and in social psychology courses in particular.

In most textbooks for such courses, although the student is briefly exposed to at least some perspective on social problems of immediate interest to him, the social problems are frequently presented in the context of artificial, simulated, experimental situations, rather than in the context of real life. The student too often is asked to learn the rules and language of a "research game," and instead of having the opportunity to relate the principles of this game to significant real-life problems, he finds himself bogged down in learning the rules of the game for their own sake.

This situation as related to many college courses concerned with experimental methodology was described very bluntly by

Popper (1963) when he observed: "Every discipline as long as
it used the Aristotelian method of definition has remained arrested
in the state of empty verbiage and barren scholasticism, and the
degree to which the various sciences have been able to make
any progress depended on the degree to which they have been able
to get rid of this essentialist method." Unfortunately, even though
students might be profitably introduced to the value of pursuing
knowledge for its own sake, this value is disproportionately applied in too many of our textbooks and lectures in introductory
psychology courses. Too often this preoccupation with the "game
of science" for its own sake develops in students a negative
attitude toward the entire field of psychology, and thus they seek
other fields which will better satisfy their interest in human problems. Such students leave introductory psychology courses with
the feeling that while they may have mastered many technical
terms or symbols and the importance of the "scientific" method,
they have not gained any truly significant perspective concerning
crucial human problems.

The present volume is an attempt to assist in dealing with this
apparent void in the training of introductory psychology students.
We have attempted to compile from the behavioral science literature a group of what we believe are unusually provocative
examples of research or analysis that are primarily directed toward
assisting the student to learn how the insights of social psychology
can aid him in gaining perspective on complex social problems.

In reading nearly two hundred reports of such social psychological examinations of human problems in real-life settings, we
decided to classify them in two ways. One group of reports might
be described as reflecting analysis or participant-observation. We
have presented such reports in Part One. This section consists
of those reports in which a social event has occurred and a social
psychologist has interpreted the event in terms of his theoretical
knowledge, thus presenting an analysis of the event within a social
psychological framework. Such efforts, of course, are neither
more nor less sophisticated than the social psychologist making
the interpretation. An example of one of the reports of this type
that we included might be cited: When the student protest movements on campuses began to occur, Kenneth Keniston compiled

an interesting social psychological analysis of the student pro-
testors, providing a fascinating insight into their backgrounds.
Another example involves participant-observation in a social
event by social psychologists. Mark Chesler and Richard Schmuck
report their experiences as members of a "super-patriot" organization and the behaviors they observed while they were members
of this group.

Part Two of this volume presents a second general type of
report, one that deals with research efforts in which an experimental manipulation by the social investigator has been effected.
Here we are dealing with the type of report where, although a
real-life situation is involved, the principal investigator either has
been in a position to manipulate some independent variable, or
has taken advantage of some "natural event or manipulation" in
the sense that he systematically controls something in the situation
so he can study its effect. For example, included in this section
is a research study (in which we participated) dealing with the
effects of various types of persuasive communications. Although
we arranged to deal with this problem in a real-life setting, we
were fortunately in the position to manipulate systematically various kinds of persuasive messages delivered. Thus we were able
to compare the effects of fear vs. pleasant appeal on a group of
teenagers as an attempt was made to modify their dental hygiene
practices, and in the process validate a new measure of behavior
change.

Through the inclusion in this volume of a number of reports by
social psychologists which reflect these two general approaches to
the examination of human behavior in real-life settings, we hope
to provide the student in the introductory general or social psychology class with an opportunity to examine real-life applications
of some of the theoretical formulations, ideas, language, or research methodology that are used in this field. Thus it is our hope
that the student may be stimulated to develop a more sophisticated social psychological perspective with respect to the crucial
social problems around him. For example, if there are civil rights
protests going on in his community and he happens to be studying
attitude theory in the classroom, it seems to us important that he
be encouraged to relate this theory to the real-life event. The

reports we include in this volume provide models of some of the ways in which this can be done.

To state our rationale for this volume in a slightly different manner, we believe that social psychology, or for that matter perhaps any introductory psychology course, should not be taught in an academic vacuum. The present volume is intended to supplement the traditional content in introductory psychology courses by directing the student to the real-life problems he might equip himself to analyze as he functions in society.

Rather than describe in this brief introduction each of the various reports selected for inclusion in the present volume, we would like to call the reader's attention to a few of its characteristics. First of all, the reader will note that each of the reports is preceded by a brief statement designed to orient the student concerning the report that follows. Second, we have included a list of references (Appendix I) that is representative of reports which we encountered in our reading as we made our selections for this volume. Although this list of references is by no means exhaustive, we feel that the reports included may be of interest and benefit to the student who wishes to pursue additional reading within the spirit of the present volume.

We had considered the possibility of "keying" the specific reports in this volume to various concepts or sections included in introductory general or social psychology courses. After much deliberation, we concluded that such attempts at keying these reports would be misleading and perhaps result in needless confusion for both instructor and student. The reason for this is that by their very nature the types of analyses included in most of these reports transcend the type of specificity in content which would usually be involved in such keying. We would suggest that various reports be assigned to students and they be asked to evaluate them critically in terms of the on-going content of their course, be it in terms of their instructor's lecture or the assignment they may be reading at the moment in their primary textbook. For example, if attitude measurement is being considered at a particular point in the course, the problems relating to attitude measurement (whether or not they were reflected in any given report we have included) could be an interesting basis for critical analysis by the student. Likewise, if at another point in the course small group theory and research are being considered, any one of the selections could be a constructive backdrop for study by the student.

It is not our intention that this collection of readings violate the instructor's or student's justifiable concern with the distinction between solid experimentation and sound interpretation on one hand, and unfounded speculation on the other. We have in fact listed a group of sources (Appendix II) that we feel reflect sound discussions of research methodology. Any one of these might be profitably examined by the student as a basis for learning about research methods which can assist him in critically examining the reports included in the present volume.

RICHARD I. EVANS
RICHARD M. ROZELLE

PART ONE

Participant-Observation

Retrospective Analysis

Description

1

The Sources of
Student Dissent

KENNETH KENISTON

While this report does not in itself reflect an actual experimental effort, it is an attempt to meaningfully interpret data and theory gathered from a variety of different examinations of a challenging current social problem—student dissent on our college campuses. The need to truly understand the structure of student dissent is of extreme importance in order to avoid premature conclusions concerning it. The social psychologist can be a valuable analyst of this problem. Unfortunately, attempts to systematically investigate this contemporary movement have been few in number. This report represents one such attempt to reveal and describe in an orderly fashion some of the sources of student dissent. Keniston distinguishes between two basic types of dissenters: the alienated and the activist. From available data the author then proceeds to investigate the differences in background and orientation of these two types of student dissenters.

From: *Journal of Social Issues*, 23(3): 108–137, 1967. Reprinted by permission of the author and The Society for the Psychological Study of Social Issues.

The apparent upsurge of dissent among American college students is one of the more puzzling phenomena in recent American history. Less than a decade ago, commencement orators were decrying the "silence" of college students in the face of urgent national and international issues; but in the past two or three years, the same speakers have warned graduating classes across the country against the dangers of unreflective protest, irresponsible action, and unselective dissent. Rarely in history has apparent apathy been replaced so rapidly by publicized activism, silence by strident dissent.

This "wave" of dissent among American college students has been much discussed. Especially in the mass media—popular magazines, newspapers, and television—articles of interpretation, explanation, deprecation, and occasionally applause have appeared in enormous numbers. More important, from the first beginnings of the student civil rights movement, social scientists have been regular participant-observers and investigators of student dissent. There now exists a considerable body of research that deals with the characteristics and settings of student dissent (see Lipset and Altbach, 1966; Block, Haan and Smith, forthcoming; Katz, 1967; Peterson, 1967 for summaries of this research). To be sure, most of these studies are topical (centered around a particular protest or demonstration), and some of the more extensive studies are still in varying stages of incompletion. Yet enough evidence has already been gathered to permit tentative generalizations about the varieties, origins and future of student dissent in the nineteen sixties.

In the remarks to follow, I will attempt to gather together this evidence (along with my own research and informal observations) to provide tentative answers to three questions about student dissent today. First, what is the nature of student dissent in American colleges? Second, what are the sources of the recent "wave of protest" by college students? And third, what can we predict about the future of student dissent?

TWO VARIETIES OF DISSENT

Dissent is by no means the dominant mood of American college students. Every responsible study or survey shows apathy and privatism far more dominant than dissent (see, for example, News-week, 1965; Katz, 1965; Reed, 1966; Peterson, 1966; Block, Haan and Smith, forthcoming). On most of our twenty-two hun-dred campuses, student protest, student alienation, and student unrest are something that happens elsewhere, or that characterizes a mere handful of "kooks" on the local campus. However we define "dissent," overt dissent is relatively infrequent and tends to be concentrated largely at the more selective, "progressive," and "academic" colleges and universities in America. Thus, Peterson's study of student protests (1966) finds political demonstrations concentrated in the larger universities and institutions of higher academic caliber, and almost totally absent at teachers colleges, technical institutes and non-academic denominational colleges. And even at the colleges that gather together the greatest number of dissenters, the vast majority of students—generally well over 95%—remain interested onlookers or opponents rather than active dissenters. Thus, whatever we say about student dissenters is said about a very small minority of America's six million college stu-dents. At most colleges, dissent is not visible at all.

Partly because the vast majority of American students remain largely uncritical of the wider society, fundamentally conformist in behavior and outlook, and basically "adjusted" to the prevailing collegiate, national, and international order, the small minority of dissenting students is highly visible to the mass media. As I will argue later, such students are often distinctively talented; they "use" the mass media effectively; and they generally succeed in their goal of making themselves and their causes highly visible. Equally important, student dissenters of all types arouse deep and ambivalent feelings in non-dissenting students and adults—envy, resentment, admiration, repulsion, nostalgia, and guilt. Such feel-ings contribute both to the selective over-attention dissenters re-ceive and to the often distorted perceptions and interpretations of them and their activities. Thus, there has developed through the mass media and the imaginings of adults a more or less stereotyped —and generally incorrect—image of the student dissenter.

The Stereotyped Dissenter

The "stereotypical" dissenter as popularly portrayed is both a bohemian and political activist. Bearded, be-Levi-ed, long-haired, dirty and unkempt, he is seen as profoundly disaffected from his society, often influenced by "radical" (Marxist, Communist, Maoist, or Castroite) ideas, an experimenter in sex and drugs, unconventional in his daily behavior. Frustrated and unhappy, often deeply maladjusted as a person, he is a "failure" (or as one U.S. Senator put it, a "reject"). Certain academic communities like Berkeley are said to act as "magnets" for dissenters, who selectively attend colleges with a reputation as protest centers. Furthermore, dropouts or "non-students" who have failed in college cluster in large numbers around the fringes of such colleges, actively seeking pretexts for protest, refusing all compromise and impatient with ordinary democratic processes.

According to such popular analyses, the sources of dissent are to be found in the loss of certain traditional American virtues. The "breakdown" of American family life, high rates of divorce, the "softness" of American living, inadequate parents, and, above all, overindulgence and "spoiling" contribute to the prevalence of dissent. Brought up in undisciplined homes by parents unsure of their own values and standards, dissenters channel their frustration and anger against the older generation, against all authority, and against established institutions.

Similar themes are sometimes found in the interpretations of more scholarly commentators. "Generational conflict" is said to underlie the motivation to dissent, and a profound "alienation" from American society is seen as a factor of major importance in producing protests. Then, too, such factors as the poor quality and impersonality of American college education, the large size and lack of close student-faculty contact in the "multiversity" are sometimes seen as the latent or precipitating factors in student protests, regardless of the manifest issues around which students are organized. And still other scholarly analysts, usually men now disillusioned by the radicalism of the 1930's, have expressed fear of the dogmatism, rigidity and "authoritarianism of the left" of today's student activists.

Activism and Alienation

These stereotyped views are, I believe, incorrect in a variety of ways. They confuse two distinct varieties of student dissent; equally important, they fuse dissent with maladjustment. There are, of course, as many forms of dissent as there are individual dissenters; and any effort to counter the popular stereotype of the dissenter by pointing to the existence of distinct "types" of dissenters runs the risk of over-simplifying at a lower level of abstraction. Nonetheless, it seems to me useful to suggest that student dissenters generally fall somewhere along a continuum that runs between two ideal types—first, the political activist or protester, and second, the withdrawn, culturally alienated student.

The Activist. The defining characteristic of the "new" activist is his participation in a student demonstration or group activity that concerns itself with some matter of general political, social or ethical principle. Characteristically, the activist feels that some injustice has been done, and attempts to "take a stand," "demonstrate," or in some fashion express his convictions. The specific issues in question range from protest against a paternalistic college administration's actions to disagreement with American Vietnam policies, from indignation at the exploitation of the poor to anger at the firing of a devoted teacher, from opposition to the Selective Service laws which exempt him but not the poor to—most important—outrage at the deprivation of the civil rights of other Americans.

The initial concern of the protester is almost always immediate, ad hoc and local. To be sure, the student who protests about one issue is likely to feel inclined or obliged to demonstrate his convictions on other issues as well (Heist, 1966). But whatever the issue, the protester rarely demonstrates because his *own* interests are jeopardized, but rather because he perceives injustices being done to *others* less fortunate than himself. For example, one of the apparent paradoxes about protests against current draft policies is that the protesting students are selectively drawn from that subgroup *most* likely to receive student deferments for graduate work. The basis of protest is a general sense that the selective service rules and the war in Vietnam are unjust to others with whom the student is identified, but whose fate he does not share. If one runs down the list of "causes" taken up by student activists, in rare cases are demonstrations directed at improving the lot of the protesters themselves; identification with the oppressed is a more important motivating factor than an actual sense of immediate personal oppression.

The anti-ideological stance of today's activists has been noted by many commentators. This distrust of formal ideologies (and at times of articulate thought) makes it difficult to pinpoint the positive social and political values of student protesters. Clearly, many current American political institutions like de facto segregation are opposed; clearly, too, most students of the New Left reject careerism and familism as personal values. In this sense, we might think of the activist as (politically) "alienated." But this label seems to me more misleading than illuminating, for it overlooks the more basic *commitment* of most student activists to other ancient, traditional and credal American values like free speech, citizen participation in decision making, equal opportunity, and justice. Insofar as the activist rejects all or part of "the power structure," it is because current political realities fall so far short of the ideals he sees as central to the American creed. And insofar as he repudiates careerism and familism, it is because of his implicit allegiance to other human goals he sees, once again, as more crucial to American life. Thus, to emphasize the "alienation" of activists is to neglect their more basic allegiance to credal American ideals.

One of these ideals is, of course, a belief in the desirability of political and social action. Sustained in good measure by the successes of the student civil rights movement, the protester is usually convinced that demonstrations are effective in mobilizing public opinion, bringing moral or political pressure to bear, demonstrating the existence of his opinions, or, at times, in "bringing the machine to a halt." In this sense, then, despite his criticisms of existing political practices and social institutions, he is a political optimist. Moreover, the protester must believe in at least minimal organization and group activity; otherwise, he would find it impossible to take part, as he does, in any organized demonstrations or activities. Despite their search for more truly "democratic" forms of organization and action (e. g., participatory democracy), activists agree that group action is more effective than purely individual acts. To be sure, a belief in the value and efficacy of political action is not equivalent to endorsement of prevalent political institutions or forms of action. Thus, one characteristic of activists is their search for new forms of social action, protest and political organization (community organization, sit-ins, participatory democracy) that will be more effective and less oppressive than traditional political institutions.

The Culturally Alienated. In contrast to the politically optimistic, active, and socially concerned protester, the culturally alienated student is far too pessimistic and too firmly opposed to "the System" to wish to demonstrate his disapproval in any organized public way.[1] His demonstrations of dissent are private: through nonconformity of behavior, ideology and dress, through personal experimentation, and above all through efforts to intensify his own subjective experience, he shows his distaste and disinterest in politics and society. The activist attempts to change the world around him, but the alienated student is convinced that meaningful change of the social and political world is impossible; instead, he considers "dropping out" the only real option.

Alienated students tend to be drawn from the same general social strata and colleges as protesters. But psychologically and ideologically, their backgrounds are often very different. Alienated students are more likely to be disturbed psychologically; and although they are often highly talented and artistically gifted, they are less committed to academic values and intellectual achievement than are protesters. The alienated student's real campus is the school of the absurd, and he has more affinity for pessimistic existentialist ontology than for traditional American activism. Furthermore, such students usually find it psychologically and ideologically impossible to take part in organized group activities for any length of time, particularly when they are expected to assume responsibilities for leadership. Thus, on the rare occasions when they become involved in demonstrations, they usually prefer

[1]The following paragraphs are based on the study of culturally alienated students described in *The Uncommitted* (1965). For a more extensive discussion of the overwhelmingly anti-political stance of these students, see Keniston (1966) and also Rigney and Smith (1961), Allen and Silverstein, 1967, Watts and Wittaker, 1967, and Wittaker and Watts, 1967.

peripheral roles, avoid responsibilities and are considered a nuisance by serious activists (Draper, 1965).

Whereas the protesting student is likely to accept the basic political and social values of his parents, the alienated student almost always rejects his parents' values. In particular, he is likely to see his father as a man who has "sold out" to the pressures for success and status in American society: he is determined to avoid the fate that overtook his father. Toward their mothers, however, alienated students usually express a very special sympathy and identification. These mothers, far from encouraging their sons toward independence and achievement, generally seem to have been over-solicitous and limiting. The most common family environment of the alienated-student-to-be consists of a parental schism supplemented by a special mother-son alliance of mutual understanding and maternal control and depreciation of the father (Keniston, 1965a).

In many colleges, alienated students often constitute a kind of hidden underground, disorganized and shifting in membership, in which students can temporarily or permanently withdraw from the ordinary pressures of college life. The alienated are especially attracted to the hallucinogenic drugs like marijuana, mescalin, and LSD, precisely because these agents combine withdrawal from ordinary social life with the promise of greatly intensified subjectivity and perception. To the confirmed "acid head," what matters is intense, drug-assisted perception; the rest—including politics, social action, and student demonstrations—is usually seen as "role playing."[2]

[2]The presence among student dissenters of a group of "nonstudents"— that is, drop-outs from college or graduate school who congregate or remain near some academic center—has been much noted. In fact, however, student protesters seem somewhat *less* likely to drop out of college than do nonparticipants in demonstrations (Heist, 1966), and there is no evidence that dropping out of college is in any way related to dissent from American society (Keniston and Helmreich, 1965). On the contrary, several studies suggest that the academically gifted and psychologically intact student who drops out of college voluntarily has few distinctive discontents about his college or about American society (Suczek and Alfort, 1966; Pervin et al, 1966; Wright, 1966). If he is dissatisfied at all, it is with himself, usually for failing to take advantage of the "rich educational opportunities" he sees

The recent and much publicized emergence of "hippie" sub-cultures in several major cities and increasingly on the campuses of many selective and progressive colleges illustrates the over-whelmingly apolitical stance of alienated youth. For although hippies oppose war and believe in interracial living, few have been willing or able to engage in anything beyond occasional peace marches or apolitical "human be-ins." Indeed, the hippie's emphasis on immediacy, "love" and "turning on," together with his basic rejection of the traditional values of American life, inoculates him against involvement in long-range activist endeavors, like education or community organization, and even against the sustained effort needed to plan and execute demonstrations or marches. For the alienated hippie, American society is beyond redemption (or not worth trying to redeem); but the activist, no matter how intense his rejection of specific American policies and practices, retains a conviction that his society can and should be changed. Thus, despite occasional agreement in principle between the alienated and the activists, cooperation in practice has been rare, and usually ends with activists accusing the alienated of "irresponsibility," while the alienated are confirmed in their view of activists as moralistic, "uptight," and "un-cool."

Obviously, no description of a type ever fits an individual per-fectly. But by this rough typology I mean to suggest that popular stereotypes which present a unified portrait of student dissent are gravely oversimplified. More specifically, they confuse the politi-cally pessimistic and socially uncommitted alienated student with the politically hopeful and socially committed activist. To be sure, there are many students who fall between these two extremes, and some of them alternate between passionate search for intensified

---

in his college. The motivations of students dropping out of college are complex and varied, but such motivations more often seem related to per-sonal questions of self definition and parental identification or to a desire to escape relentless academic pressures, than to any explicit dissent from the Great Society. Thus, although a handful of students have chosen to drop out of college for a period in order to devote themselves to political and societal protest activities, there seems little reason in general to asso-ciate the drop-out with the dissenter, whether he be a protester or an alienated student. The opposite is nearer the truth.

subjectivity and equally passionate efforts to remedy social and political injustices. And as I will later suggest, even within the student movement, one of the central tensions is between political activism and cultural alienation. Nonetheless, even to understand this tension we must first distinguish between the varieties of dissent apparent on American campuses.

Furthermore, the distinction between activist and alienated students as psychological types suggests the incompleteness of scholarly analyses that see social and historical factors as the only forces that "push" a student toward one or the other of these forms of dissent. To be sure, social and cultural factors are of immense importance in providing channels for the expression (or supression) of dissent, and in determining *which* kinds of dissenters receive publicity, censure, support, or ostracism in any historical period. But these factors cannot, in general, change a hippie into a committed activist, nor a SNCC field worker into a full time "acid head." Thus, the prototypical activist of 1966 is not the "same" student as the prototypical student bohemian of 1956, but is rather the politically aware but frustrated, academically oriented "privatist" of that era. Similarly, as I will argue below, the most compelling alternative to most activists is not the search for kicks or sentience but the quest for scholarly competence. And if culturally sanctioned opportunities for the expression of alienation were to disappear, most alienated students would turn to private psychopathology rather than to public activism.

Stated more generally, historical forces do not ordinarily transform radically the character, values, and inclinations of an adult in later life. Rather, they thrust certain groups forward in some eras and discourage or suppress other groups. The recent alternation in styles of student dissent in America is therefore not to be explained so much by the malleability of individual character as by the power of society to bring activists into the limelight, providing them with the intellectual and moral instruments for action. Only a minority of potential dissenters fall close enough to the midpoint between alienation and activism so that they can constitute a "swing vote" acutely responsive to social and cultural pressures and styles. The rest, the majority, are characterologically committed to one or another style of dissent.

THE SOURCES OF ACTIVISM

What I have termed "alienated" students are by no means a new phenomenon in American life, or for that matter in industrialized societies. Bohemians, "beatniks," and artistically-inclined undergraduates who rejected middle class values have long been a part of the American student scene, especially at more selective colleges; they constituted the most visible form of dissent during the relative political "silence" of American students in the 1950's. What is distinctive about student dissent in recent years is the unexpected emergence of a vocal minority of politically and socially active students.[3] Much is now known about the characteristics of such students, and the circumstances under which protests are likely to be mounted. At the same time, many areas of ignorance remain. In the account to follow, I will attempt to formulate a series of general hypotheses concerning the sources of student activism.[4]

It is abundantly clear that no single factor will suffice to explain the increase of politically motivated activities and protests on American campuses. Even if we define an activist narrowly, as a student who (a) acts together with others in a group, (b) is concerned with some ethical, social, ideological or political issue, and

[3]Student activism, albeit of a rather different nature, was also found in the nineteen thirties. For a discussion and contrast of student protest today and after the Depression, see Lipset (1966a).

[4]Throughout the following, I will use the terms "protester" and "activist" interchangeably, although I am aware that some activists are not involved in protests. Furthermore, the category of "activist" is an embracing one, comprising at least three sub-classes. First, those who might be termed *reformers*, that is, students involved in community organization work, the Peace Corps, tutoring programs, Vista, etc., but not generally affiliated with any of the "New Left" organizations. Second, the group of *activists proper*, most of whom are or have been affiliated with organizations like the Free Speech Movement at Berkeley, Students for a Democratic Society, the Student Non-violent Coordinating Committee, or the Congress on Racial Equality, or the Vietnam Summer Project. Finally, there is a much publicized handful of students who might be considered *extremists*, who belong to doctrinaire Marxist and Trotskyite organizations like the now-defunct May Second Movement. No empirical study with which I am acquainted has investigated the differences among students in these three sub-groups. Most studies have concentrated on the "activist proper," and my remarks will be based on a reading of their data.

(c) holds liberal or "radical" views, the sources of student activism and protest are complex and interrelated. At least four kinds of factors seem involved in any given protest. First, the individuals involved must be suitably predisposed by their personal backgrounds, values, and motivations. Second, the likelihood of protest is far greater in certain kinds of educational and social settings. Third, socially-directed protests require a special cultural climate, that is, certain distinctive values and views about the effectiveness and meaning of demonstrations, and about the wider society. And finally, some historical situations are especially conducive to protests.

THE PROTEST-PRONE PERSONALITY

A large and still growing number of studies conducted under different auspices, at different times, and about different students, presents a remarkably consistent picture of the protest-prone individual (Aiken, Demerath and Marwell, 1966; Flacks, 1967; Gastwirth, 1965; Heist, 1965, 1966; Lyonns, 1965; Somers, 1965; Watts and Whittaker, 1966; Westby and Braungart, 1966; Katz, 1967; and Paulus, 1967). For one, student protesters are generally outstanding students; the higher the student's grade average, the more outstanding his academic achievements, the more likely it is that he will become involved in any given political demonstration. Similarly, student activists come from families with liberal political values; a disproportionate number report that their parents hold views essentially similar to their own, and accept or support their activities. Thus, among the parents of protesters we find large numbers of liberal Democrats, plus an unusually large scattering of pacifists, socialists, etc. A disproportionate number of protesters come from Jewish families; and if the parents of activists are religious, they tend to be concentrated in the more liberal denominations—Reform Judaism, Unitarianism, the Society of Friends, etc. Such parents are reported to have high ethical and political standards, regardless of their actual religious convictions.

As might be expected of a group of politically liberal and academically talented students, a disproportionate number are drawn from professional and intellectual families of upper middle class status. For example, compared with active student conservatives, members of protest groups tend to have higher parental incomes, more parental education, and less anxiety about social status (Westby and Braungart, 1966). Another study finds that high levels of education distinguish the activist's family even in the grandparental generation (Flacks, 1967). In brief, activists are not drawn from disadvantaged, status-anxious, underprivileged, or uneducated groups; on the contrary, they are selectively recruited from among those young Americans who have had the most socially fortunate upbringings.

Basic Value Commitments of Activists

The basic value commitments of the activist tend to be academic and non-vocational. Such students are rarely found among engineers, future teachers at teachers colleges, or students of business administration. Their overall educational goals are those of a liberal education for its own sake, rather than specifically technical, vocational, or professional preparation. Rejecting careerist and familist goals, activists espouse humanitarian, expressive, and self-actualizing values. Perhaps because of these values, they delay career choice longer than their classmates (Flacks, 1967). Nor are such students distinctively dogmatic, rigid or authoritarian. Quite the contrary, the substance and style of their beliefs and activities tends to be open, flexible, and highly liberal. Their fields of academic specialization are non-vocational—the social sciences and the humanities. Once in college, they not only do well academically, but tend to persist in their academic commitments, dropping out *less* frequently than most of their classmates. As might be expected, a disproportionate number receive a B.A. within four years and continue on to graduate school, preparing themselves for academic careers.

Survey data also suggest that the activist is not distinctively dissatisfied with his college education. As will be noted below, activists generally attend colleges which provide the best, rather than the worst, undergraduate education available today. Objectively then, activists probably have less to complain about in their

undergraduate educations than most other students. And subjec-
tively as well, surveys show most activists, like most other
American undergraduates, to be relatively well satisfied with their
undergraduate educations (Somers, 1965; Kornhauser, 1967).
Thus, dissatisfaction with educational failings of the "impersonal
multiversity," however important as a rallying cry, does not appear
to be a distinctive cause of activism.

In contrast to their relative satisfaction with the quality of their
educations, however, activists *are* distinctively dissatisfied with
what might be termed the "civil-libertarian" defects of their college
administrations. While no doubt a great many American undergraduates distrust "University Hall," this distrust is especially pronounced among student protesters (Kornhauser, 1967; Paulus,
1967). Furthermore, activists tend to be more responsive than
other students to deprivations of civil rights on campus as well as
off campus, particularly when political pressures seem to motivate
on-campus policies they consider unjust. The same responsiveness
increasingly extends to issues of "student power": i.e., student
participation and decisions affecting campus life. Thus bans on
controversial speakers, censorship of student publications, and
limitations on off-campus political or social action are likely to
incense the activist, as is arbitrary "administration without the
consent of the administered." But it is primarily perceived injustice
or the denial of student rights by the Administration—rather than
poor educational quality, neglect by the faculty, or the impersonality of the multiversity—that agitates the activist.

Most studies of activists have concentrated on variables that are
relatively easy to measure: social class, academic achievements,
explicit values, and satisfaction with college. But these factors
alone will not explain activism: More students possess the demographic and attitudinal characteristics of the protest-prone personality than are actually involved in protests and social action
programs. Situational, institutional, cultural, and historical factors
(discussed below) obviously contribute to "catalysing" a protest-
prone personality into an actual activist. But it also seems that,
within the broad demographic group so far defined, more specific
psychodynamic factors contribute to activism.

Activists . . . Not in Rebellion

In speculating about such factors, we leave the ground of established fact and enter the terrain of speculation, for only a few studies have explored the personality dynamics and family constellation of the activist, and most of these studies are impressionistic and clinical (e.g., Coles, 1967; Ehle, 1965; Draper, 1965; Fishman and Solomon n.d., 1964; Gastwirth, 1965; Newfield, 1966; Schneider, 1966; Solomon and Fishman, 1963, 1964; Zinn, 1965). But certain facts are clear. As noted, activists are *not*, on the whole, repudiating or rebelling against explicit parental values and ideologies. On the contrary, there is some evidence that such students are living out their parents' values in practice; and one study suggests that activists may be somewhat *closer* to their parents' values than nonactivists (Flacks, 1967). Thus, any simple concept of "generational conflict" or "rebellion against parental authority" is clearly oversimplified as applied to the motivations of most protesters.

Activists . . . Living Out Parental Values

It does seem probable, however, that many activists are concerned with *living out expressed but unimplemented parental values.* Solomon and Fishman (1963), studying civil rights activists and peace marchers, argue that many demonstrators are "acting out" in their demonstrations the values which their parents explicitly believed but did not have the courage or opportunity to practice or fight for. Similarly, when protesters criticize their fathers, it is usually over their fathers' failure to practice what they have preached to their children throughout their lives. Thus, in the personal background of the protester there is occasionally a suggestion that his father is less than "sincere" (and even at times "hypocritical") in his professions of political liberalism. In particular, both careerism and familism in parents are the objects of activist criticisms, the more so because these implicit goals often conflict with explicit parental values. And it may be that protesters receive both covert and overt support from their parents because the latter are secretly proud of their children's eagerness to implement the ideals they as parents have only given lip service to. But whatever the ambivalences that bind parents with their activist children, it would be wrong to overemphasize them; what is most impressive is the solidarity of older and younger generations.

Activists . . . Family Structure

While no empirical study has tested this hypothesis, it seems probable that in many activist-producing families, the mother will have a dominant psychological influence on her son's development. I have already noted that the protester's cause is rarely himself, but rather alleviating the oppression of others. As a group, activists seem to possess an unusual *capacity for nurturant identification*— that is, for empathy and sympathy with the underdog, the oppressed, and the needy. Such a capacity can have many origins, but its most likely source in upper middle class professional families is identification with an active mother whose own work embodies nurturant concern for others. Flacks' finding that the mothers of activists are likely to be employed, often in professional or service roles like teaching and social work, is consistent with this hypothesis. In general, in American society, middle class women have greater social and financial freedom to work in jobs that are idealistically "fulfilling" as opposed to merely lucrative or prestigious. As a rule, then, in middle class families, it is the mother who actively embodies in her life and work the humanitarian, social, and political ideals that the father may share in principle but does not or cannot implement in his career.

Given what we know about the general characteristics of the families of protest-prone students, it also seems probable that the dominant ethos of their families is unusually egalitarian, permissive, "democratic," and highly individuated. More specifically, we might expect that these will be families where children talk back to their parents at the dinner table, where free dialogue and discussion of feelings is encouraged, and where "rational" solutions are sought to everyday family problems and conflicts. We would also expect that such families would place a high premium on self-expression and intellectual independence, encouraging their children to make up their own minds and to stand firm against group pressures. Once again, the mother seems the most likely carrier and epitome of these values, given her relative freedom from professional and financial pressures.

The contrast between such protest-prompting families and alienating families should be underlined. In both, the son's deepest emotional ties are often to his mother. But in the alienating family, the mother-son relationship is characterized by maternal control and intrusiveness, whereas in the protest-prompting family, the mother is a highly individuating force in her son's life, pushing him to independence and autonomy. Furthermore, the alienated student is determined to avoid the fate that befell his father, whereas the protesting student wants merely to live out the values that his father has not always worked hard enough to practice. Finally, the egalitarian, permissive, democratic, and individuating environment of the entire family of the protester contrasts with the over-controlling, over-solicitous attitude of the mother in the alienating family, where the father is usually excluded from major emotional life within the family.

These hypotheses about the family background and psychodynamics of the protester are speculative, and future research may prove their invalidity. But regardless of whether these particular speculations are correct, it seems clear that in addition to the general social, demographic, and attitudinal factors mentioned in most research, more specific familial and psychodynamic influences contribute to protest-proneness.

THE PROTEST-PROMOTING INSTITUTION

However we define his characteristics, one activist alone cannot make a protest: the characteristics of the college or university he attends have much to do with whether his protest-proneness will ever be mobilized into actual activism. Politically, socially, and ideologically motivated demonstrations and activities are most likely to occur at certain types of colleges; they are almost unknown at a majority of campuses. The effects of institutional characteristics on protests have been studied by Cowan (1966) and Peterson (1966).

In order for an organized protest or related activities to occur, there must obviously be sufficient *numbers* of protest-prone students to form a group, these students must have an opportunity for *interaction* with each other, and there must be *leaders* to initiate and mount the protest. Thus, we might expect—and we indeed find—that protest is associated with institutional size, and particularly with the congregation of large numbers of protest-prone students in close proximity to each other. More important than sheer size alone, however, is the "image" of the institution: certain institutions selectively recruit students with protest-prone characteristics. Specifically, a reputation for academic excellence and freedom, coupled with highly selective admissions policies, will tend to congregate large numbers of potentially protesting students on one campus. Thus, certain institutions do act as "magnets" for potential activists, but not so much because of their reputations for political radicalism as because they are noted for their academic excellence. Among such institutions are some of the most selective and "progressive" private liberal arts colleges, major state universities (like Michigan, California at Berkeley, and Wisconsin) which have long traditions of vivid undergraduate teaching and high admissions standards (Lipset and Altbach, 1966), and many of the more prestigious private universities.

Once protest-prone students are on campus, they must have an opportunity to interact, to support one another, to develop common outlooks and shared policies—in short, to form an *activist subculture* with sufficient mass and potency to generate a demonstration or action program. Establishing "honors colleges" for talented and academically motivated students is one particularly effective way of creating a "critical mass" of protest-prone students. Similarly, inadequate on-campus housing indirectly results in the development of off-campus protest-prone sub-cultures (e.g., co-op houses) in residences where student activists can develop a high degree of ideological solidarity and organizational cohesion.

But even the presence of a critical mass of protest-prone undergraduates in an activist sub-culture is not enough to make a protest without leaders and issues. And in general the most effective protest leaders have not been undergraduates, but teaching assistants. The presence of large numbers of exploited, underpaid, disgruntled, and frustrated teacher assistants (or other equivalent graduate students and younger faculty members) is almost essential for organized and persistent protest. For one, advanced students tend to be more liberal politically and more sensitive to political issues than are most undergraduates—partly because education seems to have a liberalizing effect, and partly because students who persist into graduate school tend to be more liberal to start than those who drop out or go elsewhere. Furthermore, the frustrations of graduate students, especially at very large public universities, make them particularly sensitive to general problems of injustice, exploitation, and oppression. Teaching assistants, graduate students, and young faculty members also tend to be in daily and prolonged contact with students, are close enough to them in age to sense their mood, and are therefore in an excellent position to lead and organize student protests. Particularly at institutions which command little institutional allegiance from large numbers of highly capable graduate students (Lipset and Altbach, 1966) will such students be found among the leaders of the protest movement.

The Issues of Protest

Finally, issues are a necessity. In many cases, these issues are provided by historical developments on the national or international scene, a point to which I will return. But in some instances, as at Berkeley, on-campus issues are the focus of protest. And in other cases off-campus and on-campus issues are fused, as in the recent protests at institutional cooperation with draft board policies considered unjust by demonstrating students. In providing such on-campus issues, the attitude of the university administration is central. Skillful handling of student complaints, the maintenance of open channels of communication between student leaders and faculty members, and administrative willingness to resist public and political pressures in order to protect the rights of students—all minimize the likelihood of organized protest. Conversely, a university administration that shows itself unduly sensitive to political, legislative, or public pressures, that treats students arrogantly, ineptly, condescendingly, hypocritically, or above all dishonestly, is asking for a demonstration.

Thus one reason for the relative absence of on-campus student protests and demonstrations on the campuses of private non-denominational "academic" colleges and universities (which recruit many protest-prone students) probably lies in the liberal policies of the administrations. As Cowan (1966) notes, liberal students generally attend non-restrictive and "libertarian" colleges. Given an administration and faculty that supports or tolerates activism and student rights, student activists must generally find their issues off-campus. The same students, confronting an administration unduly sensitive to political pressures from a conservative board of regents or State legislature, might engage in active on-campus protests. There is also some evidence that clever administrative manipulation of student complaints, even in the absence of genuine concern with student rights, can serve to dissipate the potentialities of protest (Keene, 1966).

Among the institutional factors often cited as motivating student protest is the largeness, impersonality, atomization, "multiversitification," etc., of the university. I have already noted that student protesters do not seem distinctively dissatisfied with their educations. Furthermore, the outstanding academic achievements and intellectual motivations of activists concentrate them, within any college, in the courses and programs that provide the most "personal" attention: honors programs, individual instruction, advanced seminars, and so on. Thus, they probably receive relatively *more* individual attention and a *higher* caliber of instruction than do non-protesters. Furthermore, protests generally tend to occur at the best, rather than the worst colleges, judged from the point of view of the quality of undergraduate instruction. Thus, despite the popularity of student slogans dealing with the impersonality and irrelevance of the multiversity, the absolute level of educational opportunities seems, if anything, positively related to the occurrence of protest: the better the institution, the more likely demonstrations are.

Nor can today's student activism be attributed in any direct way to mounting academic pressures. To be sure, activism is most manifest at those selective colleges where the "pressure to perform" (Keniston, 1965b) is greatest, where standards are highest, and where anxieties about being admitted to a "good" graduate or professional school are most pronounced. But, contrary to the argument of Lipset and Altbach (1966), the impact of academic pressure on activism seems negative rather than positive. Protest-prone students, with their superior academic attainments and strong intellectual commitments, seem especially vulnerable to a kind of academic professionalism that, because of the enormous demands it makes upon the student's energies, serves to cancel or preclude activism. Student demonstrations rarely take place during exam periods, and protests concerned with educational quality almost invariably seek an improvement of quality, rather than a lessening of pressure. Thus, though the pressure to perform doubt-less affects *all* American students, it probably acts as a deterrent rather than a stimulus to student activism.

Deprivation of Expectations

What probably does matter, however, is the *relative* deprivation of student expectations. A college that recruits large numbers of academically motivated and capable students into a less than first-rate education program, one that oversells entering freshmen on the virtues of the college, or one that reneges on implicit or explicit promises about the quality and freedom of education may well produce an "academic backlash" that will take the form of student protests over the quality of education. Even more important is the gap between expectations and actualities regarding freedom of student expression. Stern (1967) has demonstrated that most en-tering freshmen have extremely high hopes regarding the freedom of speech and action they will be able to exercise during college: most learn the real facts quickly, and graduate thoroughly dis-abused of their illusions. But since activists, as I have argued above, are particularly responsive to these issues, they are apt to tolerate disillusion less lightly, and to take up arms to concretize their dashed hopes. Compared to the frustration engendered by disillusionment regarding educational quality, the relative depriva-tion of civil libertarian hopes seems a more potent source of protests. And with regard to both issues, it must be recalled that protests have been *fewest* at institutions of low educational quality and little freedom for student expression. Thus, it is not the absolute level either of educational quality or of student freedom that matters, but the gap between student hopes and institutional facts.

THE PROTEST-PROMPTING CULTURAL CLIMATE

Even if a critical mass of interacting protest-prone students forms in an institution that provides leadership and issues, student protests are by no means inevitable, as the quiescence of American students during the nineteen fifties suggests. For protests to occur, other more broadly cultural factors, attitudes and values must be present. Protest activities must be seen as meaningful acts, either in an instrumental or an expressive sense; and activists must be convinced that the consequences of activism and protest will not be overwhelmingly damaging to them. During the 1950's, one much-discussed factor that may have militated against student activism was the conviction that the consequences of protest (blacklisting, F.B.I. investigations, problems in obtaining security clearance, difficulties in getting jobs) were both harmful to the individual and yet extremely likely. Even more important was the sense on the part of many politically-conscious students that participation in left-wing causes would merely show their naiveté, gullibility, and political innocence without furthering any worthy cause. The prevailing climate was such that protest was rarely seen as an act of any meaning or usefulness.

Academic Support

Today, in contrast, student protesters are not only criticized and excoriated by a large segment of the general public, but—more crucial—actively defended, encouraged, lionized, praised, publicized, photographed, interviewed, and studied by a portion of the academic community. Since the primary reference group of most activists is not the general public, but rather that liberal segment of the academic world most sympathetic to protest, academic support has a disproportionate impact on protest-prone students' perception of their own activities. In addition, the active participation of admired faculty members in protests, "teach-ins," and peace marches, acts as a further incentive to students (Kelman, 1966). Thus, in a minority of American colleges, sub-cultures have arisen where protest is felt to be both an important existential act—a dignified way of "standing up to be counted"—and an effective way of "bringing the machine to a halt," sometimes by disruptive acts (sit-ins, strikes, etc.), more often by calling public attention to injustice.

Universalism

An equally important, if less tangible "cultural" factor is the broad climate of social criticism in American society. As Parsons (1951, 1960), White (1961), and others have noted, one of the enduring themes of American society is the pressure toward "universalism," that is, an increasing extension of principles like equality, equal opportunity, and fair protection of the law to all groups within the society (and in recent years, to all groups in the world). As affluence has increased in American society, impatience at the slow "progress" of non-affluent minority groups has also increased, not only among students, but among other segments of the population. Even before the advent of the student civil rights movement, support for racial segregation was diminishing. Similarly, the current student concern for the "forgotten fifth" was not so much initiated by student activists as it was taken up by them. In this regard, student activists are both caught up in and in the vanguard of a new wave of extension of universalism in American society. Although the demands of student activists usually go far beyond the national consensus, they nonetheless reflect (at the same time that they have helped advance) one of the continuing trends in American social change.

A contrasting but equally enduring theme in American social criticism is a more fundamental revulsion against the premises of industrial—and now technological—society. Universalistic-liberal criticism blames our society because it has not yet extended its principles, privileges, and benefits to all: the complaint is injustice and the goal is to complete our unfinished business. But alienated-romantic criticism questions the validity and importance of these

same principles, privileges and benefits—the complaint is material-
ism and the goal is spiritual, esthetic, or expressive fulfillment. The
tradition of revulsion against conformist, anti-esthetic, materialistic,
ugly, middle class America runs through American writing from
Melville through the "lost generation" to the "beat generation"
and has been expressed concretely in the bohemian sub-cultures
that have flourished in a few large American cities since the turn
of the century. But today the power of the romantic-alienated
position has increased: one response to prosperity has been a
more searching examination of the technological assumptions upon
which prosperity has been based. Especially for the children of
the upper middle class, affluence is simply taken for granted, and
the drive "to get ahead in the world" no longer makes sense for
students who start out ahead. The meanings of life must be sought
elsewhere, in art, sentience, philosophy, love, service to others,
intensified experience, adventure—in short, in the broadly esthetic
or expressive realm.

Deviant Views

Since neither the universalistic nor the romantic critique of
modern society is new, these critiques affect the current student
generation not only directly but indirectly, in that they have influenced the way many of today's college students were raised.
A few of today's activists are children of the "radicals of the
1930's" (Lipset and Altbach, 1966); and Flacks comments on the
growing number of intellectual, professional upper middle class
families who have adopted "deviant" views of traditional American
life and embodied these views in the practices by which they
brought up their children. Thus, some of today's activists are the
children of bohemians, college professors, etc. But in general, the
explanation from parental "deviance" does not seem fully convincing. To be sure, the backgrounds of activists are atypical in a
statistical sense, and thus might be termed empirically deviant.
It may indeed turn out that the parents of activists are distinguished by their emphasis on humanitarianism, intellectualism, and
romanticism, and by their lack of stress on moralism (Flacks,
1967). But it is not obvious that such parental values can be

termed deviant in any but a statistical sense. "Concern with the plight of others," "desire to realize intellectual capacities," and "lack of concern about the importance of strictly controlling personal impulses"—all these values might be thought of as more normative than deviant in upper middle class suburban American society in 1966. Even "sensitivity to beauty and art" is becoming increasingly acceptable. Nor can the socio-economic facts of affluence, freedom from status anxiety, high educational levels, permissiveness with children, training for independence, etc., be considered normatively deviant in middle class America. Thus, the sense in which activists are the deviant offspring of subculturally deviant parents remains to be clarified.

Psychological Flexibility

Another explanation seems equally plausible, at least as applied to some student activists—namely that their activism is closely related to the social and cultural conditions that promote high levels of psychological flexibility, complexity, and integration. As Bay (1966) has argued, social scientists may be too reluctant to entertain the possibility that some political and social outlooks or activities are symptomatic of psychological "health," while others indicate "disturbance." In fact, many of the personal characteristics of activists—empathy, superior intellectual attainments, capacity for group involvement, strong humanitarian values, emphasis on self-realization, etc.—are consistent with the hypothesis that, as a group, they are unusually "healthy" psychologically. (See also Heist, 1966). Similarly, the personal antecedents of activists—economic security, committed parents, humanitarian, liberal, and permissive home environments, good education, etc.—are those that would seem to promote unusually high levels of psychological functioning. If this be correct, then former SDS president Tom Hayden's words (1966) may be a valid commentary on the cultural setting of activism:

> Most of the active student radicals today come from middle to upper middle class professional homes. They were born with status and affluence as facts of life, not goals to be striven for. In their upbringing, their parents stressed the right of

children to question and make judgments, producing perhaps the first generation of young people both affluent and independent of mind.

In agreeing with Bay that activists may be more psychologically "healthy" as a group than nonactivists, I am aware of the many difficulties entailed by this hypothesis. First, complexity, flexibility, integration, high levels of functioning, etc., are by no means easy to define, and the criteria for "positive mental health" remain vague and elusive. (See Jahoda, 1958). Second, there are obviously many individuals with these same "healthy" characteristics who are not activists; and within the group of activists, there are many individuals with definite psychopathologies. In any social movement a variety of individuals of highly diverse talents and motivations are bound to be involved, and global descriptions are certain to be oversimplified. Third, the explanation from "psychological health" and the explanation from "parental deviance" are not necessarily opposed. On the contrary, these two arguments become identical if we assume that the preconditions for high levels of psychological functioning are both statistically and normatively deviant in modern American society. This assumption seems quite plausible.

Whatever the most plausible explanation of the socio-cultural sources of activism, the importance of prevailing attitudes toward student protest and of the climate of social criticism in America seems clear. In the past five years a conviction has arisen, at least among a minority of American college students, that protest and social action are effective and honorable. Furthermore, changes in American society, especially in middle class child rearing practices, mean that American students are increasingly responsive to both the universalistic and romantic critique of our society. Both strands of social criticism have been picked up by student activists in a rhetoric of protest that combines a major theme of impatience at the slow fulfillment of the credal ideals of American society with a more muted minor theme of esthetic revulsion at technological society itself. By and large, activists respond most affirmatively to the first theme and alienated students to the second; but even within the student protest movement, these two themes coexist in uneasy tension.

THE PROTEST-PRODUCING HISTORICAL SITUATION

To separate what I have called the "cultural climate" from the "historical situation" is largely arbitrary. But by this latter term I hope to point to the special sensitivity of today's student activists to historical events and trends that do not immediately impinge upon their own lives. In other nations, and in the past, student protest movements seem to have been more closely related to immediate student frustrations than they are in America today. The "transformationist" (utopian, Marxist, universalistic, or democratic) aspirations of activist youth in rapidly developing nations often seem closely related to their personal frustrations under oppressive regimes or at "feudal" practices in their societies; the "restorationist" (romantic, alienated) youth movements that have appeared in later stages of industrialization seem closely connected to a personal sense of the loss of a feudal, maternal, and "organic" past. (See Lifton, 1960, 1963, 1964.) Furthermore, both universalistic and romantic youth movements in other nations have traditionally been highly ideological, committed either to concepts of universal democracy and economic justice or to particularistic values of brotherhood, loyalty, feeling, and notion.

Anti-Ideological

Today's activists, in contrast, are rarely concerned with improving their own conditions and are highly motivated by identification with the oppressions of others. The anti-ideological bias of today's student activists has been underlined by virtually every commentator. Furthermore, as Flacks notes, the historical conditions that have produced protest elsewhere are largely absent in modern America; and the student "movement" in this country differs in important ways from student movements elsewhere. In many respects, then, today's American activists have no historical precedent, and only time will tell to what extent the appearance of organized student dissent in the 1960's is a product of locally American conditions, of the psycho-social effects of a technological affluence that will soon characterize other advanced nations, or of widespread changes in identity and style produced by psycho-historical factors that affect youth of all nations (thermonuclear warfare, increased culture contact, rapid communications, etc.).

Sensitivity to World Events

But whatever the historical roots of protest, today's student protester seems uniquely sensitive to historical trends and events. In interviewing student activists I have been impressed with how often they mention some world-historical event as the catalyst for their activism—in some cases, witnessing via television of the Little Rock demonstrations over school integration; in another case, watching rioting Zengakuren students in Japan protesting the arrival of President Eisenhower; in other cases, particularly among Negro students, a strong identification with the rising black nationalism of recently-independent African nations.

Several factors help explain this sensitivity to world events. For one, modern means of communication make the historical world more psychologically "available" to youth. Students today are exposed to world events and world trends with a speed and intensity that has no historical precedent. Revolutions, trends, fashions, and fads are now world-wide; it takes but two or three years for fashions to spread from Carnaby Street to New York, New Delhi, Tokyo, Warsaw, Lagos, and Lima. In particular, students who have been brought up in a tradition that makes them unusually empathic, humanitarian, and universalistic in values may react more intensely to exposure via television to student demonstrations in Japan than to social pressures from their fellow seniors in Centerville High. Finally, this broadening of empathy is, I believe, part of a general modern trend toward the *internationalization of identity*. Hastened by modern communications and consolidated by the world-wide threat of nuclear warfare, this trend involves, in vanguard groups in many nations, a loosening of parochial and national allegiances in favor of a more inclusive sense of affinity with one's peers (and non-peers) from all nations. In this respect, American student activists are both participants and leaders in the reorganization of psycho-social identity and ideology that is gradually emerging from the unique historical conditions of the twentieth century (Lifton, 1965).

A small but growing number of American students, then, exhibit a peculiar responsiveness to world-historical events—a responsiveness based partly on their own broad identification with others like them throughout the world, and partly on the availability of information about world events via the mass media. The impact of historical events, be they the world-wide revolution for human dignity and esteem, the rising aspirations of the developing nations, or the war in Vietnam, is greatly magnified upon such students; their primary identification is not their unreflective national identity, but their sense of affinity for Vietnamese peasants, Negro sharecoppers, demonstrating Zengakuren activists, exploited migrant workers, and the oppressed everywhere. One of the consequences of security, affluence, and education is a growing sense of personal involvement with those who are insecure, non-affluent, and uneducated.

THE FUTURE OF STUDENT ACTIVISM

I have argued that no single factor can explain or help us predict the future of the student protest movement in America: active expressions of dissent have become more prevalent because of an *interaction* of individual, institutional, cultural, and historical factors. Affluence and education have changed the environment within which middle class children are raised, in turn producing a minority of students with special sensitivity to the oppressed and the dissenting everywhere. At the same time, technological innovations like television have made available to these students abundant imagery of oppression and dissent in America and in other nations. And each of these factors exerts a potentiating influence on the others.

Given some understanding of the interaction of these factors, general questions about the probable future of student activism in America can now be broken down into four more specific questions: Are we likely to produce (a) more protest-prone personalities? (b) more institutional settings in which protests are likely? (c) a cultural climate that sanctions and encourages activism? and (d) a historical situation that facilitates activism? To three of the questions (a, b, and d), I think the answer is a qualified yes; I would therefore expect that in the future, if the cultural climate remains the same, student activism and protest would continue to be visible features on the American social landscape.

Consider first the factors that promote protest-prone personalities. In the coming generation there will be more and more students who come from the upper middle class, highly educated, politically liberal professional backgrounds from which protesters are selectively recruited (Michael, 1965). Furthermore, we can expect that a significant and perhaps growing proportion of these families will have the universalistic, humanitarian, egalitarian, and individualistic values found in the families of protesters. Finally, the expressive, permissive, democratic, and autonomy promoting atmosphere of these families seems to be the emerging trend of middle class America: older patterns of "entrepreneurial-authoritarian" control are slowly giving way to more "bureaucratic-democratic" techniques of socialization (Miller and Swanson, 1958). Such secular changes in the American family would produce a growing proportion of students with protest-prone personalities.

Institutional factors, I have argued, are of primary importance insofar as they bring together a critical mass of suitably protest-predisposed students in an atmosphere where they can interact, create their own subculture, develop leadership and find issues. The growing size of major American universities, their increasing academic and intellectual selectivity, and the emphasis on "quality" education (honors programs, individual instruction, greater student freedom)—all seem to promote the continuing development of activist sub-cultures in a minority of American institutions. The increasing use of graduate student teaching assistants in major universities points to the growing availability of large numbers of potential "leaders" for student protests. Admittedly, a sudden increase in the administrative wisdom in college deans and presidents could reduce the number of available on-campus issues; but such a growth in wisdom does not seem imminent.

Cultural Climate May Change

In sharp contrast, a maintenance of the cultural climate required for continuation of activism during the coming years seems far more problematical. Much depends on the future course of the war in Vietnam. Continuing escalation of the war in Southeast Asia will convince many student activists that their efforts are doomed to ineffectuality. For as of mid-1967, anti-war activism has become the primary common cause of student protesters. The increasing militancy and exclusivity of the Negro student civil rights movement, its emphasis on "Black Power" and on grass-roots community organization work (to be done by Negroes) is rapidly pushing white activists out of civil rights work, thus depriving them of the issue upon which the current mood of student activism was built. This fact, coupled with the downgrading of the war on poverty, the decline of public enthusiasm for civil rights, and the increasing scarcity of public and private financing for work with the underprivileged sectors of American society, has already begun to turn activists away from domestic issues toward an increasingly single-minded focus on the war in Vietnam. Yet at the same time, increasing numbers of activists overtly or covertly despair of the efficacy of student attempts to mobilize public opinion against the war, much less to influence directly American foreign policies. Continuing escalation in Southeast Asia has also begun to create a more repressive atmosphere toward student (and other) protesters of the war, exemplified by the question "Dissent or Treason?" Already the movement of activists back to full-time academic work is apparent.

Thus, the war in Vietnam, coupled by the "rejection" of white middle class students by the vestigial black civil rights movement, is producing a crisis among activists, manifest by a search for issues and intense disagreement over strategy and tactics. At the same time, the diminution of support for student activism tends to exert a "radicalizing" effect upon those who remain committed activists—partly because frustration itself tends to radicalize the frustrated, and partly because many of the less dedicated and committed activists have dropped away from the movement. At the same time, most activists find it difficult to turn from civil rights or peace work toward "organizing the middle class" along lines suggested by alienated-romantic criticisms of technological society. On the whole, activists remain more responsive to universalistic issues like peace and civil rights than to primarily expressive or esthetic criticisms of American society. Furthermore, the practical and organizational problems of "organizing the middle class" are overwhelming. Were the student movement to be forced to turn away from universalistic issues like civil rights and peace to a romantic critique of the "quality of middle class life," my argument here implies that its following and efficacy would diminish considerably. Were this to happen, observations based on student activism of a more universalistic variety would have to be modified to take account of a more radical and yet more alienated membership. Thus, escalation or even continuation of the war in Vietnam, particularly over a long period, will reduce the likelihood of student activism.

Yet there are other, hopefully more permanent, trends in American culture that argue for a continuation of protests. The further extension of affluence in America will probably mean growing impatience over our society's failure to include the "forgotten fifth" in its prosperity: as the excluded and underprivileged become fewer in number, pressures to include them in American society will grow. Similarly, as more young Americans are brought up in affluent homes and sub-cultures, many will undoubtedly turn to question the value of monetary, familistic, and careerist goals, looking instead toward expressive, romantic, experiential, humanitarian, and self-actualizing pursuits to give their lives meaning. Thus, in the next decades, barring a major world conflagration, criticisms of American society will probably continue and intensify on two grounds: first, that it has excluded a significant minority from its prosperity; and second, that affluence alone is empty without humanitarian, esthetic, or expressive fulfillment. Both of these trends would strengthen the climate conducive to continuing activism.

World-Wide Protest-Promoting Pressures

Finally, protest-promoting pressures from the rest of the world will doubtless increase in the coming years. The esteem revolution in developing nations, the rise of aspirations in the impoverished two-thirds of the world, and the spread of universalistic principles to other nations—all of these trends portend a growing international unrest, especially in the developing nations. If young Americans continue to be unusually responsive to the unfulfilled aspirations of those abroad, international trends will touch a minority of them deeply, inspiring them to overseas activities like the Peace Corps, to efforts to "internationalize" American foreign policies, and to an acute sensitivity to the frustrated aspirations of other Americans. Similarly, continuation of current American policies of supporting anti-Communist but often repressive regimes in developing nations (particularly regimes anathema to student activists abroad) will tend to agitate American students as well. Thus, pressures from the probable world situation will support the continuance of student protests in American society.

In the next decades, then, I believe we can forsee the continuation, with short-range ebbs and falls, of activism in American society. Only if activists were to become convinced that protests were ineffectual or social action impossible is this trend likely to be fundamentally reversed. None of this will mean that protesters will become a majority among American students; but we can anticipate a slowly growing minority of the most talented, empathic, and intellectually independent of our students who will take up arms against injustice both here and abroad.

IN SUMMARY

Throughout this discussion I have emphasized the contrast between two types of students, two types of family backgrounds, and two sets of values that inspire dissent from the Great Society. On the one hand I have discussed students I have termed alienated, whose values are apolitical, romantic, and esthetic. These students are most responsive to romantic themes of social criticism; that is, they reject our society because of its dehumanizing effects, its lack of esthetic quality, and its failure to provide "spiritual" fulfillment to its members. And they are relatively impervious to appeals to social, economic, or political justice. On the other hand I have discussed activists, who are politically involved, humanitarian, and universalistic in values. These students object to our society not because they oppose its basic principles, but because it fails to implement these principles fully at home and abroad.

In the future, the tension between the romantic-alienated and the universalistic-activist styles of dissent will probably increase. I would anticipate a growing polarization between those students and student groups who turn to highly personal and experiential pursuits like drugs, sex, art, and intimacy, and those students who redouble their efforts to change American society. In the past five years, activists have been in the ascendant, and the alienated have been little involved in organized political protests. But a variety of possible events could reverse this ascendancy. A sense of ineffectuality, especially if coupled with repression of organized dissent, would obviously dishearten many activists. More important, the inability of the student protest movement to define its own long-range objectives, coupled with its intransigent hostility to ideology and efficient organization, means that *ad hoc* protests are too rarely linked to the explicit intellectual, political, and social goals that alone can sustain prolonged efforts to change society. Without some shared, sustaining vision of the society and world they are working to promote, and frustrated by the enormous obstacles that beset any social reformer, student activists would be likely to return to the library.

How and whether this tension between alienation and activism is resolved seems to me of the greatest importance. If a growing number of activists, frustrated by political ineffectuality or a mounting war in Southeast Asia, withdraw from active social concern into a narrowly academic quest for professional competence, then a considerable reservoir of the most talented young Americans will have been lost to our society and the world. The field of dissent would be left to the alienated, whose intense quest for *personal* salvation, meaning, creativity, and revelation dulls their perception of the public world and inhibits attempts to better the lot of others. If, in contrast, tomorrow's potential activists can feel that their demonstrations and actions are effective in molding public opinion and, more important, in effecting needed social change, then the possibilities for constructive change in postindustrial American society are virtually without limit.

REFERENCES

AIKEN, M., DEMERATH, N. J., and MARWELL, G. Conscience and confrontation: some preliminary findings on summer civil rights volunteers. University of Wisconsin, 1966. (mimeo)

ALLEN, M., and SILVERSTEIN, H. Progress report: creative arts—alienated youth project. New York: March, 1967.

BAY, CHRISTIAN. Political and apolitical students: facts in search of theory. *Journal of Social Issues*, 1967, 23, (3).

BERNREUTER, ROBERT G. The college student: he is thinking, talking, acting. *Penn State Alumni News*, July, 1966.

BLOCK, J., HAAN, N., and SMITH, M. B. Activism and apathy in contemporary adolescents. In J. F. Adams (Ed.), *Understanding adolescence*. Boston: Allyn and Bacon, 1968.

COLES, ROBERT. Serpents and doves: non-violent youth in the South. In Erik Erikson (Ed.), *The challenge of youth*. New York: Basic Books, 1963.

COLES, ROBERT. *Children of crisis*. Boston: Little, Brown, 1967.

COWAN, JOHN LEWIS. Academic freedom, protest and university environments. Paper read at APA, New York, 1966.

DRAPER, HAL. *Berkeley, the new student revolt*. New York: Grove, 1965.

EHLE, JOHN. *The free men*. New York: Harper and Row, 1965.

ERIKSON, ERIK H. (Ed.) *The challenge of youth*. New York: Basic Books, 1963.

FISHMAN, JACOB R., and SOLOMON, FREDERIC. Psychological observations on the student sit-in movement. *Proceedings of the Third World Congress of Psychiatry*. Toronto: University of Toronto/Mcgill, n.d.

FISHMAN, JACOB R., and SOLOMON, FREDERIC. Youth and social action. *The Journal of Social Issues*, 1964, 20, (4), 1–28.

FLACKS, RICHARD E. The liberated generation: an exploration of the roots of student protest. *Journal of Social Issues*, 1967, 23, (3).

GASTWIRTH, D. Why students protest. Unpublished paper, Yale University, 1965.

HAYDEN, T. Quoted in *Comparative Education Review*, 1966, 10, 187.

HEIST, PAUL. Intellect and commitment: the faces of discontent. sion for Higher Education and the Center for the Study of Higher *Order and freedom on the campus*. Western Interstate Commis-Education, 1965.

HEIST, PAUL. The dynamics of student discontent and protest. Paper read at APA, New York, 1966.

JAHODA, MARIE. *Current concepts of positive mental health.* New York: Basic Books, 1958.

KATZ, J. The learning environment: social expectations and influences. Paper presented at American Council of Education, Washington, D.C., 1965.

KATZ, J. The student activists: rights, needs and powers of undergraduates. Stanford: Institute for the Study of Human Problems, 1967.

KEENE, S. How one big university laid unrest to rest. *The American Student,* 1966, 1, 18–21.

KELMAN, H. D. Notes on faculty activism. *Letter to Michigan Alumni,* 1966.

KENISTON, KENNETH. American students and the 'political revival.' *The American Scholar,* 1962, 32, 40–64.

KENISTON, KENNETH. *The uncommitted.* New York: Harcourt, Brace and World, 1965a.

KENISTON, KENNETH. The pressure to perform. *The Intercollegian.* September, 1965b.

KENISTON, KENNETH. The faces in the lecture room. In R. S. Morison (Ed.), *The American university.* Boston: Houghton Mifflin, 1966a.

KENISTON, KENNETH. The psychology of alienated students. Paper read at APA, New York, 1966b.

KENISTON, KENNETH, and HELMREICH, R. An exploratory study of discontent and potential drop-outs at Yale. Yale University, 1965. (mimeo)

KORNHAUSER, W. Alienation and participation in the mass university. Paper read at American Ortho-Psychiatric Association, Washington, D.C., 1967.

LIFTON, ROBERT JAY. Japanese youth: the search for the new and the pure. *The American Scholar,* 1960, 30, 332–344.

LIFTON, ROBERT JAY. Youth and history: individual change in postwar Japan. In E. Erikson (Ed.), *The challenge of youth.* New York: Harper and Row, 1963.

LIFTON, ROBERT JAY. Individual patterns in historical change. *Comparative Studies in Society and History,* 1964, 6, 369–383.

LIFTON, ROBERT JAY. Protean man. Yale University, 1965. (mimeo)

LIPSET, SEYMOUR M. Student opposition in the United States. *Government and Opposition,* 1966a, 1, 351–374.

LIPSET, SEYMOUR M. University students and politics in underdeveloped countries. *Comparative Education Review*, 1966b, 10, 132–162.

LIPSET, SEYMOUR M., and ALTBACH, P. G. Student politics and higher education in the United States. *Comparative Education Review*, 1966, 10, 320–349.

LIPSET, SEYMOUR M., and WOLIN, S. S. (Eds.) *The Berkeley student revolt*. Garden City, New York: Doubleday, 1965.

LYONNS, G. The police car demonstration: a survey of participants. In S. Lipset and S. Wolin (Eds.), *The Berkeley student revolt*. Garden City, New York: Doubleday, 1965.

MICHAEL, DONALD NELSON. *The next generation, the prospects ahead for the youth of today and tomorrow*. New York: Vintage, 1965.

MILLER, DANIEL R., and SWANSON, GUY E. *The changing American parent*. New York: Wiley, 1958.

MILLER, MICHAEL, and GILMORE, SUSAN (Eds.) *Revolution at Berkeley*. New York: Dell, 1965.

NEWFIELD, JACK. *A prophetic minority*. New York: New American Library, 1966.

NEWSWEEK. Campus, 1965. March 22, 1965.

PARSONS, TALCOTT. *The social system*. Glencoe, Ill.: Free Press, 1951.

PARSONS, TALCOTT. *Structure and process in modern societies*. Glencoe, Ill.: Free Press, 1960.

PAULUS, C. *A multivariate analysis study of student activist leaders, student government leaders, and non-activists*. Cited in Richard E. Peterson, *The student Left in American higher education*. Draft for Puerto Rico Conference on Students and Politics, 1967.

PERVIN, LAWRENCE A., REIK, L. E., and DALRYMPLE, W. (Eds.) *The college drop-out and the utilization of talent*. Princeton: Princeton University, 1966.

PETERSON, RICHARD E. *The scope of organized student protest in 1964–65*. Princeton: Educational Testing Service, 1966.

PETERSON, RICHARD E. The student Left in American higher education. Draft for Puerto Rico Conference on Students and Politics, 1967.

REED, M. Student non-politics, or how to make irrelevancy a virtue. *The American Student*, 1966, 1, (3), 7–10.

RIGNEY, FRANCIS J., and SMITH, L. D. *The real bohemia*. New York: Basic Books, 1961.

SCHNEIDER, PATRICIA. A study of members of SDS and YD at Harvard. Unpublished B.A. thesis, Wellesley College, 1966.

SOLOMON, FREDERIC, and FISHMAN, JACOB R. Perspectives on the student sit-in movement. *American Journal of Ortho-Psychiatry*, 1963, 33, 873–874.

SOLOMON, FREDERIC, and FISHMAN, JACOB R. Youth and peace: a psycho-social study of student peace demonstrators in Washington, D.C. *The Journal of Social Issues*, 1964, 20, (4), 54–73.

SOMERS, R. H. The mainsprings of the rebellion: a survey of Berkeley students in November, 1964. In S. Lipset and S. Wolin (Eds.), *The Berkeley student revolt*. Garden City, New York: Doubleday, 1965.

STERN, G. Myth and reality in the American college. *AAUP Bulletin*, Winter, 1966, 408–414.

SUCZEK, ROBERT FRANCIS, and ALFERT, E. Personality characteristic of college dropouts. University of California, 1966. (mimeo)

TROW, MARTIN. Some lessons from Berkeley. Paper presented to American Council of Education, Washington, D.C., 1965.

WATTS, WILLIAM ARTHUR, and WHITTAKER, D. Some socio-psychological differences between highly committed members of the Free Speech Movement and the student population at Berkeley. *Applied Behavioral Science*, 1966, 2, 41–62.

WATTS, WILLIAM ARTHUR, and WHITTAKER, D. Socio-psychological characteristics of intellectually oriented, alienated youth: a study of the Berkeley nonstudent. University of California, Berkeley, 1967. (mimeo)

WESTBY, D., and BRAUNGART, R. Class and politics in the family backgrounds of student political activists, *American Social Review*, 1966, 31, 690–692.

WHITE, WINSTON. *Beyond conformity*. Glencoe, Ill.: Free Press, 1961.

WHITTAKER, D., and WATTS, W. A. Personality and value attitudes of intellectually disposed, alienated youth. Paper presented at APA, New York, 1966.

WRIGHT, E. O. Student leaves of absence from Harvard College: A personality and social system approach. Unpublished paper, Harvard University, 1966.

ZINN, HOWARD. *SNCC, the new abolitionists*. Boston: Beacon, 1965.

2

Participant Observation in a Super-Patriot Discussion Group

MARK CHESLER and
RICHARD SCHMUCK

By means of direct participation and careful observation, these social psychologists obtained valuable data concerning a small extremist political group. They became active members of this group through a personal invitation from one of its members, frankly identifying themselves as social psychology graduate students. Although as graduate students they possessed an unusual background compared to other members, the group seems to have accepted them, as evidenced by the open and frank discussions carried on by the other members in the presence of these "new, different" individuals.

The investigators not only describe the group and their experiences with it, but also present a social psychological analysis that attempts to explain the reasons for the existence of such extremist groups and the functions they serve for their individual members. As the authors indicate, these data represent only one such group, and any generalizations to similar groups may not be justified.

From: *Journal of Social Issues*, 19(2): 18–30, 1963. Reprinted by permission of the authors and The Society for the Psychological Study of Social Issues.

We're building a beautiful house while termites work within.
It's as though you're moving slowly through a dream while
evil spirits work like a machine.

These comments characterize the fantasies of one member of a
small discussion group, informally affiliated with the Christian
Anti-Communism Crusade. We entered this local Super-Patriot
group as a result of a personal invitation from one of the participants and attended fifteen meetings. We were identified as
graduate students involved in educational research. It is our impression that we were perceived as young and sympathetic citizens
interested in American politics. Throughout our participation in
discussion we kept careful notes on the meetings and had access
to considerable Super-Patriot literature. Each of us systematically
observed and questioned particular members from time to time.
We took notes separately and compared these after each meeting.
The observations reported in this paper represent only instances
when both sets of notes were in agreement.

This particular group consists of ten to fifteen participants. Except for the two authors and one other member they are all over
forty-five years old. The core members are real estate salesmen,
insurance salesmen, housewives, low level administrators, a clerical
worker, a female teacher, a male teacher who serves as leader, and
our retired host. For the most part these entrepreneurs and lower
echelon white collar employees maintain a lower middle class
standard of living.

Most of the members are recruited through personal contact, as
a result of occupational associations or geographic propinquity.
Many of the members interact with one another in other organizations, i.e., especially at a so-called "Conservative Club" and the
American Legion; but so far as we know, they seldom discuss
their Super-Patriot activities with non-members.

Although members come from a variety of Protestant backgrounds, the predominant religious denomination is clearly Bap-
tist-fundamentalist. They are critical of the authority and politics
of the National Council of Churches. The members often reiterate

NOTE: This is a revised version of a paper presented at the Society for
the Psychological Study of Social Issues Symposium on "Extremist Groups
in the United States," American Psychological Association meetings, September, 1962.

the prophecies and analyses of the nationally known fundamentalist minister, Carl McIntire.[1] Once, when a visiting Baptist clergyman attempted to present an apologia for the National Council of Churches, his remarks were challenged and disregarded. Some of the members are changing their church affiliations in order to escape what they consider to be the pernicious influence of the National Council.

With the exception of the two teachers, none of the participants has more than a high school education. This observation is limited to this particular study group, since leadership in the national organization includes several old family doctors and teachers. Nevertheless, members are aggressively anti-intellectual. They distrust "eggheads" and college professors who, as they say, learn about life only from books. Furthermore, they believe that Communists have infiltrated American education and have gained control of the nation's public schools and colleges in order to confuse students. As a result members feel that students are being taught that life has no ultimate design or purpose, that issues of national policy are no longer black and white, that the source of morals is in cultural and class backgrounds, and not derived from eternal truths. They protest, too, that competition is being downgraded in our schools in favor of concepts such as "social adjustment" and "mental health," and that progressive education is to blame for Johnny's not being able to read. As they see it, a Marxist-Leninist takeover of some American schools has already occurred. Their position on this issue is defined by Root (1955, 1958), Rudd (1957), and Wittmer (1956).

This discussion group is one of a reported ten thousand such small groups throughout the country. We have been told by several of its members that some thirty groups are located within their own community. This particular community is a small, midwestern, industrial city, with a population of about 25,000. The groups in this city were organized by a nucleus of American Legion members using the Legion Hall as a focal point for the commencement of anti-Communist education. A local Legionnaire

---

[1]Carl McIntire directs the "20th Century Reformation Hour" emanating from Collingswood, New Jersey, and is heard on a national radio network for thirty minutes, five days a week.

first arranged anti-Communist lectures at Legion meetings and other public events. He developed and directed discussion groups and trained enough group leaders to promulgate enterprises such as the one described here. The discussion group we observed started in the late Fall of 1961; we entered the group in December, 1961.

Meetings were held in the members' homes, every two weeks. Each meeting began with the Pledge of Allegiance. Then the leader, a high school history teacher, read from his notes. These notes often consisted of passages from J. Edgar Hoover's *Masters of Deceit* (1958) or from a manual on Communism published by the Church League of America (1961). The reading was followed by playing a tape-recorded lecture given by some renowned anti-Communist such as Herbert Philbrick, Fred Schwarz, or Cleon Skousen.[2] The tape was followed by a discussion in which earlier readings and lectures were reinforced.

The purpose of this paper is not only to present a resumé of what happened in these meetings. In addition we want to penetrate the surface of meeting events in order to speculate on some of the social psychological bases of how and why some people participate in Super-Patriot discussion and education.

SUPER-PATRIOT POSITIONS AND PROGRAMS

The avowed purpose of the group is, of course, anti-Communism. Presumably the group gathers to become educated about the principles and dangers of Communism. But this manifest goal actually masks certain latent purposes. Anti-Communism serves as an umbrella for, among other things, anti-welfarism, anti-liberalism, anti-intellectualism, and anti-internationalism. For instance, tapes, readings, and discussions suggest that members should: distrust welfare supporters because Communists often disguise their subversive activities by advocating humanitarian values; maintain an aloofness from so-called "liberals" because they are

---

[2]Some examples are: "I Led Three Lives" (Philbrick), "Communism's Appeal to the Intellectual" (Schwarz), and "Communists and Education" (Skousen).

probably Communists or most certainly Communist dupes; watch out for psychologists or teachers who are already "brainwashing" students in the direction of Communism; distrust intellectuals such as Eleanor Roosevelt because people like her are leading us to Socialism, the gateway to Communism; and understand that giving food and clothing to under-developed countries only helps the depraved Communists because then they can concentrate their resources on increased weaponry.

The national organizational strategy includes initial informative lectures to large community groups. These are to be followed by involvement in small, face-to-face discussion sessions, such as the meetings we have been attending; and finally, the eventual organization of these discussion groups in an attempt to influence legitimate political machinery directly. Already, in their community, plans are being made to channel Super-Patriots into local and state political organizations. An organization called Freedom in Action, with headquarters in Texas and regional offices throughout the country, is coordinating this local political activity.[3]

The political beliefs of the participants in this discussion group range from clearly conservative to ultra-conservative or reactionary. However, they do not owe allegiance to a particular party and are willing to cut across political lines to insure the election of a sympathetic candidate. We surmise that an ideal national ballot, for instance, would find Republican Barry Goldwater running against Democrat Strom Thurmond for President.

The members' view of the political spectrum is unique and confused. Their position is summarized in Figure 1.

They characterize Communism, on the left pole, as a totalitarian government dictating to many countries. Slightly to the right of this left pole, they designate a Fascist government as a dictatorship in control of a single nation. We interpret their view of the distinction between Communism and Fascism as the national or international character of totalitarianism. Still further to the right, in their view, is Marxist Social Democracy, the centralization of national resources via democratic decision-making. The leader noted that

[3]Eight members of this discussion group currently are involved in Freedom in Action, four of these eight are running for positions as delegates to county Republican or Democratic conventions.

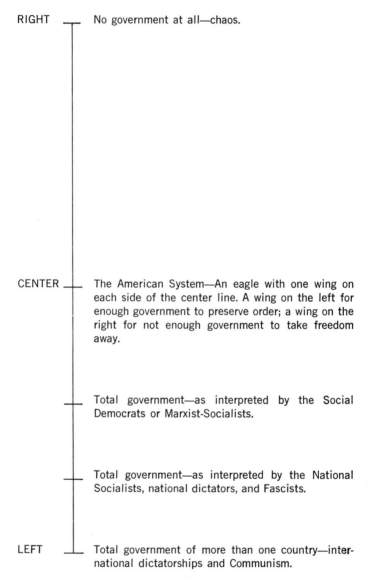

RIGHT — No government at all—chaos.

CENTER — The American System—An eagle with one wing on each side of the center line. A wing on the left for enough government to preserve order; a wing on the right for not enough government to take freedom away.

Total government—as interpreted by the Social Democrats or Marxist-Socialists.

Total government—as interpreted by the National Socialists, national dictators, and Fascists.

LEFT — Total government of more than one country—international dictatorships and Communism.

Figure 1

Social Democracy was advanced by the Fabian Socialists in England and has since been repudiated. According to him, Communists use Fascist dictators and Social Democrats to run interference for them in their attempt to take over a new nation. At the exact middle of this continuum the members place the American eagle, with a wing on either side of the center. The wing on the left represents enough government for order and security, while the wing on the right represents a balance for the protection of individual freedom. They label the right pole of the political spectrum as no government at all, a state of natural chaos. The leader explains that from the Communist position on the extreme left, all other forms of government are to the right. He adds, this helps us understand why Communists see believers in our American system, actually in the middle, as the "Extreme Right."

Despite these political perceptions, which appear similar to those of the John Birch Society, members of this group hesitate, as yet, to approve of all the means and targets of that organization; they do not indict President Kennedy directly, and do not think that Eisenhower was a self-conscious agent of the Communists. On the other hand, they support the impeachment of Chief Justice Warren, and see the Supreme Court deciding security and civil liberties issues in terms of the judges' attitudes toward Communists.

Furthermore, the members' foreign policy views are isolationist, mixed with a militant "attack and liberate the satellites" theme. They say they do not understand why the Air Force hasn't dropped a nuclear bomb on Cuba. They see disarmament as "national suicide" and remark that one of our "founding fathers," George Washington, warned us of this. They view the United Nations as a Communist technique to deprive our nation of its national identity, financial resources, and independence. The proof they present for this assertion is that two Communists, Hiss and Molotov, were primarily responsible for writing the United Nations Charter. Some additional examples of their stated historical views of world affairs are that:

> (1) Stalin put Hitler into power in Germany and encouraged him to make suicidal war so that the Communists could take over control of Europe afterwards; and

(2)   The Communist revolution in China usurped the free
      but destitute government of Chiang Kai-shek and rav-
      aged the nation as a prelude to complete social control.
      When queried as to reports of the curtailment of polit-
      ical and economic freedoms during the Chiang Kai-shek
      regime, the leader explained that Communists had in-
      filtrated the Nationalist government in order to perpe-
      trate atrocities leading to the people's loss of faith in
      the government.

Their verbalizations of socio-political problems in a dichoto-
mized moral-immoral, pro-Communist–anti-Communist framework
is similar to findings on authoritarian and dogmatic personalities
(Adorno, et al., 1950; Rokeach, 1960), as well as the reactions
of groups and individuals under stress (Menninger, 1957; Grinker
and Spiegel, 1945; Coleman, 1957). Indeed, members consider
themselves and their nation under stress—in danger from the national and international wings of the Communist Conspiracy. They
feel it is their duty as patriotic Americans to alert America to that
threat in its diverse forms.[4] It appears to us that group members
do not appreciate the complexity of issues facing national policy
makers. We will attempt to examine some of the psychological
and social bases for their views.

SUPER-PATRIOT SOCIAL ORIGINS

We suggest that certain societal changes underlie the emergence
of this Super-Patriot organization.[5] It appears that the Super-
Patriots we have observed are losing their feelings of personal
effectiveness in relation to social organizations in which they are
participating. Indeed, they are experiencing feelings of powerless-
ness and isolation (Seeman, 1959). They are being confronted
with a changing society and community with rapidly changing

---

[4]It is interesting to note that the left wing groups also consider the nation
in danger from the threat posed by the conspiracy of the "right" in its
diverse forms.

[5]Some of the essays in D. Bell, (Ed.), *The New American Right*. New
York: Criterion, 1955; notably those by R. Hofstadter, D. Reisman & N.
Glazer, and S. M. Lipset, represent other analyses of the problems.

values, while their personal social positions would have them stand still and hold onto the past. They feel that they have worked hard for their current social status. They also feel that their social standing is now threatened by new groups and "alien conspirators" who have risen more quickly than they and who have different values and styles of life. The Super-Patriots wish to find the lines of social power whereby they might once again participate effectively in community politics and move in the direction of their personal destinies. Failing in these endeavors, they look for reasons why they cannot regain this sense of power, usefulness, and involvement; and they conclude that it is due to the enemies within who have control and who prevent them from having any significant influence in determining the future.

We suggest that their frustrations have been engendered through the increased complexities involved in large-scale organizations, the gradual ascendance of a new national elite, and recent changes in international relations. In the first place, the significant growth of large-scale organizations has changed the kinds of skills required to achieve individual success in American society, particularly for persons in the middle class. One consequence of their lack of success is that they view bureaucracies as absorbing participants into one collective, making individuals anonymous and powerless. The Super-Patriots think of the "small man," the entrepreneur, and the rural individualist as no longer shaping the political and social environment directly. Instead, they see situations being shaped and decisions being made for them by bureaucrats and large organizations.

Second, new groups have risen to positions of wealth and influence, replacing the older, established families and power constellations. These new power configurations operate on the basis of new values requiring formal education and social skills and they reward these values. The Super-Patriots view the new mode of education as being opposed to hard work. They feel that "adjustment" rather than "achievement" and know-why rather than know-how are the themes of today's schools. They are concerned that society no longer rewards rugged personal commitment to hard work and the self-made individualism of the past. They feel that vast new social welfare programs work contrary to the traditional assumption that one can surely and only achieve happiness and respect by dint of personal effort and work. These welfare programs threaten them with the awesome bureaucracy of the government and the perceived antithesis of the free man and individual effort. Super-Patriots think that more power, money, information, and status are available to more people in modern America, but don't view themselves as ascending at the same rate as others. It's as though the rules of the game, the standards of success, have changed in midstream and the players feel cheated.

Third, we feel that the contemporary recognition of areas of gray in personal morality and in national decision-making are challenging older, clearer, moral and political standards. Now, too, the moral supremacy and physical inviolability of the United States is being threatened by a collectivist force. Because of these threats, the Super-Patriots feel that a defeatist internationalism has been proposed by factions at home and abroad. They object to being asked to share their cherished prosperity with people less deserving in the form of national social welfare programs and international aid programs. Group members are sure that if other countries and people had worked as hard as they, public aid would not be necessary. Thus they see the last vestiges of integrity and identity rapidly slipping away as America loses her national independence and security.

The personal dilemmas and predilections of these Super-Patriots have recently been corroborated and heightened by the election and prominence of minority group members and educated intellectuals. A team composed of young men, internationalists, and social welfarists is seen to have taken over in Washington, e.g., Arthur Goldberg, Robert Kennedy, Abraham Ribicoff, Adlai Stevenson. The status and policity frustrations these participants have feared are beginning to become manifest on the domestic and international scene. The election of John Kennedy and the intransigence of Soviet Russia, both of which have forced apparent domestic and international compromise, lend an aura of reality and reaffirmation to the concerns and fears of the Super-Patriots.

The Super-Patriots ask, what is the defense against the forces that threaten our traditional American values? Where in this advancing system of national suicide and collectivism and in the encroaching personal submersion and anomie, does a man find meaning and salvation? It is our observation that the answer has come to them through the "certain trumpets" of the leaders of the ultra-right; the way lies in the retention of traditional values— and more—it lies in the resurgence of power and the repulsion of the ideas and armies that threaten us. Their targets have been delineated clearly. Their means are an educational program designed to awaken America to her unseen peril, to save her from the grasp of her enemies and to be recognized as her true sons and saviors. It seems that this mission would be enough of an attraction for many people to remain active in Super-Patriot groups. However, other satisfactions occur for the frustrated participants as a result of their small group, face-to-face contacts with others like themselves. These include the fulfillment of psycho-social motivations, best understood by observing personal styles of individual participation in group interaction.

SUPER-PATRIOT INTERPERSONAL STYLES

Individual styles of participation in the group are quite varied. The retired gentleman, for instance, is the most sentimental and emotional member of the group. Meetings are most often held at his home. His major role as host and his strong affiliative needs place him in the position of providing socio-emotional leadership. He overcomes some of his intense personal frustrations through his participation in Super-Patriot activities. He often reiterates that he never realized how much his country meant to him until he retired and "got into this anti-Communist business." He has developed a religious devotion to his country and says of the Communists that "they're trying to kill us just as Christ was crucified." His previous occupation in a privately owned electric power company makes up much of the apperceptive mass which influences his cognitions about government activity. In fact, he once overlooked the large public expenditure in the arms industry, stressing that our government has the most control, most investment, and the most bureaucratic waste in publicly owned electric power. Generalizing from this, he distrusts most federal programs and is currently actively protesting federal medical aid for the aged.

Another member, quoted at the beginning of this paper, suspects national traitors of "filching corn from the national bin," as we continue to pour it in. His participation in the group provides him with a convenient outlet for his hostile antipathy toward new elites. The group encourages and reinforces these expressions. His behavioral orientation is to do something about the problem of creeping Socialism immediately; an investigation of the State Department going back about fifteen years to weed out the Communist scoundrels, getting out of the United Nations immediately, cutting back on foreign aid, drastically reducing welfare, etc. He is quite militant and promises to help vigorously when the group gets ready to "do something."

The task leader of the group, the high school teacher, manifests perhaps the most interesting combination of personal characteristics. His most prominent motivation seems to be a desire for power. He gains a great satisfaction out of having the correct answer immediately upon being questioned and is sometimes ostentatious about giving information. He conceives of himself as a "grass roots intellectual" familiar with governmental theory and practice, with the inconsistencies and evils of Socialism and the benefits of Capitalism. He states that he was once involved in a Doctoral program in Government, but that he left when the teacher started explaining "history according to Marx." In this group, unlike some of his past academic associations, he finds a ready audience for his particular intellectual skills. He enjoys being called upon for historical documentation and current interpretation of policy, and seems resentful and jealous when other group members fill this information-giving role.

Certain mechanisms of defense are used by more than one of the participants; among the most prevalent mechanisms are projection, denial, and rationalization. One prevalent projection involves the transfer of one's own desires for power and control to the desires for power, the intellectual prowess, and the superhuman organizational abilities of the Communists or bureaucrats in Washington. One favorite saying for the group is:

> Sir Galahad had the strength of ten men because he had a pure heart,

One Communist has the strength of ten men because he can dupe that many into working for him.

Denial and rationalization are prominent defenses used in solving problems posed by the inconsistencies of Christian altruism and hate, populist civilian interests and military elitism, democratic freedom and forced constraint of the opposition within, etc. Conflict is denied and overlooked while incompatible policy positions are upheld. An argument to curtail foreign aid was supported by an elaborate rationalization suggesting that: the surplus food we give to starving Indians or Czechs decreases the number of people the Communist rulers in these nations have to feed themselves. Thus, they are able to spend that extra money on airplanes and weapons. In order to preclude this we should not give foreign aid. In this respect, CARE is viewed as a Communist technique to "dupe" many charitable Americans into helping satellite masters prepare for world domination.

It is our observation that the style of group interaction is designed, consciously or unconsciously, to satisfy simultaneously the personal motivations of the participants and to relieve some of the shared feelings of alienation and frustration that have been built up by the changing social order. Through informal contacts and discussions, members receive affective and evaluative support for their frustrations and beliefs by interacting with people experiencing similar social and political alienation. Through social and ideological reinforcement they encourage an aggressive resolution of their frustration on a Communist scapegoat (Allport, 1958). The Communist chase actually involves, as it did for McCarthy, attacks upon liberals, intellectuals, urban aristocrats, bureaucrats, and humanitarians. By reinstituting their claim to true Americanism and as true defenders of the religious as well as the national faith, the Super-Patriot crusaders gain a new sense of status and mission. They gain a new feeling of meaning and union with their compatriots in a populist reform movement.

Each meeting is arranged to support and reinforce these predilections and expectations. All of these Super-Patriot conjectures are supported by a positive affective tone in the group. Perhaps one of the most prominent standards pervading the group, in fact,

is a tendency to emphasize informal interpersonal relations. The
predominant expectation is to feel relaxed, congenial and agree-
able. Greetings are effusive, i.e., backslapping, handshaking, and
personal inquiries are exceptionally warm and noticeable. These
characteristics are common to many lower middle class groups.
This particular enterprise is distinguished by its out-group hostility,
specific Super-Patriot content, and evaluative emphasis.

As a response to national attacks on Super-Patriots, and as a
means of supporting re-entry into social involvement, an extreme
in-group feeling has developed. The members care for one another,
defend one another when attacked, and see most sources of confusion, duplicity, and disagreement external to the group. Arguments are subtly avoided within the group. The agreement to
avoid disagreement was particularly noticeable with respect to the
treatment afforded a visiting Baptist minister when he supported
the activities of the National Council of Churches. Although his
ideas were challenged, there was little overt animosity and he was
quickly ignored and disregarded.

In addition, much approval is given to clearly stated conservative
policy positions. Support is gained from favorable publicity and
speeches made by prominent adherents. The appeal to authority is
a common technique, i.e., books, pamphlets, J. Edgar Hoover, and
the school teacher leader are constantly referred to for evaluative
support.[6] At one meeting, for instance, a prominent representative
of the national organization was present and reassured the participants that: (1) the Communist conspiracy is ever dangerous and
we just got started in time, (2) we are winning but cannot give up
or rest, (3) our power is such that the Editor of *Life* and *Time*
magazines, "an innocent dupe of the Reds and his own editorial
staff," has agreed with us, (4) there are many more of us involved
in this than you think; you're not alone, and (5) we'll be ready
to move pretty soon and all those scoundrels in Washington surely
will be surprised.

Throughout discussions virtually all of the members support one

[6]The national organization sells and supplies the host with numerous
pamphlets and materials. Among those books and pamphlets most frequently referred to are: Hoover (1958), Schwarz (1960), *The Communist
Party of the United States* (1956).

another's reasoning quite sincerely. These immediate supports and indications of cohesiveness help maintain both the friendly and congenial style of interaction, and the prominent beliefs and attitudes held by individuals. Similarly, the cohesive and friendly atmosphere helps maintain cognitive and evaluative unanimity, as well as affective support.

We attempted to explore group cohesiveness and ideological rigidity by confronting the group on two counts. The first involves sources of information and how one determines their validity; the other involves the presentation of a religious love ethic. These confrontations were handled typically by the school teacher leader. In response to the first problem, he pointed to certain "reliable" government documents, especially those put out by the House Committee on UnAmerican Activities, or to special publications like *Masters of Deceit* (Hoover, 1958) written by what he calls "reliable" government personnel. When asked at one point, "Who do we believe, Hoover or Fulbright?", he retorted quickly, "Let's let Arkansas take care of Fulbright!"[7] As a rule, it appears that good sources of political information are reactionaries and military elitists, while poor sources are domestic liberals and internationalists.

Group members seem to be quite defensive regarding the issue of a love ethic. They employ a number of different strategies to handle the problem created by the religious injunction to love all men while hating and suspecting the Communists. One way they try to solve this problem is by denying that their reactions to Communists have any religious implications at all. These Super-Patriots see Communism and Communist infiltrators as Godless, lacking moral virtue or integrity of any kind. They fear that the Communists will defeat us unless we follow the same pattern of subversion and hostility. It appears to us that what is said indirectly is that we must temporarily give up the ethic in order to preserve it. Another perhaps more psychologically economical way in which members deal with the problem is in terms of the "devil theory," which associates all people in the Communist camp with Satan.

[7]Senator Fulbright was mentioned particularly because of a memorandum and Senate address concerning the censorship of military speeches, *Congr. Rec.*, August 2, 1961, 107 (11), 14433–14439.

Since they see it as sinful to aid the devil in getting more earthly power, they have only to stop the spread of evil as militantly as possible. The spirit of this approach echoes "Onward Christian Soldiers" and helps to explain the "crusade" theme in some national Super-Patriot organizations.

It is our feeling that the phenomena discussed here will be of increasing importance to all social scientists and concerned observers. Clearly, these emergent groups and activities have not yet been subject to detailed investigation. We plan a two-fold extension of the observations presented in this paper. First, we will investigate Super-Patriot concerns and criticisms by undertaking a content analysis of extremist literature. It appears to us that these concerns and criticisms reflect value cleavages in America's history as a pluralistic society. Further, we feel that it is critical to investigate the effects Super-Patriot attacks are having on local community activities and on national policy-making. Secondly, we plan a public opinion survey of a sample of participants in Super-Patriot activities. Our interest is in the social and family background characteristics, the attitudinal and value clusters, as well as some other psychological attributes of Super-Patriots. We feel that both extensions will enhance our understanding of the character of these contemporary American phenomena.

REFERENCES

ADORNO, T. W., FRENKEL-BRUNSWIK, E., LEVINSON, D., and SANFORD, R. N. *The Authoritarian Personality*, New York: Harper, 1950.

ALLPORT, G. W. *The Nature of Prejudice*, New York: Doubleday Anchor, 1958.

BELL, D. (Ed.) *The New American Right*, New York: Criterion, 1955.

COLEMAN, J. S. *Community Conflict*, Glencoe, Ill.: Free Press, 1957.

The Communist Party of the United States: A Handbook for Americans, Washington, D.C.: United States Government Printing Office, 1956.

GRINKER, R. R., and SPIEGEL, J. P. *Men Under Stress*, Philadelphia: Blackiston, 1945.

HOOVER, J. E. *Masters of Deceit*, New York: Henry Holt, 1958.

A Manual for Survival, Wheaton, Ill.: Church League of America.

MENNINGER, K. A.   Psychological aspects of the organism under stress. *General Systems Yearbook*, 2, 146–175, 1957.

ROKEACH, M.   *The Open and Closed Mind*, New York: Basic Books, 1960.

ROOT, E.   *Brainwashing in the High Schools*, New York: Devin-Adair Co., 1958.

ROOT, E.   *Collectivism on the Campus*, New York: Devin-Adair Co., 1955.

RUDD, A. G.   *Bending the Twig*, Chicago: Heritage Foundation, 1957.

SCHWARZ, F.   *You Can Trust the Communists . . . to Be Communists.* Englewood Cliffs, New Jersey: Prentice-Hall, 1960.

SEEMAN, M.   On the meaning of alienation, *Amer. Soc. Rev.*, 24, 783–791, 1959.

WITTMER, F.   *Conquest of the American Mind*, Boston: Meador Publishing Co., 1956.

3

The Riot That Didn't Happen

ROBERT SHELLOW and
DEREK V. ROEMER

In examining examples of involvement in real-life problem situations by the social scientist, it is important to distinguish between his involvement (1) as private citizen, primarily motivated by his private political-social opinions, or (2) as scientist, objectively applying his training in experimental methodology and his professional knowledge based upon cumulated data collection and theoretical considerations. The present selection is an example of the latter case. In consulting with police, motorcyclists, and the general public, the authors demonstrate the assistance that a trained social scientist can be to a worried and apprehensive community in the time of impending public chaos.

The report also shows that for the social scientist to be effective in a community action program, he must be flexible in dealing with the public involved. In the event that some of his suggestions are not accepted he should not become personally defensive, but continue to pursue a mode of participation that reflects his scientific training in the best sense.

Although citizens traditionally rely upon police for prevention

From: *Social Problems,* 14(2): 221–233, 1966. Reprinted by permission of the authors and of The Society for the Study of Social Problems.

and control of civil riot, most police departments have only limited experience in coping with large crowds, much less full riot conditions. Moreover, it seems likely that police will be called to serve in this capacity with growing frequency as public streets become more and more the stage on which social protests and counter-protests are acted out.

This growing threat to civil order poses questions of specific relevance for social scientists. Can the approach and theories of social science be put to use in communities facing the threat or fact of civil disorder? Can social scientists study riot behavior as it develops, while at the same time sharing the responsibility for its prevention?

The authors of this paper were confronted by these two questions in the summer of 1965. A national motorcycle race was scheduled for the Labor Day weekend at Upper Marlboro, the County seat of Prince George's County, Maryland. This county of 500,000 population is adjacent to Washington, D.C., and is partly suburban, partly rural. Upper Marlboro is in a rural sector, but is only about 15 miles from well-populated suburbs.

Our involvement in what later turned out to be six weeks of planning for riot prevention began as a casual conversation between one of the authors and a detective lieutenant.[1] The news media had reported all the gory details of the Weir's Beach riot which followed the National Championship motorcycle races near Laconia, New Hampshire. The first details of the July 4th resort

NOTE: The two authors constitute the "staff" referred to in the paper. The authors wish to acknowledge the contribution of senior officers and men of the Prince George's County Police Department whose decisions and actions were ultimately responsible for the project's success. In this regard, we wish to cite especially Inspector Roland Sweitzer, Deputy Chief Vincent Free, and Captain Thomas Rogato, who carried the burden of planning and daily command decisions, and Chief George Panagoulis whose sanction of the project guaranteed the necessary flexibility in the assignment of men and equipment throughout the Labor Day weekend. We also wish to express our gratitude to the following motorcycle clubs: the D.C. Strokers, the Saddle Squires, the Draggin' Gypsies, and the D.C. Ramblers, whose members were kind enough to introduce us into the world of motorcycling.

[1]We had been consulting and collaborating with the County police on a variety of matters for some years, and had developed informal, first-name relationships with many officers.

riots were still Page One news. The lieutenant reported that shortly after the Weir's Beach episode three motorcyclists, claiming to be "Hell's Angels," were arrested and jailed for disorderly conduct by town policemen in Prince George's County. Angered by being forced to bathe for court, the cyclists threatened to return in force over Labor Day to "tear up the County."

Wishing to be kept posted on the local situation, we spoke to the Inspector responsible for police action over Labor Day. He was concerned, but he wasn't sure how seriously to take the possibility of violence. We all agreed that very little was known about these Hell's Angels and how they were likely to behave among several thousand motorcyclists amassed for a big race. Our professional curiosity aroused, we offered to try to chase down the rumors, and bring the results of our inquiries back to the police. But two weeks of search failed to turn up so much as one Hell's Angel, though the rumors of invasion and destruction were persistent and pro-liferating.[2]

When we reviewed accounts of a number of recent riots and disturbances in connection with recreational or sporting events,[3] we noted several factors which seemed to be significant in all of them. Though they are not based on a systematic review of the relevant sociological literature, we have found that the following generalizations fit rather well with at least one major theoretical analysis:[4]

---

[2]We managed to track down one individual who was alleged to be acquainted with genuine Hell's Angels. He said he could see no earthly reason why Hell's Angels or anyone else would want to leave California and come to Prince George's County. In mid-August we learned he himself had left for California on his "motor," and did not intend to return before Spring, if at all.

[3]Most of these accounts were from newspapers, with the exception of a very informative report and analysis of a 1963 riot at Garnett, Kansas, in connection with a sports car race. The report was prepared by Bill D. Schul, Juvenile Director, and is available from the Office of the Attorney General of Kansas, in Topeka.

[4]R. H. Turner and L. M. Killian, *Collective Behavior*, Englewood Cliffs, N.J.: Prentice-Hall, 1957; R. H. Turner, "Collective Behavior," in E. L. Faris (Ed.), *Handbook of Modern Sociology*, Chicago: Rand McNally, 1964. Though all the events referred to above occurred in recreational set-tings on major holidays or at national sports events, similarities to many of the race riots and political disturbances discussed by these authors can be discerned.

1) An influx of outsiders into a small town or circumscribed amusement area, where the number of outsiders was large relative to the number of local inhabitants and control personnel.

2) The outsiders were distinguished from "locals" by some common feature such as an intense interest (e.g., motorcycling), an age group (e.g., college youth), place of residence (e.g., urban areas), race, etc.

3) The distinction between "locals" and "outsiders" was often made more visible by differences between the two in dress, argot, and other expressive behavior.

The specific conditions under which exuberance and rowdiness exploded into rioting seemed to be the following:

1) Recreational, service and control facilities "flooded" by overwhelming numbers of visitors, who were then left at loose ends, ready for any kind of "action."

2) Ineffectual, often provocative attempts at control and expression of authority by police or officials.

3) Development of a sense of group solidarity among members of the crowd.

Often the locals, including the authorities, contributed to the developing cohesion by perceiving the visitors as a homogeneous mass, attributing negative characteristics to them as a class, labelling them, e.g., as "hoodlums" or "young punks," and then treating them accordingly. The effect of opposition or attack in increasing group cohesion is well documented.[5] If the opposition is ineffectual as well, many members of the developing mob begin to sense its potential power. (Several reports of disturbances attributed careful pre-planning to a small cadre of dedicated instigators, who allegedly circulated rumors before the event and selected targets on the scene. Actual proof of "planning," however, as opposed to mere repetition of common rumors, is difficult to obtain.)

It had become obvious that in order to prepare for the Labor Day weekend, much information would be needed about the organization of motorcycling, as a sport and as a way of life. Moving

---

[5]F. M. Thrasher, *The Gang*, Chicago: University of Chicago Press, 1927; M. Sherif and C. W. Sherif, *Reference Groups: Explorations into Conformity and Deviation of Adolescents*, New York: Harper and Row, 1964.

from one enthusiast to another and making contacts at the local
Harley-Davidson dealer, we made a number of discoveries.
Motorcyclists come from all walks of life. The majority are employed, and need to be, since as much as $3,000 may be tied up
in a "motor." The devotees insist that the size of the machine
separates the men from the boys. Those who own enormous Har-
ley-Davidsons and the large Triumphs or BSA's, and who engage
in competitive events such as races, "field events" and "hill climbs,"
see themselves as a breed apart from the "candy ass" owners of
Hondas and the lightweights. For the former group, the motorcycle often serves as the fulcrum of social and even family life.
They enjoy being able to take off any evening at a moment's
notice and ride, say, from Washington, D.C. to Atlantic City,
returning as the sun rises. They travel regularly to weekend field
meets and races, usually camping overnight on the scene.

Like many hobby-sports, motorcycling has its formal organization, the American Motorcycle Association (AMA) and its "sanctioned" members. AMA clubs have tight rules and tolerate little
deviance. There are other clubs, some of which aspire to AMA
membership and some of which suit those who enjoy a more
relaxed and casual organization. The latter require only that members not seriously embarrass the club in public. They tend to be
more tolerant in their attitudes regarding noisy mufflers and styling,
and less regimented during group expeditions. All get classified
by the AMA as "outlaws."

Aside from these more or less conforming clubs, the "outlaw"
class also includes groups of dedicated rowdies who pride themselves on their ability to intimidate and destroy. The *Hell's Angels
Motorcycle Club of California* is such a group, as are the *Gooses*,
from New York and New Jersey, or the *Pagans*, from the Washington area. Some groups and individuals trade on the established
reputation of the Hell's Angels, imitating their insignia, the "winged
death's head and wheel."[6]

Spokesmen for the motorcycling "Establishment" often refer to
the "one percent who cause all the trouble," and give the sport a

[6]Jackets with insignia, often brought back as souvenirs of a California
trip, can be traded around from one motorcyclist to another, each taking
his turn as a "Hell's Angel" and enjoying all the rights and privileges
attendant thereto.

bad image. The rowdies have proudly accepted "one percenter" as an honorific epithet, and often have it emblazoned on their costume as a badge of commitment. It is the "one percenter" who personifies the popular stereotype of the motorcycle gang member, as portrayed by Marlon Brando in "The Wild Ones." Current styles among these individuals include long hair, beards, earrings, oily dungarees which are never washed, and an enormous variety of bizarre, highly personalized regalia. Some affect the habit attributed to "beatniks" of never bathing.

Regardless of their reference group or status within it, motorcyclists are of one voice in complaining of police persecution, and they all report victimization on the streets by ordinary motorists. Many respectable motorcyclists, like the "rowdy outlaws," see themselves as a persecuted minority.[7]

With regard to the Labor Day weekend itself, we learned that the schedule of events was more complex than we or the police had thought. Aside from the big race on Sunday, the "Ninth Annual Tobacco Trail Classic" at the Upper Marlboro track, there were lesser races at the same track on Saturday. The main race was for the first time a National Championship event, with top riders competing for points toward the national title. At the Vista track, 14 miles away but within the same police jurisdiction, there were to be "field events" (drag races, "riding the plank," "sack races," etc.) on Saturday and Sunday and an AMA-sanctioned race meet Monday. The sponsors of the Upper Marlboro races had also scheduled a Saturday night race, at a track 30 miles away in the Baltimore suburbs, "to give people something to do and keep them out of trouble."

The Vista track had in the past operated as an "outlaw" track without AMA sanction, and most or all of the competitors and spectators had been Negroes. However, in 1965 it achieved sanctioned status, and its events were now listed in the national calendar. A dance hall, popular with Washington area Negroes, was located in the track infield and would be operating every night of the weekend. Very likely large proportions of those attending

[7]One suspects that even respectable enthusiasts found attractive as well as abhorrent elements in the outlaw image, even though they resented and suffered from its indiscriminate application to all motorcyclists by the general public.

the motorcycle events at Vista would be Negroes. The crowd at
the Marlboro track was expected to be between 3,000 and 6,000;
a much smaller crowd was anticipated at Vista. Most motorcyclists
we spoke to thought there would be a great deal of migration
during the weekend from one track to another and among the
various camping areas (assuming there were more than one),
the taverns, and other recreation spots. Easy mobility is the essence
of motorcycling.

Concluding that our staff enjoyed a special and privileged
relationship with motorcyclists, the police asked us whether or not
the race should be called off. We did not feel we could take responsibility for the decision, but we joined in the deliberations.
To cancel a public event on the basis of thin rumor alone was a
dangerous precedent to set, yet to knowingly jeopardize the safety
of innocent people was unthinkable. Finally it was decided to
permit the race to be run as scheduled, with every effort being
made to avert violence. Our shift in role from outside consultant
to partnership with the police in this project tied us much closer
to the action and events of the weekend than would have been
true in the role of detached scientist-observer.

GOALS AND STRATEGIES

The decision to permit the race made, we then developed a set
of major goals which we felt should guide our own planning and
that of the police.

First of all we encouraged sober planning for all the events
and contingencies of the long weekend. Naturally, advance planning was not foreign to a professional police department. Nonetheless we felt that the unsettled state of the Hell's Angels rumors,
plus our refusal to make pseudo-authoritative pronouncements on
the probable course of events, helped maintain a degree of controlled anxiety among police officials. This limited anxiety went
far to prevent a premature resolution of the planning process,
either through panicky reliance on harshness or toughness on the
one hand, or complacent relaxation on the other. Planning, we

felt, should have three major objectives: first, anticipation of the kinds, numbers and distribution of motorcyclists and spectators, as well as the activities they would engage in and the amount of localized roving to be expected; second, the disposition of police officers and their instructions both as to general attitude and specific actions in various contingencies; third, coordination of the several police departments concerned, including the State Police, and the local police of nearby towns and counties to which the motorcyclists might travel in search of recreation. We relied on the County police to make contact with the other departments.

The second goal was to avoid a polarization of relations between the authorities on the one hand and motorcyclists in general on the other.[8] We addressed our efforts to both groups. As we explored the "culture" of motorcycling, we tried to keep the police informed and interested in what we learned. We arranged a meeting between some local motorcyclists and police officials; films of sport motorcycling were shown, and afterwards each group gave frank expression to its gripes concerning the other. Our educational goals with the police were: 1) to show them that motorcyclists are not essentially different from other citizens, and need not be treated as a breed apart; 2) to inform them that motorcyclists are not a homogeneous class but come in a variety of shapes and sizes, some innocuous, some potentially troublesome; 3) to impress upon them that indiscriminate harsh treatment of all motorcyclists would confirm the latter's sense of persecution, increase group solidarity among them, and go far toward creating the very polarization we wished to avoid.

In working with local motorcyclists, we had two objectives: 1) to involve the organized groups in the actual control effort, asking them not only to refrain from participating in or serving as passive audience to rowdiness, but to help actively in identifying potential trouble areas, keeping police informed of large group movements, etc.; 2) to weaken the respectable motorcyclists' sense of solidarity with the "one percenters" through reinforcing their existing

[8]Cf. use of this term in J. S. Coleman, *Community Conflict*, Glencoe, Ill.: The Free Press, 1957.

concern for the deteriorating "image" of motorcycling and pointing up their vested interest in a peaceful race meet.[9]

Our third major goal was to ensure that adequate facilities were provided for the visiting motorcyclists, with an eye to both containment and entertainment. The object here was to inhibit milling behavior, a usual precursor to crowd disturbances. Specifically, we suggested that adequate and convenient camping facilities were customary and essential at motorcycle meets, and that certain informal and rather dangerous recreations (such as drag racing and stunt riding in the camp grounds), which do not impinge on the non-motorcycling citizenry, are also customary and ought to be permitted.[10]

Finally, our fourth major objective was to monitor the events of the weekend and keep a continuous flow of intelligence coming into command headquarters, so that the senior officer could make effective decisions. Here we served in something of a combined research and undercover capacity, checking out rumors, keeping current with the temper of various groups, clubs and gangs among the motorcyclists, and observing events such as fights or accidents as they occurred. We made a point of spending time in places where the county police could not routinely go.

EVENTS LEADING UP TO THE WEEKEND

Rumors of the arrival *en masse* of the Hell's Angels of California persisted through Saturday of the three-day weekend and were *never* clearly proved or disproved. However, we learned Hell's Angels were anticipated in resorts all the way from Ocean City,

[9]Organized motorcyclists viewed with alarm the possibility of wholesale cancelling of scheduled events. A major meet had been cancelled only a few weeks previously, in Pennsylvania. We ascertained that the cancellation was due to past, and threatened, rowdyism.

[10]We had noted that at Laconia the only permissible camping area was 40 to 50 miles from the track. The campers were reluctant to set out on the long return trip after each day's racing, some preferring simply to stay up all night. Thus they remained in the town of Weir's Beach long past the

Maryland, 140 miles away, to the Pacific coast. Three scattered locations (a tavern, the race track and a whole town) in Prince George's County were to be wrecked. All these rumors seemed to be circulating mostly among youth and motorcyclists. We began to see that the Hell's Angels were assuming a mythical character. They had become folk heroes, functioning both as vicarious exemplars of behavior most youth could only fantasy (unless swept away in mob activity), and as legendary champions who could come to the rescue of the oppressed and persecuted.[11] An older motorcyclist, witnessing police harassment of his fellows at a town outside Prince George's County, was heard to remark, "Just wait 'til the Angels hear about this when they come in tomorrow. They'll come down here and tear this place apart."

The police never did accept the idea of actively involving local motorcycle clubs in the control effort, even though we offered to do all the leg work in getting club representatives together for a meeting. An exception was the large club that sponsored the Marlboro races. The Inspector warned them severely that any trouble this weekend would greatly reduce the likelihood of the race being permitted next year.[12] However, he emphasized that the department would not discriminate in any way against motorcyclists, and that they by no means classified all motorcyclists with the Hell's Angels. The Inspector convinced the sponsoring club of the necessity of hiring uniformed guards for the race track. The club also assured us that adequate camping facilities would be provided.

There was little advance coordination among the various police departments in the area. The State Police initially announced a

time when they might ordinarily have returned to secluded camping areas for an evening of drag-racing, motor-reving and beer-drinking in mutually acceptable segregation from the rest of the citizenry.

[11]O. E. Klapp, *Heroes, Villains, and Fools*, Englewood Cliffs, N.J.: Prentice-Hall (Spectrum), 1962.

[12]The earlier possibility of the race being cancelled had upset the sponsoring club considerably. This was the most important national race yet scheduled here, and a substantial sum had been invested in publicity, etc. Even the national office of the AMA was moved to write an angry letter citing numerous motorcycle events attracting much larger crowds which had been held during the year without incident.

policy of "keep them moving," and said they would "get tough"
with any rowdy-looking types they encountered, but later they did
conform to the approach of the County police. The detailed
cooperation between departments that we had envisioned, like
involvement of the motorcycle clubs in police planning, was probably considered too far outside normal practice to be warranted
by the situation.

Among these largely negative circumstances, one particularly
positive development stood out. At each police roll call prior to
the Labor Day weekend, all the uniformed men were instructed
to treat all motorcyclists just as they would any motorist visiting
the County. They were told that only a very small minority of
motorcyclists were troublemakers, and that only the behavior, not
the style of dress, haircut or bodily cleanliness, was a matter of
police concern. Thus the professional police attitude of neutrality
and commitment to impartial law enforcement, characteristic of
the department's work in other special situations, was reinforced
with respect to a new group.[13]

On Saturday morning of the race weekend we and the police
were quite disturbed to learn that the sponsoring AMA club had
reneged on its promise to provide public camping facilities. Apparently they wished to avoid the expense of renting portable out-
houses, which were likely to be broken up for firewood in the
course of the weekend. We were further disturbed to learn that
early arrivals, some of whom were pretty ragged and rough looking, had already set up camp in the large field usually rented for
that purpose. This created a tricky problem for the police. They
could not legitimately enter the field, which was private property,
unless the owner complained or a violation of law occurred which
was visible from the public highway. If the police officially notified
the owner, he would be bound to ask that the trespassers be removed, because of his liability for damages incurred by people
who were on his property with his implied permission. Eviction
of the growing crowd of squatters would have meant removing a
noisy, potentially troublesome group from a location remote from

[13]R. Shellow, "Reinforcing Police Neutrality in Civil Rights Confrontations," *Journal of Applied Behavioral Science*, 1 (July–August–September,
1965), 243–254.

residences and businesses where the amount of property they could damage was limited. Furthermore they were not, at that time, visibly violating laws. There was no way to predict where they would go if evicted, but obviously they would not go home so early in the weekend. The problem might simply have been scattered all over the County, aggravating the difficulties of control while at the same time provoking resentment which could have been turned against innocent citizens.

It was decided that notification of the owner of the field was not warranted and that there were tactical advantages in keeping the field open, since it seemed to be attracting and holding the rowdier element. So long as they were all in one place, surveillance would be simple and response to trouble could be quick.

The activities on the field were kept under continuous but unobtrusive observation. Police cars were continually passing the field, occasionally pausing near the entrance; the people on the field were thus kept aware of the police presence in the general area, but not so heavily as to arouse feelings of persecution. The 45-man Civil Disturbance Unit (CDU), trained in riot control but lacking experience in full riot conditions, had been mobilized and sent out on the road the night before (Friday). Only a few motorcyclists were seen in the County and the Unit was dismissed around midnight. The usual dance at Vista track was held without incident.

From Saturday through Monday the entire force, including the CDU, was ordered on 12-hour shifts. The men were kept on the road except when responding to trouble calls, thus providing extra control for the normally heavy holiday beach traffic. We felt that the men would have been able to respond more quickly to large-scale trouble if they had been concentrated in two or three central stand-by locations rather than dispersed over the County's 486 square miles. However, police officials judged that the disadvantage of a possible delay in mobilization of force was offset by the double payoff from the same investment in overtime pay—more extensive traffic control as well as riot prevention.

An elaborate communications system was set up, employing the police radio (monitored by newspapers and wire services) and also a Civil Defense band which permitted more detailed discussion and open references to likely trouble spots. A special radio

code was established so that squad cars using the police band
could notify headquarters briefly and in confidence of the presence
of groups of motorcyclists.

THE WEEKEND AS IT DEVELOPED

On Saturday, only a few hundred spectators attended the scheduled lightweight and novice races at Marlboro. Across the highway those squatters, dusty out-of-towners and locals who preferred
the role of contestant to that of passive onlooker conducted their
own impromptu field games.[14] The entire center of the squatters'
field, despite its ruts and hummocks, became a drag strip. Groups,
clubs, even families had set up camp sites around the periphery
of the field in a broken crescent.

Groups and couples who settled on the extreme ends of the
crescent appeared to have expensive camping equipment and rather
conventional dress. Dead center at the head of the drag strip, the
most ragged troop of squatters set up headquarters in a large army
tent, its center pole flying a red flag. Sullen young men and girls
milled around this command post drinking beer and making men-
acing noises at curiosity seekers. Clusters of jackets marked "Hell's
Angels," "Pagans," or "The Gooses" were seen. Individuals
sported a nose ring, a swastika, a Halloween wig, or gold cross
earrings; many wore their hair in shoulder-length manes.

A group of mostly short-haired locals, more or less neat in
T-shirts and jeans, tried to introduce some order into the drag
races. One tried to control racing by flagging each pair of racers
to a start. He was successful for several hours but finally the
enormous quantities of beer, hard liquor, and green wine consumed by participants began to undermine his authority. Racers
roared past him without waiting for the flag. He shouted for order,
but few responded. Non-racers criss-crossed the drag strip, narrowly escaping collision. The proximity of the self-appointed track

[14]The vast majority of motorcyclists who came to see the 75-mile National race never entered the field. There was virtually no contact between
those on the field and the ten times greater number of persons who remained
at the track. A busy high-speed dual-lane highway separated the two areas.

superintendents to the encampment of long-haired outsiders and locals became abrasive. Accidents began to occur, and finally a fight broke out between a very wobbly Pagan and a helmeted short-haired local. The short-haired hero punched the Pagan unconscious, and was then successfully protected by his associates from assault by the rest of the Pagans. The victor had the poor taste and bad judgment to sit triumphantly astride the hood of a truck, waving his beer can in bravado challenge. Now all the "one percenters" joined in a confederation and charged *en masse* toward the short-haired locals. Just at that moment a drunken cyclist lost his machine to a rut in the track. His mishap was noted by police on the highway who dispatched an ambulance along with five police cruisers. The vehicles poured onto the field and fanned out in a half-circle around the casualty, thus coincidentally presenting the crowd with an array of flashing red lights. The unexpected show of power was so sudden and instantaneous that the would-be warriors at the head of the strip broke ranks and returned to their staging area. Unknowingly (since the conflict had not reached a stage where observers off the field could distinguish it as such), the police had put a stop to what might have been a bloody war, for the local motorcycle enthusiasts were far outnumbered by the combined force of Pagans, "Hell's Angels,"[15] and Gooses. Quite fortuitously, those spoiling for trouble got the message that there was a large force of police nearby, ready for action on a moment's notice.

Following the withdrawal of the police, twenty "Hell's Angels" and Gooses set out to replenish their beer supply at the Old Tavern nearby. Just as they started to throw their weight around in the bar and threaten the owner, a police sergeant and another officer entered the room. The group quieted down and waited for the action. Three cyclists moved to the window to assess the size of the sergeant's force; four cruisers were visible. The sergeant

[15]Note that "Hell's Angels" appears in quotes wherever the reference is to participants in local events. It was never established that any bona fide members of the Hell's Angels Motorcycle Club of California were present in Prince George's County. None of the persons wearing Hell's Angels' insignia who were arrested in the County gave California addresses. In any case there were less than ten people in the entire crowd wearing such insignia.

opened with "I hope you all are behaving yourselves." Remembering from a conversation with us that motorcycle chains worn loosely over the hips rather than through belt loops should be considered weapons, he asked, "What's that chain for?" "Hey, man, I lock up my motor with it." "Well, aren't you afraid someone'll steal your motor, not being locked up and all? You better come with me while we put that chain on right, son." The group tensed, then relaxed as the young man elected to go quietly and do as the sergeant suggested. Shortly after this low-key encounter the group roared back to the field and the Old Tavern was prematurely closed for the weekend.

At eleven that evening about 75 cyclists were seen by one of our staff at a rock 'n' roll beach resort in a neighboring county. The Chief of Police there had already advised the press of his intention to lock up any rowdy motorcyclists who showed up. He arranged for the State Police to back him up. Twenty state troopers in riot dress with five dogs were lined up on the main street across from the crowd of motorcycle riders, while six local policemen pushed and poked with night sticks, arresting several who took exception to their tactics. By 1:30 A.M. most of the motorcyclists had left town. Statements to the press by the Chief greatly exaggerated the numbers present and arrested, thus giving an unwarranted notoriety to the evening.

By Sunday morning 300 motorcyclists had settled on the field at Marlboro. Those who had been driven from the beach resort were in a mean mood. Under the direction of the unofficial starter drag racing resumed at a more frantic tempo than on the day before. Across the highway a steady stream of spectators poured onto the track for the afternoon race. Few took notice of the accidents that were beginning to occur on the field.

At two in the afternoon a fire was set in a railroad caboose on a siding behind the field. Fire equipment and police responded quickly; no attempt was made to find the arsonists. At three o'clock a crane was started on an adjacent construction site and tools were stolen from its cab. At four-thirty, coinciding with the Tobacco Trail Classic across the road, a young man removed the license plates from his dilapidated old car and set it afire. With another sportsman straddling the hood, the owner drove onto the drag strip and jumped free. The car rammed an accelerating motor-cycle. Both hood rider and motorcyclist were thrown on impact, both suffering broken legs. A fire truck arrived to put out the fire amid jeers from spectators. A police lieutenant supervised aid to the injured, making humorous asides to cool the excited crowd and enable the ambulance to remove the casualties to the hospital.

About six o'clock the long-haired groups demanded that the locals turn over the starting flag to a "Hell's Angel" who appeared to be one of their leaders. Fighting broke out but subsided im-mediately when one squad of the CDU (10 men) drove onto the field. This time the police had riot equipment visible—helmets, clubs, shotguns, gas masks. The crowd dispersed; the squad with-drew. Since tension on the field seemed to be building, command officers set up an observation post on a cloverleaf approach over-looking the field. At six-thirty the flagman and a delegation from his club came up to plead with command officers to clear the field of hoodlums; they threatened to bring in their own weapons if police didn't protect them. Since the delegation could not agree on who should be charged with what, police action was delayed.

At seven several men broke away from the milling crowd at the center of the field and ran to their machines. From the observa-tion post, it was clear they were returning with bars, chains and other weapons. The entire CDU was sent onto the field where they quickly assembled in riot formation. The Inspector drawled out over the bull-horn, "All right men, you've had your fun, now it's time to go home." Before he finished his sentence motorcycles began to move out of the field. Within twenty minutes the area was clear except for some peaceful campers who were allowed to finish their dinner.

Up to this time, the importance of containing troublemakers on the field was dominant in the minds of commanding officers. But if the crowd were allowed to remain overnight, fighting prob-ably would continue, but now under cover of darkness. Dispersing the squatters while it was still light would, hopefully, send them on their way home. The alternative, isolating and removing the instigators and mob leaders, was complicated by the fact that police could not remain on the field, and by the inability or unwillingness of cyclists to serve as complainants.

Fifteen minutes after the field was vacated, ten men and a girl were arrested outside the Old Tavern, where they had started to break windows. Within minutes, another ten, including the leading "Hell's Angel," were arrested as trespassers at a filling station where they refused to make way for customers. There was no further trouble in the County, at the Vista track, or at the beach resort, though an anxious lookout was maintained till early the next morning. By Monday it was obvious that the danger had passed. The final races at Vista were held without incident, although some "Hell's Angels" and Pagans were rumored to be among the spectators.

REACTIONS TO THE WEEKEND

Both the command officers and the County Commissioner responsible for police matters were satisfied that the police had conducted themselves effectively and that the control effort had been a success. They felt, however, that the situation had not warranted the extra expense and trouble. Estimates of cost ranged from $6,000 to $10,000, but certainly some of the overtime pay would have been necessary for a Labor Day weekend even without motorcyclists. The Commissioner announced that he couldn't see why the County had "to put up year after year with the influx of motorcycle tramps who camp out, drink and fight among themselves."[16]

Like the Commissioner, most of the police leadership was opposed to permitting the race next year. We refrained from offering unsolicited and premature advice on the issue of future races. The club sponsoring the Marlboro races was considering cutting down the meet to a one-day event and preventing camping altogether, in the hope that this would make the event more acceptable to authorities.

Since we were unable to maintain contacts among Pagans, Gooses, or "Hell's Angels," we could not ascertain *their* reactions to police policy and procedure. We did talk to our acquaintance

[16]Quoted in *The Prince George's Post*, Thursday, September 9, 1965, p. 9.

at the local Harley-Davidson dealership, which provides service
and parts for many out-of-town motorcyclists. He reported that
for the first time in nine years of race meets he had heard none of
the usual atrocity stories of police mistreatment of motorcyclists
in the County. The local short-haired motorcyclists who had been
in the fighting on the field felt that the police had exercised entirely
too much restraint in dealing with that situation. They did not
know, until we told them, that the field had not been rented this
year.

CONCLUSION

There was no riot in Prince George's County. The citizens and
their property emerged almost unscathed. The races and field
events were held. The campers drank, dragged and scuffled undis-
turbed for a longer period than any of them probably expected.

Was all the concern, planning and extra police activity justified?
Would the Gooses, Pagans and alleged "Hell's Angels" have been
just as peaceful anyway, despite their frightening appearance? We
think not, and cite the forays against the Old Tavern, the crane
and the caboose, the incinerated car, and the brawling which broke
out repeatedly on the field as evidence that, if unhindered and
undaunted, the hoodlum element sooner or later would have left
the camping area and sought glory and reputation in new arenas,
before new audiences. These seem to be people who need and
seek the stimulation of collective action, excitement, and violence.
Without it they become depressed and demoralized. They have
an affinity for the romantic role of outlaw, which is perhaps the
only status in which they feel they can stand out as individuals.
In it they approach the dramatic, larger-than-life identity of the
mythic Hell's Angel. And only the self-justifying power of mob
action could support such a heroic identity for youths such as
these. We see them, then, as mob seekers and mob creators.

We consider four factors to have been critical in preventing
the spread of violence to the local citizenry.

Most important was *the general police policy of strength, fair-
ness and neutrality*, which influenced all the tactics employed. Law
violations were dealt with immediately and firmly, but motorcyclists

were not harassed or deliberately antagonized. The availability of
overwhelming force, literally on a moment's notice, was demonstrated but not over-dramatized. Thus potential mob leaders were
deprived of the rallying point of "police brutality," and potential
followers never developed the sense of mob power that results
from evidence of police weakness. Well-behaved motorcyclists,
whatever their appearance, were not mistreated and thus were not
given reason for aligning themselves with the trouble-seekers and
against the police.

*The decision not to interfere with the motorcyclists camping and
drag racing* on private property, until extreme violence impended,
was also of critical importance, for several reasons. In the field the
potential troublemakers were all contained in an open area where
their activities, their comings and goings, could be easily observed.
They were segregated by the broad highway and differentiated from
the much larger mass of spectators at the track, and thus deprived
of both victims and audience.[17] The amount of property vulnerable
to damage was relatively small. Finally, they were allowed to
occupy their time with activities which were both customary and
satisfying (drinking, dragging, showing off, etc.) while not annoy-
ing other citizens. This business of "keeping them occupied" is
not trivial. Mob action, except in a catastrophe, is usually preceded
by a period of "milling," wherein people whose customary lines
of action are blocked or inappropriate to the situation seek new
guidelines. They engage in seemingly aimless behavior, which is
actually exchange of fact and rumor, and movement toward consensus. It is during such periods that mob leaders can seize the
initiative in directing the crowd toward specific objectives.[18]

A third important factor was *the continuous flow of intelligence*,
both during the weekend and over the preceding weeks. We feel
that our investigations and discussions before the holiday, aside
from their obvious utility in planning, helped break down police
stereotypes concerning motorcyclists and reinforced an attitude of
impartiality toward them.

Last but far from least was plain and simple *good luck*, which

[17]The presence of a large group of onlookers would also have been a
serious impediment to swift police response in case of trouble.

[18]Turner and Killian, *op. cit.*

favored us on several occasions. Undoubtedly there was an element of luck in the fact that the "hoodlum element" chose to remain at the camp ground rather than roam the County. The factional dispute between the short-haired locals and the "one percenters" may have been fortunate, in that it kept the warlike elements busy and precluded any alliance between the two groups. It was especially fortunate that when it finally became necessary to clear the field, most of the rowdier motorcyclists left the County entirely. The Vista track, even with its nightly dances, did not attract them. The isolation of the camp ground from the race track and from settled areas was another helpful accident.

As noted above, certain policies which we considered advisable were not carried out. We believe that the trouble which did occur can be attributed in part to those omissions.

The failure of the sponsoring club to provide camping facilities at Marlboro, as promised in the race publicity, might well have had more serious consequences than it did. Depriving the visitors of the activities ordinarily organized around camp sites logically means they will seek others; they become a group of potential malcontents, at loose ends, away from home, and with a grievance. Violence in such a situation need not be entirely spontaneous; norms from similar past situations (e.g., New Hampshire) exist to guide the group to it (see Turner, 1964, on norms in crowd behavior).

The fighting on the field might not have gone as far as it did if the local motorcycle clubs had all been actively involved in the control effort. The "short-hairs" who were brawling with the "one percenters" were all members of one club. In addition to avoiding trouble and reporting it when they saw it, local groups could have helped operate the camping area (if it was formally rented), directed the informal drag races with official sanction, and set up a registry of all groups entering the camp ground. Such a registry (including motorcycle tag numbers) might have destroyed the anonymity which allows people away from home and in a group to violate law and convention and feel safe about it.

Once coordination with the State Police contingent assigned to the County was achieved, the lack of involvement of other departments in the planning was of no consequence for the County department. It might have been, had the motorcyclists chosen to roam more. Town police at the rock 'n' roll beach resort might have benefited from coordination and consultation with the County department.

As social scientists we tried to apply in this situation the specialized knowledge and theory of our field, and found it useful. The police, logically, focus on the apprehension of persons who violate laws, protection of citizens from the acts of such persons, prevention of specifically violative behavior, and the deployment of strength in accordance with those goals. As social scientists we focused on the collection of data, the analysis of differences and similarities, the understanding of group and individual behavior, and the communication and exchange of fact and opinion.[19]

Though the events of Labor Day, 1965, in Prince George's County were of little national or long-term import in themselves, we consider the principles applied and the lessons learned to have far broader relevance—a significant practice for things to come.

[19]The clarity with which these distinctions are drawn is not meant to deny that there are policemen who think like social scientists, and vice versa.

4

The Cocktail Lounge: A Study of Heterosexual Relations in a Public Organization

JULIAN ROEBUCK and
S. LEE SPRAY

Although the cocktail lounge is generally known as a place to "socialize," few attempts have been made on the part of the social scientist to systematically describe and analyze this situation. The following report reflects an attempt to do so. By cooperating with the cocktail lounge personnel and by the use of participant-observation, the investigators were able to collect information that revealed complex and meaningful relationships among the patrons of the lounge. It is important to note that no disruption of the normal routine of the cocktail lounge was involved in collecting the data. The patrons were not aware that they were being studied in any systematic fashion. As this study demonstrates, unobtrusive measurement techniques are extremely important in obtaining accurate information which would otherwise be concealed from the social scientist investigating real-life settings.

From: *American Journal of Sociology*, 72(4): 388–395, 1967. Reprinted by permission of the authors and The University of Chicago Press.

An important setting for social contact among urban residents from the upper middle and upper classes is the cocktail lounge. Despite this obvious fact, little, if any, research has been done on such establishments. The reasons for the surprising paucity of data on this social setting seem to stem from (1) the assumption that the cocktail lounge caters to an individualized, transient population, and (2) the assumption that any organized group behavior found in such a setting is for instrumental purposes. As a result, the literature includes materials on the neighborhood bar and on taverns and restaurants where musicians, entertainers, prostitutes, criminals, and others gather for a variety of purposes. There are virtually no data available on the social organization of the plush cocktail lounge.[1]

Who frequents these quiet, well-furnished establishments where the employees are well dressed, where the bartenders often have college degrees, where the patrons are well dressed and well behaved, where formal entertainment is limited to soft music, and where one never sees a uniformed policeman? The existing popular literature suggests that attendance at a cocktail lounge is a pattern of the affluent but lonely transients without their spouses, alcoholics, call girls, young people out for kicks, men and women looking for spouses, etc. Undoubtedly all these types do frequent cocktail lounges. But is this the only support base for such an establishment, or does it, like the working class bar, also draw support from persons whose attendance is sufficiently frequent as to classify them as regulars? If so, who are they, and what are their reasons for going to the lounge? The purpose of this paper is to provide tentative answers to these questions by presenting data gathered in the course of a two-year study of an upper and upper middle class cocktail lounge in a middle-sized West Coast city (250,000 population).

NOTE: The authors are indebted to David Riesman, Robert J. Potter, Jeanne Watson Eisenstadt, John Marx, and Thomas Cottle for their helpful comments on this paper.

[1]Most of the literature dealing with establishments of this type focuses either on the extent to which the tavern or bar contributes to various "social problems" or on the deviant behavior of the patrons, rather than on the organization of the establishment. For a notable exception to this statement, see David Gottlieb, "The Neighborhood Tavern and Cocktail Lounge: A Study of Class Differences," *American Journal of Sociology*, LXII (May, 1957), 559–62.

METHODS

Our interests led to the adoption of the following methods of investigation. First, a variety of persons who were knowledgeable about the city were interviewed regarding the presence of "high class" cocktail lounges in the city. Those contacted included cab drivers, bartenders, bar owners, employees of the local Chamber of Commerce, businessmen, psychiatrists, college professors, ministers, and restaurateurs. Consensus was reached on two cocktail lounges in the central area as meeting the criteria outlined above. The attributes most often mentioned in identifying these lounges as "high class" were: (1) the quality of service was polite and attentive; (2) the clientele included successful business and professional men who frequented these bars at the cocktail hour (and later); and (3) young, attractive, sociable females were generally present. One of the two cocktail lounges was located in what was generally considered the finest hotel in the city, and it was under the general supervision of the manager of the hotel, who agreed to cooperate in the study. With the help of the manager, the cooperation of all the employees of the lounge—four bartenders (three of them college graduates), two cocktail waitresses, and a female pianist—was secured.[2] After sufficient rapport was established, the purpose of the project was explained to each employee

[2]Several factors contributed to the excellent cooperation of the employees of the lounge. First, the hotel manager was a long-time friend of one of the researchers and, hence, accepted the promise of confidentiality without question. Second, the manager had had a great deal of experience managing large, exclusive hotels throughout California and elsewhere and did not feel threatened in any way by the researchers' desire to gather data on a lounge that even the manager felt was rather typical of establishments of its kind. Third, two of the bartenders were part-time graduate students in sociology who used their experiences in the lounge to develop Masters' theses which were later written under the supervision of one of the researchers. A third bartender was a college graduate who had taken courses in sociology, understood the research objectives, and was interested in participating in the research project. These three employees were invaluable aids in assuring the other employees that the research was important and that the researchers could be trusted. Finally, it quickly became known to the patrons that the observer was a college professor (though they never knew that he was doing research in the lounge). While this fact made him somewhat "different" from the other patrons, it also carried a certain amount of prestige and gave him a "license" to ask questions which were not normally asked by other patrons.

individually, and the anonymity of their responses was guaranteed. At the same time, the necessity of keeping the data collection procedures and all information absolutely confidential was stressed. The employees initially served as informants and were told to work alone and to reveal their information to no one but the researcher.

The first step was to secure information on the characteristics of the lounge patrons. To this end, each of the employees was given four cards and instructed to list the regular male patrons on one card and the regular female patrons on another card. A "regular" was defined as a person who visited the lounge at least once a week. On the remaining two cards, the employees were instructed to list the irregular male and female patrons; an "irregular" was defined as a man or woman who visited the lounge at least once every three weeks. The employees were instructed to withhold their lists from each other so the ratings would be independent. When all the lists had been completed, they were pooled and discussed by all of the employees, the manager, and the researcher. Unanimous agreement was reached on the four lists of names composed of twenty female regulars, twenty male regulars, ten female irregulars, and ten male irregulars. Those listed were well known to all members of the group. The list of patrons was used to construct a set of cards, each containing the code number of the patron and a list of variables (22 for the men and 24 for the women) considered important to the research objectives. A set of cards was given to each employee, and the variables were defined and explained to them. The instructions were for each employee to keep the cards behind the bar and to record information acquired by listening to conversations or by occasionally asking direct questions. Information coming directly from the patrons was to be checked with information coming from other patrons about their peers in the lounge. The employees were also instructed to use any information about patrons gained from sources outside the lounge (e.g., from acquaintances of the patrons, from reading about them in the newspapers, or by driving by a patron's home and rating his house by type and neighborhood). Both direct and indirect information were recorded immediately after the period of observation. At the end of two years, the cards were examined and edited by the researcher and the hotel manager. Few inconsistencies were found in the data on each card. Since the manager was well acquainted with the study sample, he was able to resolve the few inconsistencies found.

The second method of data gathering was that of participant-observation. By participant-observation we mean that the field-worker observed and participated in the group in the sense that he had durable social relations with members of the study group.[3] The researcher was present a minimum of five hours a week in the lounge for the two-year duration of the study. A minimum of two visits per week was maintained during this period, with all hours of the day from 4:00 P.M. to 2:00 A.M. and all days of the week being covered systematically. In addition, each of the sixty members of the study sample were informally interviewed on three separate occasions over the two-year observation period, with each interview lasting approximately one hour.[4]

For the purpose of analysis, the data on regulars and irregulars of each sex were combined, since the data collected by the lounge employees and those obtained by the researchers in the interviews revealed no differences between them.

FINDINGS

In analyzing the data, it was apparent that the patrons studied spent a sufficiently large amount of time in the lounge to warrant classifying their behavior as habitual. (The men averaged ten visits per week and the women six visits per week.) The fact that the initial sample of sixty persons remained available, without attrition, for the entire two-year period of observation indicates that the voluntary relationships in the lounge were highly stable.

[3]For a discussion of this particular definition of "participant observation," see Morris Zelditch, Jr., "Some Methodological Problems of Field Studies," *American Journal of Sociology*, LXVII (March, 1962), 566–76.

[4]These informal interviews seemed to have no adverse effect on the on-going observations that were being made. For an interesting discussion of interviewing during a period of field observation see Howard Becker, "Interviewing Medical Students," *American Journal of Sociology*, LXII (September, 1956), 199–201.

Clearly, the lounge was an important center of activity for these people.

In attempting to assess the importance of engaging in the activities of the cocktail lounge, two broad alternative interpretations were available. The first alternative, which is consistent with the deviant-behavior approach to the study of activities in settings of this type, would start with two assumptions: (1) the activities in the lounge would be related to the disruption of other social ties (e.g., family, occupation, community, etc.), and (2) the importance of the lounge to the patrons would be related to the extent to which the individual has failed to achieve primary goals in other settings and has turned to the lounge as a second-best alternative setting. The second alternative, and the one considered most consistent with the findings, was to consider the importance of participating in the activities of the lounge to be related to obtaining gratifications in this setting that were not possible in other settings.

An examination of these two alternatives led to a focus on three questions: (1) What kinds of social ties characterize the regular patrons of the lounge? (2) What kinds of goals were the individuals pursuing in this particular social setting? (3) How did the social organization of the lounge contribute to the attainment of personal goals at a level sufficient to retain the participation of these persons over an extended period of time?

We will first consider some of the major social characteristics of these people. In addition to the findings presented in Table 1, it should be added that two-thirds of the men had an annual income over $10,000 (the top being $75,000) with the remainder earning between $8,500 and $10,000. (None of the employed women earned as much as $9,000 annually.) With regard to religion, two-thirds of the men were Catholics and the remainder were Protestants, while 60 per cent of the women were Catholics and the remainder were Protestants. All the respondents expressed a belief in God, and all attended church.[5] Finally, we had the employees of the lounge rate the women patrons as to their relative

[5] All of the respondents were Caucasian, and none were members of ethnic minority groups. With regard to nativity, twenty-six of the males and twenty-seven of the females were born in urban areas outside of California, while the remaining three females were born in rural areas outside of California.

TABLE 1
SOCIAL CHARACTERISTICS OF RESPONDENTS

Variable	Men (N = 30)	Women* (N = 30)
Marital status:		
Single	13%	60%
Married	70	0
Divorced or separated	17	40
Age (median: men = 39; women = 24):		
20 and under	0	13
21–25	0	37
26–30	7	37
31–35	27	13
36–40	27	0
41–45	23	0
46 and over	16	0
Occupation of father:		
Professional	37	30
Manager, official, proprietor	33	10
Clerical and sales	10	27
Craftsman	7	13
Farm manager and owner	13	20
Education of respondent:		
College graduate	53	20
Attended college	20	40
High school graduate	27	33
Less than high school graduate	0	7
Home ownership of respondent:		
Owned own home:		
Upper class (dwelling and neighborhood, $60,000 homes)	23	0
Upper-middle class (dwelling and neighborhood, $40,000–$59,000 homes)	17	0
Middle class (dwelling and neighborhood, $30,000–$39,000 homes)	37	3
Rented apartment	23	83
Lived with parents	0	13
Occupation of respondent:		
Professional	40	10
Manager, official, or proprietor	53	—
Farm owner and manager	7	—
Secretary	—	33
Clerk	—	17
Cocktail waitress	—	17
Service worker	—	3
College student	—	20

*The percentages do not always total to 100 because of rounding error.

attractiveness. The following distribution resulted: "Very Sharp" = 30 per cent; "Sharp" = 50 per cent; "Average" = 20 per cent.[6]

Table 1 clearly indicates a general difference between the men and women in terms of social status, although none of the patrons was lower class in origin or current position. Specifically, the men who frequent the cocktail lounge tend to be older, married men of high class position while the women are young, attractive, unattached and of somewhat lower class position. What influence does this status differential have on the development of social relationships in the lounge? Does it provide support for a distinct sex-role differentiation in the cocktail lounge that the patrons believe is absent in their relationships outside the lounge? Or is it simply irrelevant because the regular patrons frequent the lounge to engage in "retreatist," "criminalistic," or "escapist" sexual deviation and drinking behavior? To answer the last question first, the interviews revealed that none of these men and women considered themselves, or were considered by their peers, to have a drinking problem. This was further supported by the employees of the lounge who believed that only four of the men and four of the women could be considered to be relatively heavy drinkers. Similarly, while both men and women admitted to occasional sexual relations with other regular patrons, none of the women was considered, either by themselves or by the employees and other patrons, to be a prostitute or call girl. None of the patrons had a delinquent or criminal history. None of the male patrons had illegitimate children, and only one female had an illegitimate child. Finally, with regard to personal abberation, we had the employees classify the patrons according to their personality stability. The results shown in Table 2 indicate that the vast majority of both the men and women were considered to be reliable, predictable persons.

The evidence indicates, then, that the regular patrons of the cocktail lounge were not anomic, personally disorganized or disturbed individuals driven to frequent the lounge for deviant purposes. Rather, these people seemed to visit the lounge because it

[6]The terms used to classify the women as to their attractiveness were those given by the employees of the lounge. While these are very general categories, they were commonly defined by the employees of the lounge inasmuch as they were able to reach complete consensus on which of the three categories each of the women should be placed in.

TABLE 2
PERSONALITY CHARACTERISTICS OF REGULAR PATRONS

Type of Personality*	Men (N = 30)	Woman† (N = 30)
Stable	80%	80%
Unstable	20	20

*While the terms "stable" and "unstable" may not be satisfactory from a clinical point of view, they were the terms used by the employees of the lounge and seemed to be very meaningful to them. Using these terms, the employees were able to achieve complete agreement in classifying the patrons of the lounge.

†Two of the women were referred to as "Very Unstable," while none of the men was referred to in this manner.

was a preferred recreational pattern. Furthermore, this particular preference did not seem to set them apart from other persons of similar social status. Finally, the other activities they mentioned as preferred recreational activities were quite standard. For example, when the women were asked to list their preferred recreational patterns, they most often mentioned dancing, going to parties, and listening to jazz music, while the men mentioned playing golf, fishing, and hunting. Given these findings the important question becomes one of determining what it is about the cocktail lounge that makes it such a desirable setting for these individuals.

In the interviews, each respondent was asked to list his reasons for frequenting the cocktail lounge. Table 3 presents the answers given by the men and women. In examining these findings, it is apparent that they are direct extensions of the various dimensions of feminine and masculine roles. That is, the emphasis the women placed on financial dependence and the maintenance of a "good reputation" combined with the emphasis the men placed on having earned the rewards of relaxation with attractive young women portrays sex-role differentiation in a heightened form. The fact that a great emphasis was placed on conducting these heterosexual activities between married men and unattached women according to a specific code of "proper" behavior clearly indicates that the behavior was institutionalized. Basically, what these men and women had done was to accept the definition of appropriate behavior for one age level (youth) and certain settings (marital) and apply them to new age categories (those represented in the lounge) and new social settings (the lounge and hotel). The popularity of the cocktail lounge, then, stems from the fact that it is a setting in which casual sexual affairs between unattached women

TABLE 3
REASONS FOR FREQUENTING THE COCKTAIL LOUNGE

Reasons Stated by Respondents	Percentage*
Male (*N* = 30):†	
To meet attractive women	73
To relax	23
To meet male friends	20
To meet business acquaintances	14
Female (*N* = 30):‡	
To meet men with money who could take her out	48
To meet men who would keep quiet about sexual and drinking behavior	19
To meet men who did not want to get involved	15
To enjoy the company of older men	10
To meet eligible men for marriage	7

*The percentage figures do not total 100 because multiple reasons for frequenting the lounge could be given by each respondent.
†Total number of reasons = 51. Total number of sex-linked reasons = 48.
‡Total number of reasons = 52. Total number of sex-linked reasons = 52.

and higher-class men can be conducted in a context of respectability. From the standpoint of the patrons, these activities tend to be viewed more in terms of reaffirming social identities than rejecting social norms.

The above argument implies that participating in the activities of the cocktail lounge may not necessarily disrupt marital and other social ties. To gain evidence on this point, we asked the respondents to evaluate their behavior in and related to the lounge. The men explained their behavior in the following terms:

1. They accepted part of their behavior as wrong in a technical-legal sense but not in a social sense.

2. They insisted that certain extenuating circumstances (e.g., busy wives, family pressures, business pressures, "cold" wives, etc.) created a need for extracurricular activities in the cocktail lounge.

3. They deserved romantic interludes with attractive, decent women because earlier in life they did not have the time for such interludes, and such women were not available to them.

4. They did not permit themselves or the young women with whom they consorted to become emotionally involved.
5. They maintained friendly relationships with the young women which were devoid of exploitation.
6. The women were not *virgins*.
7. They were discreet and protective of the women and themselves in securing safe places of assignation and in preventing pregnancy.
8. They believed in the double standard.
9. They remained good husbands and fathers at home where they were loved and loved in return.
10. They did not feel guilty but would feel shame if caught.

The female respondents' rationale for consorting with older married men, as reported during the interviews, closely parallels the reasons they gave for frequenting the cocktail lounge. In sum, with men who were older, married, sophisticated, protective, and friendly, they could enjoy sex and companionship in pleasant and discreet circumstances without having to play a competitive, exploitive courtship game. They all insisted that they were not interested in breaking up any man's home. Moreover, they did not feel that their behavior in the lounge in any way precluded or endangered their social and occupational roles in the larger community.[7] As in the case of the male respondents, the women

[7]A follow-up study, conducted two years after the completion of the original study, indicated that the women's views were correct. By this time, slightly more than one-half of the women were married and no longer frequented the cocktail lounge. By all available evidence, the women had made "good" marriages with high-status men. However, none of the women had married regular patrons of the cocktail lounge. The follow-up study also revealed that the women who left the cocktail lounge were replaced by other young, unattached women with similar characteristics. Much less attrition had occurred among the men, involving at most five of the regular patrons. The reason given by the employees for the disappearance of these men was that they had either become too old for the activities in the cocktail lounge or they had moved out of the area. Among the married men, none was known to have been divorced since the study ended. Finally, observation (averaging three times per week over a three-month period) during the follow-up study revealed that the same pattern of behavior among the patrons still persisted even though the personnel had changed somewhat.

expressed no guilt feelings about their behavior but did express the fear of shame if exposed.

Given these findings we have to conclude that participation in the activities of the cocktail lounge does not lead to a disruption of family ties. Further, it seems clear that the married men were not driven to participate in the activities of the lounge by disintegrating marriage and family relations. Finally, if the cocktail lounge does provide a setting in which gratifications can be obtained, which cannot be achieved in other settings, it becomes important to ask what type of social organization makes this possible. To throw some light on this question, we will turn to a consideration of the structural properties of the cocktail lounge.

In investigating the social organization of the cocktail lounge, it was expected that the strongest normative regulation of behavior would be found in areas having the greatest consequence to the group, such as the motives that brought the people together and the activities affecting the maintenance of the group. As we have indicated, most of the norms surrounded heterosexual interaction. These included the following patterns, which were rarely violated by the regular patrons. First, women usually came in alone and did not sit at the bar unless a previous date had been arranged with a man already at the bar. The men came in alone or in pairs and took a position at the bar. Women who did not have dates sat at a table, and men who were well acquainted with them might ask if they could join them at a table. The usual pattern was for one couple to occupy a table, but occasionally two couples would share a table. When this happened, however, the interaction still took place primarily on a couple basis and not as a group. Men who were not acquainted with the women sitting at tables would watch them and look for social cues defining their status. Women who were waiting for a date pointedly looked at their watches, asked the waitresses and the bartenders if the awaited party had been in yet, and in other ways signaled their unavailability. The unattached males at the bar who were interested were expected to wait out a woman through one drink, during which time they made inquiries to the bartenders and/or cocktail waitresses about them and their attachments. If they found the woman unattached, they would ask that she be served a drink of her choice. By accepting the drink and nodding her thanks, the woman indicated her willingness to engage in conversation. It was only at that time that the man could go over to the woman's table. At times the invitee would ask the cocktail waitress for a rundown on the inviter before accepting the drink.

In short, the bartenders and cocktail waitresses played an important mediating role in the proper introduction; they knew the male and female patrons well, and they accepted the responsibility of facilitating contact between people who would be compatible. They knew the social, emotional, and physical attributes that appealed to the various patrons. Occasionally the bartender or waitress would parry an introduction by politely remarking something as follows: "Lorraine, I tried to check Joe's play. I told him you were not his type. I know you can't stand bald-headed fat men, but he insisted. It's up to you now. Do you want to drink with him or not?" The regular patrons who were well acquainted were very informal in their polite salutations. However, they invariably made their "play" through the hired help. The exceptions to this rule occurred among the patrons who were first-timers or who came in very infrequently. The aggressive male or female who bypassed the hired help in a direct approach to an unknown person was referred to as a "burglar." He was not appreciated by his fellows, the hired help, or the unknown person contacted. At times such a person would be "called down" by any one or all three of these categories of persons; the expression used by the employees would be something like: "Charlie, slow down and use a little class. If she is available and interested, everything will work out. You know what is right. Of course, you do what you want." The women, of course, by declining or accepting a drink, exerted some control over the choice; but they did not enjoy unlimited freedom. Should an unattached woman (alone or in twos or threes) decline more than two invitations, she took the chance of losing the aid of the employees. The bartenders and waitresses could and did discourage other males from making further invitations. As one bartender put it, "If they come to play, O.K., we'll help, but if they get too choosy or just come to build their egos and look pretty, let them hustle their drinks elsewhere." In essence, the expectations were that polite behavior was to be used at all times, and the power of initiating interaction always resided in the men but was supposed to be channeled through the employees of the lounge.

CONCLUSION

Popular myth has it that the cocktail lounge is a place where strangers pick up sexual partners. The major role of the high-class cocktail lounge studied was to facilitate casual sexual affairs in the context of respectability but not among strangers. In fact, the regular patrons of the lounge constituted a highly stable group of persons who considered the lounge to be an important center of activity. The implication is that the cocktail lounge (1) provides gratifications that may not be available in other spheres of life for these people, and (2) serves to drain off energies which might otherwise be invested in change by the individuals of other aspects of their life situations. For the unattached women this means that the availability of the "consort status" at the lounge may operate as a substitute for, or enable them to postpone, the ordinary heterosexual concern of women their age—the location of a suitable marriage partner.[8] For the married men, the relationships established in the cocktail lounge may actually serve to maintain marital ties that would otherwise be dissolved. In general, then, the cocktail lounge seems to perform many of the functions frequently attributed to the "mistress complex" in society and may, in fact, be related to the practical disappearance of this pattern in American society. This suggests, if true, that other public organizations (e.g., ski lodges, resorts, night clubs, etc.) may perform similar functions and that one key to understanding the sexual norms in upper middle and upper class society lies in the study of such settings.

[8]This idea was suggested by Jeanne Watson Eisenstadt in a personal communication.

ABSTRACT

This paper covers a body of data in a relatively neglected area of research, namely, the society found in a high status public organization. Using a variety of methods (participant-observation interviews, having the employees of the organization systematically gather data on the clientele), it was found that the cocktail lounge was frequented by regular patrons who engaged in organized activities around which stable expectations for "proper" behavior had developed. The major function of the cocktail lounge was the facilitation of casual sexual affairs between high status married men and young unattached women. The organization of the cocktail lounge is described, and the relationship between activities in the lounge and outside social ties is discussed.

5

An Abortion
Clinic Ethnography

DONALD W. BALL

Deviant behavior is a topic of much importance in social
science, but reliable data concerning it are rare. The major
reason for this lack of data is the difficulty in its collection
due to such factors as fear of legal punishment on the part
of the informants, distrust of the scientist, and general resistance to be "studied" in a systematic fashion.

This report is an example of how such data may be collected through cooperation with the people actually involved
in the deviant behavior, with the agreement, of course, that
they remain anonymous. First, there is a description of the
abortion clinic and the procedures which it follows. Next, the
investigator discusses his data in terms of a "rhetoric of
legitimization," or the attempt to create a situation that, although it is illegal, appears to be "legitimate" and respectable.

From: *Social Problems*, 14(3): 293–301, 1967. Reprinted by permission
of the author and of The Society for the Study of Social Problems.

Traditionally, the study of deviant behavior, however defined, has suffered from a lack of primary data. Materials available to students of various forms of deviance have usually been, in some degree, removed from the actual phenomena under investigation. Thus all too often reports dealing with unconventional social behavior and/or its organization have been based on official statistics produced by variously concerned agencies and on self-reports by the apprehended violators of formal rules and regulations. Neither of these sources is likely to produce an unbiased sample of deviant actors, their actions, and the social organization of these phenomena.[1]

An alternative method of pursuing the study of deviance (one rarely utilized) is to develop contacts with unapprehended deviants themselves, i.e., to go directly to unconventional actors and their subcultures; it is only with such procedures that the natural context of deviance can be studied without the skewedness typical of the usual sources of data.[2] The report which follows is an effort of this alternative: An attempt to utilize actual direct contact with deviant actors in their natural habitat—in this case an abortion clinic—in order to shed light on selected aspects of this relatively unstudied area of social life.[3]

More specifically, what follows is an effort to describe ethnographically certain aspects of a particular abortion clinic, especially as such data may illuminate the presentational strategies employed

NOTE: I am grateful to Stanford Lyman for his critical comments on an earlier draft of this paper, to Theodore Ravetz for help at various stages of the project, and to Carma Westrum Coon for clerical assistance. I cannot adequately express my debt of gratitude to the anonymous contacts and informants who made this study possible. Portions of this material were presented to the panel on Medical Sociology, Pacific Sociological Association meetings, Vancouver, British Columbia, April 7, 1966.

[1]The sources of bias in official statistics are too well known to require citation, e.g. differentials in organizational actions, variances in definitions, etc.; to deal with apprehended violators only is to study the *technically unskilled and the politically unconnected*.

[2]See the penetrating discussion of the ethical problems involved in this method by Ned Polsky, quoted in Howard B. Becker, *Outsiders*, New York: The Free Press of Glencoe, 1963, pp. 171–172.

[3]For a recent summary which demonstrates how little is known see Edwin M. Schur, *Crimes Without Victims*, Englewood Cliffs, N.J.: Prentice-Hall, 1965, pp. 11–16.

by an habitually deviant establishment in its dealing with a situationally deviant clientele.

For the clinic's staff, participation in an action legally defined as deviant, i.e., criminal abortion, is habitual; that is to say, it is regularly repeated on a routine, businesslike basis. For patrons, however, participation is occasional, irregular, and frequently a once-in-a-lifetime engagement in this form of deviance. Most of them are members of otherwise law abiding cultures. Unlike the staff, their involvement in this deviant setting is not an aspect of a career, but an accidental consequence of an unwanted pregnancy.

In the context of the clinic, therefore, the deviant transaction ordinarily is enacted by two kinds of actors: those habitually involved in such exchanges, i.e., the staff; and those only situationally deviant, the otherwise conventional actors in their clinic-related roles as patrons. It becomes of some interest, then, to consider how the clinic manages and fosters impressions for this audience constituted of actors drawn from outside its habitually deviant, abortion-oriented subculture, and some of the characteristics of such strategies. Put another way, the focus herein will be upon techniques used by the clinic to key itself to the demands and expectations of a patronage drawn from the conventional culture.

Suffice to say, strictures of confidence prevent any elaborate discussion of method, problems of access, etc. Let it be noted, however, that the materials reported and interpreted herein are based upon: (1) sufficiently lengthy observation of a clinic's routine (exclusive of specifically medical procedures, which are not strictly relevant to the problem) to establish the patterns of its everyday functioning; (2) extensive interviews with a necessarily small number of patrons, some of whom were also observed within the clinic; and (3) limited discussions with some of the clinic's non-medical staff. Additionally, supplementary and confirmatory data have been drawn from interviews with individuals who have utilized other, similar facilities. Unfortunately, any more detailed methodological description would, not surprisingly, violate promises of anonymity guaranteed to the subjects involved; for similar reasons, no direct quotations will be presented.[4]

[4]For those interested in procedural minutiae as criteria of validity, the only answer can be: Go out and replicate using your own design. Though

BACKGROUND

The clinic studied is located, along with several like establishments, in a border town along the California-Mexico line. Its staff includes two practitioners or abortionists, ostensibly physicians, the younger of whom is in an apprentice relationship to the senior man; a practical nurse; a receptionist-bookkeeper; a combination janitress and custodian; a chauffeur-errand boy; and a telephone-appointments secretary.

As costs for such procedures go, the clinic is a relatively expensive one, with fees averaging $500 per abortion. The rate is somewhat less for other medical personnel and students, who are eligible for a discount; and more for persons desiring post-operative overnight observation, or else beyond the tenth week of pregnancy. In terms of finances, the clinic studied is probably representative of others catering to a middle and upper middle class clientele.

In order to obtain a better picture of the establishment, a brief natural history of a typical involvement between clinic and patron is useful at this point.

Preliminarily, it should be recognized that the ideal-typical practitioner-patient model is not appropriate for the analysis of abortion. Like veterinarians and pediatricians, abortionists frequently have patients for whom financial, if not moral, responsibility is an aspect of the role of some other person, i.e., a client. For abortionists such clients include boyfriends, husbands, and parents. Along with persons such as accompanying friends, they comprise for the patient what might be classified as *supportive others*: persons attending the clinic along with the patient in order to provide psychological support and reinforcement in this crisis situation. Not surprisingly, it is rare for a patient to go to the clinic completely alone, without some morally supportive other. Thus, within the context of abortion, the typical practitioner-patient dyad usually becomes a triad, comprising practitioner, patient, and supportive other.[5]

---

precise comparisons would not be possible, such confirmation or refutation would be most desirable.

[5]In this discussion the general label patron will be used in reference to patients, clients, and supportive others, unless reference is specifically limited to one of the roles in this category.

After referral, usually by a physician, less often by friend or acquaintance, the patron makes original contact with the clinic by telephone. The typically tentative, noncommital, but implicitly urgent communication of the patron is immediately treated in a matter-of-fact manner by the telephone girl. In appropriate middle class speech patterns she asks the length of the pregnancy, extolls the skills of the staff, sets up a tentative appointment, and discusses the fee and its mode of payment. Treating as routine the patron's problem helps minimize anxiety inherent in such situations. Parallel to this is a "medicalization" of the situation, also helping to disarm the patron vis-à-vis the deviant nature of the proposed transaction; at all times, the terminology is that of conventional medicine and surgery. Later, ordinarily two or three days prior to the appointment, the patron again calls the clinic, this time to get confirmation of date and time.

Usually patrons spend the night before their appointment at a hotel or motel near the clinic. Early in the morning of the scheduled date they call the clinic once again, this time to get directions to the only then revealed place of rendezvous where they are picked up and transported to the clinic by one of the staff members in a large, late model station wagon.

It is at this time that patrons find that they are not alone in their dilemma as there are also several others picked up at the same time, filling the station wagon to capacity. Although propinquity might argue for it, there is little deliberate interaction among the patrons during the ride to the clinic, uncertainty effectively immobilizing them in this ambiguous situation.

Upon arrival at the clinic site, where the wagon and all related cars of the staff are hidden from street view, the patrons are ushered into a large, well furnished waiting room. The clinic itself resembles a roomy private home, both externally and internally in its non-medical areas, and is located in a prestigious residential neighborhood.

Once in, the patrons find seats for themselves and settle into a waiting period of hushed expectancy. Conversation is limited to patients and their respective supportive others, i.e., to those previously known to one another. After a short interval of perhaps five minutes, the receptionist appears and calls out the name of the first patient. The pair, patient and receptionist, then retire out of sight of the remaining patrons and into the medical wing of the clinic.

The first stop in the medical wing is an office. After first explaining the procedure in explicitly medical terminology, the receptionist shifts to her bookkeeper role and requests the fee (in cash or traveler's checks) from the patient, frequently finding that it is being held by an accompanying supportive other still in the waiting room. Following this discussion and collection of the fee, the patient is then sent to a bathroom, well appointed in terms of luxury rather than gynecology, to remove her street clothes and put on a surgical gown. Once gowned, the patient is directed to the room where the actual abortion will take place.

Those specifically involved in the procedure include, in addition to the patient, the two practitioners, senior and apprentice, and a practical nurse. Although an anesthetic is administered, at no time is the patient allowed to lose consciousness; a necessity born of the possible need for quick removal in the event of visitation by legal agents. Immediately upon completion of the procedure the patient leaves the table and is sent to another room to rest for fifteen minutes to an hour and a half. Finally, after receiving medication and instruction regarding post-operative care from the receptionist, the patient and any supportive others are returned to the site of the original rendezvous and thus to their conventional worlds.

ANALYSIS

With this brief, oversimplified picture it is now possible to turn to more specifically sociological concerns: the aforementioned presentational strategies which make up what may be called, for the clinic, a *rhetoric of legitimization*.

Sociologically, a rhetoric is a vocabulary of limited purpose; that is to say, it is a set of symbols functioning to communicate a particular set of meanings, directed and organized toward the representation of a specific image or impression. Such vocabularies are not only verbal but also include visual symbols such as objects, gestures, emblems, etc.[6]

In the case of the clinic the rhetoric operates to subvert the conventional world's view of abortion, and to generate a picture of legitimate activity. Fundamentally, the question thus becomes: What techniques are utilized via this rhetoric to *neutralize* the context of deviance in which the clinic operates, so as to enhance parallels with conventional medical and social situations and thus derive a kind of "rightness" or legitimization.[7] How, in other words, are the setting and actions *qua* impressions manipulated to maximize the clinic's image over and above successful performance of its task and contradict the stereotypic stigma of deviance? Specifically, how does the clinic (1) minimize the possibilities of trouble with frightened or recalcitrant patrons; (2) generate the patron satisfaction necessary for referral system maintenance; and (3) present an image which will provide the most favorable self-image or identity for the actors involved, whether patron or staff?[8]

For conceptual purposes, the clinic's rhetoric of legitimization

[6]The concept of rhetoric as used herein is similar to but independent of the work of Kenneth Burke. As a theoretical point it should be noted that rhetorics are not necessarily the same thing as ideologies, although this may empirically be the case. The conceptual difference between the two is that rhetoric speaks to communication, both style and content, while ideology refers to perception and justification in terms of the ideologue's conception of the relevant portions of the world. It is quite conceivable that individual actors will utilize a rhetoric without any ideological convictions as regards its validity, but with recognition of its pragmatic efficacy; and similarly, that ideological dedication does not automatically assume any developed rhetoric to attempt its maintenance or furtherance.

[7]Compare Gresham M. Sykes and David Matza, "Techniques of Neutralization: A Theory of Delinquency," *American Sociological Review*, 22 (December, 1957), pp. 664–670, where the analysis is individual rather than institutional; also Matza, *Delinquency and Drift*, New York: John Wiley and Sons, 1964.

[8]The second and third problems are, in effect, special cases of the first. Minimization of trouble is not motivated by fear of patron complaints to legal agents, which would involve the complainants in admitting complicity, but by desire to maintain referrals and enhance self-images. Additionally, such minimization produces a smoother, easier work-flow for the staff; a similar rationale in conventional medical settings sometimes dictates the use of general anesthetics when, in terms of patient pain, locals would be adequate.

may be treated by employing Goffman's delineation of *front* and its constituents of setting, appearance, and manner;[9] originally a framework for analyzing the presentation of self, it seems extendible to the strategies of establishments and institutions as well. Essentially, front consists of those communications which serve to define the situation or performance for the audience: standardized expressive equipment including *setting*, the spatial/physical background items of scenery in the immediate area of the interaction; *appearance*, the sign-vehicles expressing the performer's social status or type; and those expressions which warn of a performer's demeanor, mood, etc., i.e., *manner*.

Examining each of these elements for evidence of how they are manipulated to make up a rhetoric will show the central themes and dimensions of the clinic's presentational strategies. Although the combination of the conceptions of rhetoric, neutralization, and front produces an admittedly loose theoretical scheme, the character of the data does not suggest the need for further rigor.

Setting

A paramount feature of the clinic's rhetoric is its physical and spatial characteristics. Especially important for patrons generally is the stereotype-contradicting waiting room, the first impression of the clinic itself—and the dominant one for supportive others. The waiting room is likely to be the only room in which the supportive others will be present during their entire visit to the clinic, save the possibility of a short interval in the office if they happen to be holding the fee, a frequent occurrence, especially if the other is also a client.

Spatially, the waiting room is L-shaped and extremely large, approximately 75 feet long and 50 feet wide at the base leg. Its size is accentuated by the fact that most of the room is sunken about three feet below other floor levels. Fully and deeply carpeted, well furnished with several couches, arm chairs, large lamps, and tables, the room speaks of luxury and patron consideration,

[9]Erving Goffman, *The Presentation of Self in Everyday Life*, Garden City, N.Y.: Doubleday Anchor, 1959, pp. 22–30. This scheme formed the observational framework for data collection as well as a perspective for preparing the data.

also implied by the presence of a television set, a small bar, and a phonograph, in addition to the usual magazines present in waiting room situations.

Both the size of the room and the placement of the furniture function to provide private islands which need not be shared; space is structured so as to create withdrawal niches for each set of patrons. Couches and chairs are arranged along the walls of the room, maximizing distance between groupings and minimizing the possibilities of direct, inter-group eye contact between the various patron-sets who, despite their shared problem and the recently experienced forced propinquity of the ride to the clinic, tend to keep their anxieties private. Thus, interaction among patrons in the waiting room is closed, confined to patients and their own accompanying supportive others only.

Turning to the medical wing: The picture is a far cry from the shabby and sordid image of "kitchen table abortion" drawn in the popular press; it is one of modern scientific medicine, and with it comes assurance to the patient. Once the patient has donned a gown, her next stop is the operating room, a designation used without exception by the staff. In addition to a gynecological table, the room contains familiar (to the lay patient) medical paraphernalia: surgical tools, hypodermic syringes, stainless steel pans and trays, bottles and vials enclosing various colored liquids, capsules, pills, etc.—props effectively neutralizing the negative stereotypes associated with abortion as portrayed in the mass media.

After the procedure has been completed, the patient is moved from the scientific arena of the operating room and back again into luxury. As is the waiting room, the rooms in which the patients spend their short period of post-operative rest are expensively furnished.

Ultimately, after resting, the patient returns to the waiting room and, for most, to supportive others, and receives a final post-operative briefing before being returned to the rendezvous site. Parenthetically it may be noted that throughout the entire episode piped-in music has pervaded every room in which patrons are present.

In terms of setting, the clinic presents itself as not unlike a small hospital albeit with a decorator-designed interior. For patient and supportive others the scenery and props have functioned to communicate an image of assurance and protection through the devices of cost and luxury along with scientific medicine, to minimize the deviant nature of the transaction, and to emphasize cultural values, thus efficiently counteracting the stereotypic image.

Appearance and Manner

A widespread device for visibly differentiating various social categories or types is clothing.[10] Items of dress may function as insignia or uniforms to label the persons so garbed as members of particular social groups, occupations, etc. Such institutionalized symbols act as both identifiers and identities; to be attired in certain ways is to be a certain kind of person, not only in the eyes of the audience, but also in terms of the actor's perception of himself. Dress is an integral aspect of social identity.

So it is with the staff of the clinic: practitioners, patient, nurse —all wear the appropriate symbols, from the layman's point of view, of dress for surgically centered roles. White tunics are worn by the practitioners; the patient is surgically gowned; the nurse and even the janitress wear white uniform dresses. This element of the rhetoric is highlighted at the beginning of the procedure when both practitioners ostentatiously don surgical gloves, visibly emphasizing their, and the clinic's, concern with the necessities of asepsis. This ritualistic activity also serves to forcefully identify these actors in their roles as defined by the rhetoric.

The medical model is further underscored by the pre-operative medical history which is taken and recorded upon a standard, multi-carboned form (the destiny of these duplicate copies is unknown). Actions such as this, along with dress, provide major modes of stressing the medical legitimacy of the clinic, its staff, and its task.

[10]Mary Ellen Roach and Joanne Bubolz Eicher (eds.), *Dress, Adornment, and the Social Order*, New York: John Wiley and Sons, 1965.

From the receptionist on up through the clinic's hierarchy, behavior, particularly verbal, emphasizes medical and professional
aspects of the clinic's operation. Nowhere is this more apparent
than in the area of vocabulary; it is strictly medical, with no
effort either made or implied to speak down to the less knowledgeable lay patron. It is also noteworthy that at no time is the word
abortion used in the presence of a patron; rather, it is referred
to as the operation, the procedure, or as a D and C (dilation and
curettage). Similarly, as noted above, the room in which the procedure takes place is at all times designated by the staff as the
operating room.

Other elements of staff behavior which further the medical impression are (1) the post-operative consultation and medication
which effectively contrast with the popular view of abortion as an
"off-the-table-and-out" procedure, and (2) the presence of an
apprentice practitioner and its obvious analogy, at least to the
medically sophisticated, with a teaching hospital. For the patient,
the teaching aspects of the senior practitioner's role help to generate confidence in his skill, a matter which is verbally reinforced
by other staff members in their interactions with the patrons.

As with appearance, the manner of the staff is essentially directed toward the medical elements of the clinic's rhetoric; their
demeanor is professional at all times, with one exception. This
exception is the receptionist-bookkeeper, whose role is, by definition, outside the strictly medical aspects of the clinic. As a result,
freed of the obligations of professional mien, the receptionist is
able to interact with patrons in a reassuring and supportive manner; in effect, her presentation of the rhetoric is through expressive
strategies, while the manner of other staff members is more in-
strumentally oriented.[11]

Before turning to the central themes engendered among the
patrons by the clinic's rhetorical strategies, it may be well to at
least take note of some flaws in the presentation, even though they
may escape the usual patron's attention. These may be considered
under the general rubrics of pseudo-sterility and miscellaneous
delicts.

[11]Excluded from this consideration is the telephone girl who is never in
face-to-face interaction with the patrons but is also supportive in her
demeanor.

Pseudo-Sterility

Although ostentation is the rule as regards the emphasis of aseptic and antiseptic precautions, there are also omissions less readily obvious. It will be recalled that measures apparently designed to minimize infection and also at the same time maximize parallels with legitimate medicine included the wearing of tunics by the practitioners, their donning of surgical gloves prior to the procedure, and the display of the tools and paraphernalia of medicine and surgery in the operating room.

It should be pointed out that, aseptically, tunics are no substitute for full surgical gowns, that full precautionary tactics would also include items such as face masks, caps, etc.; and that it is highly irregular for an operating room to lack an autoclave (for the sterilization of instruments) and changeable covering for the table, and for surgical instruments to stand on display, exposed to the air for long periods of time. Additionally, it may be noted that the portion of the pre-operative medical history which is taken by the senior practitioner is recorded by him after his elaborate display of putting on the surgical gloves—a less than ideal practice for sterility.

These breaches of standard procedure suggest that much of what is passed to the lay patron as concern with aseptic and antiseptic practices is actually rhetoric, designed to communicate to the audience a standard of medical rigor which does not in fact exist.

Miscellaneous Delicts

Within this category are included additional practices at variance with the fostered impression.

Perhaps the most glaring of these is the lack of privacy afforded the patient in comparison with more conventional medical settings. The fact that patients are handled in groups, and moved and serviced in what in comparison with a hospital is a small and not systematically designed space, leads to a good deal of enforced contact between patients and staff involved in various stages of the process. Of necessity this leads to invasions of privacy, at least as perceived by patients accustomed to more traditional medical situations. Thus, for instance, the room used as an office also doubles as a resting room, and a patient lying there for postoperative rest may suddenly find herself witness to a financial transaction as a later-scheduled patron pays the fee; the resting patient is thus treated, in effect, as an object, becoming in Goffman's phrase, a non-person,[12] i.e., an actor not accorded the usual deferences given as minimal acknowledgements of a person's moral worth simply by virtue of that person's being human.

Also of interest is the function of the music, piped into every room including the one for the procedure. When the patrons first arrive at the clinic the music is quiet, soothing, and relaxing in style; but with the entrance of the first patient into the medical wing, the tempo and timbre increase. The volume of the music then operates to drown out any untoward sounds which might emanate from the medical wing and alarm those patrons still in the waiting room.

Another delict involves the marked contrast in vehicles used in picking up and returning, patrons to the rendezvous. In keeping with the symbolism of cost and luxury presented to the prospective patron, the station wagon which brings them to the clinic is an expensive late model. By contrast, for the return to the rendezvous, which is not done en masse as is the initial pick up, and by which time presentational strategies are less necessary, the car driven by the chauffeur-errand boy is an old, rather decrepit foreign sedan of low cost and questionable reliability.

Another item at variance with traditional medical procedures is the emphasis, especially by the practitioners, on the necessity of the patient's cooperation to assure the procedure's success. The patient is in effect invited, if not commanded, to become an active participant in the ongoing activity.[13] She is told, for instance, of the desirability of her concentrating on other matters, e.g., "think of something else and all will go smoothly and rapidly." This

[12]Goffman, *The Presentation of Self*, pp. 151–152.

[13]See the discussion of the patient as basically helpless and passive in Talcott Parsons, *The Social System*, Glencoe, Ill.: The Free Press, 1951, pp. 439–447. An alternative approach is indicated in Robert Leonard's work. See his several papers in James Skipper, Jr. and Leonard, *Social Interaction and Patient Care*, Philadelphia: J. P. Lippincott, 1965.

assigning an active role to the patient stands in marked contradiction to her objectification as regards matters of privacy, and implies expediency as a more central concern of the clinic's operation than is patient welfare.

Finally, it may be noted that though the practitioners are verbally represented by others on the staff as physicians—gynecologists, in fact—no evidence of medical training in the form of certificates or diplomas is available for patron scrutiny.

DISCUSSION

From this selective ethnographic description of various aspects of the clinic's front, two broad dimensions appear essential to its rhetoric of legitimization: (1) luxury and cost, and (2) conventional medical practices and procedures. It is these two themes which are emphasized in the clinic's efforts to neutralize its aura of habitual deviance before an audience of situationally deviant patrons drawn from the world of conventional culture. Thus, the rhetoric draws its vocabulary from meaningful and positive values of the patron's culture.

Within these two valued themes, four elements may be specified as contributing to the two broader dimensions of luxury and cost and conventional medicine: cleanliness, competence, conventionality, and concern for the patron.

Cleanliness and competence are both elements of the instrumental aspects of medicine. Albeit with significant flaws, unrecognized by most lay patrons anyway, the clinic's presentational strategies enhance these impressions, if not to the same extent their actualities. The obvious symbols of dress and equipment are presented to the patient in the medical wing of the clinic where anxiety and uncertainty are high. The symbols are readily recognizable and imply the conventionality of the situation; they provide, in effect, a set of familiar expectations drawn from past experience with legitimate medicine. In a similar allaying manner, the practitioner's skill and competence is repeatedly voiced by the staff from the time of the initial telephone contact until the beginning of the actual abortive procedure itself.

Conventionality here means a realization of the middle class values of most patrons. One of these values is, of course, a positive view of professional medicine, a view which the clinic attempts to exploit. Throughout the patron's experience with the clinic, parallels with this model are highlighted; but it is in another area that this element of the rhetoric functions most effectively.

This is the waiting room setting. The obvious expense, comfort, and general decor of this room are such as to disarm all but the most fearful and suspicious patron. This room and the first impressions it presents are such as to immediately link the clinic to the safe, known world of respectable middle class conventionality. In the process of this linkage, the clinic is, in the patron's perception, divorced from the usually illicit image conjured by abortion; if not rendered totally respectable, the clinic is at least brought within the context of the definitions and expectations of mundane, everyday experience. Because of its crucial location in the process, being the patron's first direct exposure to the clinic milieu, it is fair to say that this room is the most successful presentation strategy in the clinic's legitimizing rhetoric.

The comfort of the waiting room is but one of the forms of expression of concern for the patron which help to create a legitimizing presentation. Other strategies include the telephone girl's supportive routinization of the patron's problem at the time of the initial contact; the similarly solicitous demeanor of the receptionist; and the post-operative consultation. This involves not only the dispensing of drugs to facilitate the patient's convalescence, but also a brochure specifically detailing an expected course of progress and steps to be taken in case of complications.

By demonstrating concern, the clinic affirms its subscription to the values of its patrons, and thus asserts its basically conventional nature, i.e., the congruence of its operation with the norms of those upon whom its income relies.

All of these factors combine to help construct a rhetoric of legitimacy: a set of presentational strategies which allows the clinic to minimize problems inherent in typically anxious and fearful patrons, and thus to function more effectively; and in addition to generate the reputation necessary for an establishment of its kind, dependent upon referrals from physicians.

Additionally, whether manifest or latent, the rhetoric also has consequences for the identities of the actors involved. Both habitual deviants, the staff, and situational deviants, the patrons, are able to partake of the rhetoric so as to enhance their own self-images. The rhetoric helps the staff define their participation in the clinic's habitually deviant activities, despite the occasional flaws, as involvement in a professionally operating establishment with the trappings of conventional medicine. For patrons, though they too are admittedly involved in a deviant situation, the rhetoric blunts this hard truth. By accepting the presentational strategies as part of the clinic's image, the patron is allowed to define the situation through the symbols drawn from his conventional everyday experience. Thus, for both patron and staff alike, the rhetoric allows for a minimization of the threat to identity which is built into their illicit transaction.

Unfortunately, the confidential nature of this research does not allow one of the usual canons of science to be met, i.e., that regarding exact replication; and no claim regarding the typicality of the clinic described herein can be made. Hopefully, however, the materials have shed some light on a relatively little known area of social behavior. Given the incidence of abortion, it may be hoped that similar analyses can be conducted by others.[14] Additionally, it may be suggested that the concept of rhetoric provides a useful tool for examining the dramas of social life, whether deviant or conventional, spontaneous or routine, unusual or mundane.

[14]A step in this direction is the dissertation (in progress) of Nancy L. Howell, "Information Channels and Informal Networks in the Distribution of Source Information," Department of Social Relations, Harvard University.

6

The Hustler

NED POLSKY

Combining the richness of personal interest and intuition with his disciplined but imaginative approach as a social scientist, this investigator presents a detailed description of an uncommon "profession" and, indeed, way of life. Any systematic or highly controlled collection of data with a representative sampling of poolroom "hustlers" in such real-life settings would be virtually impossible. However, in spite of such built-in methodological limitations the investigator proceeded to collect data as carefully as possible. He thus reflected the attitude of many social scientists, especially those conducting natural setting research, "do the best you can with what you have." In this spirit, this investigator presents us with a highly revealing, informative, and insightful contribution to social psychology.

From Ned Polsky, *Hustlers, Beats, and Others* (New York: Doubleday Anchor Books, 1969), pp. 31–108. Reprinted by permission of the author and Aldine Publishing Company.

Such a man spends all his life playing every day for small stakes. Give him every morning the money that he may gain during the day, on condition that he does not play—you will make him unhappy. It will perhaps be said that what he seeks is the amusement of play, not gain. Let him play then for nothing; he will lose interest and be wearied.

Blaise Pascal

They talk about me not being on the legitimate. Why, lady, nobody's on the legit when it comes down to cases; you know that.

Al Capone[1]

The poolroom hustler makes his living by betting against his opponents in different types of pool or billiard games, and as part of the playing and betting process he engages in various deceitful practices. The terms "hustler" for such a person and "hustling" for his occupation have been in poolroom argot for decades, antedating their application to prostitutes. Usually the hustler plays with his own money, but often he makes use of a "backer." In the latter event the standard arrangement is that the backer, in return for assuming all risk of loss, receives half of the hustler's winnings.

The hustler's offense in the eyes of many is not that he breaks misdemeanor laws against gambling (perhaps most Americans have done so at one time or another), but that he does so daily. Also—and again as a necessary and regular part of his daily work —he violates American norms concerning (a) what is morally correct behavior toward one's fellow man and (b) what is a proper and fitting occupation. For one or another of these related reasons the hustler is stigmatized by respectable outsiders. The most knowledgeable of such outsiders see the hustler not merely as a gambler but as one who violates an ethic of fair dealing; they regard him as a criminal or quasi-criminal not because he gambles but because he systematically "victimizes" people. Somewhat less

NOTE: Approximately the first third of this chapter appeared, in slightly different form, in *Social Problems*, Vol. 12, No. 1 (Summer, 1964), pp. 3–15.

[1] The Pascal quotation is from *Pensées*, V. Al Capone's remark is quoted in Paul Sann, *The Lawless Decade* (New York: Crown Publishers, 1957), p. 214.

knowledgeable outsiders put down the hustler simply because gambling is his trade. Still less knowledgeable outsiders (perhaps the majority) regard hustlers as persons who, whatever they may actually do, certainly do not hold down visibly respectable jobs; therefore this group also stigmatizes hustlers—"poolroom bums" is the classic phrase—and believes that society would be better off without them. Hustling, to the degree that it is known to the larger society at all, is classed with that large group of social problems composed of morally deviant occupations.

However, in what follows I try to present hustlers and hustling on their own terms. The material below avoids a "social problems" focus; to some extent, I deliberately reverse that focus. Insofar as I treat of social problems, they are not the problems posed by the hustler but for him; not the difficulties he creates for others, but the difficulties that others create for him as he pursues his career.

This approach "from within" has partly dictated the organization of my materials. Some sections below are built around conceptual categories derived less from sociologists than from hustlers, in the hope that this may help the reader to see hustling more nearly as hustlers see it. The disadvantage for the scientifically-minded reader is that the underlying sociological framework may be obscured. Therefore I wish to point out that this framework is basically that of Everett Hughes's approach to occupational sociology.

I try mainly to answer three types of questions: (*a*) *The work situation.* How is the hustler's work structured? What skills are required of him? With whom does he interact on the job? What does he want from them, and how does he try to get it? How do they make it easy or hard for him? (*b*) *Careers.* Who becomes a hustler? How? What job risks or contingencies does the hustler face? When and how? What is the nature of colleagueship in hustling? What are the measures of success and failure in the career? In what ways does aging affect the hustler's job skills or ability to handle other career problems? What leads to retirement? (*c*) *The external world.* What is the place of the hustler's work situation and career in the larger society? What changes in the structure of that society affect his work situation or career?

PREVIOUS RESEARCH

A bibliographic check reveals no decent research on poolroom hustling, sociological or otherwise. Apart from an occasional work of fiction in which hustling figures, there are merely a few impressionistic accounts in newspapers and popular magazines. With a couple of exceptions, each article is based on interviews with only one or two hustlers. No article analyzes hustling on any but the most superficial level or provides a well-rounded description. The fullest survey of the subject not only omits much that is vital, but contains numerous errors of fact and interpretation.[2]

The desirability of a study of hustling first struck me upon hearing comments by people who saw the movie *The Hustler* (late 1961, re-released spring 1964). Audience members who are not poolroom habitués regard the movie as an accurate portrait of the contemporary hustling "scene." The movie does indeed truly depict some social characteristics of pool and billiard hustlers and some basic techniques of hustling. But it neglects others of crucial importance. Moreover, the movie scarcely begins to take proper account of the social structure within which hustling techniques

---

[2]Jack Olsen, "The Pool Hustlers," *Sports Illustrated*, Vol. 14 (March 20, 1961), pp. 71–77. Jack Richardson's "The Noblest Hustlers," [*Esquire*, Vol. IX (September, 1963), pp. 94, 96, 98] contains a few worthwhile observations, but it is sketchy, ill-balanced, and suffers much from editorial garbling, all of which makes it both confusing and misleading for the uninitiated. One article conveys quite well the lifestyle of a particular hustler: Dale Shaw, "Anatomy of a Pool Hustler," *Saga: The Magazine for Men*, Vol. 23 (November, 1961), pp. 52–55, 91–93. Useful historical data are in Edward John Vogeler's "The Passing of the Pool Shark," *American Mercury*, Vol. 8 (November, 1939), pp. 346–51. For hustling as viewed within the context of the history of pool in America, see Robert Coughlan's "Pool: Its Players and Its Sharks," *Life*, Vol. 31 (October 8, 1951), pp. 159ff.; although Coughlan's account of the game's history contains errors and his specific consideration of hustling is brief (p. 166), the latter is accurate.

Among novels that deal with hustling, Walter Tevis's *The Hustler* (New York: Harper, 1959) has the most external documentary detail; but Don Carpenter's *Hard Rain Falling* (New York: Harcourt, Brace & World, 1963) is much superior in its exploration of a hustler's character, as well as more satisfying stylistically.

are used and which strongly affects their use. *The Hustler* is a reasonably good but highly selective reflection of the poolroom hustling scene as it existed not later than the mid-1930's. And as a guide to today's hustling scene—the terms on which it presents itself and on which the audience takes it—the movie is quite misleading.

METHOD AND SAMPLE

My study of poolroom hustling extended over eight months in 1962 and 1963. It proceeded by a combination of: (a) direct observation of hustlers as they hustled; (b) informal talks, sometimes hours long, with hustlers; (c) participant observation—as hustler's opponent, as hustler's backer, and as hustler. Since methods (b) and (c) drew heavily on my personal involvement with the poolroom world, indeed are inseparable from it, I summarize aspects of that involvement below.

Billiard playing is my chief recreation. I have frequented poolrooms for over 20 years, and at one poolroom game, three-cushion billiards, am considered a far better than average player. In recent years I have played an average of more than six hours per week in various New York poolrooms, and played as much in the poolrooms of Chicago for most of the eight years I lived there. In the course of traveling I have played occasionally in the major rooms of other cities, such as the poolrooms on Market Street in San Francisco, West 25th Street in Cleveland, West Lexington in Baltimore, and the room on 4th and Main in Los Angeles.

My social background is different from that of the overwhelming majority of adult poolroom players. The latter are of lower-class origin. As with many American sports (e.g., baseball), pool and billiards are played by teenagers from all classes but only the players of lower-class background tend to continue far into adulthood. (And as far as poolroom games are concerned, even at the teenage level the lower-class contributes a disproportionately large share of players.) But such differences—the fact that I went

to college, do highbrow work, etc.—create no problems of acceptance. In most good-sized poolrooms the adult regulars usually include a few people like myself who are in the poolroom world but
not of it. They are there because they like to play, and are readily
accepted because they like to play.

The poolroom I play in most regularly is the principal "action
room" in New York and perhaps in the country, the room in
which heavy betting on games occurs most often; sometimes, particularly after 1:00 A.M., the hustlers in the room well outnumber
the non-hustlers. Frequently I play hustlers for money (nearly
always on a handicap basis) and occasionally I hustle some non-
hustlers, undertaking the latter activity primarily to recoup losses
on the former. I have been a backer for two hustlers.

I know six hustlers well, and during the eight months of the
study I talked or played with over 50 more. All are now usually
based in New York, except for two in Chicago, two in Cleveland,
one in Philadelphia, one itinerant hustler whose home base is
Boston and another whose home base is in North Carolina. However, the hustlers based in New York are of diverse regional
origins; almost a third grew up and started their hustling careers
in other states.

It is not possible to demonstrate the representativeness of this
sample because the universe (all U.S. pool and billiard hustlers)
is not known exactly. But the hustlers I asked about the number
of real hustlers in America, i.e., the number of people whose exclusive or primary occupation is hustling, generally agree that
today the number is quite small. In response to my queries about
the total number of poolroom hustlers, one hustler said "thousands" and another said "there must be a thousand," but the next
highest estimate was "maybe 400" and somewhat lesser estimates
were made by nineteen hustlers. Moreover, the three hustlers making the highest estimates have rarely been out of New York,
whereas over half the others either come from other parts of the
country or have made several road trips. It seems safe to assume
that the sample is at least representative of big-city hustlers. Also,
it is probable that it includes the majority of part-time hustlers in
New York, and certain that it includes a good majority of the
full-time hustlers in New York.

POOLROOM BETTING: THE STRUCTURE OF "ACTION"

Hustling involves betting against one's opponent, by definition. But the converse is not true. The majority of poolroom contests on which opponents bet do not involve any element of hustling. In order to understand how hustling enters the picture, one must first establish a perspective that encompasses all betting on poolroom games, hustled or not.

In pool or billiard games, the betting relationship has three possible modes: (1) player bets against player; (2) player against spectator; (3) spectator against spectator. In most contests only the first mode occurs, but combinations of the first and second are frequent, and slightly less so are combinations of the first and third. Combinations of all three are uncommon, but do occur when there is more "ready action" offered to the players by the spectators than the players can or wish to absorb. I have never seen the second mode occur alone, nor a combination of second and third. I have seen the third mode occur alone only twice—at professional tournaments. The betting relationship, then, involves the mode player-vs.-player, whatever additional modes there may be.

If two mediocre players are betting, say, upward of $15 per game, and at another table two excellent players are playing for only a token amount, the first table will invariably draw many more people around it. The great majority of spectators, whether or not they bet much and whatever their own degree of playing skill, are attracted more by the size of the action than the quality of the performance. (A visiting Danish billiardist tells me this is not so in Europe, and also that betting on poolroom games is far less frequent there than in America.)

There is an old American poolroom tradition that players should make some kind of bet with each other, if only a small one. This tradition remains strong in every public poolroom I know. (It is weak in the pool or billiard rooms of private men's clubs and YMCAs, weaker still in student unions, and virtually non-existent in faculty clubs.) When one player says to another, "Let's just play sociable," as often as not he means that they should play for only a dollar or two, and at the very least means that they should play "for the time" (the loser paying the check). It is only some of the newer and least skilled players who refuse to bet at all (who want to "split the time"), and nearly always they rapidly become socialized to the betting tradition by a carrot-and-stick process—the stick being that it is often hard to get a game otherwise, the carrot that better players are always willing to give poorer ones a handicap (a "spot"). Most of the regular players will not even play for the check only, but insist on a little money changing hands "just to make the game interesting."[3] The player who claims that just playing the game is interesting enough in itself is regarded as something of a freak.

Few serious bettors, hustlers excepted, care for big action; but nearly all, including hustlers, want fast action. Although they may not want to bet much per game, they want the cash to change hands fairly quickly. Consequently, in an action room the standard games are redesigned for this purpose. Some are simply shortened: players gambling at snooker will remove all the red balls but one; or three-cushion billiard players will play games of 15, 20, or 25 points instead of the usual 30, 40, or 50. In straight pool (pocket billiards), where the standard game is 125 or 150 points, good players are usually reluctant to play a much shorter game because scoring is so easy—any really good player can occasionally run more than 50 balls—that shortening the game makes it too much a matter of chance. Therefore, in an action room one finds most of the pool players playing some variant of the game that not only requires high skill but also minimizes chance, and that therefore can be short (taking only 5 to 20 minutes per game). Today the chief of these variants are "nine ball" and "one pocket" (also called "pocket apiece"), although there are several others, such as "eight ball," "bank pool," and "rotation."

Every poolroom has at least one "No Gambling" sign on display, but no poolroom enforces it. The sign is merely a formal gesture for the eyes of the law (and in some cities required by law). It is enforced only in that the proprietor sometimes may

[3]This attitude has of course existed among some regular players elsewhere. For example, see chapter 1 of Alexander Pushkin's novella *The Captain's Daughter* (1836).

ask players to keep payoffs out of sight—not to toss the money on the table after the game—if the room is currently "heaty," e.g., if an arrest has recently been made there. Police are hardly ever concerned to stop the gambling on poolroom games, and everyone knows it. (But police sometimes check to see that the minimum age law is observed, so proprietors will often ask youths for identification.) Betting is so taken for granted that in most poolrooms the proprietor—the very man who displays a "No Gambling" sign over his desk—will on request hold the players' stake money.

However, in no poolroom does the house take a cut of the action; the proprietor gets no fee for permitting gambling or holding stake money, and wouldn't dream of asking for one. His payment from bettors is simply that they comprise most of his customs in equipment rental. And hustlers, as he and they well know, count in this regard far beyond their numbers, for they play much oftener and longer than other customers; indeed, they virtually live in the poolroom.

The only non-bettor whose payment is somewhat related to the size of the action is the rack boy (if one is used), the person who racks up the balls for the players after each frame. The bigger the action, the larger the tip he can expect, and if one player comes out very much ahead he tips the rack boy lavishly. The rack boy's position is thus analogous to that of the golf caddie, except that a rack boy is used in only about half of hustler-vs.-hustler contests and in but a tiny fraction of other contests. Sometimes he is an employee (sweeper, etc.) of the poolroom, but more often he is a spectator performing as rack boy on an *ad hoc* basis.

NON-HUSTLED POOLROOM GAMBLING

Hustling is *not* involved when the games played for money are any of the following:

(a) *Non-hustler vs. non-hustler.* A "sociable" game in which the bet is a token one. The only betting is player vs. player.

(b) *Non-hustler vs. non-hustler.* A game for significantly more than a token amount. The players play even-up if they are fairly equal. If they are aware of a significant difference in skill levels, the weaker player is given an appropriate handicap. Usually the betting is just between players; rarely, one or both players will bet spectators; spectators do not bet each other.

(c) *Hustler vs. non-hustler.* The players are aware of the difference in skills, and this is properly taken into account via an appropriate spot. Usually the betting is only player vs. player, though sometimes spectators bet players or each other. The hustler tries to avoid this type of game, and agrees to it only when he has nothing better to do.

(d) *Hustler vs. hustler.* Each player knows the other's mettle, if only by reputation ("Minnesota Fats" vs. "Fast Eddy" in *The Hustler*, for example). The hustler, contrary to the impression given by the movie, does *not* prefer this type of game (though he does prefer it to the foregoing type) and does *not* regard it as hustling. But he plays it often because he often can't get the kind of game he wants (a true "hustle") and this alternative does offer him excitement—not only the greatest challenge to his playing skill, but the most action. The average bet between two hustlers is much higher than in any other type of poolroom contest.[4] And betting modes 2 and 3 (player vs. spectator, spectator vs. spectator) occur much more often.

Be that as it may, the hustler much prefers to hustle, which means to be in a game set up so as to be pretty much a sure thing for him, a game that "you're not allowed to lose" as the hustler puts it. In order to achieve this, to truly hustle, he engages in deception. The centrality of deception in pool or billiard hustling is perhaps best indicated by the fact that the poolroom hustler's

[4]When two high-rolling hustlers agree to play each other there is often a real race among poorer spectators to offer rack-boy services because, as previously noted, if one is engaged for such a session he can expect a good tip. I witnessed one six-hour session between hustlers in which the winning hustler came out $800 ahead and tipped the rack boy $50.

argot originated the widespread American slang dictum, "never give a sucker an even break."[5]

THE HUSTLER'S METHODS OF DECEPTION

The structure of a gambling game determines what methods of deception, if any, may be used in it. In many games (dice, cards, etc.) one can deceive one's opponent by various techniques of cheating. Pool and billiard games are so structured that this method is virtually impossible. (Once in a great while, against a particularly unalert opponent, one can surreptitiously add a point or two to one's score—but such opportunity is rare, usually involves risk of discovery that is judged to be too great, and seldom means the difference between winning and losing anyway; so no player counts on it.) One's every move and play is completely visible, easily watched by one's opponent and by spectators; nor is it possible to achieve anything via previous tampering with the equipment.

However, one structural feature of pool or billiards readily lends itself to deceit: on each shot, the difference between success and failure is a matter of a small fraction of an inch. In pool or billiards it is peculiarly easy, even for the average player, to miss one's shot deliberately and still look good (unlike, say, nearly all card

[5]Its pool-hustler origin is noted by Vogeler, *op. cit.*, p. 347. It is recorded in none of the slang sourcebooks (Mencken, Mathews, Berrey and Van den Bark, *et al.*) except Harold Wentworth and Stuart Berg Flexner, *Dictionary of American Slang* (New York: T. Y. Crowell, 1960), p. 527. Wentworth and Flexner do not attempt to account for the phrase's origin. They claim that it dates to around 1835, but this seems impossibly early. The only source they cite is its use as the title of a 1941 W. C. Fields movie.

Actually, Fields used the phrase earlier in his *Poppy* (1936), where it is his exit line and the last line of the movie. Fields's partiality to "never give a sucker an even break" is thoroughly in keeping with Vogeler's account of the origin of the phrase: Fields was the son of a Philadelphia poolroom owner, spent much of his boyhood in his father's poolroom, was an excellent player, and built his funniest vaudeville act around his pool-playing skill (at the act's climax he sank fifteen balls with one shot). Cf. Douglas Gilbert, *American Vaudeville* (New York: Whittlesey House, 1940), pp. 273–74.

Another of Fields's pool-playing vaudeville skits became the core of his first movie, a one-reeler of 1915 entitled *Pool Sharks*. Cf. Donald Deschner, *The Films of W. C. Fields* (New York: Citadel, 1966), p. 35.

games, where if one does not play one's cards correctly this is soon apparent). On all shots except the easiest ones, it is impossible to tell if a player is deliberately not trying his best.

The hustler exploits this fact so as to deceive his opponents as to his (the hustler's) true level of skill (true "speed"). It is so easily exploited that, when playing good opponents, usually the better hustlers even disdain it, pocket nearly every shot they have (intentionally miss only some very difficult shots), and rely chiefly on related but subtler techniques of failure beyond the remotest suspicion of most players. For example, such a hustler may strike his cue ball hard and with too much spin ("english"), so that the spin is transferred to the object ball and the object ball goes into the pocket but jumps out again; or he may scratch (losing a point and his turn), either by "accidentally" caroming his cue ball into a pocket or by hitting his cue ball hard and with too much top-spin so that it jumps off the table; or, most commonly, he pockets his shot but, by striking his cue ball just a wee bit too hard or too softly or with too much or too little english, he leaves himself "safe" (ends up with his cue ball out of position, so that he hasn't another shot). In such wise the hustler feigns less competence than he has.

Hustling, then, involves not merely the ability to play well, but the use of a kind of "short con." Sometimes the hustler doesn't need to employ any con to get his opponent to the table, sometimes he does; but he always employs it in attempting to keep his opponent there.

The best hustler is not necessarily the best player among the hustlers. He has to be a very good player, true, but beyond a certain point his playing ability is not nearly so important as his skill at various kinds of conning. Also, he has to possess personality traits that make him "rocklike," able to exploit fully his various skills—playing, conning, others—in the face of assorted pressures and temptations not to exploit them fully.

THE HUSTLER'S CARDINAL RULE

As the foregoing indicates, the hustler's cardinal rule is: *don't show your real speed.* Of course, an exception is permitted if by some miracle the hustler finds himself hustled, finds himself in a game with someone he thought would be easy but who turns out to be tough. But this is not supposed to happen, and it rarely does. For one thing, hustlers generally know each other, or of each other, and their respective skill levels. Secondly, any pool or billiard game is overwhelmingly a game of skill rather than luck— even in the chanciest type of poolroom game the element of skill counts for much more than in any card game whatsoever—and this means it is possible to rate the skill levels of various players (to "handicap" them) along small gradations with a high degree of accuracy. For example, if one has seen the three-cushion billiard players X and Y play various people over a period of time, it is possible to arrive at the judgment "On a 30-point game, X is two or three points better than Y" and to be dead right about it in at least eight out of ten contests between them.

The corollaries of the hustler's chief rule are: (a) The hustler must restrain himself from making many of the extremely difficult shots. Such restraint is not easy, because the thrill of making a fancy shot that brings applause from the audience is hard to resist. But the hustler must resist, or else it would make less believable his misses on more ordinary shots. (b) He must play so that the games he wins are won by only a small margin. (c) He must let his opponent win an occasional game.

It may be thought that once a hustler has engaged an opponent, a bet has been agreed upon and the stake money put up, and the game has started, the hustler might safely let out all the stops. This would be terribly short-sighted.

In the first place, as noted earlier, the typical non-hustler bets only a small amount on the game. The hustler's only hope of making real money, therefore, is to extend the first game into a series of games, entice his opponent into doubling up when he is behind, etc. If the hustler does this well, the opponent will hang on for a long time, may even come back after the first session to play him on another day, turn into a real "fish" (the poolroom term for an inferior opponent who doesn't catch on that he's outclassed, and keeps coming back for more). And when the opponent starts demanding a spot, as sooner or later he will, the hustler can offer him his (the hustler's) average winning margin, or even a little better, and still have a safe game.

Secondly, there are spectators to take into account. Some of them will bet the hustler if he offers the non-hustler a seemingly fair spot. More importantly, some of them are potential opponents. Nearly all poolroom spectators are also players. The hustler doesn't want to look too good to spectators either.

He knows that as he beats various opponents his reputation will rise, and that increasingly he'll have to offer spots to people, but he wants to keep his reputation as low as possible as long as possible with as many people as possible. He also knows that he has to play superbly on occasion—that he will play fellow hustlers when there's no other action around, and that then he must show more skill—but he wants to keep these occasions few. (It helps considerably, by the way, that because hustler-vs.-hustler games occur when hustlers give up hope of finding other action, these games usually take place after midnight when there aren't so many non-hustler potential victims around to watch.)

The sooner everyone in the poolroom knows the hustler's true speed, the sooner he exhausts the real hustling possibilities among the room's regular players. Such a situation constitutes one of the career crises that every hustler has to face. (For reasons which will become apparent below, he now has to face it earlier in his career than hustlers formerly did.) When it occurs, either he must move on to a poolroom where he's less known or, if he stays in the room, he has to take games he shouldn't take or else restrict his pickings to strangers who wander in.

JOB-RELATED SKILLS AND TRAITS

Although the hallmarks of the good hustler are playing skill and the temperamental ability to consistently look poorer than he is, there are other skills and traits that aid him in hustling. Some are related to deceiving his opponent, some not.

Chief of these is argumentative skill in arranging the terms of the match, the ability to "make a game." The prospective opponent, if he has seen the hustler play, may when approached claim that the hustler is too good for him or ask for too high a spot, i.e., one that is fair or even better. The hustler, like the salesman, is supposed to be familiar with standard objections and with "propositions" for overcoming them.

Another side of the ability to make a game reveals itself when the prospective opponent simply can't be argued out of demanding a spot that is unfair to the hustler, or can be convinced to play only if the hustler offers such a spot. At that point the hustler should of course refuse to play. There is often a temptation to do otherwise, not only because the hustler is proud of his skill but because action is his lifeblood (which is why he plays other hustlers when he can't find a hustle), and there may be no other action around. He must resist the temptation. In the good hustler's view, no matter how badly you want action, it is better not to play at all than to play when you are disadvantaged; otherwise you are just hustling yourself. (But the hustler often will, albeit with much argument and the greatest reluctance, agree to give a fair spot if that's the only way he can get action.)

The hustler, when faced, as he very often is, with an opponent who knows him as such, of course finds that his ability to make a game assumes greater importance than his ability to feign lack of skill. In such situations, indeed, his game-making ability is just as important as his actual playing ability.

On the other hand, the hustler must have "heart" (courage). The *sine qua non* is that he is a good "money player," can play his best when heavy action is riding on the game (as many non-hustlers can't). Also, he is not supposed to let a bad break or distractions in the audience upset him. (He may pretend to get rattled on such occasions, but that's just part of his con.) Nor should the quality of his game deteriorate when, whether by miscalculation on his part or otherwise, he finds himself much further behind than he would like to be. Finally, if it is necessary to get action, he should not be afraid to tackle an opponent whom he knows to be just about as good as he is.

A trait often working for the hustler is stamina. As a result of thousands of hours of play, all the right muscles are toughened up. He is used to playing many hours at a time, certainly much more used to it than the non-hustler is. This is valuable because sometimes, if the hustler works it right, he can make his opponent forget about quitting for such a "silly" reason as being tired, can extend their session through the night and into the next day. In

such sessions it is most often in the last couple of hours, when the
betting per game is usually highest, that the hustler makes his
biggest killing.

Additional short-con techniques are sometimes used. One hustler, for example, entices opponents by the ancient device of
pretending to be sloppy-drunk. Other techniques show more imagination. For example, a hustler preparing for a road trip mentioned to me that before leaving town he was going to buy a
soldier's uniform: "I walk into a strange room in uniform and
I've got it made. Everybody likes to grab a soldier."

One of the most noted hustlers of recent years, Luther "Wimpy"
Lassiter, reports that in his own forays he has sometimes worn a
wedding band and flashed a wallet (because the typical hustler
is unmarried and, like dedicated gamblers generally and lower-
class gamblers especially, carries his money loose in his pocket).

Finally, the hustler—the superior hustler at any rate—has
enough flexibility and good sense to break the "rules" when the
occasion demands it, will modify standard techniques when he
encounters non-standard situations. An example: Once I entered
a poolroom just as a hustler I know, X, was finishing a game with
non-hustler Y. X beat Y soundly, by a higher margin than a hustler should beat anyone, and at that for only $3. Y went to the
bathroom, whereupon I admonished X, "What's the matter with
you? You know you're not allowed to win that big." X replied:

> Yeah, sure but you see that motherfucking S over there?
> [nodding discreetly in the direction of one of the spectators].
> Well, about an hour ago when I came in he and Y were talk-
> ing, and when S saw me he whispered something to Y. So
> I had a hunch he was giving him the wire [tipping him off]
> that I was pretty good. And then in his middle game it looked
> like Y was stalling a little [missing deliberately] to see what
> I would do, so then I was sure he got the wire on me. I had
> to beat him big so he'll think he knows my top speed. But
> naturally I didn't beat him as big as I *could* beat him. Now
> he'll come back cryin' for a spot and bigger action, and I'll
> nail him.

And he did nail him.[6]

[6]This sort of situation is unusual. One part of the poolroom code, ad-
hered to by nearly all regular players, holds that a player is supposed to
watch out for himself in the matches he gets into, find out for himself

THE ART OF DUMPING

As we saw, the structure of a pool or billiard game makes it virtually impossible for the hustler to cheat his opponent. By "stalling" (deliberately missing some shots, leaving himself out of position, etc.) and by "lemoning" or "lemonading" an occasional game in the session (winning in a deliberately sloppy and seemingly lucky manner, or deliberately losing the game), the hustler keeps his opponent on the hook and entices him into heavier action, but such deception falls short of outright cheating. However, in examining betting we saw that there is considerable variation in the interpersonal superstructure of the game, i.e., that there are several types of betting relationships between and among players and spectators. One of these varieties does lead to outright cheating by the hustler—not cheating his opponent, but cheating some spectators.

When two hustlers play each other, not only is the betting between players relatively heavy, but the betting of spectators against players is also, typically, at its height. Therefore, two hustlers sometimes will agree before their session that if, on any game, there is a good disparity between the amounts of action that each gets from spectators, the player with the most to gain from side bets with spectators will win the game and the players will later share the profits. The amount that spectators bet each other is of course irrelevant to such calculations, and in such circumstances the amount that the players bet each other automatically becomes a phony bet, strictly for deluding the spectators.

For example, one such game I know of went as follows: Hustler A played hustler B for $70. A's side bets with spectators totaled $100 and B's side bets with spectators totaled $380. Therefore A deliberately lost to B, paying him $70 and paying $100 to spectators, with B collecting $70 from A and $380 from spectators.

---

whom he can and cannot beat. Ordinarily one does not warn a player about who is superior or who the hustlers are, unless one is a close friend of that player. (And even if one is a friend, the code demands that such a warning be given only before any match is in prospect; that is, once a player has started to "make a game" with another, third parties are supposed to stay out.)

Later, in private, B gave A $310 (the $70 that A had "lost" to B, the $100 that A had paid to the audience, plus $140 or one-half the overall amount won from the audience). Each player thus made $140 on the deal.

Sometimes the hustlers will set up the audience for such disparity in side betting, via previous games in the session. An example: Hustler X played hustler Y for $20 per game. By pre-arrangement, both players refused to make side bets with spectators on the first three games and player Y deliberately lost the first three games. At the end of the third game Y became enraged, claiming that bad breaks had beat him, that X was just lucky, etc.; he raised his bet with X to $50 and also offered to bet spectators. Naturally, he got lots of action from spectators—and just as naturally he won the fourth game.

More commonly, however, such setting up does not occur. Rather, the hustlers will agree before their session that they will play each other in earnest and the bets between them will be real, but that if there is a disparity in side betting with spectators on a given game and one player gives the other a prearranged signal (gives him "the office," as the hustler's argot has it), the player with the most side action will win.

In the hustler's argot, the above type of deliberate losing is called "dumping." It is always distinguished from "lemoning" (where deliberate losing is strictly a means of conning one's opponent). Though all hustlers use the verb "to dump" in referring to a game that the hustler deliberately loses for the purpose of cheating spectators, hustlers vary in the object they attach to the verb. Some hustlers would say that the hustler who lost "dumped the game," others that he "dumped to" his opponent, and others that he (or both players in collaboration) "dumped the bettors." Some hustlers on occasion prefer a nominal use: "the game was a dump."

Because dumping involves outright cheating and could lead to serious, in fact violent, reprisals if discovered, it is the aspect of hustling that hustlers are most evasive about. No hustler likes to own up to dumping, even in talk with other hustlers. One learns about dumping indirectly, via hustlers' comments on other hustlers,

and only rarely via a hustler's direct admission that he has engaged in it. It is my impression that such reticence is always pragmatic rather than moral, i.e., that no hustler has strong compunc-
tions about dumping and that every long-time hustler has dumped
at least on occasion.

Although dumping is a possibility whenever two hustlers playing each other make unequal amounts of side bets with spectators,
it actually occurs in only a minority of such situations.[7] For dumping is risky even when it is not literally discovered; sometimes
the spectators' suspicions are aroused even though nothing can be
proven, and hustlers can't afford to have this happen often, because it would kill their chances of side betting.

In this regard there are two kinds of spectator-bettors that the
hustler distinguishes and takes account of: First, there are the
ignorant majority of spectators who don't know about dumping;
the hustler doesn't want talk, much less actual knowledge, of
dumping to reach their ears. Second—and equally important to
the hustler because, though they are in the minority, they bet more
—there are some knowledgeable spectators (including other hustlers) who know about dumping but *also* know that it occurs in
only a minority of hustler-vs.-hustler contests and therefore will
often risk a bet. That is to say, just as some horse players assume
that at certain tracks there probably will be one race per day that
is fixed (one race "for the boys") and are willing to discount this
because it's only one race out of nine or ten, similarly there are
poolroom spectators who will bet on one hustler against another
because they know that dumping occurs but seldom. (Among the
knowledgeable spectators there are also, of course, some cautious
types who refuse to make such bets because of a possible dump,
even though they know the odds are against it.)

In sum, the fact that spectators will bet players in hustler-
vs.-hustler games not only permits dumping but at the same time
restrains its extent. Hustlers must severely limit their dumping,
both to prevent it becoming known to the ignorant and, just as
importantly, to prevent knowledgeable spectators from feeling that
hustlers *generally* dump when they play each other. No hustler

[7]Under certain special circumstances, dumping can also occur when there
are no bets with spectators or such bets are approximately equal on both
sides; see below.

wants to get a reputation as a dumper; therefore he cautiously picks his spots. As a result, dumping provides only a small portion of his true hustling income, i.e., his "sure-thing" income. The great bulk of such income derives from his games with non-hustler opponents.

THE HUSTLER AND HIS BACKER

The hustler frequently uses a backer, who pays the losses if the hustler loses and receives 50 per cent of any winnings. A backer hardly ever assumes any managerial function. All he does is put up the hustler's stake money in return for a half share in the profits.

Once in a very great while, a hustler will work out a standing agreement for backing, that is, have someone agree to back him regularly. There is no time limit specified for such an arrangement; the deal lasts only as long as both parties consent to it.

But almost always the hustler has no standing agreement with a backer. Rather, he looks for backing on an *ad hoc* basis as the occasion for backing arises. The "occasion" is not that the hustler decides, in the abstract, to play on someone else's risk capital; it is a specific match with a particular opponent, whose handicap terms (if any) the hustler has already arranged or knows he can get. Indeed, even a top-notch hustler rarely can get backing without being able to tell the backer who the prospective opponent is and what the terms of the game are; the hustler has to convince the backer that the particular deal is a good one.

After tentatively arranging a game with his opponent, the hustler asks one of his acquaintances in the room to back him, and if he can't find backing in the room he phones a potential backer to hurry on down with some cash. Sometimes the hustler enters the poolroom with his backer in tow.

The backer specifies the maximum amount per game that he is willing to invest, but makes no guarantee about a total investment. That is, if the hustler starts to lose, the backer can pull out after any game. And if the hustler starts winning, he cannot then bet only his "own" money and dispense with the backer; the backer is in for 50 per cent of the profit made on the entire session.

Under what conditions does the hustler seek a backer? The obvious answer is that when the hustler is broke or nearly broke (as he very often is), he looks for backing, and when he has his own money to invest he plays with that. This is indeed how the average hustler operates. The superior hustler, however, figures more angles. As one of the most intelligent hustlers explained to me:

> If you've got lockup action [a game impossible to lose] and you're broke or maybe you need a bigger stake, you should first try like hell to *borrow* the dough. It's crazy to cut somebody in on action like that unless you have to. The other big thing—what some of these jerks don't understand—is that when you have a real tough game you should *always* look for a backer, even if you've got the dough. You should take out insurance.

The backer, then, should not assume he is being approached for backing because the hustler can raise stake money no other way (though this is usually the case), but has to consider the possibility that it's because the hustler has a very difficult game he wants to "insure."

Also, the backer must consider the possibility that he may be dumped by the hustler: If the hustler is playing a colleague, they may have agreed that one of them will win the good majority of games and that they will later split the profits. (When both hustlers making such an agreement are using backers, the decision as to which hustler will lose is more or less arbitrary. If one hustler is using a backer and the other is not, it is of course the former who agrees to lose.) Or, if the hustler is playing a non-hustler with whom no such collusion is possible, he may deliberately lose on the backer's money until the backer quits, and then, after the backer has left the room or on some other occasion, the hustler, playing with his own money, will slaughter the opponent he has set up on the backer's money.

All in all, it takes as much sophistication to be a good backer as to be a good hustler.

THE HUSTLER AS CON MAN

As several parts of this study illustrate in detail, hustling demands a continuous and complicated concern with how one is seen by others. Attention to this matter is an ineluctably pervasive requirement of the hustler's trade, and is beset with risks and contradictions. The hustler has not only the concerns that one ordinarily has about being esteemed for one's skills, but develops, in addition to and partly in conflict with such concerns, a complex set of special needs or desires about how others should evaluate him, reactions to their evaluations, and behaviors designed to manipulate such evaluating.

The hustler is a certain kind of con man. And conning, by definition, involves extraordinary manipulation of other people's impressions of reality and especially of one's self, creating "false impressions."[8] If one compares the hustler with the more usual sorts of con men described by David Maurer in *The Big Con*, part of the hustler's specialness is seen to lie in this: the structural contexts within which he operates—the game, the setting of the game within the poolroom, the setting of the poolroom within the larger social structure—are not only more predetermined but more constraining. Structures do not "work for" the poolroom hustler to anywhere near the extent that they often do for other con men, and hence he must involve himself in more personal ways with active, continuous conning.

The point is not simply that the hustler can't find an ideal structural context, but that much less than the ordinary con man is he able to bend a structure toward the ideal or create one *ab ovo* (come up with an analogue of the con man's "store"). That

[8]Of course, conning is only a matter of degree, in that all of us are concerned in many ways to manipulate others' impressions of us, and so one can, if one wishes, take the view that every man is at bottom a con man. This form of "disenchantment of the world" is central to Herman Melville's *The Confidence-Man* (one of the bitterest novels in all of American literature) and to the sociological writings of Erving Goffman. Its principal corollary is the view expressed by hustlers, by other career criminals, and by Thorstein Veblen, that all businessmen are thieves.

is, the hustler is far less able to be a "producer" or "director" of
ideal social "scenes." To a much greater extent he must work in
poor settings, and to a correspondingly greater extent he must
depend on being a continuously self-aware "actor."[9] (In this connection, note the ease with which many passages of this essay
could be restated in dramaturgical or Goffmaniacal terms.)

There is another significant respect in which the hustler's conning differs structurally from the work of ordinary con men. The
latter's work, according to Maurer, falls into one or the other of
two structurally distinct types of con games: the short con, in
which the mark is played for the money he happens to be carrying, or else the big con, in which an essential feature is that the
mark is "put on the send" to withdraw much larger sums from
his bank. (Some con men also on occasion "throw the send into"
a short-con game, but this is unusual.) There is no analogous
distinction made by pool hustlers in theory or practice. Virtually
every hustle is in Maurer's sense a short con, i.e., the sucker is
simply taken for the cash he has on him at the time, or as much
of it as he will allow himself to lose.

There are two situations in which the hustler's conning involves
his victim going on the send, but they are accidental and rare;
the hustler doesn't expect them, though he is of course pleased
when one or the other of them happens: (a) As we have noted,
the ideal kind of sucker is the "fish" who doesn't realize he can
never win and makes himself available on other days for return
matches, much like the sort of mark whom con men call an
"addict." In order to reinforce any propensity his victim might
have for being or becoming a fish, the hustler tries to win the last

[9]The kinds of structural problems faced today by the pool or billiard
hustler are by no means all endemic; some are the result of recent social
change (see pp. 145–148 below). On the other hand, such change has not
created structural problems for all types of hustling. Today the golf hustler,
for example, finds that with precious little "acting" he can (a) get heavy
action from non-hustlers, (b) lose the majority of the eighteen holes and
still clean up, and at the same time (c) not be suspected as a hustler. The
structure of the game of golf itself, the peculiar structurally predetermined
variations in the betting relationship as one makes the round of the course
("presses," etc.), and the present setting of the game within the larger
society—all these combine to create a situation that is tailor-made for
hustling. But that is another story.

game of a match by only a small margin even though he *knows* it is the last game, i.e., knows that after he beats the sucker the latter will quit because he is cleaned out or unwilling to risk the small amount he may have left. On very rare occasion, to the hustler's surprise and delight, when the sucker is thus cleaned out he may not end the match but instead become a sort of instant fish (my term, not used by hustlers): he may have the hustler wait while he (the sucker) runs out to get more cash and comes back with same. (b) As a result of having watched the hustler stall with some other opponent (or in solitary practice), the sucker may decide that before he challenges the hustler, or accepts the hustler's challenge, he should go get more of a bankroll so he can make bigger bets.

Although in both of the above situations the victim goes on the send as a result of the hustler's actions, such actions are not, strictly speaking, calculated to achieve that result. The sucker essentially puts himself on the send.

The hustler, in any case, needs to be continually concerned about evaluation of him by other persons. But the nature and degree of his concern vary with the particular kind of "others" that these persons represent. The victim or prospective victim, the hustler's orientation toward whom we have discussed at several points, is only one kind of other. Obviously the hustler must take cognizance of at least two additional types of significant others: outsiders and colleagues. Let us look at how he relates to them.

OUTSIDERS

By "outsiders" I do not mean those poolroom players and spectators who aren't hustlers (most such people most of the time are considered by the hustler to be prospective victims), but rather the public at large whose interests lie outside the poolroom world entirely. As far as the hustler is concerned, the central fact about such people is that they are not potential sources of income for him.

Another relevant fact about such people was noted at the beginning of this essay: nearly all of them, insofar as they have any knowledge or opinion about hustling at all, stigmatize the hustler and his trade. But this fact—and here hustlers differ in a major way from other socially deviant groups—is not at all important in hustler thinking. The fact that hustlers are put down by society at large is extraordinarily rare as a topic of hustlers' conversation or consciousness. Nor, despite the fact that hustlers come from a subculture whose values differ from those on the basis of which they are stigmatized, do they bother to develop a definite counter-ideology about why outsiders should themselves be put down. In this respect hustlers seem to be unlike, say, most drug users, homosexuals, bohemians and jazz musicians, and unlike the great majority of career criminals.

To be sure, the hustler is aware that outsiders in general stigmatize him. But he is aware of it less often, and less strongly, than other people are aware of their negative status in the larger society —for he comes in contact with it far less. The homosexual may elicit negative reactions in a variety of "straight" work situations and other public situations unless he is successful in disguising his homosexuality (and even then he hears a lot of putdowns of "queers"); the Negro, even if he elects to live in the heart of his ghetto and remain as "black" as possible, is raised on white mass media and at the least cannot help internalizing white ideals of physical attractiveness; the typical criminal cannot pick up a newspaper or look at TV without being faced with the fact that the public rejects him and his kind. The hustler's lifespace and lifeways, however, cut him off much more fully from outsiders' negative judgments. Unlike Negroes, he is segregated not only from his "betters" but from their opinions of him. There are three reasons for this.

(1) My statement earlier that hustlers "virtually live in the poolroom" was meant literally. About four-fifths of the hustlers are unmarried. Moreover, almost every unmarried hustler resides by himself in one small furnished room or hotel room, hardly conducive to developing a "home life." His real psychological home is the job site, the poolroom. This is where he spends almost all his waking hours. This is not only where he works but where he loafs, plays, and as often as not eats—and also where he sleeps

when he can't make room rent. In fine, it is his leisure-place as much as his work-place.

The typical hustler has very few interests outside the poolroom and reads nothing except (sporadically) the racing page of the newspaper. Even his few outside interests are intermittent: watching sports events on TV once or twice a week, occasionally making a pickup in a bar and getting laid, once in a while seeing a movie, going to the track several times a year, now and then playing cards—that's the sum total of non-poolroom life for most hustlers.

(2) When the hustler does temporarily take a non-hustling job, it tends to be one that takes him out of the poolroom not at all or hardly at all, or else provides only fleeting, fragmented contacts with the non-poolroom world.

(3) The hustler seldom runs into non-hustler players who put him down. First of all, most non-hustler poolroom habitués not only accept the poolroom tradition that all players should bet, but tend in varying degrees to accept the "sporting life" ethic accompanying it (especially the notion that if a player overmatches himself that's his own problem), and their attitudes toward hustlers range from ignorance or indifference to tolerance to sympathy to outright admiration. Certainly such attitudes (except for ignorance) are true of nearly all those non-hustlers who play regularly in "action rooms."

As for the players who strongly object to hustlers: whether they play regularly or infrequently, they seldom are in the action rooms where hustlers hang out but prefer the sedater poolrooms (or, if upper class, prefer to play in private clubs). Also, more often than not such players are so unperceptive of all but the crudest hustling that they can't tell a hustler when they see one. Many a player who believes he has never played a hustler has in fact been hustled by several.

Of course, the hustler doesn't proclaim his trade to the outside world, for typically he has neither a masochistic urge to be put down nor the reactive hostility to majority opinion that one finds in the flamboyant homosexual or "professional Negro" or "professional Jew" and the like. On the other hand, he isn't much concerned with hiding his trade from outsiders so long as openness would not adversely affect his income. He actually runs into put-downs so seldom and his world is so self-contained that the majority's negative opinion neither significantly affects his life-chances nor bruises his psyche.

In other words, though the hustler cares about what the outside world thinks of his role, he cares about it much less than other deviants do. Outsiders as a class may comprise a significant other for the hustler, but they are not a genuine "reference group" for him: he has not even the most latent of aspirations to membership in their world, and thus is not about to change his behavior to accord with their moral standards. As a result he is likely to practice a peculiar kind of inconsistency about revealing his occupation to outsiders—an inconsistency that has the mark not of "conflict" or "ambivalence" but rather of genuine flexibility and free choice, i.e., choice based on rational calculation of what, in any given situation with outsiders, might be most to his advantage.

An example of this flexibility or rational inconsistency in the presence of outsiders may be seen by comparing two samples from the behavior of the man known among hustlers as Wimpy, America's foremost nine-ball hustler, and known to larger circles as a professional player under his real name, Luther Lassiter (on the relation between hustling and professional playing, see below). In April, 1963, he won the World Professional Pocket Billiard Tournament. One day during the tournament—after he had won a game that made it almost certain he would be the next champion —a few spectators, including myself, were talking with him when a reporter from the Associated Press came up and started interviewing him. The reporter asked, among other things, how Mr. Lassiter made his living—and did he make it playing pool? Wimpy smiled and said no; he said that he lived with his mother, that he had a rich brother who helped him out, and that it just seemed that the good Lord looked after him. Yet only a few weeks later he appeared on a nationwide TV program called *To Tell the Truth*, in which the panelists were to guess which one of three persons, including Lassiter, was a pool hustler, and in which his occupation was revealed. In the first situation, there was nothing to be gained from revealing his occupation to the reporter, and possibly negative consequences for the "image" of pocket billiards

—which both the players and the sponsors of the tournament were concerned to improve.[10] In the second situation, there was a nice fee for him in going on TV to own up publicly to his trade.

COLLEAGUESHIP

Colleagueship among hustlers is partly typical of colleagueship in occupations generally, and partly not. One way in which it is untypical has to do with entry to and expulsion from the occupation.

In most kinds of work, the colleague group can debar someone from entry, either by formal means (e.g., deny him job training, or a license, or tools, or union membership) or by informal means (e.g., ostracize him socially, refuse to work with him, deny him the recommendations needed to get work). But entry to hustling does not involve elements that can be effectively controlled by colleagues. There are no formal entrance criteria such as examinations or licenses or diplomas. And job training (the development of playing and conning ability) is publicly available to anyone, as are the tools of the trade (playing equipment), a workplace (the poolroom), and the market for one's skill (suckers). In most of his job activities, and in all that are truly essential, each hustler is basically an individual entrepreneur. For this reason also, the colleague group cannot really "expel" anyone from hustling.

It is true enough that to enjoy colleagueship means first of all to be recognized and accepted as a colleague by others. But it does not always follow that to be denied colleagueship is to be denied work. It may make the work situation tougher, but by no means

[10]Apropos of the public relations or "image-making" aspect of this tournament: members of its sponsoring group, the Billiard Room Proprietors Association of America, admitted to me that because of their desire not to jeopardize the game's comeback attempt (this was the first world tournament held in several years), they had not invited two players who doubtless were superior to at least one of the ten contestants invited. The two uninvited players might have damaged the "image" that the tournament was trying to convey: one of them had recently been in jail on a felony charge, and the other was noted for, among other things, his refusal to wear a tie and the unrelieved profanity of his speech.

impossible. Thus, if a hustler is denied acceptance by other hustlers, it can rule out dumping and other forms of cooperation between him and them, but it has no discernible effect on his main job activity, which is to lure suckers into games with him.

In any case, outright rejection of a hustler by his colleagues, by refusal to cooperate or associate with him, is actually quite rare. It is invoked only on those whose personalities can cause associates plenty of grief. An example: after this study was under way for three months I began avoiding games with one of the hustlers I had until then played billiards with—this on the advice of other hustlers, who warned me that my playing companion was both armed and unpredictably short-tempered.

A colleague group creates *esprit de corps*, a feeling of "we-ness." It also creates awareness that although colleagues are equals, some colleagues are more equal than others; that is, it creates an intra-occupational stratification system, mostly along the dimension of prestige. I mention these together because in the hustling world the two are peculiarly intertwined: Non-rigged games between hustlers—ever more frequent these days, for reasons to be indicated later—constitute on the one hand intense, focused interaction between friendly colleagues, in the context of an audience consisting largely or exclusively of other colleagues, and thus such games contribute much to group identity feelings. But on the other hand, they are also serious, fierce competitions, whose results provide colleagues with their chief basis for rating a hustler's playing skill, which rating is in turn a major ingredient of his general prestige rank. Thus the *esprit de corps* of the hustling world and its internal stratification system are to some degree functions of each other. That noted, we can now look at each separately.

At the bottom of the prestige hierarchy are those few players with so little skill that, even though they hustle, colleagues question their right to be regarded as hustlers at all. Thus, of one hustler it was contemptuously remarked:

> He calls himself a hustler but he always dogs it for the cash.
> I guess his old lady supports him.

And of another:

I've hardly never seen him take down the cash. That movie turned him on to thinking he was a hustler, but he ain't. You could give him 12 on 30 [points in three-cushion billiards] and still have a lock. He should get a job.

At the top of the hierarchy are, of course, the players of outstanding skill. Although most hustlers can play any poolroom game well—and in addition many can, if need be, offer a sucker the handicap of shooting with the hand other than the one they normally use—they tend to specialize in one game or another. A hustler's standing among colleagues is based on this functional specialization, and he may be rated highly in one game but not in another (or not even thought of in connection with the other). Thus Wimpy, though he can play any pool game superbly, is known chiefly as the outstanding nine-ball hustler, Eddy Taylor (the Knoxville Bear) is rated best at bank pool, and so on. Some hustlers are noted for their ability to make a difficult shot with great frequency and to win bets thereby; e.g., Don Willis is admired especially for his consistency in making "wing shots" (in which you shoot at an object ball that is moving rapidly down the table away from you, and pocket it in a far corner).

There is by no means unanimity about who is the best in each specialty. Usually there are two or three candidates for that rating among the hustlers. For example, there is disagreement about who is the most adept specialist in the "I'll play you one-handed" routine; Lusitay has hustler partisans who claim he is best and so does Miami. And one can always get a good argument going among hustlers by asking who is the best one-pocket specialist, Ronnie Allen or Jersey Red or Marv Henderson.

Although hustlers specialize, most of them will, as noted above, play a game that's not their specialty if it is the only game the sucker will play. So if a hustler is a specialist in versatility, as it were, this also can confer status. It is in fact the basis of the extraordinary prestige that Boston Shorty enjoys among his colleagues. Hustlers do not rate him at the top in any specialty (except for a few who say he is probably the best at three-cushion billiards), but they are quick to point out that he is near the top in almost every specialty. By unanimous agreement, Boston Shorty is our country's best "all around" hustler. His great prestige derives

not so much from his excellence at the whole gamut of pool games
(a few other hustlers are probably his equals here), but from
the fact that he is, at the same time, the best or nearly best hustler
at three-cushion billiards. Hardly any hustlers shuttle between
pocket and three-cushion games to the extent that Shorty does,
and none with such success as he; the reason is that although
basic skills (such as how to hold a cue stick, or how to aim) are
readily transferable, some advanced skills are not and, more importantly, actually interfere with each other.[11] That is why virtually
all regular players, hustlers included, tend over time to concentrate
entirely or almost entirely on either pool or three-cushion billiards.

It is assumed that every hustler knows how to "make a game,"
and this aspect of his work influences prestige rank among colleagues only if he is especially inept at it:

> X has got the heart and he's got the stroke. But he'll never
> be a good hustler, 'cause he's always giving away too many
> points. He's part sucker, that's what he is.

Another aspect of maladroitness in making a game was put
down by Brooklyn Johnny, with whom I was watching a game in
which hustler Y managed to eke out a win over a very tough
non-hustler. I said something about hustler Y's great playing, and
Johnny replied:

> But it's dumb. Look at the takedown [amount of cash] he
> got for it. It's dumb to make a game where you have to show
> the room your top speed for only $5.

[11]This is especially true of one's stroke: developing a perfect stroke at
pool makes it almost impossible simultaneously to have a perfect stroke at
three-cushion billiards, and vice versa. (An exact parallel exists in the
playing of keyboard instruments, where the touch someone develops in
becoming an outstanding pianist precludes his being an outstanding harpsi-
chordist, and vice versa.) In the entire history of pool and three-cushion
billiards only two professional players, Alfredo DeOro and Johnny Layton,
ever managed to win championships at both (and Layton was able to win
these only at widely separated points in his career).

Studies of transferability of motor skills—the main ones are summarized
in Woodward and Schlosberg's *Experimental Psychology*—have to a slight
extent dealt with negative transfer effects. But the type of situation discussed above, in which attaining the highest level at one motor skill inhibits
a similar level of performance at a closely related motor skill, seems not
to have been studied at all.

Without exception, hustlers contend that "heart" (courage or toughness) is as essential to hustling as playing ability is. We saw earlier that they view it as basic to the job. The point here is that hustlers, in their preoccupation with it, often use judgments about "heart" to confer or withhold prestige. Some examples of such judgments that hustlers have made to me are these (each applies to a different hustler):

> You can't bet on A because you don't know how he's going to stand up for more than $20. No heart.

> Take B over there, thinks he's such a hotshot. But you'll never see him put up his own dough. He's got no heart, that's why. He's gotta have backing even when the game is a lock. B wouldn't play on his own dough unless the sucker had one foot in the grave, the other on a banana peel, and both arms in a cast.

> C don't have the heart for it. He only does okay when he gets out in front early.

> Weenie Beanie's got real heart. He's no locksman. A real strong gambler.

> I tell you one thing about Boston Shorty, the real great thing, is that the guy kisses icewater. He don't frighten out. One time I seen a game where some dude runs over 100 balls on him, and Shortly comes right back with 89 and out. It takes plenty heart to do that.

The *esprit de corps* of a colleague group, especially if it is a deviant group, tends to be strengthened by a well-developed hostility toward outsiders. But as we saw earlier, hustlers, for special reasons, do not have an elaborate ideology or strong feelings about this. They do, of course, sometimes speak contemptuously of outsiders; but in developing solidary feelings they rely much more on emphasizing the joys of hustling, talking of its virtues (such as autonomy and heart), rating each other, discussing its technology, telling tales of its heroes and villains, and so on. When a hustler says of hustling that "it beats working," his emphasis is not on putting down the workaday world; his primary meaning is, rather, a positive one—that hustling is infinitely more pleasurable than any other job he could find.

The fact that the hustler's work-place is to so great an extent also his leisure-place not only lessens his need for putting down the outside world, but at the same time increases those collegial interactions which foster *esprit de corps* by other means. One of those means, as should be obvious by now, is the use of an elaborate argot; I have placed my analysis of hustlers' argot in an appendix to this chapter, for reasons explained there.

Colleagueship involves an obligation to cooperate and rewards for doing so. Cooperation among hustlers takes several forms: (1) The main one, already discussed, is the cooperative swindle known as "dumping." (2) Often a hustler will tell a colleague about a fault he has noticed in the latter's game, although there appears to be no clearly defined collegial obligation to do this. (3) A clearly defined obligation, the strongest element in the hustlers' colleague code, has to do with regulating the competition for opponents: when a hustler has started to make a game (be it with a sucker or another hustler), any hustler who is a third party is not supposed to cut in with a better offer or otherwise queer the pitch; as previously noted, this sanction is observed not only by hustlers but by regular poolroom players generally. (4) When a hustler from out of town is cleaned out by some local hustler, the latter is obligated to give the former, on request, "get-out-of-town money." And whatever the winner's personal feelings about the loser, he doesn't fail to honor the request, so severe would be the castigation from his colleagues otherwise. (5) When a hustler is preparing for a road trip to towns he doesn't know, or hasn't visited in a long time, colleagues who have recently been to those places provide him with information on where the action is, who the best players are, what kind of cons they go for, and what their skill levels are. Conversely, when he returns from the road he fills in his colleagues with any new information he has gleaned on these matters.

More than a word needs to be said about the relationships between hustlers and professional players. The hustler and the professional have quite distinct occupational roles if we view them as ideal types, but empirically there is some overlap, especially today, and it leads to collegial relations between them that are extensive, complex, ambiguous and ambivalent.

The professional's income, years ago when professionalism paid well, derived mainly from tournament prizes, exhibition fees, endorsements of billiard products or representation of billiard supply firms, and teaching fees. Today, except for two or three top professionals, income from such sources is negligible. It is doubtful if even the current titleholder makes as much as $15,000 from them. (Compare this with Hoppe's 1925 estimate that the title was worth as much as $50,000 per year to whoever held it.) Professionals gain their income mostly from other occupations, especially managing a poolroom or owning a piece of one. One of these "other" occupations is hustling, and it appears that even in the earlier period many professionals also hustled on occasion. But it also appears that, except for a few professionals, they have done so infrequently. The great majority of professionals have often made big bets with opponents and spectators, but in situations where their skill levels were known to all concerned, i.e., not true hustling situations. In sum: many, possibly most, professionals have hustled—but seldom; and possibly a majority, certainly a large minority, of professionals either have never hustled at all or hustled only in early youth.

The very large majority of hustlers, on the other hand, have never tried to become professionals: they have stayed out of tournaments—in order, of course, to stay out of the limelight. At least, that's the reason most hustlers give. An additional reason, which they don't give, is that not many hustlers have been good enough to hold their own with the top professionals. However, if a hustler feels that his skill is already so well known that he has nothing much to lose by appearing in professional tournaments, and also feels that maybe he could win all the marbles, he will "go professional." And with the decline of potential income from hustling (see below), such feelings are becoming more common and the percentage of players in professional tournaments who have long hustling backgrounds has been going up rapidly—so that now, perhaps, the majority of professionals have such backgrounds.

Of course, if a hustler appears often in tournaments he severely reduces his chances of true hustling. And should he attain professional stardom, he effectively takes himself out of hustling altogether, whether he wants to or not. For example, as a result of his 1963 and later tournament victories, plus the numerous paid public exhibitions he was able to give after 1963 (including several on television), Wimpy cannot really be a hustler any more—regardless of what his current desire or self-conception may be. Today there is scarcely a poolroom in America, and certainly none with significant action, where he would not be recognized as soon as he walked in the door. He can still play for big bets (and does), but only with top players and, at that, by giving them tremendous handicaps.

All of the above-mentioned blurring and criss-crossing of occupational lines has led to some uneasy relations between the professionals and the hustlers. (1) A good number of professionals who were never hustlers have been against hustlers because the latter give the game a bad "image." There were many such "respectable" professionals in the old days (Hoppe is as good an example as any) and there are still some today (e.g., Irving Crane). On the other hand, even these professionals have a grudging respect for the skill of top hustlers and recognize that they are, after all, in the same sort of trade and have the same love of the game. (2) Most of the professionals who hustled a bit in their earliest days, or who have combined professional play with occasional hustling for a significant part of their careers, or who were basically hustlers before turning professional, don't put down hustlers at all, hang around with them, and in general find their company more congenial than the company of "respectable" professionals. But at the same time they are concerned to improve their chances of income from professional play, and agree with the equipment manufacturers and poolroom owners that the best way of doing so lies in improving the game's public "image"; as a result, they will sometimes be publicly and calculatedly evasive about their hustling backgrounds. (3) A few (very few) players who formerly hustled not only have gone professional but, upon doing well at it, have gone respectable. As one would expect, they become more royalist than the king. For example, Willie Mosconi has been given to making contemptuous remarks in public about "hustlers" such as Wimpy—this despite the fact that Mosconi was himself quite a hustler in his youth. Needless to say, Mosconi's present contempt for hustlers is returned by them.

AN OCCUPATION IN DECLINE

Outsiders who saw *The Hustler* gathered that a good pool or billiard hustler can make big money or an excellent living by exercising his skills. In this matter as in some others, the movie falsified by offering past history as if it were the present. The days when the poolroom hustler could readily find non-hustlers willing to play for high stakes are long gone, and probably gone forever. Structural changes in American sporting life over the past thirty years have had disastrous consequences for the hustler (as for the professional player).

The major datum is, of course, the radical decline of American interest in pool or billiards. In the entire history of the United States, no other sport of nationwide appeal seems ever to have had such a proportionate drop in its popularity.[12] As we have seen in Chapter 1, the chief aspect of this decline is that today, even after the recent "revival," the number of American poolrooms is only about a fourth what it was in the 1920's. From talks with oldtimers, I gather that the decline in action rooms has been proportionately even greater. For the hustler this means, among other things, that it is much harder to stay unknown. There are so few action rooms remaining that he cannot space his visits to them far enough apart to avoid damaging his reputation, i.e., to avoid getting too good a reputation. And, in addition, there are simply many less players and therefore many less bettors.

As if this were not enough, there has been a devastating shift (devastating for the hustler) in the ideology of the regular players who remain or enter the poolroom. They still adhere to the tradition that players should bet, but they bet far smaller amounts,

[12]Along with negative consequences for the hustler from decreased participation in pool or billiard playing, there has come disaster for the professional player in the form of decreased spectator interest. Today the final match of a professional tournament is lucky to draw 300–500 people, and the champion is lucky to draw 75 people to an exhibition. But it was not always thus. When Willie Hoppe played George Slosson for the championship in 1906, there were over 4,000 paying spectators (Cf. Hoppe, *Thirty Years of Billiards* [New York: Putnam, 1925], p. 103). And high spectator interest continued into the 1930's; see Mosconi's remark noted in [Polsky, *Hustlers, Beats, and Others*] Chapter 1, p. 19.

absolutely as well as relatively, than they did thirty years ago. The decline of the game's hold on the American sporting imagination has meant that, even among the regular players, it is no longer considered the skill game on which to plunge. The big betting by non-hustlers on their playing skill has shifted to other sports. There are now many golf hustlers living high—several make upward of $25,000 a year—for they find plenty of cocky amateurs willing to stand heavy action. (Joe Louis is one such amateur. Part of the reason he went broke is that the golf hustlers took him so often.) And some bowling hustlers do fairly well. But the pool or billiard hustler cannot make out. It is doubtful if today there are more than half a dozen poolroom hustlers who make even $7000 per year by their hustling.

Today, when the poolroom hustler plays a sucker, as often as not the action is "sociable," two or three dollars per game; the average (mean) action is perhaps $5. $10 or $15 is considered quite good action, $20 and up is uncommon, and games for as much as "half a yard" ($50) or more are downright rare. And, it must always be remembered, the hustler often has to go a good while between games that are true hustles for him. If he makes $90–$100 per week hustling, he's doing much better than average. True, almost any hustler will on the proper occasion tell of a big score he made off a sucker—say, $600 in one session. But if you pin him down as to how many times in the past few years he's made a score like that, it rarely turns out to be more than three or four times.

Games for $50 and more certainly do take place, on occasion, when hustlers play each other. (I have witnessed one series of games between two hustlers for $1,000 per game, and at least a dozen such series for $300–$800 per game.) But even here, really heavy action is uncommon; in hustler-vs.-hustler contests, the mean action is perhaps $15 or $20 per game. And in any case, though hustlers get a great kick out of the relatively big action when they play each other, they know that basically they are just taking in each other's washing.

There are certain peaks of these cannibalistic hustler-vs.-hustler contests: (a) Since 1961 there has been an annual tournament for hustlers in Johnston City, Illinois (pop. 3,900), with cash prizes but much more bet on the side between the players. It is sponsored by the Jansco brothers of that city, whose increased motel and bar business during the tournament makes up for the prize money they offer.[13] (b) When professional tournaments are held, hustlers from various cities come together as spectators and consequently adjourn to the local action room late at night for games with each other. (c) When word spreads that a poolroom has come up with a new local player willing to stand big action, hustlers flock to the room—and more often than not end up playing each other. For example, in 1962, New York City hustlers got the wire that a sucker in Lodi, New Jersey, would gamble heavily, and they began traveling across the river to seek him out; of a weekend night there would often be eight or ten hustlers in Lodi, with only the one non-hustler willing to provide decent action, so naturally many hustler-vs.-hustler games developed to pass the time.

But neither the bigger action involved in hustler-vs.-hustler contests, nor their frequency, nor their great fascination, should lead us to blink the crucial fact that they constitute occupational cannibalism. No hustler seriously expects to make a living from playing other hustlers. He wants to find opponents whom he can truly hustle, and in this connection his never-ending problem is, Where's the big action?

A room where suckers play for decent money is so rare these days that when one does turn up, it is likely to be ruined through over-exploitation. An example: In 1962 a new poolroom opened in one of Cleveland's fancier suburbs, and the area's wealthy high school students began playing each other for sizeable stakes even

[13]A good description of this scene is Tom Fox's "Hustler's Holiday in the Lion's Den," *Sports Illustrated*, Vol. 15 (December 4, 1961), pp. 53–56, 59–61; a grossly inadequate one is "Battle of the Hottest Sticks," *Sports Illustrated*, Vol. 18, No. 8 (February 25, 1963), pp. 32–37. Students of mass communications may be interested to know that in connection with the 1963 tournament a typical bit of TV fakery took place. Games between Luther Lassiter (Wimpy) and Eddy Taylor (The Knoxville Bear) were videotaped and later broadcast, on December 22, 1963, as a CBS *Sports Spectacular*. Although the tournament was for hustlers, CBS did everything possible to create the impression that it was not: the screen title was simply "World Pocket Billiard Championship," and the word "hustler" was never mentioned on the program.

though most of them scarcely knew how to hold a cue stick. Word got out and the hustlers descended—first the local hustlers from Cleveland's West 25th Street, and soon hustlers from all over the country. At its peak several hustlers were each pulling out as much as $400 per week from the room. But they tore it down; there were just too many hustlers taking too much money from too many kids, and mounting pressure from parents and police forced the room to close.

The professional three-cushion billiard player, Arthur Rubin, recently summed up the general situation as follows:

> In the old days when the hustler got too well known in his home town he just went on the road for a while. He did fine. Every town in America had its local champion willing to play for high stakes; and if the champion didn't have money himself, he always had plenty of backers willing to put it up. Today, the hustlers are more and more reduced to playing each other. And when that happens, that's not hustling— that's gambling.

The poolroom hustler, then, is a highly skilled man whose skills no longer find a lucrative outlet. His occupation, once quite rewarding financially, now can support very few people, and these barely. Why does the hustler hang on? How? What does he do if he can't? How did he come to be a hustler anyhow?

HANGING ON, CAREER CONTINGENCIES, AND RETIREMENT

The question, Why does the hustler hang on?, is somewhat misleading as applied to most hustlers. It implies that because hustling once was lucrative and now is not, today's hustler once had something valuable—a good living at his trade—that he now tries to "hang onto" after it has gone. But in my sample of *ca.* 59 hustlers (give or take a couple), 40 to 45 of them are under 50 years old and over half are under 40 years old. Now, if the good majority of hustlers are under 50, this means that they never had much to hang onto. The majority of today's hustlers entered hustling after its decline. The question to ask about them is, Why in the world did they become hustlers in the first place—and if they initially had false notions about its lucrativeness, why didn't they quit when they saw the reality (which indeed nearly all do see)? But let us look at the older group first.

The hustlers over 50 years old, who are truly "hanging on," are generally nostalgic, full of stories about famous matches and high stakes in the old days. It is only to be expected, I think, that a number of people who entered hustling when it was still big-time, or at least were in poolrooms when it was big-time, just won't give up hustling. What really needs explaining, it seems to me, is why so few such people are on today's hustling scene.

By all surmises, including their own, the active U.S. hustlers between 50 and 70 can comprise at the very most 5 per cent of living persons in this age group who once were hustlers. There must be hundreds of living ex-hustlers over 50 who loved the game, i.e., the whole lifestyle involved in the game, just as much as the old hustlers who haven't quit. If one can assume what strikes me as two reasonable assumptions, that "love of the game" is no greater in the younger generation than in the older and that hustlers over 50 can draw sustenance from memories of the big-time that the young hustlers cannot, it remains to be explained why more old-timers are not still hustling.

The reader familiar with sports in general will know an obvious answer: if the good young hustler has trouble making ends meet, the old-timer's income from hustling must be worse yet—simply because, as we know from a variety of sports, one's skill level declines rapidly after reaching one's forties. But the obvious answer won't do. Pool and billiards are peculiar, nay unique, in that one can play at or very near one's top game well into old age—usually even to compensating fully for the hand tremors that often accompany old age. Of course, the older man doesn't have the stamina he once had, can't engage in all-night sessions very often. But otherwise, unless and until his sight becomes uncorrectable even with bifocals, he has no skill problem.

True, when the hustler's eyes no longer can be helped a great deal with glasses, he has had it. The ex-hustler Tugboat Whaley (so called because part of his con was pretending to be a tugboat captain) reports as follows:

I'm 65. I haven't played for big stakes in 10 years. This game
isn't like baseball—your legs don't give out, your eyes do.
You don't lose your stroke. Your eyes go bad, you can't see
the edge of the ball.[14]

However, it must be emphasized that the eyes of most hustlers
are correctable or almost entirely correctable with glasses far into
old age, and that consequently most hustlers can keep playing well.

An index of this peculiarity about the game is that the record
time-span over which a player in any sport or game was still
winning world championships is held by billiards: Willie Hoppe
won his first world championship in 1906 and his last in 1952,
forty-six years later (whereupon he retired, at the age of 65). It is
true that Hoppe's skill level may have been unique.[15] But he was
by no means unique in the number of years he was able to play
his best. Nor can it be said that this is due to the particular
varieties of the game that he played (balk-line and three-cushion
billiards). For example, in the professional pocket billiard (pool)
championship tournaments held between 1963 and 1965, there
were four competitors over 55 years old out of a combined field
of 23 different players in the three tournaments; i.e., four players
over 55 were ranked among the best 23 players in the world—
and one of these four was 69 years old. And I have played several
opponents who, though not of championship calibre, were still
superb players well past the age of 70.

Nor is there a decline in the old hustler's temperamental ability
to feign less playing skill than he has, or in his ability to "make
a game" or his other conning skills. Furthermore, his age does not
make him suspect as someone whose accumulated knowledge and

[14]Quoted from Tom Fox, *op. cit.*, p. 59.

[15]And maybe not. Some old-timers claim that whenever Johnny Layton
was even halfway sober (seldom), he beat Hoppe.

In recent three-cushion tournaments the current world champion, Ray-
mond Ceulemans of Belgium, has surpassed Hoppe's tournament scoring
average—but this does not necessarily indicate his basic skill level is
greater. Averages today are generally higher than they used to be. This is
because three-cushion billiards, unlike pool, requires mastery of a large
body of knowledge that is still being developed and extended. (The difference between the two games in this respect is as vast as, say, the difference
between checkers and chess.) Today good three-cushion players can make
certain shots that nobody knew how to make thirty years ago.

experience might prove too strong. On the contrary, the older hustler finds that once in a while his age, as such, helps him to hustle: sometimes an ignorant sucker will assume that a decrepit-looking old man couldn't possibly play a decent game any more, and finds out the hard way.

For some hustlers, as they get older, over-indulgence in alcohol becomes a severe problem. It has wrecked the careers both of hustlers and of professionals (e.g., to mention only the most famous among the dead, Ralph Greenleaf). However, alcoholism seems no more frequent among hustlers than in most other segments of our society.

Rather, the scarcity of old hustlers is explained by an aspect of the hustler's way of life today that is particularly hard to take in old age: today the periods in any hustler's career when he goes completely broke are more frequent and of longer duration. A young man may not be too shaken by the fact that once in a great while he can't even pay room rent in a fleabag hotel and has to grab his sleep in the poolroom for two or three days, or that he may get down to just one change of clothes, for he knows that one decent hustle—bound to come along in a couple of days if he keeps sharp eyes out—will get him started again. But an older man finds himself looking for more security than that, finds himself less adaptable to the more frequent and more severe down-turns that are a contingency of the hustling career today.

In addition, an indeterminate number of hustlers give up the poolroom life because they eventually get married and find, when they do, that this poses another great occupational problem. That is one reason why the great majority of career hustlers are career bachelors. Marriage is of course a contingency that can adversely affect careers in many occupations, as in, say, the case of the aspiring organization man whose spouse is not a proper organization wife; but in hustling, much more frequently and intensely than in most occupations, marriage precipitates a genuine career crisis.

Perhaps because bachelor ideology had so recently played a prominent part in his thinking, when the hustler does get married he is notably less successful than, say, a jazz musician, in finding a woman to put up with his irregular working hours. Whatever the cause may be, it appears that most women who marry hustlers can't or won't readily—or even unreadily—adjust to the erratic hours that hustling entails, or that are entailed when one wishes to watch or engage in games between hustlers (which, for reasons already indicated, take place mostly between the hours of 1:00 and 6:00 A.M.). Instances of such difficulties are frequently told in the hustling world, being cited most often, of course, by the bachelor majority as reason enough for their continued bachelorhood. Apart from erratic hours as such, the small and unpredictably fluctuating nature of the hustler's income poses an equally severe marriage-vs.-career problem, one that only a few hustlers have been able to ease by finding wives who will work steadily while they (the husbands) continue hustling.

Some hustlers solve this career crisis by eventually walking out on the wife; others solve it by eventually walking out on the poolroom. The latter solution appears to be more frequent, though how much more so I do not have enough data to say.

It is reasonable to speculate—though again I have no data— that some decades ago a hustler's marriage did not pose such a critical problem for him. In the old days hustlers had much more opportunity for good action with suckers in daytime and early evening hours (as opposed to today's frequently fruitless hunt during such hours), far lesser need to play each other, and consequently both greater choice of working hours and greater dependability of income.

The twin factors discussed above—crises posed by financial insecurity in old age and by marriage—strongly suggest that today's young hustlers, as they get older, will also show a very high dropout rate.

Hustlers who retire when young sometimes return to the poolroom for visits, to see friends or watch contests. But the older hustlers who drop out, and the young retired hustlers as they get older, tend to abandon the poolroom world entirely. Among the many old men who hang around or work in poolrooms, there are few former hustlers.

Perhaps the best known of such former hustlers is Carl Zingale, now 70, whose monicker in the poolroom world is Cue Ball Kelly (an illustration, incidentally, that it is not always safe to infer

someone's ethnic origin from his ethnic monicker). He was hustling by the age of 10:

> I was what you might call on the hustle. The dough wasn't
> too bad for a kid and I figured that I could make more money
> this way than I could in school. There were many days that
> I would win three or four games and come home with my
> pockets jingling. . . . After a few years I suddenly realized
> that I wasn't the greatest pool player around. So I decided to
> start picking up some money by refereeing and booking games
> [professional games]. I've refereed for every top player in the
> past 40 years and I've also handled bookings for them.

Although Kelly has made a fair living from professional tournaments by alternately refereeing and entertaining the audience with
trick shots, the business really isn't big enough to support more
than one such person in this manner (and even Kelly has had
rough going at times). Retired hustlers who want to stay around
the game have to take ordinary jobs in the poolroom. If they are
lucky, they end up with ownership or part ownership of a poolroom, but rarely are they that lucky. For the most part they face
only ill-paid and dead-end poolroom jobs (desk man, sweeper)
and as a result tend to drift out of the poolroom to other jobs
that, although also unskilled, pay a bit better.

RECRUITMENT AND INDUCTION

Hustlers arise in all regions of the country, and in small cities
as well as big ones. (But the decline in action rooms forces the
small-town hustlers to move to one or another of America's big
cities, and also means that road trips to small towns are far rarer
than they were thirty years ago.) The only significant factor common to their backgrounds appears to be that of social class.

At least four-fifths of the hustlers in my sample are of lower-
class origin, and those who are not come, by anybody's definition,
from the lower reaches of the middle class. One index: with a
solitary exception, none of the hustlers attended college (not even
those who could have done so on the GI Bill), and probably over

half of them, certainly well over a third, did not finish high school. Hustlers' origins are also, by and large, in keeping with ethnic succession in the lower class.[16] For example, most of the Jewish hustlers are over 55; and Puerto Rican hustlers, virtually unknown until ten or fifteen years ago, now are much in evidence among the younger hustlers (one is often reputed to be the best one-handed player in the country).

Hustlers are social deviants, in the sense that they gamble for a living and, in the process, violate societal norms of "respectable" work and of fair dealing (and do worse things, as will emerge presently). However, psychopathology as such has nothing to do with either the origin or maintenance of their hustling. Many a psychiatrically oriented observer might indeed find that hustlers as a group seem to show more mental disorder than people he knows in general, but this would be merely to say that his "in general" includes little acquaintance with the lower class, where, as several researchers have amply demonstrated, the burden of mental illness in our society mainly falls. As a matter of fact, hustlers as a group may well be psychologically healthier than those members of the lower class whose teens were spent in more respectable places than poolrooms; this would not be out of keeping with the data, reported by the Gluecks and others, which indicate that in lower-class neighborhoods of high delinquency the non-delinquents have higher neuroticism rates than the delinquents.

The causes relevant to hustling are not psychopathological but subcultural. In the context of American lower-class subcultures, hustlers are not nearly so "deviant" as they appear to the middle- or upper-class outsider. For one thing, in lower-class areas pool playing is a much commoner pastime and the poolroom is more frequently a neighborhood institution.

Secondly, the "social norms" that the hustler transgresses carry less weight in the lower class than elsewhere, and correspondingly the hustler is stigmatized less. After all, in lower-class subcultures the successful neighborhood racketeer or political thief is frequently admired, and hustlers *qua* hustlers are less violative of basic social

[16]This holds as well for the origins of professional players; see Chapter 1, note 42. See also Dudley Kavanagh's prideful observation in 1869: "Ireland, the mother of the majority of billiard professionals. . . ." (Kavanagh, *The Billiard World* [N.Y.: Kavanagh & Decker, 1869], p. 45).

norms than such people. Nor does the fact that hustling isn't a "steady job" carry in the lower class the stigma that it does elsewhere.

Thirdly, and crucially: hustling, notably unlike most American occupations, represents a career line that is almost completely open to members of the lower class, an occupation where social origin bars one neither from entry nor advancement.

I say "almost" completely open because there is some discrimination against Negroes—not, however, by white hustlers, but by white poolroom owners. Even so, racial integration in the poolroom has been significantly in advance of that in the world outside it. Two examples: (a) Negroes were an accepted part of the Times Square poolroom scene by the early 1940's, in the days when their patronage of Times Square movies was discouraged and they simply couldn't get served by most restaurants in the area. (b) When I visited Cleveland in 1963, its public places were still so segregated that even in the action poolrooms on West 25th Street, the owners would pull the "club members only" routine to keep Negroes out. But the white hustlers objected strongly to this practice, and, moreover, would frequently travel to the Negro section for matches with the better Negro players (hustlers or otherwise). At the main Negro action room, on 105th and Massey, it was expected that white players would drop in, and quite okay for them to do so.[17] This relative lack of anti-Negro discrimination by white hustlers is part of a larger phenomenon: the social bonds uniting members of any deviant subculture tend to override race prejudice in large degree, and thus nearly every such subculture is more racially integrated than is "respectable" society.[18]

[17]During the course of this study Howard Becker interviewed for me a San Francisco hustler, Harry the Russian, who indicated that in recent years the decline of pool hustling has made it more difficult for a white hustler to move in Negro neighborhoods without being rousted by police. The Russian says that when he went into the Fillmore (the Negro section of San Francisco) in the old days, the police knew he was there to hustle pool and let him alone, but now they assume he is there to score for drugs or girls, stop him, and make him explain his presence.

[18]America's most racially integrated deviant subculture is probably the homosexual. For example, the homosexuals' annual "drag ball," held on Halloween in several cities, is one of our country's chief interracial events. And the Negro community knows it; e.g., at the Chicago drag ball I attended in 1955, the guest of honor was America's second most powerful

Hustling, then, is fully open to lower-class whites, and more open to lower-class Negroes than are most jobs. Except for the discrimination faced by Negroes, success depends entirely on individual skills. And, still more importantly, it depends on the kind of skills that a lower-class youth has a good chance to acquire—unlike, say, the skills whose acquisition depends on parental encouragement of reading.

In hustling, nepotism or knowing people who are "well connected" counts for naught; the manly virtue of self-reliance counts for plenty. Hustling distributes its rewards strictly on the basis of individual talent and hard work, thus fulfilling two cardinal tenets of the Horatio Alger "myth" (as distinguished from the reality of the Alger novels themselves, where, as the late Richard Wohl noted, fortuitous events always play a key role in success).[19]

All in all, for a number of lower-class youths, hustling as a possible ladder of social ascent seems very real. As Boston Shorty put it to me: "If I hadn't got interested in pool when I was a kid, I might have ended up a bum or in jail."

The induction process in hustling has remained unchanged over the decades; it is the same for today's newcomer as it was for the old-timer. The difference is only that far fewer youths enter the career these days because of the decreased chances to earn good money from it. But some continue to enter; in our larger cities, each year the hustling scene reveals a few new young faces.

Negro political leader, U.S. Congressman William Dawson. (It perhaps needs explaining that Halloween has a latent function as a sort of homosexual national holiday because at that time transvestites can go forth in women's clothing ["drag"] without fear of arrest. Mardi Gras has a similar function for homosexuals.)

It is also obvious that among homosexual couples who live together and define themselves as "married" to each other, the interracial "marriage" rate is far higher than in the heterosexual world. A hypothesis I hope to test is that these interracial homosexual couples, much more often than interracial heterosexual couples, settle in neighborhoods that had previously been entirely white, and thus play an important pioneering role in opening up such neighborhoods to Negroes generally.

[19]Cf. R. Richard Wohl, "The 'Rags to Riches Story': An Episode of Secular Idealism," in Reinhard Bendix and Seymour Martin Lipset, eds., *Class, Status and Power* (Glencoe, Illinois: The Free Press, 1953), pp. 388–95.

In general the process goes like this: hustlers, even those who finished high school, played truant from school often, and in so doing found themselves in poolrooms much more frequently than either their classmates or their fellow-truants. Since the development of pool or billiard skill is, at least in the first several years of play, largely a matter of the number of hours one practices, they quickly developed superiority over their age-mates and were able to earn some fair change thereby. Naturally they wanted to keep a good thing going, and in the process many dropped out of school entirely, while nearly all passed up job experience and training; almost without thinking about it they became hustlers, as much by drift as by decision. The only significant exception to this general line of development is that some hustlers, now in their forties, had an extra reason for spending much of their youth in poolrooms, namely, their teens were Depression years when there were no jobs around.

Because in hustling there is neither a formal entrance requirement nor formal recognition of entry (no examination, license, *rite de passage*, union membership, etc.) and, especially, because the poolroom tradition that all players should bet makes it nearly impossible to recall (or even to distinguish at the time) any hustling analogue of one's "first real job," the transition from non-hustler to hustler status is smooth and almost imperceptible to the person involved. The transition never seems to involve a conscious decision to *become* a hustler, but rather a recognition that one already *is* a hustler, and is good at it. Here is a typical response to my queries about entry:

> How I got to be a hustler? Well it wasn't any special deal, you know. When I was a kid around 14 I was shootin' pool for money like the other kids, only I got to be the best, and after a while you can't get a game if you let on how good you are. And pretty soon I was beating lots older guys, 'cause right away I come up with a real good stroke, you know. And me with my baby face, they didn't know what was happenin' until I took down the cash. I was better at hustlin' pool than anything else, so I figured I would keep on doin' it.

And here is an account by the man sometimes regarded as America's best one-pocket hustler, Jersey Red:

> I thank them, every one of them down there in the New
> YMCA. That's where I got my start. I hustled for Cokes and
> change, and if they had some that folded and some nerve,
> I would unfold it for them. I started in there when I was 13
> and when I was 14 I got my stroke. I got my stroke and
> learned to count [pocket the balls]. I beat every kid in the Y
> and then I started lookin' around. I just kept looking.[20]

Although the hustler's career decision—if one can call it that—
may come late, acquisition of the playing skills requisite to hustling
must start early. Every first-rate pool or billiard player, hustler
or not, began playing regularly no later than his early teens.[21]

Once embarked in the hustling life, hustlers prefer to stay in it:
it's exciting, it has a tradition and ideology that can make them
feel heroic, it's fun (the game is enjoyable as such), it's not routine, and so on. The point is that these characteristics of the
occupation, appealing as they might be to, say, the readers of this
book, are still more appealing to lower-class youths. The hustling
career partakes deeply, often passionately, of every one of the
orientations that Walter Miller finds to be distinctive "focal concerns" of American lower-class subcultures: trouble (with the
law), smartness (in the sense of being able to con and of being
no one's dupe), excitement, fate, toughness ("heart"), and autonomy.[22]

The existence of such orientations in hustling has tremendous
positive consequences both for the entry of lower-class youths and
for their continuing with the career in the face of frequent financial
adversity. And on top of all that, "love of the game" is an important element in the makeup of most hustlers—the same kind
of "hangup" on a game, as such, that one finds in chess bums,
tennis bums, et al. (and that is the main basis of my relationship
with hustlers). Thus, although numerous problems confront the
hustler, "alienation" from his work is emphatically not one of
them. It is small wonder that when asked why he stays in the
occupation, many a hustler replies: "It beats working."

However, despite the fact that the typical hustler supports only

[20]Quoted from Dale Shaw, op. cit., p. 91.

[21]See Chapter 1, pp. 19–20.

[22]Cf. Walter Miller, "Lower Class Culture as a Generating Milieu of
Gang Delinquency," Journal of Social Issues, Vol. XIV (1958), pp. 5–19.

himself and pays no income tax,[23] it is frequently hard to make ends meet, and sometimes impossible. The rate of failure is high, and the hustler knows it. For example, when a hustler *un*intentionally misses a shot, sometimes he will curse himself with the exclamation "Get a job!," whereby he recognizes, if only ironically, that he is in a very tough racket where only the best survive and he may not make it.

Some hustlers do indeed give up when still young. It is not uncommon for a young hustler who hasn't been in the poolroom for a while to say, when he finally does show up to see his friends and is queried about his absence, "I'm retired." But most hustlers, once they have entered the career, stick it out tenaciously for a number of years. The action (in all senses) provides too many pleasures for them to worry that much about being broke.

But sooner or later even the best and most determined hustler finds that if he is to keep hustling he must, at least on occasion, obtain other sources of income. That is, he finds that if he is not to retire, then he must moonlight. In many cases, when hustlers are moonlighting, the major share of their income derives from the latter source. Sometimes the hustler gets to depend on, or actually to like, his moonlighting job, and moonlights permanently to all intents and purposes.

MOONLIGHTING

The purpose of moonlighting is not merely to provide more income but to provide it in a way that allows you to keep your primary job, the one you prefer. The job the hustler takes, therefore, is one that allows him to hustle. Such jobs fall into two types:

[23]The extent to which hustlers live beyond the ken of our society's record-keeping bureaucracies is truly remarkable. Most hustlers, for example, are not counted in the U.S. Census, and many of them—probably the majority—do not even have Social Security numbers. In a recent pool tournament held at a Las Vegas hotel, three hustlers finishing in the money had difficulty collecting their prizes because the management insisted on paying by check, for which purpose it needed Social Security numbers, and these three had no such numbers to give. (The problem was eventually solved.)

(1) Poolroom-based. The hustler may take a job as a desk clerk, general handyman, lunch-counter man, etc., in the poolroom. More often, he will engage in some illegal activity that either can be headquartered in the poolroom or, because its "working hours" are short and sporadic, permits him to hang around the poolroom most of the time. His lower-class origin, his lack of legitimate job training, the availability of contacts in the poolroom for criminal jobs, the ethic of hustling life—all these facilitate taking criminal jobs when moonlighting.

He may moonlight at being a booster, or fence, or drug pusher, or loan shark, or numbers runner, or forger, or burglar, or bookie, etc. Several hustlers in my sample are also skilled card cheats ("mechanics," in the argot). Three hustlers are also pimps, have women who "hustle" in the usual sense. (One has rather high poolroom status because his girl always gets at least $50 per trick.) At least three members of the sample, perhaps more, are "heavy men" in their moonlighting roles, i.e., their moonlighting involves the use or potential use of armed violence.

Among hustlers who have moonlighted at crimes that society defines as more serious than hustling itself, the frequency of participation varies all the way from the hustler who has undertaken such activity only once or twice to the hustler who undertakes it more or less continuously. My point is that over half the hustlers have, apparently, undertaken such moonlighting at least once.

But the point as far as the hustler is concerned is that such a job allows him to hustle. In either kind of poolroom-based job, legal or illegal, the hustler is on hand to grab whatever pool-playing action might present itself.

(2) Not poolroom-based. A job based in the poolroom is of course preferable to any other kind of moonlighting; it allows the hustler to stay in the poolroom all or nearly all the time. But if the hustler wanting to moonlight can't get such a job, he tries to make sure that the job he takes at least permits him to drop into the poolroom often. It can't be an office or factory or retailing job, for these would tie him down to another location. It has to let him move around the city, and have somewhat flexible hours

if possible, so that he can spend at least some time checking on the action in poolrooms. Among such jobs: window washer, outside salesman, cab driver.

A few (very few) hustlers have become wealthy from outside activities. One made oil investments that paid off; another is associated with racketeers and in a lucrative vending machine business; another is a major bookmaker; another owns restaurants; another has made a fortune cheating at cards; and another has, at this writing, six prostitutes working for him. But poolroom hustling remains their true love. For example, the hustler grown rich from vending machines spends two days a week looking after his business and five days a week in poolrooms. It is entirely possible that a few hustlers who somehow struck it rich from moonlighting may have thereupon retired from hustling, but I have never heard of such. There are, of course, a number of people who retired from hustling and then did well in the other occupations they entered, for example, the baseball pitcher Bo Belinsky.[24]

THE OCCASIONAL HUSTLER

So far, except for noting that professional players have hustled, I have considered only the hustling done by hustlers, that is, persons whose primary occupational identification is with pool or billiard hustling and who engage in it as a full-time career whenever they are not forced to moonlight. There are, however, a number of casual laborers in the field.

Over 99 per cent of the more-or-less regular adult poolroom players are not hustlers. Only a small minority of them are even good enough to hustle. But a minority of this minority, such as myself, do hustle on occasion, e.g., "stall" and "lemon" so as to keep opponents playing and betting. However, their primary occupational identification lies elsewhere. I am rather untypical of such persons not only because of my middle-class background, but because most of them have jobs that allow them much more

[24]On Belinsky's hustling background see, for example, Walter Lee Jackson, "Bo Belinsky: Baseball's 'Beau'," *Modern Man*, Vol. 12, No. 11 (May, 1963), pp. 36–38, 51.

time in the poolroom—are traveling salesmen, professional criminals, holders of political sinecures, etc. The late jazz pianist Jelly
Roll Morton was an occasional hustler of this kind.[25]

However, virtually none of these persons is as skilled as the
typical hustler. They hustle very little, not merely because they
wish to do so less often than the hustler but because they must
be more cautious than he in picking opponents. They account for
only a tiny fraction of all hustled games, perhaps 1 per cent.

Secondly, of the many players who are high school students
not yet entered into society's occupational structure, some hustle.
A few of the best will eventually become hustlers by trade, though
most will not. They hustle their agemates primarily, as few are
skilled enough to beat the more experienced players. They account,
I would guess, for perhaps 2 or 3 per cent of all hustled games.

A third group, however, accounts for quite a significant percentage of hustled games, at a guess about 15 per cent.[26] This
group consists of people who are no longer students but who have
no occupational identity whatever. When indicating how he makes
his living, such a person may say that he "scuffles," or that he
"gets by" by doing "a little of this and a little of that." His varied
activities are more often than not illegal. Often he may say that
he "hustles," but he means this in the generalized slang sense that
he undertakes any short-term activity for a fast buck. Pool-playing
skill is merely one element of his armamentarium. He may be
hustling at pool one night, in a crooked dice game the next, hustling his own ass in a gay bar the next, and so on. It is my impression—though the sample is too small to permit sure generalization
—that this group shows a greater incidence of mental disorder than
other poolroom groups and also that Negroes are heavily over-
represented in it.[27]

[25]In his talking and singing autobiography, recorded at the Library of
Congress in 1938, Morton has left some fascinating recollections of his
pool hustling in the years 1900–1908. Listen to the Jelly Roll Morton Library of Congress recordings, as follows: volume 5, *Georgia Skin Game*,
Riverside RLP 9005 (side 1, "Aaron Harris" bands 1 and 2); volume 9,
Jack the Bear, Riverside RLP 9009 (side 1, "Jack the Bear" bands 1, 2,
and 3; side 2, "Alabama Bound" bands 3 and 4).

[26]N.B. that all the remarks above about "percentages" of hustled games
are strictly guesses, though informed guesses.

[27]A valuable autobiography of one such "hustler" or "scuffler," transcribed from tape-recorded interviews, is Henry Williamson's *Hustler* (New

THE HUSTLER IN HISTORY

Although the techniques of deception that can be used in a gambling game are modified by the game's social context, these techniques flow fundamentally, as we noted at the beginning, from the inner structure of the game itself. Thus we might reasonably suspect analogues of the modern hustler's techniques to have been used in the earliest forms of billiard games.

But it doesn't help much to state, as a *terminus a quo* for hustling, the date when something like billiards first was played, because nobody has demonstrated what that date might be. Billiard historians have indeed proposed several dates and places for the origin of the game; however, as indicated in Chapter 1, such historians are hopelessly incompetent. (Many of them, for example, state that billiards was known in ancient Egypt, the "evidence" being that Shakespeare has Cleopatra say "Let's to billiards.") Until research on the subject that I have under way is completed—if my hunch is right, it will demonstrate that billiards began in fifteenth-century France—we had best skip this matter and turn from the origin of billiards to the question of what the historical record might have to say, if anything, about billiard players' conscious use of hustling techniques as such. And it does say something.

The earliest evidence of hustling I have found so far (let me reiterate that my research is not completed) reveals that not only hustling techniques, but the poolroom hustler as a distinct occupational type, had arisen in Europe by the time of the Industrial Revolution. The basic strategies and tactics of present-day hustling were adumbrated by the workers of *ancien regime* France.

To be sure, there were differences because the structure of billiard games and the superstructure of betting relationships differed somewhat from today's practice. But by the 1770's, in the

York: Doubleday, 1965). Its accounts of pool hustling are at pp. 73, 93 ff., and 156 ff. Williamson's vocational drifting (or versatility) is entirely criminal and concentrates on felonies, chiefly armed robbery. Pool hustling, as it merely breaks misdemeanor laws against gambling, constitutes his nearest approach to a legitimate occupation. For the life history of another such "hustler," see Edwin Lemert, *Social Pathology* (New York: McGraw-Hill, 1951), pp. 332–37.

poolrooms of Paris, there had developed clear-cut equivalents of today's stalling, lemoning, and dumping. There had also emerged the professional gambler who lived off his bets on hustlers, the prototype of today's backer, and indeed his was more often a full-time occupational role than that of the hustler.

In addition, the subtle art of "making a game" was highly developed, the principal difference being that in pre-revolutionary Paris, non-playing bettors participated fully in arranging the handicap terms of a match. And the eighteenth-century hustler had a remarkably modern bag of ancillary short-con routines, e.g., he too would pretend to be upset by an unlucky break and to be badly thrown off his game thereby.[28]

A number of modern hustlers, like some other regular players, have so great a love of the game that for all their lack of formal education they show much genuine interest in and knowledge of billiard history. Not only are they more historically minded than other deviant groups, not only has much material written by billiard historians—true and untrue—filtered down to them, but they have preserved a good bit of billiard history and playing technique by means of a long oral tradition. For example, it was from a hustler that I first learned exactly how the structure of the game played by Phelan and Seereiter in 1859 differed from today's game.[29] Or, to give an example from playing technique, many refinements and extensions of the mathematical systems for calculating three-cushion billiard shots have never been published, but have been simply passed on orally from one generation of players—including hustlers—to the next.[30] So it did not seem to me fantastic on the face of it to wonder if modern American hustlers knew anything of their European predecessors. I found

[28]I take all this material on Parisian hustling in the 1770's from the eyewitness account of Restif de la Bretonne; see his *Les Nuits de Paris* (Paris: Hachette, 1960), as follows: "Les Billards: Acteurs," pp. 116–19; "Suite du Billard: Le Prête-Nom," pp. 119–22; "Suite du Billard: La Revanche," pp. 124–26; "Suite: Le Coup de Grace," pp. 127–30.

[29]On the significance of this game, see Chapter 1.

[30]The fullest published information on mathematical systems for three-cushion billards can be found in Willie Hoppe, *Billiards as It Should be Played* (Chicago: Reilly and Lee, 1941), pp. 64 ff. But full as it may be, it is only a small part of what the best older students of the subject know, use in their playing, and pass on orally to younger players.

that a few hustlers and also some non-hustlers did indeed have knowledge, or folklore, about hustlers who were active before they were born, but that this material extended neither beyond the 1890's nor beyond America.

That the oral tradition, strong though it is, knows nothing of American hustlers earlier than the 1890's doesn't rule out the possibility that there were such hustlers. But it led me to think that in comparing modern American hustling with early European predecessors, I was probably seeing "history" where none existed, that what really was involved was not cultural diffusion but independent invention. Such facts as I have been able to gather support this latter interpretation.

Before one can talk of cultural diffusion one must demonstrate cultural contact. For example, it would be absurd to suggest that the syncopation in Negro jazz derives from syncopation's prior appearance in Beethoven's Ninth Symphony (absurd because the slaves didn't go to Beethoven concerts), but sensible to suggest that it derives from the syncopation in West African music (sensible because the slaves did come from West Africa). Now, billiards did not come to America from the sort of poolrooms and persons described by Restif de la Bretonne, nor from similar milieux in England. All the evidence we have indicates that it diffused from the British tradition of upper-class private playing (see Chapter 1). Public tables made their appearance in America very soon afterward, but that was a native development rather than an importation, i.e., private playing by the American upper class quickly "trickled down" to become public playing by the middle and lower classes, at first on tables in taverns and inns, later in poolrooms as such.

Moreover, if we consider Michael Phelan's 1850 comment about the number of public tables in earlier days, it is obvious that there wouldn't have been much point for American hustlers to have existed before, say, 1825, because there wouldn't have been anything like the "opportunity structure" that existed in the Paris of Restif. And the *New York Times* correspondent in Detroit in 1859, reporting on preparations for the Phelan-Seereiter match, wrote that in addition to the good players who had come from all over the country to see the contest, there were also in town "a great many black-legs, sharpers, and the like, and probably some pickpockets," but significantly didn't mention hustlers (neither "black-leg" nor "sharper" had that meaning in America).[31]

The lack of hustlers in 1859 wasn't due to any lack of poolrooms or players; there were plenty of both by then. But one key element of the opportunity structure was still missing: heavy action. The poolroom tradition that all players should bet on themselves—not merely on those battling it out for a championship—was just getting started. In 1850, Michael Phelan correctly noted that billiards was

> sometimes desecrated to purposes of gambling . . . yet, as a general thing, playing for money is prohibited in the Billiard Rooms and Saloons of this country; in truth, it is a very unusual circumstance to hear, that money is wagered on Billiards at present.[32]

And in 1869 Dudley Kavanagh could still write, with absolute honesty and only slightly less accuracy, that

> Betting on billiards is not common in this country between the players engaged. In England a game is scarcely thought to be worth playing unless for a stake, however small. This is also the custom in Continental Europe. The very little betting which is done here (besides large bets on professional matches) is for the expense of the game and the accompanying refreshments.[33]

But note that Kavanagh says there were "large bets on professional matches." Since that would mark the true beginning in America of the requisite opportunity structure, it is where one would expect to find the first recorded instance of American hustling—and where one does find it: the early professionals Carme and Rudolphe, in a match played on November 18, 1868, acted in collusion to dump the bettors.[34] American hustling was started by the professional players themselves.

As more and more of the ordinary players began betting on

[31]*New York Times*, April 14, 1859, *Supplement*, [p. 2], col. 3.

[32]Michael Phelan, *Billards Without a Master* (New York: D. D. Winant, 1850), p. 7.

[33]Dudley Kavanagh, *op. cit.,* p. 67.

[34]*Ibid.*, p. 32.

their own matches in addition to the professionals' matches, hustling arose as an occupation distinct from professional play. For
example, one player's recollection (published in 1914) of billiards
in South Michigan during the period 1860 to 1890, describes the
emergence of hustlers "along near the end of this period," and
tells how rumors of a fine young player in Plainville, Michigan,
"attracted the attention of what today would be called the 'sharks'
in Chicago, Detroit, and other cities."[35] It would seem that the
earliest date for American hustlers preserved in today's oral tradition is not far off the mark after all.

By about 1890, then, through an independent line of development, American poolrooms had become what their French and
English predecessors had long been: full-fledged action rooms,
with suckers ready to plunge on their own skill and hustlers ready
to take them. The words of wisdom for players in E. White's
British billiard book of 1807 (which, as I indicated, is probably
swiped from a French book), by the 1890's applied to America
also:

> No billiard room of any notoriety is free from men who
> are gamesters by profession, and who are constantly in wait-
> ing to catch the ignorant and unsuspecting, who occasionally
> drop in, from motives either of curiosity or amusement; and
> by constant practice they acquire a degree of dexterity, that
> enables them to obtain an easy advantage over the general-
> ity of their opponents. Their grand object is to conceal their
> skill from their adversary, and to accommodate their play to
> his, in such a manner, as to appear to obtain the conquest
> more in consequence of good fortune than good play. In
> order to effect this, they . . . chiefly depend upon those
> strokes, the intent of which are apparent only to those who
> are intimately acquainted with the minutiae of the game.
> They generally suffer their adversary to gain some few games
> . . . but in the end, it is well for him indeed, if he escapes
> being fleeced of all the ready money he may happen to have
> about him.[36]

That's what the hustler did, and does.

[35]George Hersch, "Billiards in South Michigan from 1860 to 1890 (Second Installment)," *Billiards Magazine*, Vol. 1, No. 11 (February, 1914),
pp. 17–19.
[36]E. White, *A Practical Treatise on the Game of Billiards* (London:
W. Miller, 1807), p. 2.

CONCLUSIONS

Throughout this study I have used a special orientation toward the material, an orientation not generally found in other studies of people who make their living from illegal work.[37] If, nevertheless, I have managed to make sociological sense out of the data, then it follows that the special orientation provides the most significant lesson of this study for the future of criminological research. The lesson is this: criminologists stand to lose little and gain much in the way of sociological understanding if, when studying people dedicated to an illegal occupation, they will overcome their fascination with the "illegal" part long enough to focus on the "occupation" part. After all, any theory of illegal occupations can be but a special case, albeit an important one, of general occupational theory.

Criminologists, following the lead of the late Edwin Sutherland, recognize that one hallmark of the career criminal—be he engaged in major crime or, like the hustler most of the time, in violating generally unenforced criminal law—is that the illegal activity in question constitutes his regular job.[38] Yet their researches seem thoroughly untenanted by what occupational sociologists have learned about how to look at someone's regular job. An example: one of the best recent criminological studies of a specific type of career criminal is Roebuck and Cadwalleder's research on Negro armed robbers.[39] But for all its useful findings —and there are plenty—the study is also a story of missed re-

[37]I know of only one other study of an illegal occupation that has an orientation similar to mine: James Bryan's "Apprenticeships in Prostitution," *Social Problems*, Vol. 12, No. 3 (Winter, 1965), pp. 287–97. Howard Becker's *Outsiders* (New York: Free Press of Glencoe, 1963), although it does not deal with illegal work, is the pioneering application of this framework to the sociology of deviance; Becker employs it to analyze avocational lawbreakers (marihuana users) and people whose work is legal but who are nevertheless stigmatized (jazz musicians).

[38]See, for example, Marshall Clinard, *Sociology of Deviant Behavior*, rev. ed. (New York: Holt, Rinehart & Winston, 1963), pp. 210–11.

[39]Cf. Julian Roebuck and Mervyn Cadwalleder, "The Negro Armed Robber as a Criminal Type," *Pacific Sociological Review*, Vol. 4 (Spring, 1961), pp. 21–26.

search opportunities because it proceeds with blissful inattention to what sociology has had mainly to say about one's "career" and its relation to other matters.

What is especially surprising about criminology's neglect of these occupational aspects as such, is that people dedicated to an illegal occupation actually *tell* the criminologist these aspects are central in their thinking and, moreover, under the right conditions can be observed to behave in accord with their statements on the matter. Thus one would think that the criminologist, even if he had read little or no occupational theory, would become inescapably aware of its possible relevance just as soon as he began seriously to study a career-oriented deviant. (This is in fact how I first became aware of its possible relevance—although not, as it happened, out of acquaintance with hustlers but out of acquaintance with a burglar.)

But the criminologist doesn't reach such awareness because he doesn't appreciate the career deviant's statements indicating the centrality of occupational concerns. (For example, when a professional criminal describes himself as being "like a businessman" or "just in a different line of business," the criminologist takes this to be merely a rationalization. It is a rationalization all right, but it is by no means merely that, and often it is not even primarily that.) The reason the criminologist doesn't appreciate such statements is that he doesn't confirm them from his own observation. And the reason he doesn't confirm them from his own observation is that he doesn't study the deviant under proper conditions.

As to the possible gain for criminology in the orientation I suggest, consider, for example, one theoretical implication of what the hustler often does when he needs additional sources of income. It suggests the possibility that many of the data criminologists refer to by rubrics such as "the occasional criminal" or "occasional crime" would be more sharply conceptualized and better understood under the heading "crime as moonlighting." This is for two reasons. First, as soon as we think of crime in this way, it becomes clearer that much serious crime (e.g., bank robbery) is undertaken by people who are neither "mentally ill" nor "white-collar criminals" nor oriented to serious crime as a career nor even oriented to milder crime as a career (unlike the hustler), but who are employed in and identify with perfectly legitimate lower-class jobs, get way behind in their bills, and see temporary or "one shot" criminal activity as a way to get solvent without giving up their regular jobs. It would also become clearer that the same often holds true for milder crimes, e.g., non-victim crimes such as prostitution, which is frequently undertaken in a moonlighting way by typists, salesgirls, and the like. (Moonlighters in prostitution are so frequent that the professionals have even developed argot terms for them; they are called "weekenders" by the professional prostitutes in Las Vegas and "party girls" by the professionals in New York.)

Second, a major precondition of moonlighting, according to Wilensky, is the existence of "occupations and industries on flexible work schedules which provide opportunity for part-time help,"[40] and more recent analysis by labor economists confirms the point: "The industries in which 'moonlighters' found their second jobs were typically those providing opportunities for part-time work."[41] Most crime fits these descriptions perfectly. Indeed, one of the most genuinely appealing things about crime to career criminals and part-timers alike—though one would hardly gather this from the criminology texts—is that for most crimes the working hours are both short and flexible.

Criminological research informed by the orientation I suggest would also, of course, turn up material both new and germane to the sociological study of work as such. In the present study, I have noted some such findings in the section on colleagueship. Here I would like to point out certain other findings that seem to have no analogue in the literature of occupational sociology.

(1) The work situation. We saw that the hustler must be not only a skilled player, but that he must be skilled at pretending *not* to

---

[40]Cf. Harold Wilensky, "The Moonlighter: A Product of Relative Deprivation," *Industrial Relations*, Vol. 3, No. 1 (October, 1963), pp. 106 ff.

[41]Forrest Bogan and Harvey Hamel, "Multiple Jobholders in May 1963," *Monthly Labor Review* (U.S. Dept. of Labor), Vol. 87, No. 3 (March, 1964), p. 249.

have great playing skill. The latter requirement is one thing that distinguishes him from the usual con man (who often, on the contrary, feigns more expertise than he has). And it also distinguishes him from the usual professional gambler. The latter indeed sometimes pretends to be other than he is and disclaims real skill ("I guess I'm just lucky tonight"), but he relies basically on playing skill alone, or else on a combination of playing with cheating skill—being able to switch dice into and out of a game, or to deal seconds or thirds or bottom cards, etc. Pretending to lack of skill is not a basic requirement of the gambler's job, as it is for the hustler. As far as I know, this hustling reliance on competence at feigning incompetence is unique, and nowhere treated in the occupational literature.

(2) Careers. Certain occupational roles require youthfulness by definition (e.g., acting juvenile parts), and thus enforce unusually early retirement.[42] In certain other occupations (airline pilots, for example) age-related career contingencies also force early retirement. It is common to cite competitive sports or games requiring high physical skills as examples of this type—but pool or billiard playing doesn't fit the pattern. And because such faulty generalizing about sports occurs not only among occupational sociologists but among the populace at large, sometimes old age actually helps the hustler in his con.

In textbooks and treatises on the sociology of work, the attention paid to the moonlighter is notable for its scantiness. To the extent that occupational sociologists have studied the subject, they agree with Wilensky's conclusion that the moonlighter "is a man caught in a life-cycle squeeze—he has many dependents."[43] But this pattern obviously doesn't apply to hustlers—nor, for that matter, to the aforesaid typists and shopgirls who moonlight in prostitution.

[42]The earliest documented retirement of this kind I have run across is the following: "Chattanooga, Jan. 7 (UPI)—Chris Haley retired from county government service yesterday at the age of 9. Chris had been drawing names for Hamilton County grand jurors since 1959. The law requires such tasks to be performed by children under 10. The boy will be 10 in March." From the New York *Daily News*, January 8, 1964, p. 42.

[43]Wilensky, *op. cit.*, p. 110.

(3) The external world. We saw that changes in American sporting life over the past three decades have severely damaged the
hustler's work situation and career. These changes have reduced
the number of places he can hustle in, the time-span in which he
can stay unknown, the number of people he can hustle, and the
average amount of money he can get from someone he hustles.
Hustling is a dying trade.

Whenever an occupational group faces a disappearance or
major decline of the market for its skills and a consequent inability
to make ends meet, we conceptualize this situation as "technological unemployment." But this concept doesn't fit the situation
of hustlers at all well. They suffer not from a shift in technology
but from a shift in America's demographic structure, i.e., the
decline of the bachelor subculture that populated poolrooms so
heavily, and secondarily from a shift in fashion, i.e., the decline in
the average amount of money bet on poolroom games. In origin,
the hustler's problem is utterly unlike that of, say, the order clerk
displaced by the introduction of electronic data processing. There
is nothing whatever in the present technological structure of our
society to prevent hustling (and poolroom life generally) from
having or regaining its former place in America. It would seem,
then, that occupational theory needs to complement the notion of
"technological unemployment" with notions such as "demographic
unemployment" and "fashion unemployment."

A more general lesson of this essay is that sociology has unduly
neglected the study of people who engage in sports or games for
their livelihood. The sociological reason for this neglect is that
sociology is compartmentalized into "fields" that tend to make
such people, for all their visibility to the sociologist as citizen,
invisible to him in his role as sociologist: such people are neglected
by students of leisure because the latter are by definition concerned
with sports involvement only in its impact on avocational life;
and because sports involvement is for the very great majority of
people strictly avocational, and those who earn a living at it
constitute a minuscule fragment of the labor force, the study of
the latter is neglected by occupational sociologists. Thus a largely
unexplored area of social research consists of the people who work
at what most of us play at.

APPENDIX: THE HUSTLER AND HIS ARGOT

Outsiders usually find a deviant group's argot to be one of the most interesting things about that group. But analysis of the argot requires an amount of space disproportionate to its importance in an over-all account of the group. To attenuate this conflict I have followed David Maurer's practice (in *The Big Con*) and relegated argot analysis to an appendix. Moreover, what follows is in no sense a full-scale study of hustlers' argot; it does not even contain a full vocabulary list. Instead, it examines the argot merely in its more sociological aspects—in its relation to hustling life and to the structural and functional features of argots in general.

A myth that dies very hard, even among linguists and social scientists, is that the special language or slang developed by a socially deviant group functions importantly to protect the group, has secrecy as a primary motive and mainspring. It dies hard because any outsider quickly notices on first acquaintance with such language that (a) it has terms for various shady processes and techniques, (b) it has terms to distinguish insiders from outsiders, and (c) he can easily be spotted as an outsider because he doesn't know, or misuses, some of the language. "Common sense" tells him that all this greatly aids group secrecy. But all it shows *eo ipso* is that the argot of any special group (deviant or otherwise) includes many terms for things peculiar to that type of group, is in good part a technical vocabulary that must be learned. The hustlers' argot is no exception.

Like all other American deviant argots I know of, it also reveals numerous facets that testify against a "secrecy" interpretation. Some examples: (1) Hustlers always use their argot among themselves when no outsiders are present, where it could not possibly have a secretive purpose. (2) The argot itself is not protected but is an "open secret," i.e., its meanings are quite easily learned by any outsider who wishes to learn them and is an alert listener or questioner. (3) The argot is elaborated far beyond any conceivable need to develop a set of terms for deviant phenomena, and even far beyond any need to develop a full-scale technical vocabulary (which subsumes the terms for deviant phenomena).

   That last point indicates the true mainsprings of argot: in various specialized groups, be they deviant or merely specialized occupational groups, argots develop partly to provide a shorthand way of referring to technical processes but partly also as an elaborately inventive, ritualistic, often rather playful way of reinforcing group identity or "we-feeling." Thus the argot of hustlers sets them off not for the purpose of secrecy, but rather by way of helping their sense of colleagueship and *esprit de corps*.[44]

   Any secrecy function the argot serves is incidental, a bonus as it were, and hustlers certainly do not count on it. The hustler, like the members of secret societies discussed by Georg Simmel, knows that the only way to maintain group secrets is to keep his mouth shut about them in the presence of outsiders—not discuss them even in esoteric terms, which would, if anything, only make the outsider highly suspicious. For this reason hustlers actually use their argot much less when outsiders are present than when they are absent. To the very small extent that hustlers' collaborative swindling (dumping) requires some secretive communication in the presence of the swindled, such communication is, as we have seen, carried out not via argot at all but by a pre-arranged *ad hoc*

[44]Linguists commonly distinguish between two types of specialized slang: (a) a noncriminal group's specialized slang, called *argot*, which of course is unintelligible to outsiders (and thus may occasionally be used for secrecy), but nevertheless is developed and used primarily to meet the need for technical terms and secondarily as a way of bolstering group solidarity; and (b) a criminal group's specialized slang, called *cant*, which is designed and used primarily to make the group's conversation unintelligible to outsiders.

   This distinction may have some validity when applied to the criminal speech of certain other countries in certain historical periods, but it is often uncritically assumed to hold good for American criminal speech also (see, for example, H. L. Mencken's *American Language*, 4th ed., p. 578). A lot of myth and nonsense about American criminals' so-called "cant" has been generated by linguists bookishly familiar with the history of specialized slang but unfamiliar with the actual lifeways of American criminals. I contend that "cant," in the linguists' sense of the term, has not been demonstrated to exist, and cannot be demonstrated to exist, for any American criminal group whatsoever.

   An honorable exception among linguists is David Maurer. His discussion of the language of con men in his *The Big Con* (New York: Pocket Books, 1949, pp. 282–88) is, with one exception noted below, a model of sociological sense.

signal ("the office") that is not standard argot and in fact is usually nonverbal.

The lexicon of hustler argot overlaps that of some other argots. First, there is considerable overlapping with general poolroom argot. I estimate that most regular poolroom players understand at least a third of hustler argot. (And since the portion they understand is not restricted to "innocent" technical terms but includes such items as "fish," this is further evidence against a secrecy function.) Hustler argot subsumes that of the poolroom world; it is poolroom argot plus about twice as many additions and elaborations. And, as one would expect from the fact that hustlers have a greater sense of collective identity than poolroom habitués in general, that portion of the argot understood by non-hustlers isn't used by them with anywhere near the frequency that hustlers use it.[45]

Secondly, and quite understandably in view of the nature of hustling life, there is lexical admixture from other professional criminal argots, especially gamblers' argot. The most important such term is "action," used variously in the senses of "a bet" or "betting" or "an opportunity to bet" or "a situation involving betting." As the reader may have gathered by now, it is the most ubiquitous argot word in hustler speech. Some other criminal terms used by hustlers are: "the office"; "the wire" (in the phrase "to send" or "give" someone "the wire," to tip him off— not in the professional con man's sense); "score" (noun: an amount of money or goods won or taken; verb: to win or take money or goods); "mechanic"; "yard" ($100); "the joint" (jail), etc.

Finally, one should note—though it is technically part of general slang admixture rather than argot—that a huge dimension of the hustler lexicon is in the use of obscene exclamations ("mother-

---

[45]A portion of poolroom argot, and consequently of hustler argot, is also used by that dwindling band of upper-class billiard players who play entirely or almost entirely in private men's clubs. For example, I find the hustler term "shortstop" (meaning an excellent player but of the second rank, one who can stop all but the top players) used in a billiard book issued by an upper-class club. [*Amateur Billiard Championship of America (Class A): A Souvenir. . . .* (New York: Knickerbocker Athletic Club, 1899), p. 18].

fucker," "rat bastard," "cocksucker," *"chinga su madre,"* etc.). The hustler is particularly given to these exclamations when he unintentionally misses a shot. His use of such terms is far more frequent than one would expect simply from his lower-class origins. There are two reasons for this: (a) In general, obscenities are used oftener in the poolroom than elsewhere in lower-class life, because the main inhibition against their use (for all classes) is the presence of women—and the poolroom, like the army, is ordinarily an all-male institution. (b) The hustler spends more time than anyone else in this non-inhibiting milieu of the poolroom, and thus tends to develop greater habitual use of obscenity than other poolroom players. For these reasons also, when a woman does enter an action poolroom it is the hustlers who are likely to feel most resent-ful, for they suffer the greatest inhibition of their characteristic mode of discourse.

An argot has a geography, which means not merely that it is used in various localities of a country but that typically its content varies a bit, at any given time, from one locality to another. Such variation takes two main forms: (a) The same thing may be referred to differently. Thus in one locality the usual criminal term for police may be "the Man," in another it may be "the fuzz," in another "the nabs," in another "busters," etc. (b) The same term may be used for different things. Thus the term "gun-sel" among Illinois criminals means a homosexual who takes the female role, but among California criminals it means an armed robber. Both kinds of variation occur not only from one city to another, but in larger cities they sometimes occur from one neigh-borhood or friendship clique to another. Hustler argot seems unusually bare of such variations; the only significant exception is that one kind of hustling game is usually called "one pocket" in some cities and "pocket apiece" in others. The argot is strikingly uniform from one city to the next and, within large cities, from one poolroom to the next.

It is tempting to attribute this relative uniformity to intercity and inter-poolroom communication, to the fact that hustlers pos-sibly move about oftener than members of most other argot-using groups. But intercity communication is not sufficient to deter the preserving of local linguistic patterns. (For example, many linguists once assumed that the rapid spread of radio ownership in the 1920's and 1930's would tend to level out American regional differences in pronunciation and semantic patterns, but the *Linguistic Atlas of the United States and Canada* abundantly disproved this assumption.) Rather, it seems attributable mostly to the hustler's strong traditionalism—something that will emerge more clearly when we look at the argot historically.

An argot varies in time as well as space. Over the years it adds and drops words; and some other words, though they remain in the argot throughout, have their meanings changed. (For example, the criminal term "gunsel," some of whose current meanings are given above, once meant—among other things—an apprentice safecracker.) Such historical change is more rapid in argot than in the language at large (though less rapid than change in general slang); compendia of argot get out of date much sooner than a general dictionary does. Furthermore, the argots of socially deviant groups (e.g., drug addicts, jazz musicians, professional criminals) tend to change even more rapidly than argots of respectable trades; when an argot word of such a group gets to be common coin among outsiders, the insiders often replace it—again, not for purposes of secrecy, but by way of reaffirming their separateness and "in-groupness." (Thus, only outsiders these days still refer to a marihuana cigarette as a "reefer.") But despite these strong predisposing factors, the hustlers' argot shows hardly any evidence of historical change.

Of course the argot of pool and billiard hustlers didn't spring full-formed from Zeus's head; there must have been a developmental period in which words were added and others dropped. But this period, whenever it was, certainly antedated World War I. For as far back as I have been able to trace the argot of hustlers —about sixty years—it has been remarkably stable. During this entire time it seems that: (a) no new words have been introduced; (b) no words have become obsolete; (c) no words are obsolescent (used or understood only by oldtimers); (d) only one word has become more generalized in its meaning; and (e) only three words have become more specialized in their meanings.

I believe this is related to the strong element of traditionalism in hustler ideology, to the fact that the hustler has more awareness of, involvement with, and reverence for his outstanding predecessors and their accomplishments than other kinds of deviants have for their historical counterparts—more than the usual professional criminal or drug addict; more, even, than the homosexual or jazz musician.[46] Certainly it is not due to any lack of linguistic inventiveness or playfulness on the hustler's part (as we shall see when we consider hustler's nicknames).

A stigmatized group counter-stigmatizes by having at least one pejorative term for outsiders as a class. Outsiders (in this context think of all non-hustlers, in or out of the poolroom world) are likely to encounter this term at least as frequently as any other in the argot; that is why the term applied to outsiders by, for example, jazz musicians and many criminal groups, "squares," is now understood by nearly all outsiders and is indeed used by so many of them that it has ceased to be just an argot word and has become part of general American slang. A few argot words for outsiders, though, remain fairly esoteric, e.g., the homosexual term "jam." Hustler argot is unusual in that its term for outsiders, "suckers," is properly speaking not an argot word at all; that is, it did not originate with hustlers, or even in other deviant groups that use it, but was adopted from general American slang. This possibly may relate to the fact, noted earlier, that hustlers are unusually indifferent to the opinions of those who put them down, and hence would feel little need to develop counter-stigmatizing terms of their own.

Criminal or quasi-criminal groups commonly have a name for those outsiders considered to be prospects, for their actual or potential "victims." This is especially so for deviants who do their "victimizing" in a primary, face-to-face situation. Thus the con man has his "mark," the prostitute has her "john" or "trick," etc. But the hustler has no such special term. A few decades ago, when

[46]The homosexual's interest in famous predecessors tends to be limited to citing them for the purpose of self-justification. The jazz musician's interest in famous predecessors or their accomplishments tends to be limited to those few major breakthroughs of the recent past, such as the innovations of Charlie Parker, from which current developments are deemed to stem. (Jazz fans are often more involved with past history—much to the annoyance of the musician, who would prefer that his questioner stop bugging him to recall details of a recording date of 25 years ago and concentrate instead on current sounds.) The historical attitude of most pool and billiard hustlers is quite different; even teenage hustlers are often full of respectful and prideful lore about their forebears.

pool hustlers were also (and usually) called pool "sharks," their actual or potential victims were often called "fish." But for fifteen or twenty years now the term "shark" has not been used in this sense among hustlers themselves and among poolroom habitués generally (though it is still so used among older outsiders whose acquaintance with poolrooms ended years ago), and the term "fish" has been restricted to cover only a small minority of victims —those rare ones who keep returning for more beatings.[47] (The hustler's "fish" is thus comparable to the con man's "addict" rather than his "mark.") Today, hustlers use the term "sucker," which formerly had only one meaning (outsiders as a whole, i.e., all non-hustlers), indiscriminately to refer to (a) outsiders as a whole or (b) that particular class of outsiders who are actual or potential victims. Which of these meanings it has depends on the context, and in some contexts it can mean both at once (as in one hustler's remark to me, "The trouble today is that most of the suckers are wise").

Perhaps the most striking aspect of the pool and billiard hustlers' argot is its development and use of nicknames. Well over half of all full-time hustlers have nicknames which they use regularly. My impression is that the percentage of them who have nicknames is not only higher than among either professionals or hustlers in other sports, but is higher than in any other adult group in America except for certain criminal groups (notably con men). A few hustlers acquired their nicknames in their pre-hustling childhood or adolescence—this is especially likely if the nickname refers to a physical characteristic of the hustler—but the good majority acquired such names after they entered hustling.

[47]"Shark" survives in poolrooms with a specialized meaning as a transitive verb: to "shark" one's opponent means to upset or distract him while he's shooting, for example, by making a sudden movement in his line of sight when he is aiming. In addition to the specialization of "shark" and "fish," the word "hustler" itself has taken on a specialized meaning among hustlers. When they referred to themselves as "sharks" in the old sense, they often used "hustler" in the general slang sense of anyone who's alert and willing to take on any sort of odd job for a quick buck; now, of course, they use "hustler" in the narrower meaning of a member of their profession. For the early usages, and the period of overlap between the meanings of "shark" and "hustler," cf. Vogeler, *op. cit., passim.*

The following are the nicknames of some hustlers recently or currently active: Brooklyn Jimmy, Cornbread Red, Spanish Eddy, Sleepy, Blueshirt, Glendale Johnny, Fats, Wimpy, Harry the Russian, Snake, Whitey (three hustlers), Connecticut Johnny, Detroit Whitey, Brooklyn Johnny, Jersey Red, Blacky, Fifth Avenue Red, Miami, Shoes, Cicero, Gigolo, Subway, Country, Peter Rabbit, Weenie Beanie, Skinny Eddy, Squirrel, Fast Eddy,[48] Gypsy (two hustlers), Tallahassee, Boston Shorty, Rockaway Abe, Brooklyn Charlie, Johnny Irish, Big Gene, Charlie the Hat, the Knoxville Bear,[49] Derby, Dago Frankie, Lefty (three hustlers), Iron Joe, Bob the Destroyer, Jimmy Sure-Shot, Daddy Warbucks, and Tommy the Sailor.

Nicknames formed on similar principles were borne by hustlers active before 1920: Cowboy Weston, Boston Whitey, the Sicily Kid, Seattle Slim, Farmer Jones, Johnny Icewater, West Coast Willie, Dago Joe, Bowery Al.[50]

I had assumed at first that certainly this part of the argot, if no other, was used for purposes of secrecy or disguise. A nickname, I thought, would help a hustler to con because he, whose poolroom reputation is known via his nickname, could disguise his identity from the non-hustler by introducing himself by his real name (could con by "honestly" introducing himself). This hypothesis was completely disproven. The hustler doesn't keep his nickname from his opponent or anybody else in the poolroom; he is always pleased to use it and be referred to by it. For example: at the start of a game with a hustler I'd seen but never met, I introduced myself by saying, "I'm Ned," and the hustler replied, "They call me Shoes." Most hustlers never use their real names (except occasionally with outsiders encountered outside the poolroom), not because these need to be hidden but simply because they prefer to be nicknamed. Like many other argot terms, these nicknames exist because, to quote the words of more than one hustler, "they lend a little color to the game."

[48]Fast Eddy was nicknamed after the character in the movie *The Hustler* —but ironically, for he exasperates opponents by shooting quite slowly.

[49]The Knoxville Bear is, however, more frequently referred to among hustlers by his real name, Eddy Taylor.

[50]These nicknames of pre-1920 hustlers are taken from Vogeler, *op. cit.*, p. 346.

This is to say that the hustler's nickname is a *monicker*, not an *alias*. True enough, the monicker of a hustler (or other criminal) may incidentally aid him when he is being sought by police, for the latter may be seeking him only under his real name whereas most of his colleagues and friends have never heard that name and know him only by his monicker. It is also true that hustlers sometimes have to dodge the police because of trouble over their criminal moonlighting jobs. But the hustler (or other criminal) trying to avoid arrest never depends on his monicker for this purpose; on the contrary, when on the lam and faced with any situation in which he must give his name—e.g., meeting new people, renting a room, buying a plane ticket—he uses neither his real name nor his monicker but temporarily adopts yet another name, a true alias.[51]

Although the chief reason for hustlers' use of monickers is, as indicated above, the furtherance of *esprit de corps*, additional factors bolster such use. Taken together, they probably account for the extremely high percentage of hustlers—old and young alike—with monickers. (a) Hustlers are overwhelmingly from the lower class, which makes more frequent use of nicknames in adulthood than other classes. (b) The hustlers' world overlaps other criminal circles that have high monicker rates (especially, other types of gamblers). (c) Hustlers are historically minded, and the use of monickers is one way of maintaining a long-standing craft tradition (the old-time hustlers also had monickers). (d) The monickers may also reflect a continuance of certain male-alliance aspects of adolescence. Relevant here is the fact that the poolroom world— at least the world of action rooms—is exclusively male, except on infrequent occasion.[52]

[51]Unfortunately David Maurer's discussion of monickers (*op. cit.*, p. 286), in failing to note the functional distinction between a monicker and an alias, misleadingly conflates the two.

[52]After this book was in press one hustler, whose monicker is "Fats" and who alleges he is the model for "Minnesota Fats" in *The Hustler*, published a book of reminiscences: Minnesota Fats with Tom Fox, *The Bank Shot and Other Great Robberies* (Cleveland: World Publishing Company, 1966). Fats is a delightful storyteller, but his imagination and ego have resulted in a book that presents, along with much fact, much fiction as if it were fact.

7

They Saw a Game: A Case Study

ALBERT H. HASTORF and
HADLEY CANTRIL

Most of us, at one time or another, have had experiences similar to those described in this report. Discussing a sporting event such as a football game with someone who is a fan of the opponent usually reveals that you and the other fan have seen two quite different games!

The present report is a social scientific account of just such an occurrence and dramatically demonstrates how people perceive events in terms of their individual needs and desires. What may be thought of initially as an objective "fact" is nothing more than a consensus of subjective interpretations, depending upon what "side" a person is on.

From: *Journal of Abnormal and Social Psychology*, 49: 129–134, 1954. Reprinted by permission of the authors and of American Psychological Association.

On a brisk Saturday afternoon, November 23, 1951, the Dartmouth football team played Princeton in Princeton's Palmer Stadium. It was the last game of the season for both teams and of rather special significance because the Princeton team had won all its games so far and one of its players, Dick Kazmaier, was receiving All-American mention, had just appeared as the cover man on *Time* magazine, and was playing his last game.

A few minutes after the opening kick-off, it became apparent that the game was going to be a rough one. The referees were kept busy blowing their whistles and penalizing both sides. In the second quarter, Princeton's star left the game with a broken nose. In the third quarter, a Dartmouth player was taken off the field with a broken leg. Tempers flared both during and after the game. The official statistics of the game, which Princeton won, showed that Dartmouth was penalized 70 yards, Princeton 25, not counting more than a few plays in which both sides were penalized.

Needless to say, accusations soon began to fly. The game immediately became a matter of concern to players, students, coaches, and the administrative officials of the two institutions, as well as to alumni and the general public who had not seen the game but had become sensitive to the problem of big-time football through the recent exposures of subsidized players, commercialism, etc. Discussion of the game continued for several weeks.

One of the contributing factors to the extended discussion of the game was the extensive space given to it by both campus and metropolitan newspapers. An indication of the fervor with which the discussions were carried on is shown by a few excerpts from the campus dailies.

For example, on November 27 (four days after the game), the *Daily Princetonian* (Princeton's student newspaper) said:

> This observer has never seen quite such a disgusting exhibition of so-called "sport." Both teams were guilty but the blame must be laid primarily on Dartmouth's doorstep. Princeton, obviously the better team, had no reason to rough up Dartmouth. Looking at the situation rationally, we don't see why the Indians should make a deliberate attempt to cripple Dick Kazmaier or any other Princeton player. The Dartmouth psychology, however, is not rational itself.

The November 30th edition of the *Princeton Alumni Weekly* said:

> But certain memories of what occurred will not be easily
> erased. Into the record books will go in indelible fashion the
> fact that the last game of Dick Kazmaier's career was cut
> short by more than half when he was forced out with a broken
> nose and a mild concussion, sustained from a tackle that came
> well after he had thrown a pass.
>
> This second-period development was followed by a third
> quarter outbreak of roughness that was climaxed when a Dart-
> mouth player deliberately kicked Brad Glass in the ribs while
> the latter was on his back. Throughout the often unpleasant
> afternoon, there was undeniable evidence that the losers'
> tactics were the result of an actual style of play, and reports
> on other games they have played this season substantiate this.

Dartmouth students were "seeing" an entirely different version
of the game through the editorial eyes of the *Dartmouth* (Dartmouth's undergraduate newspaper). For example, on November
27 the *Dartmouth* said:

> However, the Dartmouth-Princeton game set the stage for
> the other type of dirty football. A type which may be termed
> as an unjustifiable accusation.
>
> Dick Kazmaier was injured early in the game. Kazmaier
> was the star, an All-American. Other stars have been injured
> before, but Kazmaier had been built to represent a Princeton
> idol. When an idol is hurt there is only one recourse—the tag
> of dirty football. So what did the Tiger Coach Charley Cald-
> well do? He announced to the world that the Big Green had
> been out to extinguish the Princeton star. His purpose was
> achieved.
>
> After this incident, Caldwell instilled the old see-what-
> they-did-go-get-them attitude into his players. His talk got
> results. Gene Howard and Jim Miller were both injured. Both
> had dropped back to pass, had passed, and were standing
> unprotected in the backfield. Result: one bad leg and one
> leg broken.
>
> The game was rough and did get a bit out of hand in the
> third quarter. Yet most of the roughing penalties were called
> against Princeton while Dartmouth received more of the
> illegal-use-of-the-hands variety.

On November 28 the *Dartmouth* said:

> Dick Kazmaier of Princeton admittedly is an unusually able
> football player. Many Dartmouth men traveled to Princeton,

not expecting to win—only hoping to see an All-American in action. Dick Kazmaier was hurt in the second period, and played only a token part in the remainder of the game. For this, spectators were sorry.

But there were no such feelings for Dick Kazmaier's health. Medical authorities have confirmed that as a relatively unprotected passing and running star in a contact sport, he is quite liable to injury. Also, his particular injuries—a broken nose and slight concussion—were no more serious than is experienced almost any day in any football practice, where there is no more serious stake than playing the following Saturday. Up to the Princeton game, Dartmouth players suffered about 10 known nose fractures and face injuries, not to mention several slight concussions.

Did Princeton players feel so badly about losing their star? They shouldn't have. During the past undefeated campaign they stopped several individual stars by a concentrated effort, including such main-stays as Frank Hauff of Navy, Glenn Adams of Pennsylvania and Rocco Calvo of Cornell.

In other words, the same brand of football condemned by the *Prince*—that of stopping the big man—is practiced quite successfully by the Tigers.

Basically, then, there was disagreement as to what had happened during the game. Hence we took the opportunity presented by the occasion to make a "real-life" study of a perceptual problem.[1]

PROCEDURE

Two steps were involved in gathering data. The first consisted of answers to a questionnaire designed to get reactions to the game and to learn something of the climate of opinion in each institution. This questionnaire was administered a week after the game to both Dartmouth and Princeton undergraduates who were taking introductory and intermediate psychology courses.

The second step consisted of showing the same motion picture of the game to a sample of undergraduates in each school and having them check on another questionnaire, as they watched the

[1]We are not concerned here with the problem of guilt or responsibility for infractions, and nothing here implies any judgment as to who was to blame.

film, any infraction of the rules they saw and whether these infractions were "mild" or "flagrant."[2] At Dartmouth, members of two
fraternities were asked to view the film on December 7; at Princeton, members of two undergraduate clubs saw the film early in
January.

The answers to both questionnaires were carefully coded and
transferred to punch cards.[3]

RESULTS

Table 1 shows the questions which received different replies
from the two student populations on the first questionnaire.

Questions asking if the students had friends on the team, if
they had ever played football themselves, if they felt they knew
the rules of the game well, etc., showed no differences in either
school and no relation to answers given to other questions. This
is not surprising since the students in both schools come from
essentially the same type of educational, economic, and ethnic
background.

Summarizing the data of Tables 1 and 2, we find a marked
contrast between the two student groups.

Nearly all *Princeton* students judged the game as "rough and
dirty"—not one of them thought it "clean and fair." And almost
nine-tenths of them thought the other side started the rough play.
By and large they felt that the charges they understood were being
made were true; most of them felt the charges were made in order
to avoid similar situations in the future.

When Princeton students looked at the movie of the game, they
saw the Dartmouth team make over twice as many infractions as

[2]The film shown was kindly loaned for the purpose of the experiment by
the Dartmouth College Athletic Council. It should be pointed out that a
movie of a football game follows the ball, is thus selective, and omits a
good deal of the total action on the field. Also, of course, in viewing only
a film of a game, the possibilities of participation as spectator are greatly
limited.

[3]We gratefully acknowledge the assistance of Virginia Zerega, Office of
Public Opinion Research, and J. L. McCandless, Princeton University, and
E. S. Horton, Dartmouth College, in the gathering and collation of the data.

TABLE 1
DATA FROM FIRST QUESTIONNAIRE

Question	Dartmouth Students (N = 163)%	Princeton Students (N = 161)%
1. Did you happen to see the actual game between Dartmouth and Princeton in Palmer Stadium this year?		
Yes	33	71
No	67	29
2. Have you seen a movie of the game or seen it on television?		
Yes, movie	33	2
Yes, television	0	1
No, neither	67	97
3. (Asked of those who answered "yes" to either or both of above questions.) From your observations of what went on at the game, do you believe the game was clean and fairly played, or that it was unnecessarily rough and dirty?		
Clean and fair	6	0
Rough and dirty	24	69
Rough and fair*	25	2
No answer	45	29
4. (Asked of those who answered "no" on both of the first questions.) From what you have heard and read about the game, do you feel it was clean and fairly played, or that it was unnecessarily rough and dirty?		
Clean and fair	7	0
Rough and dirty	18	24
Rough and fair*	14	1
Don't know	6	4
No answer	55	71
(Combined answers to question 3 and 4 above)		
Clean and fair	13	0
Rough and dirty	42	93
Rough and fair*	39	3
Don't know	6	4
5. From what you saw in the game or the movies, or from what you have read,		

TABLE 1   (continued)

Question	Dartmouth Students (N = 163)%	Princeton Students (N = 161)%
which team do you feel started the rough play?		
Dartmouth started it	36	86
Princeton started it	2	0
Both started it	53	11
Neither	6	1
No answer	3	2
6. What is your understanding of the charges being made?**		
Dartmouth tried to get Kazmaier	71	47
Dartmouth intentionally dirty	52	44
Dartmouth unnecessarily rough	8	35
7. Do you feel there is any truth to these charges?		
Yes	10	55
No	57	4
Partly	29	35
Don't know	4	6
8. Why do you think the charges were made?		
Injury to Princeton star	70	23
To prevent repetition	2	46
No answer	28	31

*This answer was not included on the checklist but was written in by the percentage of students indicated.

**Replies do not add to 100% since more than one charge could be given.

TABLE 2
DATA FROM SECOND QUESTIONNAIRE CHECKED WHILE
SEEING FILM

		Total Number of Infractions Checked Against			
		Dartmouth Team		Princeton Team	
Group	N	Mean	SD	Mean	SD
Dartmouth students	48	4.3*	2.7	4.4	2.8
Princeton students	49	9.8*	5.7	4.2	3.5

*Significant at the .01 level.

their own team made. And they saw the Dartmouth team make over twice as many infractions as were seen by Dartmouth students. When Princeton students judged these infractions as "flagrant" or "mild," the ratio was about two "flagrant" to one "mild" on the Dartmouth team, and about one "flagrant" to three "mild" on the Princeton team.

As for the *Dartmouth* students, while the purality of answers fell in the "rough and dirty" category, over one-tenth thought the game was "clean and fair" and over a third introduced their own category of "rough and fair" to describe the action. Although a third of the Dartmouth students felt that Dartmouth was to blame for starting the rough play, the majority of Dartmouth students thought both sides were to blame. By and large, Dartmouth men felt that the charges they understood were being made were not true, and most of them thought the reason for the charges was Princeton's concern for its football star.

When Dartmouth students looked at the movie of the game they saw both teams make about the same number of infractions. And they saw their own team make only half the number of infractions the Princeton students saw them make. The ratio of "flagrant" to "mild" infractions was about one to one when Dartmouth students judged the Dartmouth team, and about one "flagrant" to two "mild" when Dartmouth students judged infractions made by the Princeton team.

It should be noted that Dartmouth and Princeton students were thinking of different charges in judging their validity and in assigning reasons as to why the charges were made. It should also be noted that whether or not students were spectators of the game in the stadium made little difference in their responses.

INTERPRETATION: THE NATURE OF A SOCIAL EVENT[4]

It seems clear that the "game" actually was many different games and that each version of the events that transpired was just as "real" to a particular person as other versions were to other people. A consideration of the experiential phenomena that

[4]The interpretation of the nature of a social event sketched here is in part based on discussions with Adelbert Ames, Jr., and is being elaborated in more detail elsewhere.

constitute a football game for the spectator may help us both to account for the results obtained and illustrate something of the nature of any social event.

Like any other complex social occurrence, a football game consists of a whole host of happenings. Many different events are occurring simultaneously. Furthermore, each happening is a link in a chain of happenings, so that one follows another in sequence. The football game, as well as other complex social situations, consists of a whole matrix of events. In the game situation, this matrix of events consists of the actions of all the players, together with the behavior of the referees and linesmen, the action on the sidelines, in the grandstands, over the loud-speaker, etc.

Of crucial importance is the fact that an "occurrence" on the football field or in any other social situation does not become an experiential "event" unless and until some significance is given to it: an occurrence becomes an *event* only when the happening has significance. And a happening generally has significance only if it reactivates learned significances already registered in what we have called a person's assumptive form-world (1).

Hence the particular occurrences that different people experienced in the football game were a limited series of events from the total matrix of events *potentially* available to them. People experienced those occurrences that reactivated significances they brought to the occasion; they failed to experience those occurences which did not reactivate past significances. We do not need to introduce "attention" as an "intervening third" (to paraphrase James on memory) to account for the selectivity of the experiential process.

In this particular study, one of the most interesting examples of this phenomenon was a telegram sent to an officer of Dartmouth College by a member of a Dartmouth alumni group in the Midwest. He had viewed the film which had been shipped to his alumni group from Princeton after its use with Princeton students, who saw, as we noted, an average of over nine infractions by Dartmouth players during the game. The alumnus, who couldn't see the infractions he had heard publicized, wired:

> Preview of Princeton movies indicates considerable cutting of important part please wire explanation and possibly air mail missing part before showing scheduled for January 25 we have splicing equipment.

The "same" sensory impingements emanating from the football field, transmitted through the visual mechanism to the brain, also obviously gave rise to different experiences in different people. The significances assumed by different happenings for different people depend in large part on the purposes people bring to the occasion and the assumptions they have of the purposes and probable behavior of other people involved. This was amusingly pointed out by the New York *Herald Tribune's* sports columnist, Red Smith, in describing a prize fight between Chico Vejar and Carmine Fiore in his column of December 21, 1951. Among other things, he wrote:

> You see, Steve Ellis is the proprietor of Chico Vejar, who is a highly desirable tract of Stamford, Conn., welterweight. Steve is also a radio announcer. Ordinarily there is no conflict between Ellis the Brain and Ellis the Voice because Steve is an uncommonly substantial lump of meat who can support both halves of a split personality and give away weight on each end without missing it.
>
> This time, though, the two Ellises met head-on, with a sickening, rending crash. Steve the Manager sat at ringside in the guise of Steve the Announcer broadcasting a dispassionate, unbiased, objective report of Chico's adventures in the ring. . . .
>
> Clear as mountain water, his words came through, winning big for Chico. Winning? Hell, Steve was slaughtering poor Fiore.
>
> Watching and listening, you could see what a valiant effort the reporter was making to remain cool and detached. At the same time you had an illustration of the old, established truth that when anybody with a preference watches a fight, he sees only what he prefers to see.
>
> That is always so. That is why, after any fight that doesn't end in a clean knockout, there always are at least a few hoots when the decision is announced. A guy from, say, Billy Graham's neighborhood goes to see Billy fight and he watches Graham all the time. He sees all the punches Billy throws, and hardly any of the punches Billy catches. So it was with Steve.
>
> "Fiore feints with a left," he would say, honestly believing that Fiore hadn't caught Chico full on the chops. "Fiore's knees buckle," he said, "and Chico backs away." Steve didn't see the hook that had driven Chico back. . . .

In brief, the data here indicate that there is no such "thing" as a game existing "out there" in its own right which people merely "observe." The game exists for a person and is experienced by him only in so far as certain happenings have significances in terms of his purpose. Out of all the occurrences going on in the environment, a person selects those that have some significance for him from his own egocentric position in the total matrix.

Obviously in the case of a football game, the value of the experience of watching the game is enhanced if the purpose of "your" team is accomplished, if the happening of the desired consequence is experienced—i.e., if your team wins. But the value attribute of the experience can, of course, be spoiled if the desire to win crowds out behavior we value and have come to call sportsmanlike.

The sharing of significances provides the links except for which a "social event" would not be experienced and would not exist for anyone.

A football game would be impossible except for the rules of the game which we bring to the situation and which enable us to share with others the significances of various happenings. These rules make possible a certain repeatability of events such as first downs, touchdowns, etc. If a person is unfamiliar with the rules of the game, the behavior he sees lacks repeatability and consistent significance and hence "doesn't make sense."

And only because there is the possibility of repetition is there the possibility that a happening has a significance. For example, the balls used in games are designed to give a high degree of repeatability. While a football is about the only ball used in games which is not a sphere, the shape of the modern football has apparently evolved in order to achieve a higher degree of accuracy and speed in forward passing than would be obtained with a spherical ball, thus increasing the repeatability of an important phase of the game.

The rules of a football game, like laws, rituals, customs, and mores, are registered and preserved forms of sequential significances enabling people to share the significances of occurrences. The sharing of sequential significances which have value for us provides the links that operationally make social events possible.

They are analogous to the forces of attraction that hold parts of an atom together, keeping each part from following its individual, independent course.

From this point of view it is inaccurate and misleading to say that different people have different "attitudes" concerning the same "thing." For the "thing" simply is *not* the same for different people whether the "thing" is a football game, a presidential candidate, Communism, or spinach. We do not simply "react to" a happening or to some impingement from the environment in a determined way (except in behavior that has become reflexive or habitual). We behave according to what we bring to the occasion; and what each of us brings to the occasion is more or less unique. And except for these significances which we bring to the occasion, the happenings around us would be meaningless occurrences, would be "inconsequential."

From the transactional view, an attitude is not a predisposition to react in a certain way to an occurrence or stimulus "out there" that exists in its own right with certain fixed characteristics which we "color" according to our predisposition (2). That is, a subject does not simply "react to" an object. An attitude would rather seem to be a complex of registered significances reactivated by some stimulus which assumes its own particular significance for us in terms of our purposes. That is, the object as experienced would not exist for us except for the reactivated aspects of the form-world which provide particular significance to the hieroglyphics of sensory impingements.

REFERENCES

1. CANTRIL, H. *The "Why" of Man's Experience.* New York: Macmillan, 1950.
2. KILPATRICK, F. P. (Ed.) *Human Behavior from the Transactional Point of View.* Hanover, N. H.: Institute for Associated Research, 1952.

8

How Good Are the Rating Services?

RICHARD I. EVANS

Most television viewers are becoming increasingly aware of the great influence that the television rating services have upon the range and quality of television programs that are made available to the public. Most, however, are not aware of the problems involved in obtaining and interpreting these ratings of viewers watching various television programs. This report presents the major pitfalls encountered in surveys that attempt to discover what programs people watch on television. A complex of sampling and interviewing techniques are involved and, as this report shows, no completely reliable methods have as yet been devised.

Although this report concerns itself specifically with television ratings, the problems discussed are well known to any social scientist who has ever been involved in survey research of any type. The report is a good example of how the trained social scientist can apply his skills and ideas to a form of communication which no doubt has been, and will continue to be, one of the most influential in information dissemination, entertainment, and attitude formation and change within the context of everyday living.

From: *National Association of Educational Broadcasters Journal (NAEB Journal)*, Jan.–Feb., 1961, 39–50. Reprinted through the courtesy of Educational Broadcasting Review.

The recent history of television rating services, as all of you know, has led to a kind of confusion, distortion, and downright frustration on the part of all the important decision makers in the television industry. Some comments (such as the one made by a famous comedian, who asked how his program could be rated when he had never known anyone who had been asked if he watched it) reflect an almost complete lack of knowledge of sampling techniques. In other words, the very basic assumptions of audience research are apparently not very well understood.

Another point of confusion seems to center around the apparent differences in ratings of the same program reported by different rating services. As a result of this, there seems to develop a game of selecting for sales purposes the rating service most favorable to the program being represented by a particular advertising agency or television station. But even then the one selected may prove disappointing at the next comparative go-round, when still another rating service will appear which rates the program higher than the favorable rating service selected the previous month.

Still another point of confusion has centered around the whole concept of audience size as a criterion by which television programs are or should be judged. The widely stated example of the "I Love Lucy" show and Philip Morris cigarettes illustrates this quite well. As you know, "I Love Lucy" was consistently top rated by all of the major rating services for a period of time, but Philip Morris cigarettes, the sponsor's product, continued to stand fourth in national sales throughout the entire period. Finally, the tobacco company cancelled its sponsorship of the program. Perhaps the most optimistic statement in defense of the audience size criterion concerning this was the reported remark by the advertising agency account executive representing the program, who stated that without the program the sales of Philip Morris cigarettes might have actually declined. This implied that the success of the program in terms of audience size contributed to the continuing success of a failing product, a comment undoubtedly not relished by the Philip Morris executives.

I should like to discuss very briefly the major audience rating services, their techniques of contacting the television homes that they select in their respective samples, the nature of their samples, and some of the advantages and disadvantages of their respective approaches. In order to base this analysis on the most fundamental data, we wrote to each of the major rating services and requested as much of this information as they had available. It is interesting to note that some of the rating services were extremely cooperative, supplying comprehensive reports of their sampling and measuring techniques, while others apparently limited their information to advertising "blurbs." In these instances, it was necessary to seek more detailed information about their sampling and measuring instruments from other sources, which may or may not be author- itative or up to date.

The final point in my presentation will be an attempt to look at this problem in general and make some suggestions as to how audience studies in depth could conceivably supply new insights concerning the television audience and their responsiveness to programs in terms of buying behavior with respect to the sponsors' products. Such insights might conceivably challenge the notion that programing policy should bow to the criterion of the size of the audiences which programs can command.

SAMPLING THE AUDIENCE

In attempting to assess audience reaction to a given television program, probably the first question that should be raised is: Who exactly is the intended target for the program? Educational televi- sion, for example, as well as some public service programing, is admittedly not designed to attract all interest groups. On the other hand, a good deal of, if not most, commercial programing seems to be designed as a kind of "shotgun" technique to gain viewers simultaneously from as broad a base as possible. In other words, there is no doubt that the average commercial television program is designed to appeal, if possible, to interests in as large an audi- ence as possible. Assuming for a moment that we are now inter- ested in assessing the audience for such a program on one of the major television networks, what we technically define as the universe for the program automatically becomes all of the televi- sion homes in the United States. It is apparent that every member of the universe cannot be reached for the purpose of audience studies. Sampling theory would therefore require that a random or truly representative sample of this universe be contacted. Let me illustrate this point with an analogy. If a physician wishes to learn something about the structure of a patient's blood, he does not have to drain all of the blood out of the patient's body and examine it. He can study even a single drop of blood and form an accurate picture of the structure of this patient's blood in general. (Incidentally, this example is not intended to suggest what some of you may already believe—that television rating is a bloody business!)

In theory, a sample is truly representative only if every item in the universe has an equal opportunity to be selected. To insure this, tables of random numbers are typically used. Alphabetical lists of all the items in the universe may be used instead. In some cases, for that matter, all of the items could simply be put into a hat, shaken up, and a sample drawn.

Now, the critical point here is that if every television home in the universe has an equal opportunity of being selected, then, in terms of probability theory, how many television homes have to be selected in order to have a truly representative sample? Here we apply a variation of a statistical formula designed to give us the standard error of a percentage, based on the levels of confidence we desire. For example, in a study that we did of the over 300,000 television homes in the signal area of Channel 8 in Houston, this formula estimated that we would have to interview respondents in approximately 600 television homes to be accurate within 5 per cent. On a national survey of voters, to take another example, surprisingly great precision could be obtained by sampling in the neighborhood of 10,000 randomly selected voters. Such statistical license to sample, I repeat, can be exercised only when every single item in the universe has an equal opportunity of being selected.

Another very important, fundamental point relative to this problem is that if we are considering a universe of all television homes in the United States, and we draw a sample which represents this large group, then breakdowns in terms of subgroups of the total universe, such as, say, a large metropolitan area like Houston, cannot be reliably estimated from the sample selected for the over-all United States universe. In order to get a true representation of the metropolitan Houston area, the universe would now have to be defined, as in our earlier-mentioned Channel 8 study, as the television homes in the Houston signal area, and a sample in terms of this particular universe would have to be drawn. It is entirely possible, for example, that on a national sample of the universe of all television homes in the United States, sampling rigor could be theoretically exercised when only nine or ten television homes in the Houston area are contacted. This, how-ever, would hardly be a statistically sound basis for making infer-ences about the Houston market.

These few remarks about the elements of sampling should emphasize the necessity of rigorous adherence to theoretically justified sampling procedures, since any departures from such procedures, slight though they may be, can completely invalidate the significance of the data obtained. Suppose, for example, a cer-tain rating service wishes to obtain a sample for the entire United States. Their statisticians select a random sample based on one of the area sampling methods. They even list the specific television home in every part of the United States that is to be contacted by the interviewer. Now let's assume that, among other things, electronic recording devices must be installed in the televi-sion sets in these homes. Certain individuals refuse to allow such devices to be installed in their homes. If the residents of a home that has been selected in the sample refuse to participate, a rating service representative might proceed to knock on doors in the immediate vicinity until more cooperative television viewers are found. This procedure introduces what we technically refer to as a biased sampling error. Without proof, we have no reason to believe that individuals who allow electronic devices to be placed in their homes are basically similar in personality characteristics, such as television viewing behavior, to individuals who do not allow such devices to be placed in their television sets. In this example, we might have a well-defined sample, carefully selected by expert statisticians working out of the rating service headquar-ters; we might have a very accurate electronic device, at least in the sense of actually recording when and to what channel the television set is tuned; yet all this precision is vitiated by the introduction of a biased sampling error at the field contact level. Many other possible sources of sampling errors in audience research could be cited.

MAJOR RATING SERVICES EVALUATED

Of the marketing organizations engaged in television audience research, four have emerged as the leaders in establishing program ratings. These are the A. C. Nielsen Company, Trendex, the Pulse, Inc., and the American Research Bureau. These organizations are staffed, in my opinion, with competent statisticians and research methodologists trained in such fields as psychology, sociology, and marketing. When critically evaluating the validity of reports by these firms, therefore, one is seldom, if ever, justified in asserting that deficiencies or inaccuracies are due to incompetence or lack of sophistication in the theoretical planning stages of their audience studies. Most of the problems critically affecting validity, as we shall see, appear to emerge in the operational stages of the studies.

Among such possible sources of error in audience studies, one of the most important is the interview instrument itself. Any inaccuracies arising from defects in the structure of the interview form or recording device are referred to as instrument errors. If their form or content tends to bias responses in any way, an instrument error is operative. For example, when the aided recall method is used in an interview, the interviewee is given a list of all the television programs presented in the area on the previous day and asked to indicate those he viewed. He may be inclined to mention programs that he viewed only briefly or inattentively simply because they are listed before him—programs which, without the aided recall technique, he would probably have failed to remember. The fact that he recognizes the name of a program on the list cannot be taken as an indication that he viewed the entire program with attention. This would be particularly true of the advertising message tied in with the program.

The so-called viewing diary is also susceptible to instrument errors since data recording is done entirely by the respondent without supervision. Theoretically, the viewer places the diary on top of his television set and records programs at the time of viewing. Actually, he may not fill in the diary until the end of the week or later, relying on memory when he does so. This time lapse introduces the possibility of faulty recall, which may completely distort the record of his week's viewing.

Another factor affecting the validity of the diary method is what we might call a combination instrument and sampling error. The moment an individual is selected to maintain a diary of viewing behavior, he becomes atypical. As a result, he may alter reports of his viewing to create a particular image of himself, to reflect what he conceives to be his ideal behavior rather than his actual behavior. Such a viewer might actually watch a number of western programs, for example, but omit them from his report, substituting, for the sake of his self-esteem, programs which he believes to have more intellectual or artistic merit.

The A. C. Nielsen Company employs an electronic device, the Audimeter, which is attached to the television set and records the time it is turned on and the channel to which it is tuned. Nielsen maintains Audimeters in 1,000 television homes selected on the basis of an approximation of random area sampling. The participating family is paid 25 cents per week and one-half the cost of any set repairs for allowing the Audimeter to be attached to the set.

When first introduced, this device was hailed as the ultimate solution to the problem of accurate audience measurement, one which would insure reliable results. It obviously does not depend on individual recall of programs watched nor does it require any particular effort on the part of the viewer. Yet it soon became evident that this was not the final, foolproof method of audience evaluation. For one thing, the great expense of installing and maintaining the Audimeter makes it economically unfeasible to utilize a sample of the statistically most desirable size. It was soon revealed, moreover, that from 5 to 8 per cent of the Audimeters were out of order or not functioning properly at any given time. Another obvious flaw in this instrument is that, even when it is working properly, it supplies only a part of the desired information. While it clearly reveals set operation, it does not indicate who, if anyone, is watching the set, a matter of great importance. As many of you will recall from the old days of radio, almost continuous operation of the radio, whether anyone was listening or not, became a habit in many households, where radio was part of the background of family life. There is already some evidence that a similar habit is being formed with respect to television.

Another limitation of the Audimeter in terms of program planning is that it may take three weeks or more of processing to adequately evaluate the data obtained. Still another criticism, to emphasize an earlier example, which applies not only to the Audimeter but to every method which requires some kind of co-operation from the television viewer, is that, no matter how carefully a sample of television homes is selected, there is always the possibility that some individuals in the sample may be unwilling to cooperate. As a result, the sample actually used is not a sample of all television homes in the universe under consideration but rather a sample of all television homes whose residents are willing to participate in audience studies. This certainly suggests the possibility of a biased sampling error, since one would suspect that individuals who refuse to participate in such studies differ significantly from those who agree to participate.

In recognition of possible sources of error affecting the Audimeter, Nielsen began partially verifying Audimeter results by employing viewing diaries. Again, as noted earlier, viewing diaries also present possibilities of instrument error. Furthermore, since Nielsen apparently uses a relatively small sample in its diary surveys, it would hardly be feasible to analyze the results in terms of national markets. There is no reason to suppose, moreover, that one less than perfect measuring technique, the Audimeter, supplemented by another still less adequate measuring device as used herein, the diary, will necessarily provide a more accurate audience measurement than either technique by itself.

TELEPHONE USED

The late C. E. Hooper pioneered an audience evaluation technique called the telephone coincidental method. Trendex, an off-shoot of the old C. E. Hooper group, which apparently no longer specializes in radio and TV audience research, employs the telephone coincidental method in twenty cities throughout the United States. This method has the virtues of easy analysis, immediacy, and great flexibility. The limitations of samples based on telephone listees, however, have been conspicuously apparent at least since 1936, when the *Literary Digest* flatly predicted on the basis of a poll based in part on a sample of telephone homes that Alfred Landon would defeat Franklin Roosevelt in a landslide. In those depression days, of course, telephone subscribers were relatively wealthier, on the whole, than the general population and therefore more likely, in those days, to be Republicans. Today, of course, telephone listees are more representative of the total population, yet samples drawn from telephone subscribers may still reflect definite biases. It is well known, for example, that in many metropolitan areas, new housing developments are often without telephone service for a considerable time. Television viewing behavior in such developments may not be adequately represented in samples based on telephone listees. A still more serious limitation of telephone surveys centers around the "time-of-contact" problem. Telephone calls to viewers for the purpose of surveys can hardly be placed later than, say, 10 P.M. without the risk of disturbing sleeping households and precipitating great wrath.

The Pulse, Inc., bases its ratings on personal interviews using the aided recall type of instrument which was discussed earlier. The sample apparently consists of approximately 8,000 television homes per day. Because of cost considerations involved in such large numbers, such interviews must be completed quickly. Therefore, their aided recall instrument allows for interview lengths of only approximately eight minutes. Such rapid interviewing is open to serious question, since without time to establish sufficient rapport even the most skillful interviewer would be hard pressed to get accurate responses from interviewees. From our own experience in audience research, we discovered that short interviews often result in hasty decisions on the part of interviewees, who invariably sense the "let's get it over with" attitude that interviewers in such situations are prone to project. We noted earlier the possibilities of instrument errors inherent in the aided recall technique in general.

The American Research Bureau has made an especially careful effort to obtain accurate data through utilization of viewing diaries. This organization not only attempts to sample with precision 2,000 representative television homes in the national television market, but also demonstrates sampling precision in local television markets. In an attempt to prevent the development of the artificiality in responses referred to earlier, ARB changes its sample of diary-television homes every month. The viewer is asked to maintain a diary record for one week, recording the name of the program, the time, and the channel when he sets the dial. As suggested earlier, the less conscientious viewers may fill in the required information not after watching each program but at the end of the week, thus introducing the possibility of recall errors. Perhaps the most basic criticism of the ARB method, however, concerns the percentage of diaries returned. Although ARB claims as a selling point that from 60 per cent to 70 per cent of the diaries are returned each week, the fact that around 35 per cent are not returned introduces a very significant biased sampling error. After all, even though a television viewer has agreed to participate in maintenance of a diary, one cannot force him to complete and return the diary, nor can one assume that those who are negligent in this respect do not differ appreciably from those who fully cooperate.

In the last several months, the American Research Bureau has introduced an electronic meter, the Arbitron, which is perhaps the most dramatic development in audience measurement devices to date. These instruments, which are placed in representative television homes, are connected to a central data center in which information concerning the operation of the television sets is instantaneously recorded. With the use of electronic computers, it appears to fulfill the need for immediate audience assessment. However, the elimination of the three-week period for data processing seems to be its only major advantage over the Nielsen Audimeter, since even the most amazing electronic device will not solve the sampling problem created by viewers who simply do not wish to have such devices attached to their television sets because they regard them as an unwarranted intrusion on their privacy. At present the Arbitron is operating, of course, in such a few markets

(apparently only seven cities) that it has had only a limited application, so a truly fair evaluation of its potential could not, of
course, be made at this time.

PROBLEMS IMPAIR ACCURACY

In this brief discussion of the various audience rating services,
we have seen that the methods of every single one of them are
susceptible to either instrument or sampling errors. As mentioned
earlier, I am convinced that the major audience rating services,
without exception, have excellent researchers planning their studies, but because of the nature of the behavior that is being studied
—television viewing—the operational end of such research is
bound to be affected by the kinds of errors that we mentioned
which, unfortunately, cannot be easily offset by even the best planning. Therefore, aside from anything further that can be said about
audience ratings, these problems involved in implementing such
audience studies tend to seriously impair their accuracy. They
also provide at least a partial explanation, of course, of the frequent inconsistencies among the reported results of the various
services.

Incidentally, another basis for this inconsistency lies in the fact
that a kind of rank order of television programs is drawn from
the rating data. Since a margin of error has to be contended with
in the rating of any specific program during a particular rating
interval, such error may cause chance rank order differences among
the various rating services. In order to overcome this source of
error, it would have to be recognized that comparisons of the rankings of specific programs over several rating intervals to determine
long-term trends should ideally be incorporated. In the opinion of
Dr. Samuel Becker, chairman of the NAEB Research Committee,
such analysis of program rankings would demonstrate greater reliability than could be obtained from making comparisons among
the services on the basis of any given week's ratings.

To confound the picture even more, however, the data obtained
by the rating services are placed in the hands of individuals who
see them in the setting of advertising economics and use them in

a manner which tends to distort further the over-all picture of audience ratings. If you were the account executive of an advertising agency, the temptation would be great to cite only the results of the rating service which rated your program most advantageously. Moreover, if only national program results are purchased, and these national results are favorable to the program being sold, it might be a great temptation to misrepresent national results as being applicable to certain regions in which sponsorship for the program is sought, when such representation, as we pointed out earlier, is by no stretch of the imagination based on a representative sample. To remedy this situation, most of the rating services also sell regional surveys, of course. But these regional surveys are often sold on a cost-per-sample-television-home basis, which, due to cost-cutting efforts, frequently results in the purchase of rating information not only beset by all of the sampling and instrument errors referred to earlier, but also by the additional problem of samples of inadequate size.

Still another problem in interpretation is the reduction of television ratings to what is technically referred to as a percentile standard score system, which was pioneered by the late C. E. Hooper. This system reduces any audience rating to a kind of percentage basis, with 100 being optimal. The transformation of audience sizes into percentiles leads to an illusion of uniformity which may not be statistically valid. When comparing ratings of 30, for example, on any level, regional or national, we must also take into consideration such problems as the number of viewers or television homes in the universe (depending on which is used as the basis of audience size), the number of television stations in the market, the number of television sets that could be expected to be operating at given times, and so on. You have divided your program schedules into such designations as A, B, and C periods in an attempt to indicate relative numbers of sets that could be expected to be tuned in at various times. Ratings must take such factors into consideration when percentiles are projected into the size of the audience claimed for any program.

It is interesting to note that in the interest of more precision, cumulative viewing patterns are now being considered by some of the rating services. This is important in comparing programs that have multiple weekly presentations with those that have bi-weekly presentations, and so on.

Another example of the kind of problem that is now recognized by some of the rating services is the factor of overlapping viewing behavior, particularly in the case of longer programs such as the so-called "spectaculars." We know that viewers may watch the first portion of one program, switch to another program, and then later switch back to the original program. This kind of behavior on the part of the viewer cannot be ignored in an adequate evaluation of viewing behavior.

These are all examples of the kinds of complex interaction variables that should be very seriously considered in interpreting rating service results and which further underline the difficulties in correctly applying rating service data. As an approach to solving these problems, a form of motivation research, which has begun to permeate the field of market research generally, is now being employed in television audience studies to a greater and greater extent. The basic assumption underlying motivation research as used here is that data obtained from a smaller number of individuals interviewed intensively, although obviously less representative in terms of sampling size, may reveal significant unique audience interests that, from the standpoint of programing strategy, could be a good deal more valuable than simple quantitative statements of sheer audience size, such as most rating services traditionally report.

If we ponder for a moment the notion of a television program designed as a background for the delivery of advertising messages, we may begin wondering whether the kind of quantitative mass appeal so often employed in program content may not eventually create indifference to the advertising message. The viewer, as he becomes more sophisticated, may begin to perceive the fact that the program is designed for a universal target group. He may then tend to react to the sponsor's messages much as he does to form letters, ignoring them in general as having little interest for him as a unique human being. Is it not possible that advertising messages might be more effective in a context of programing directed to a somewhat smaller audience but clearly appealing to the members of that audience as *individuals?*

An example of characteristics of special audiences was apparent in a recent audience study that we completed under terms of a grant from the National Educational Television and Radio Center. In this study in depth of the educational television audience in the Channel 8 signal area, we discovered as we expected, that the size of educational television audiences was very small—so small, in fact, that our criteria of frequency of viewing had to be very crude. We had to designate as "frequent" viewers those who viewed the station as seldom as two times per week or more. A surprising number of respondents viewed the station as infrequently as once a month. Yet even by our crude definition of frequent viewers, the frequent viewers differed significantly from the infrequent or non-viewers. To quote from our research report distributed by the National Educational Television and Radio Center in 1958, "The frequent viewer of educational television does seem to differ from the infrequent or non-viewer in that to a statistically significant extent he is more likely to vote more frequently in elections. He actively discusses the content of the educational television programs he watches with friends, and he appears to feel that he benefits from such discussions. His leisure time activity seems to be dominated by participative self-improvement activities. . . . He is generally more active, information-minded, self-improvement-seeking, and civic-minded than the non-viewer. . . . The frequent viewer appears to be a viewer who counts in the sense that he is inclined to actually put into practice information that he receives."

As you can see, this picture of a minority audience is very provocative since it suggests that the true impact of educational television programing extends beyond the group of actual viewers. Another illustration of the effectiveness of programing directed to a smaller audience can be found in the loyalty of the growing numbers of FM radio listeners. The members of this audience appear to demonstrate their appreciation of special programing by their response to sponsors' appeals. Most reports indicate that FM listeners are more responsive to advertisers' messages than audiences reached through the typical "shotgun" kind of programing which is intended for almost everybody.

If marketing research organizations would expend as much

effort in examining such qualitative aspects of the behavior of television audiences as they do on the usual nose-counting techniques, they would, in my opinion, discover that buying behavior could sometimes be stimulated more successfully by recognizing unique needs of certain individuals in the television audience than by appealing at all times to a mythical common denominator. This is not to say that programing for a mass audience would have no place in the industry but rather it suggests that such upgrading of programing in terms of the interests of different audience groups could not only reduce the intensity of some of the basic criticisms of commercial programing, but also, in the long run, increase the effectiveness of programing as a means of influencing the viewer's buying behavior. This would also, of course, require a vast program for the re-education of advertisers. At a minimum, however, this appears to be a crucial hypothesis that should be thoroughly tested.

Not everyone will agree with all of the observations I have made. But perhaps one might think seriously about the possibilities for upgrading programing which could result from unshackling ourselves from such a limited criterion of programing success as audience size!

9

The "Phantom Anesthetist" of Mattoon: A Field Study of Mass Hysteria

DONALD M. JOHNSON

A retrospective social psychological analysis of the hysteria in a small midwestern town revealed that the cause of the community's concern was nothing more than human imagination. A critical lesson can be learned from this study concerning how fantasy and distortion of facts could even lead to destructive action such as riots. This study is an example of how social psychological methods can assist in deciphering seemingly unexplainable events.

From: *Journal of Abnormal and Social Psychology*, 40: 175–186, 1945. Reprinted by permission of the author and the American Psychological Association.

The story of the "phantom anesthetist" begins in Mattoon, Illinois, on the first night of September 1944 when a woman reported to the police that someone had opened her bedroom window and sprayed her with a sickish, sweet-smelling gas which partially paralyzed her legs and made her ill. Soon other cases with similar symptoms were reported, and the police organized a full-scale effort to catch the "gasser." Some of the Mattoon citizens armed themselves with shotguns and sat on their doorsteps to wait for him; some even claimed that they caught a glimpse of him and heard him pumping his spray gun. As the number of cases increased—as many as seven in one night—and the facilities of the local police seemed inadequate to the size of the task, the state police with radio-equipped squad cars were called in, and scientific crime detection experts went to work, analyzing stray rags for gaseous chemicals and checking the records of patients recently released from state institutions. Before long the "phantom anesthetist" of Mattoon had appeared in newspapers all over the United States, and Mattoon servicemen in New Guinea and India were writing home anxiously inquiring about their wives and mothers. After ten days of such excitement, when all victims had recovered and no substantial clews had been found, the police began to talk of "imagination" and some of the newspapers ran columns on "mass hysteria"; the episode of the "phantom anesthetist" was over.

Journalistically the story died in a few weeks. In the police records the last attack was reported on September 12. Scientifically, however, the episode demands attention as a fascinating psychological phenomenon. Only one case of a "mental epidemic" has been reported in recent years: an outburst of hysterical twitching in a Louisiana high school was described by Schuler and Parenton.[1] They were unable to find any reference in the standard sources to hysterical epidemics in the United States for over forty years, and

NOTE: The writer is indebted to the Research Board of the University of Illinois for financial support of this project, and to Police Commissioner T. V. Wright for his friendly cooperation during the field work at Mattoon. Dr. R. P. Hinshaw kindly looked over the manuscript.

[1] E. A. Schuler and V. J. Parenton, "A Recent Epidemic of Hysteria in a Louisiana High School," *J. Soc. Psychol.*, 1943, XVII, 221–235.

they raise the question whether these phenomena are disappearing. The writer, therefore, undertook an investigation of the Mattoon case, with two general aims: (1) to preserve, for the sake of the record, an accurate account of the events, and (2) to attempt an analysis of the psychological factors involved in these events. The investigation consisted chiefly of an analysis of the records in the Police Department and interviews with those who reported physical symptoms from the gas. The study was begun in the middle of September and continued until the end of the year, but most of the interviewing was done in October. All the work was done by the writer, who assumes responsibility for this report.

THE FACTS OF THE CASE

Mattoon is a small Illinois city, located about 50 miles southeast of the center of the state. The population, according to the 1940 census, was 15,827, of which 98 percent were native-born white. It is surrounded by rather prosperous farm land, and its economy is largely determined by this fact. In addition, it is a junction for the Illinois Central and the New York Central railroads, both of which maintain repair shops at this point. There are a few small industries, a shoe factory, a furniture factory, diesel engine works, a foundry, and the like. All in all it is a fairly typical midwestern city. As a result of the war it has enjoyed a mild boom, but not an upsetting one.

The outlines of the story can be quickly set down as a background for discussion of specific questions. On September 1 about midnight Mrs. A had a friend telephone the police that she and her daughter had been gassed. The police found no signs of an intruder, but Mr. A reported that, when he came home about two hours later, he saw a man run from the window. The police were called again, and again they found nothing. The next evening the Mattoon *Daily Journal-Gazette* carried a front-page story on the "gas attack" and a headline: "ANESTHETIC PROWLER ON LOOSE."

On the following day, Sunday the third, Mr. B reported to the police that he and his wife had had a similar occurrence. In the middle of the night of August 31—the night before Mrs. A's attack—he woke up sick, and retched, and asked his wife if the gas had been left on. When she woke up she was unable to walk. At first they had attributed these symptoms to hot dogs eaten the evening before. About the same time Mr. C, who works nights, told the press that his wife and daughter had likewise been attacked. The daughter woke up coughing and, when Mrs. C got up to take care of her, she could hardly walk. They did not suspect gas until they read the papers next day. These two accounts appeared in the Mattoon paper on September 5, since no paper was printed on Sunday the third or Labor Day the fourth.

On the evening of September 5 two new attacks were recorded. Mrs. D came home with her husband about 10:30, picked up a cloth from the porch, smelled it, and reported that the fumes burned her mouth and lips so badly that they bled. Mr. E, who works nights, reported that his wife heard someone at the bedroom window, smelled gas, and was partially paralyzed by it.

On the sixth three more cases occurred, according to the police records. On the seventh, none; on the eighth, four; on the ninth, five; and on the tenth, seven. This apparently was the climax of the affair, for no cases were reported on the eleventh, only one on the twelfth, and none thereafter.

The symptoms reported were nausea and vomiting, palpitations, paralysis of the legs, dryness of the mouth and throat and, in one case at least, burns about the mouth. All cases recovered rapidly, hence there was little possibility for outside check on the symptoms. Four cases were seen by physicians, who diagnosed all cases as hysteria.

In at least three cases, so the testimony goes, the family dog "must have been gassed also" since he did not bark at the intruder.

Those who reported smelling the gas described it as "a musty smell," "sickish," "like gardenias," or "like cheap perfume." In some cases, though symptoms were reported, the gas was not smelled.

Police activity took several directions. Most important, probably, was the attempt to catch the "mad gasser" *in flagrante delicto*. The police answered all telephone calls as soon as possible and, when the state police came into the picture with modern radio equipment, were often able to surround a house, in the words of the Commissioner of Police, "before the phone was back on the hook." Despite all this and despite the amateur efforts of an excited citizenry, no one was ever apprehended "in the act." Less direct procedures revolved around examination of a few objects found near houses where attacks had been reported, particularly chemical analysis of the cloth found by Mrs. D, and the usual round-up of suspicious characters. The results of these attempts were also negative. On the eleventh the Commissioner of Police put a note in the paper requesting that "roving bands of men and boys should disband," and that guns be put away "because some innocent person may get killed." About the same time the police adopted the policy of having the victims sent to a hospital for examination.

GAS OR HYSTERIA?

Obviously something extraordinary took place in Mattoon, and for its explanation two hypotheses have been advanced. The "gasser" hypothesis asserts that the symptoms were produced by a gas which was sprayed on the victims by some ingenious fiend who has been able to elude the police. This explanation was disseminated by newspapers throughout the country, at the beginning of the episode at least, and it is widely believed in Mattoon at present. The alternative hypothesis is that the symptoms were due to hysteria.

The evidence for the "gasser" hypothesis comes from the reports of the victims concerning their symptoms, reports which are notoriously difficult to check. The fact that vomiting did occur was authenticated in a few cases by outside testimony but, since vomiting could be produced by gas or hysteria or dietary indiscretions, this fact is not crucial. There is plenty of evidence from the police and other observers that the victims were emotionally upset by their experiences, but this too is not a crucial point.

Another difficulty with the "gasser" hypothesis is the self-contradictory demands it makes on the gas. In order to produce effects of the kind reported when sprayed through a window it would have to be a very potent stable anesthetic with rapid action, and at the same time so unstable that it would not affect others in the same room. It would have to be strong enough to produce vomiting and paralysis, and yet leave no observable aftereffects. Study of a standard source on anesthetics and war gases[2] and consultation with medical and chemical colleagues at the University of Illinois indicates that the existence of such a gas is highly improbable. Chemists are extremely skeptical of the possibility that such an extraordinary gas could be produced by some "mad genius" working in a basement.

Several people reported seeing a prowler who might be the "anesthetist." This too is not an important matter since prowlers have been reported to the police in Mattoon once or twice a week for several years. And, of course, prowlers do not produce paralysis or dry throats.

A minor weakness in the gas hypothesis is the lack of a motive. No money was stolen, and the circumstances were such that there would be little gratification for a peeper.

The best evidence for the hysteria hypothesis is the nature of the symptoms and the fact that those cases seen by physicians— though there were only four—were diagnosed as hysteria. All symptoms reported are common in hysteria and can be found in the medical literature for many years back. For example, here is a description of a mild hysterical attack dated about a hundred years ago. Janet[3] quotes it from Briquet:

> I choose, for an example, what happens to a woman somewhat impressionable who experiences a quick and lively emotion. She instantly feels a constriction at the epigastrium; experiences oppression, her heart palpitates, something rises in her throat and chokes her; in short, she feels in all her limbs a discomfort which causes them in a way to drop; or else it is an agitation, a necessity for movement, which causes a contraction of the muscles. This is indeed the exact model of the most common hysterical accident, of the most ordinary hysterical spasm.

The hypothesis of hysteria accounts for the rapid recovery of all victims and the lack of aftereffects. It explains why no "gasser"

[2]L. Goodman and A. Gilman, *The Pharmacological Basis of Therapeutics* (New York: The Macmillan Co., 1940).

[3]P. Janet, *The Mental State of Hystericals* (New York: G. P. Putnam's Sons, 1901), pp. 376–377.

was found in spite of mobilization of local and state police and volunteers. It accounts for the fact that nothing was stolen and that dogs did not bark. The objections to the hypothesis of hysteria come from the victims themselves—quite naturally—and from others who do not realize the intensity and variety of effects which are produced by psychological forces.

Some who like compromises may argue that these two explanations are not exclusive, that there may have been a "gasser" at first even though the later spread of the symptoms was an hysterical phenomenon. The "anesthetist" soon became scared and ceased his fiendish activities. We may grant the charm of compromise as a general thing but insist that the above arguments still hold—for the first part of the episode as well as the last. The hypothesis of hysteria fits all the evidence, without remainder.

QUANTITATIVE DATA ON CHRONOLOGY

If we consider the whole affair as a psychogenic one, as a "mental epidemic" due chiefly to suggestion, the sequence of events takes on a particular significance, and fortunately a more or less objective chronology of the case is furnished by records of telephone calls to the Police Department. In the Mattoon Police Department the desk sergeant regularly records the date and time of all calls and a brief note of the nature of the call and subsequent police action. From these records calls specifically reporting a "gassing" were easily segregated. Another category of calls, usually designated as "prowler calls" by the police, was found to be useful. This designation means that someone phoned and reported that a man was acting strangely on the street, or that noises were heard on the back porch, and that, when the police answered the call, they could find no evidence of any damage or break-in. The records were broken down in this way for the period of the excitement and a few weeks before and after.[4] Figure 1 shows the trends which appear when these data are grouped into weekly intervals.

[4]The writer is very grateful to Sgt. Edward Davidson for carrying out a day-by-day analysis of these records.

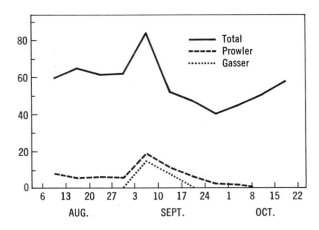

Figure 1.   Analysis of records of telephone calls to the Mat-toon police department. Gasser calls begin on September 2, increase rapidly, and decrease rapidly to zero. Prowler calls, which develop out of an unstructured situation, begin in this graph at their average level, rise with the excitement of the gasser episode, and fall to zero as contrasuggestibility develops. Total calls at the police station begin at the average level, rise with the increase in gasser activities, decline as contrasuggestibility develops, then return to the average level.

The "gasser" curve starts from zero, reaches a peak rapidly, and rapidly returns to the baseline, as one would expect. (The decline is actually quite sharp, as noted earlier, though in the figure it appears more gradual than the rise because of the grouping into weekly intervals.) The "prowler" curve rises and falls with the "gasser" curve, a parallel which cannot be merely coincidental. Since the police do not list a call as a "prowler" call if they find evidence of damage or entry, it is likely that these calls result, in many cases at least, from psychological causes operating in a vague or ambiguous perceptual situation. Thus, during a period of great excitement like a manhunt, when anticipation is intense, the number of "prowler" calls would increase. Similarly, as the excitement subsides, the number of such calls would subside. The most striking fact is that there were so few "prowler" calls in the last part of September and none whatever in October until just before Hallowe'en. This is very unusual, according to the police, and a check of the records for the same months in 1943 discloses no similar fluctuations. The only plausible explanation is that the lack of "prowler" calls results from the development of contrasuggestibility. After hearing of the "phantom anesthetist" and then of "imagination" and "hysteria," the people who ordinarily would have called the police when they heard a suspicious noise became critical and inhibited their "imagination."

The curve for total calls is similar. Police business in general increased sharply during the "gasser" episode, then declined for a few weeks before coming back to normal.

In the light of the evidence presented thus far it seems proper to speak of a wave of excitement or a "mental epidemic" sweeping through Mattoon. The people who succumbed to the epidemic can be grouped into three classes according to the intensity of their response. In the first class are those who merely put off their evening stroll and locked their windows more carefully than usual. Such conduct would of course be called "sensible" and hardly requires any explanation, but it must be remembered that there were many in Mattoon—perhaps a majority—who completely ignored the incident. In the second class are those who reported to the police that they saw or heard a prowler. A report of this kind indicates a higher level of susceptibility since it means that suggestion enters into and complicates perception. The third class is made up of those who reported physical symptoms from "gassing." The occurrence of the physical symptoms indicates a high degree of suggestibility, on the average at least, and perhaps some constitutional predisposition to physical complaints as well.

AGENCIES OF COMMUNICATION

How was the suggestion carried to all these people so quickly and uniformly? There are three possibilities: direct face-to-face contact between victims, indirect conversation or gossip, and the newspapers. In talking to the victims the investigator attempted to determine when and how each had first heard of the "phantom anesthetist." The replies gave very little evidence of face-to-face contact. With the exception of four cases in which two people lived together and were "attacked" at the same time, it seems that the victims were practically unknown to each other. The possibility of indirect contact through neighborhood chatting is a more likely one, and one which is difficult to check. The chief argument against this avenue of communication is that it takes time, and the "epidemic" spread rapidly. The cases were widely scattered throughout the town, and, as we shall see later, only about a third of the victims had telephones.

As a means of communication the newspaper is, of course, the most effective. According to 1941 figures,[5] 97 percent of Mattoon families read the Mattoon *Daily Journal-Gazette* every evening except Sunday. This is the only paper with a large circulation in Mattoon, and obviously it is the source to which most residents would turn for information in a case of this kind. It is necessary, therefore, to examine the *Journal-Gazette*'s treatment of the story and to analyze its psychological influence.

The Mattoon *Daily Journal-Gazette*, which usually runs to about eight pages, resembles other small newspapers both in size and in editorial policy. In general its treatment of the news is conservative, and one would expect that its readers have confidence in its reliability. No one would consider it a "sensational" paper. When a headline, "ANESTHETIC PROWLER ON LOOSE," appeared, therefore—as it did Saturday evening, September 2—it was no doubt taken at face value. The story, which ran on the front page in a full column headed "Mrs. (A) and Daughter First Victims," was written as a straightforward news item. Including the headline it covered 47 square inches.[6] In retrospect it makes rather interesting reading. The careful reader's eye is caught particularly by the word "First" in the heading, since only the one case is mentioned. Whether this was an instance of prophetic insight or merely an error is not known, but the word does now, and probably did then, arouse a tingle of anticipation.

[5]Illinois Daily Newspaper Markets. Paul L. Gorham, Leland Bldg., Springfield, Ill.

[6]Measurement of newspaper space, as for our purposes, is not well standardized. In the present analysis the square inch is used, and the figure given include headlines and photographs as well as text. Those who like to think in terms of the column inch can halve these figures and get the length of a *standard two-inch column* which would contain the material.

On the next two days, Sunday and Labor Day, no paper was printed, but on Tuesday, the fifth, 26 square inches appeared on page six. On the sixth there were 40 square inches, including a headline, on the front page. On the seventh, 29 square inches were used, including a headline, "MAD ANESTHETIST STRIKES AGAIN." No headline was used on the eighth and only 28 square inches of space. Objectively and in terms of newspaper space the excitement seemed to be dying down. But note the first paragraph:

> Mattoon's "mad anesthetist" apparently took a respite from his maniacal forays Thursday night and while many terror stricken people were somewhat relieved they were inclined to hold their breath and wonder when and where he might strike next.

Several attacks were reported that night, and on the evening of the ninth a three-quarter-inch headline was used, crowding the war news to a secondary position. In all, the story took up 51 square inches of space. Evidently the climax is approaching. Up to this point the reader is treated to an absorbing horror story—with a mysterious marauder whose "maniacal forays" increase in a fantastic crescendo, a frightful new scientific device for gassing the victims, and a succession of tantalizing clews. His interest may be aroused to the point where he participates in the manhunt—vicariously, through reading about the scientific investigations of the state crime-detection experts or trying out his own hunches, or actually, by following the police cars or patrolling the streets. In other cases it was not the thrill of the chase which was aroused but apprehension and fear. It was in these people that the hysterical symptoms appeared.

On the eleventh (the tenth was Sunday) the tone of the story changes. Although 62 square inches were given to the story, the headline contained the phrase "few real" and the treatment is critical. No headline was used on the twelfth and the keynote phrase was "hysteria abates"; the story took up 28 square inches. The next evening a comical twist is given to the affair, expanding it to 59 square inches about two false alarms which turned out to be a black cat and a doctor trying to break into his own office after he had forgotten his keys. On the fourteenth the account falls to 19 square inches, and next evening it is put back on page six with only 14 square inches, although a box of 10 square inches appeared on the front page telling how widely the story had been circulated.

The *Journal-Gazette* dropped the affair from this point to the twentieth, when an editorial was printed, apparently in reply to some ribbing by a Decatur paper. The editorial asserted that, although much of the excitement may have been due to hysteria, there really had been some odors in Mattoon—perhaps blown up from Decatur. With this epilogue the drama takes its leave from the columns of the Mattoon *Daily Journal-Gazette*.

Of the out-of-town newspapers the *Chicago Daily Tribune* and the *Chicago Daily News* have the largest circulations in Mattoon, with coverages of 24 percent and 20 percent respectively.[7] The *Tribune* started the story on the sixth with 10 square inches and gave it 20 to 30 square inches each day thereafter until the fifteenth. The editorial viewpoint of the story became skeptical about the twelfth. The *Daily News*'s treatment was similar except that it ran photographs and did not question the authenticity of the "anesthetist." These papers have enough circulation in Mattoon to have an important influence but, since they came in late and since their readers read the local paper also, their influence was probably merely one of emphasis and reinforcement.

The *Chicago Herald-American*, though its coverage in Mattoon is only about 5 percent,[8] handled the story most thoroughly and most sensationally. Its text and photographs were often cited to the investigator. It started late—on the eighth—with 41 square inches, including a photograph. The opening paragraphs of the front-page story which appeared on the tenth are worth quoting:

> Groggy as Londoners under protracted aerial blitzing, this town's bewildered citizens reeled today under the repeated attacks of a mad anesthetist who has sprayed a deadly nerve gas into 13 homes and has knocked out 27 victims.
>
> Seventy others, dashing to the area in response to the alarm, fell under the influence of the gas last night.
>
> All skepticism has vanished and Mattoon grimly concedes it must fight haphazardly against a demented phantom adversary who has been seen only fleetingly and so far has evaded traps laid by city and state police and posses of townsmen.

[7]Illinois Daily Newspaper Markets, *op. cit.*
[8]*Ibid.*

By the eleventh the story was up to 71 square inches, including a 1½-inch headline: "STATE HUNTS GAS MADMAN." On the twelfth it was given 95 square inches, with pictures of crying babies on the front page. After that the account becomes somewhat critical but continues to carry hints that the "gasser" may be a woman, or an apeman, and the like. On Sunday, the seventeenth, however, after the other papers had dropped the story, the *Herald-American* printed a long interview with a psychiatrist, Dr. Harold Hulburt, beginning at the top of the front page above the headline, and covering 196 square inches, with several photographs. This article discusses the dynamics of hysteria in general and includes some sympathetic conjectures regarding unconscious motives of Mrs. A. Further articles resulting from the interview with the psychiatrist appeared on the eighteenth and the twentieth. On December 3 *The American Weekly*, a Sunday supplement of the *Herald-American*, carried a full-page article by Donald Laird entitled "The Manhunt for Mr. Nobody."

The story was carried by the press services and was used or ignored by newspapers throughout the country according to their editorial policies. The *New York Times*, for instance, did not refer to it, while *PM* had 12 square inches on the seventh and 5 on the twelfth. The *Stars & Stripes* (London Edition) carried 7 square inches on the eleventh. Among the weeklies, *Newsweek* for September 18 carried 20 square inches, while *Time* for the same date carried 26. Both of these accounts were skeptical—*Time* was even sarcastic—but neither dared come to any definite conclusions. *Time* elevated the number of cases at the peak from seven to seventeen. *Dispatch*, a weekly of the Persian Gulf Command, gave it 13 square inches on the eighteenth.[9]

Striking evidence of the interest aroused by these accounts comes from the large number of letters and telegrams—estimated at about 300—which were received by Mattoon officials from all over the United States. The writer examined a sample of 30 of these and found half of them more-or-less sensible, though ill-informed, containing suggestions for capturing the "menace." The other half

---

[9]Radio treatment of the story was not considered important enough to warrant study. There is no radio station at Mattoon, and no one in Mattoon or elsewhere mentioned a radio account to the investigator. In general, radio editors treat these stories conservatively.

could be judged psychopathic—on the basis of ideas of self-reference, intensity of affect, and the combination of poor judgment with good vocabulary and expression. Paranoid trends were common.

CHARACTERISTICS OF THE SUSCEPTIBLE SAMPLE

Thus far in our investigation we have treated the Mattoon affair as a social phenomenon. The next question, and perhaps the most important, concerns the individuals in the affair. Why were some people susceptible while their next-door neighbors were not? Phrased in more workable form the question becomes one of finding differences between the susceptible sample and the rest of the population of Mattoon. The experimental literature on suggestibility and the clinical literature on hysteria offered several attractive hypotheses for check, but the nature of the case put a distinct limitation on the methods which could be used. It was apparent from the first few interviews that the victims, while they would talk about the "gassing," and their symptoms, and similar superficial matters, would not be willing to cooperate in any inquiry directed toward, for example, unconscious motivation. They had been victimized twice: once by the concatenation of factors, environmental and personal, which produced the symptoms, and later by publicity and gossip, which carried the implication that people who have hysterical attacks are more peculiar, or less sincere, than their neighbors. For these reasons the best one could hope for was a description of the sample in respect of a few objective characteristics.

The 1940 Census Reports[10] give data on a number of characteristics of the Mattoon population; getting the same data for our sample would permit a comparison in these respects. Those characteristics were selected which seemed easy to verify and of possible significance for the present problem: age, sex, schooling, economic level, and occupation. Age was estimated and, in doubtful cases, checked by the estimates of acquaintances. To get a picture of the

[10]U.S. Bureau of the Census, *16th census of the U.S.* (Washington, D.C.: U.S. Govt. Printing Office, 1942).

economic level of the sample four conveniences were used as indices: radio, mechanical refrigerator, electricity, and telephone. Percentages for the first three are given in the Census Reports. The number of residential telephones in Mattoon was kindly furnished by the manager of the local telephone agency, and the percentage computed in reference to the number of occupied dwelling units given in the Census Reports. The Census Bureau's descriptions of their occupational categories were studied before the interviewing began so that the necessary data could be obtained. For example, the Reports state specifically that railway brakemen are classed as "Operatives" while locomotive engineers and firemen are classed as "Craftsmen, Foremen and Kindred Workers." Furthermore in a small town like Mattoon the variety of jobs is limited and cross-checking is relatively easy. Hence placing the occupations of the sample into the Census Bureau's categories offered less difficulty than might be expected. A woman's occupation was used if she worked, otherwise her husband's. (Only two women had husbands in military service. One of these worked, hence her own occupation was used. In the other case the husband had been inducted only recently, so his civilian occupation was used.) All these data are brought together in Table 1 for comparison with similar data for the total population of Mattoon.

Statistically speaking, the sample is small; the number of cases on which the percentages in Table 1 are based varies from 14 for schooling to 29 for sex. The table includes, however, nearly all the cases in which physical symptoms were reported. The investigator checked police records and newspaper accounts for names and found a few others while interviewing. Two people could not be found at home despite repeated calls. Three had left town. One would not talk to the investigator. Some of the data on these were obtained from acquaintances. Table 1 gives us at least a partial description of the people who were most intensely affected by the excitement.

To begin with, the sample has a much greater proportion of women than the general population of the city. This is in agreement with the laboratory studies on suggestibility[11] and the clinical

[11]C. Bird, *Social Psychology* (New York: D. Appleton-Century Co., 1940).

TABLE 1
THE SAMPLE OF "GASSER" VICTIMS COMPARED WITH THE TOTAL
POPULATION OF MATTOON IN RESPECT TO CERTAIN
OBJECTIVE CHARACTERISTICS

	Percentage of sample	Percentage of population
Sex		
Women	93	52
Age		
Below 10	0	14
10–19	0	18
20–29	37	17
30–39	16	15
40–49	21	13
50–59	16	10
60–69	10	7
Over 70	0	6
Education		
Grade school only	71	58
Some high school	29	32
Some college	0	10
Indices of Economic Level		
Electricity	80	95
Radio	80	91
Mechanical refrigerator	28	46
Telephone	33	60
Occupational Categories		
Professional and semi-professional	0	7
Proprietors, managers, and officials	16	13
Clerical, sales, and kindred workers	32	21
Craftsmen, foremen, and kindred workers	5	16
Operatives	37	24
Laborers, farm laborers, and farm foremen	10	5
Domestic service workers	0	5
Service workers, except domestic	0	9

reports on hysteria.[12] All of the cases have been married but one, who was about twenty years old.

Since children are more suggestible than adults,[13] why were there not more children in the sample? Many children probably did accept the suggestion in the sense that they reported to their parents that they saw the "gasser" or smelled the gas. While the dynamics of symptom-formation are not well understood and may be different in each case, it does seem likely that adults would be more inclined to the withdrawing, incapacitating sort of symptoms which appeared in this "epidemic" than children. In the case reported by Schuler and Parenton[14] among high school children the symptoms were of a more positive, lively nature.

In education the sample is below the total population. This too might have been predicted from the literature on suggestibility.

From the economic indices it seems clear that the sample is less prosperous than the population at large, at least in respect to these four conveniences. It is noteworthy that no attacks occurred in either of Mattoon's two high income areas.

Our sample, then, is characterized by low educational and economic level. These two characteristics go together in our culture. In a study similar in some respects to the present study Cantril[15] found that those people who were most strong influenced by the Orson Welles 1938 broadcast, "War of the Worlds," were likewise of low educational and economic level. No doubt it is education which is more directly related to suggestibility. Cantril found that the better educated were more critical in that they made more and better outside checks on the authenticity of the broadcast and thus were less frequently panicked.

The data on occupation are not clear-cut since the categories used by the Census Bureau were not constructed for studies of this kind. As the number of cases on which good occupational

[12]A. J. Rosanoff (ed.), *Manual of Psychiatry* (New York: John Wiley & Sons, Inc., 1920); W. S. Sadler, *Theory and Practice of Psychiatry* (St. Louis: The C. V. Mosby Co., 1936).

[13]Bird, *op. cit.*

[14]*Op. cit.*

[15]H. Cantri, *The Invasion from Mars* (Princeton, N.J.: Princeton University Press, 1940).

data were available was only 19, the number in some categories was small, and some rearrangement was advisable. The category "Farmers and farm managers" was eliminated as there were none in the sample and less than 1 percent in the general population. Professional and semi-professional classes were combined. "Laborers, except farm" was combined with "Farm laborers and farm foremen." The category "Proprietors, managers, and officials" is a broad one which could include a wide variety of people, hence it is of little use to us. The proprietors in our sample were proprietors of small shops and rooming houses.

As it stands Table 1 shows a lack of any professional or semi-professional people, which agrees with the data on educational level. A fairly clear-cut vertical comparison can be made if we consider the craftsmen and foremen as skilled workers, the operatives as semi-skilled, and the laborers as unskilled. The proportion of the sample in these three groups decreases—in comparison with the proportion in the population at large—as the amount of skill increases.

The interviews, one can easily realize, were conducted under rather unfavorable conditions. It was not possible to get any insight into personality makeup of the victims except in a very superficial way. But it was possible usually for the investigator to work in a few general questions about the victim's health. In only fourteen cases was any information obtained in this way, but, of these, eight, or over half, replied with such phrases as "always been nervous," "never sleep much," and "doctoring for nerves." We have no control data for the total population, but the percentage does seem extraordinarily high. The interview data do not go far, but they reinforce the diagnosis of hysteria and show, as far as they go, that, extraordinary as the Mattoon affair may be on the surface, psychologically it follows a familiar pattern.

CONCLUSIONS

Analysis of records available at Mattoon together with the results of interviews with most of the victims leads to the conclusion that the case of the "phantom anesthetist" was entirely psychogenic. There is always the possibility of a prowler, of course, and it is quite likely that some sort of gas could be smelled at various times in Mattoon. But these things do not cause paralysis and palpitations. Hysteria does. The hypothesis of a marauder cannot be supported by any verifiable evidence. The hypothesis of hysteria, on the other hand, accounts for all the facts.

What, then, produced this mass hysteria? There are some gaps in the story, to be sure, but a fairly clear picture can now be drawn. Mrs. A had a mild hysterical attack, an event which is not at all uncommon, which is, on the contrary, familiar to most physicians. The crucial point is that her interpretation of her symptoms was rather dramatic—a quick look through any textbook (e.g., footnote 12) will convince any reader that hysterical symptoms usually are dramatic—arousing the interest of the press, with the result that an exciting uncritical story of the case appeared in the evening paper. As the news spread, other people reported similar symptoms, more exciting stories were written, and so the affair snowballed.

But such acute outbursts are necessarily self-limiting. The bizarre details which captured the public imagination at the beginning of the episode became rather ridiculous when studied more leisurely. The drama of the story lost its tang with time and the absurdities showed through. For example, the volatility of the gas, which was such an asset in penetrating physical barriers, became a liability when anyone tried to capture the gas and examine it. The facts seemed to evaporate as rapidly as the agent which produced them. At last the failure of the police and volunteers to find anyone or anything tangible (the best the news photographers could do was to pose women pointing at windows, babies crying, and men holding shotguns) combined with the statements of city officials in the paper produced a more critical public attitude. The attacks ceased. The critical attitude increased and spread, however; police business struck a new low. It is proper to say that the wave of suggestibility in Mattoon left a wave of contrasuggestibility in its wake. Objective records document this generalization.

Naturally the more suggestible people accepted the story at face value. Of these only a small percentage reported physical symptoms from "gassing," presumably because of some personal motivation toward, or gratification from, such symptoms. As might be predicted from psychological and psychiatric literature, those who succumbed to the "mental epidemic" were mostly women and were, on the average, below the general population in educational and economic level. This supports the above analysis and puts the "phantom anesthetist" of Mattoon, in some aspects at least, into a familiar psychological pattern.

10

The Connecticut Speed Crackdown: A Study of the Effects of Legal Change

H. LAURENCE ROSS and
DONALD T. CAMPBELL

As the present paper demonstrates, the social psychologist can make valuable contributions in assessing the actual, long-term effects of social and legal reforms. Through the use of ingenious methodological analyses, the present investigators reveal that what was thought to be an effective legal procedure, an intensive crackdown on speeding, actually created no more reduction in the accident rate than would have been expected to occur without a crackdown over a period of time.

This application of social psychological methodology points to the necessity for careful and systematic evaluation of various social programs to discover those that truly contribute to the advancement of mankind.

From: H. L. Ross, ed., *Perspectives on the Social Order*, Second Edition (New York: McGraw-Hill Book Co., 1968), pp. 30–35. Reprinted by permission of the authors and publisher.

In 1955, the state of Connecticut introduced a campaign to
reduce highway fatalities through enforcement of speed limit laws.
We report here the results of a study of this campaign, with two
goals in mind. First, with our methodology we wish to illustrate
some pitfalls of uncritical interpretations of change and to demonstrate some more dependable ways in which to evaluate the effects
of changes in law and other systems of social control. Second,
although our findings are limited to the case at hand, we wish to
suggest some problems and unforeseen results that may accompany attempts to change behavior by law enforcement.

Automobile accidents caused 324 deaths in Connecticut in 1955.
This was a record high for the decade of the fifties. As the hazardous Christmas holidays approached, Governor Abraham Ribicoff
initiated an unprecedented attempt to control traffic deaths by law
enforcement, in the form of a crackdown on speeders. He acted
in the belief that excess speed was a common contributing factor
in traffic deaths, that control of speed would result in diminished
fatalities, and that this control could be accomplished by enforcing speed limits. On December 23, Governor Ribicoff announced
that in the future all persons convicted of speeding in Connecticut
would have their licenses suspended for thirty days on the first
offense, with longer periods of suspension for repeating offenders.
The decree was put into force through the Governor's power of
appointment over local judges, who were told that reappointment
in 1957 would be denied to those who appeared lax in conviction
of speeders, or who did not recommend to the Motor Vehicle
Department the suspension of drivers' licenses for this offense.

In the first three months of 1956, license suspensions for speeding numbered 2,855, an increase of almost 2,700 over the corresponding period in 1955. There were 10 fewer fatalities, and
765 fewer arrests for speeding. The Governor was quoted as saying: "This is positive proof that operators are not only driving
slower, but are driving better."

By the end of June there were 22 fewer fatalities than in the
first six months of 1955, representing a 15 per cent reduction.
Suspensions for speeding had risen from 231 to 5,398, and arrests

had declined from 4,377 to 2,735. Ribicoff announced: "Connecticut has succeeded in stopping the upward surge in highway deaths, and in the first six months of this year, contrary to the national trend, we have saved lives. Fewer people died on the highways this year than in the same period last year, in Connecticut. We did it by enforcing the law, something the safety experts said couldn't be done because the people wouldn't be behind it."

In the late summer Connecticut experienced a very high number of traffic fatalities, and by the beginning of September deaths almost equaled those of the previous year. However, fatalities were fewer in the fall, and by the end of the year Connecticut counted a total of 284 traffic deaths, as compared with 324 in 1955. Governor Ribicoff concluded: "With the saving of forty lives in 1956, a reduction of 12.3 per cent from the 1955 motor vehicle death toll, we can say the program is definitely worthwhile."

Our study of the Connecticut speed crackdown is based on analysis of mileage death rates, i.e., the number of deaths per 100 million miles driven in the state. This corrects for the fact that more deaths would be expected in Connecticut during the decade merely because more miles were being driven.

Figure 1 presents the mileage death rates for Connecticut for the years 1955 and 1956, on which Governor Ribicoff based his claims for the effectiveness of his program. If we think of these data as similar to a classical experiment, the 1955 data constitute a pretest, the crackdown is like an experimental treatment, and the 1956 data constitute a posttest.[1] Governor Ribicoff believed the difference between the pretest and the posttest to be the effect of the treatment, an inference that might be valid if the study had

[1]Quasi-experimental methodology is discussed in, e.g., Donald T. Campbell and Julian S. Stanley, "Experimental and Quasi-experimental Designs for Research on Teaching," in Nathan L. Gage, Ed., *Handbook of Research on Teaching*, Chicago: Rand McNally, 1963, pp. 171–246; Donald T. Campbell, "From Description to Experimentation: Interpreting Trends as Quasi-experiments," in Chester W. Harris, Ed., *Problems in Measuring Change*, Madison: University of Wisconsin Press, 1963; Donald T. Campbell and Keith N. Clayton, "Avoiding Regression Effects in Panel Studies of Communication Impact," *Studies in Public Communication*, No. 3, Chicago: Department of Sociology, University of Chicago, 1961, pp. 99–118, reprinted in Bobbs-Merrill Reprints in Sociology as S-353.

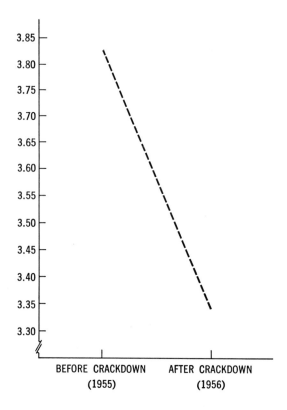

Figure 1.   Pre- and Posttest Measures of Connecticut Traffic
Fatalities per 100 Million Driver Miles.

truly been a classical experiment, subject to controls and randomization of extraneous variables. As the latter was not the case, this
situation, which we term "quasi-experimental," requires independent evidence to rule out several possible alternative explanations
of the observed difference. Some of these, briefly stated, are as
follows:

1. History. This term denotes specific events, other than the
treatment, occurring between the pretest and posttest, which might
independently account for the change. For instance, 1956 might

have had less snow and ice than 1955, this fact rather than the speed crackdown producing the lower death rate.

2. Maturation. This term is taken from psychology, where it refers to changes correlated with the passage of time per se, such as growing older or more tired. Its use is not limited to organic changes, however. Maturation may refer to any general, secular, time-linked changes not the result of discrete events. Potential causes of the change in the Connecticut death rate subsumed under this heading are improved roads and more competent medical care.

3. Testing. A change may occur as a result of the pretest, even without the treatment. In the present instance, the assessment of the death rate for 1955 constitutes the pretest. It is conceivable that publicizing the high death rate for that year may have changed driver caution, and hence changed the death rates for the following year.

4. Instrumentation. This term refers to a shifting of the measuring instrument independent of any change in the phenomenon measured. Such changes are common in sociology, for example, artificial rises in crime rates which occur due to changes in the administration of police records.

5. Regression. Statistical theory tells us that when a group is selected for study because of extreme scores on one test, their scores on a subsequent test will tend to be less extreme, merely as a statistical artifact. As high accident rates for 1955 were cited to justify the crackdown, lower rates for 1956 would be expected due to regression.

6. Instability. A ubiquitous problem in quasi-experimentation is to distinguish "true" changes in a measure from random changes due either to a small population base on which observations are made or to large numbers of change-producing events which, taken individually, we have called history.

The plausibility of these alternative explanations can be evaluated by the systematic use of series of data which are commonly available to the researcher in the situations similar to this. If data are gathered for the years directly prior to and following the treatment, they are usually available for other years as well. A fairly long sequence of observations before and after the treatment allows us to apply the logic of the quasi-experimental model termed the Interrupted Time-Series Design. Figure 2 presents the relevant data for Connecticut.

The data of Figure 2 help us to evaluate maturation and, on certain assumptions, testing as causes of the observed change of Figure 1. For these explanations to be plausible, the observed change should be part of a long-term, secular trend. They would be implausible—and our preferred explanation in terms of the

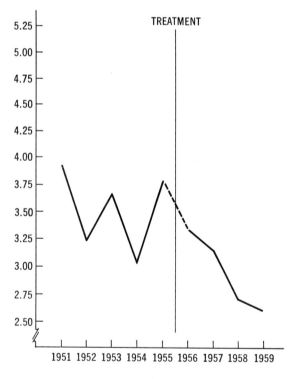

Figure 2.   Interrupted Time-Series Presentation of Connecticut Traffic Fatalities per 100 Million Vehicle Miles.

treatment would be more plausible—if an abrupt change took place at the time of treatment and nowhere else in the series. Unfortunately for Governor Ribicoff's claims, the changes in 1955–1956 seem to be well in accord with these alternative explanations. The fact that 1955–1956 is the third abrupt downward jump in five years, and the smallest of the three, certainly argues against imputing any special causal effects to events occurring at that point.

The likelihood of regression is also supported by the data of Figure 2. The largest upswing in the series occurs in 1954–1955, just prior to the crackdown. This peak is seen even more strongly in the raw death statistics, presented for comparison in Figure 2a. It thus seems quite likely that the high figures of 1955 caused the crackdown, and thus less likely that the crackdown caused the low figures of 1956, for such a drop would have been predicted on grounds of regression in any case.

The graphic presentation of the precrackdown years provides evidence of the general instability of the accidental death rate and makes the supposed effect of Figure 1 now look trivial. Box and Tiao[2] have developed an analytical technique for estimating and making inferences about change in the level of a nonstationary time series, and this technique was applied to our data (in monthly units) by Gene V. Glass.[3] The test was unable to show a significant shift at the time of the crackdown.

In the case at hand it was possible to improve on the methodology discussed up to now by constructing a type of control group of adjacent and similar states: New York, Massachusetts, Rhode Island, and New Jersey. This is a Multiple Time-Series Design. It provides a quasi-experimental control for history, which is not possible with single Interrupted Time-Series, and acts as an additional check on maturation, testing, and instrumentation. The data are presented in Figure 3. A significant fact in this comparison is that prior to the crackdown Connecticut's rate is rising relative to the other states, but afterwards its rate is falling. Glass's

[2]E. P. Box and G. C. Tiao, "A Change in Level of a Non-stationary Time Series," *Biometrika*, 52 (1965), pp. 181–192.

[3]Gene V. Glass, "Analysis of Data on the Connecticut Speeding Crackdown as a Time-Series Quasi-experiment," Research Paper #1, Laboratory of Educational Research, University of Colorado, July, 1967.

analysis applied to these data does show a statistically significant reduction in fatalities associated with the speed crackdown. However, the change appears minute, and the continuing possibility of regression as a cause of the shift renders enthusiastic support of the hypothesis very difficult.

Some additional analyses were made to illustrate further the use of time-series methodology, and to show that the crackdown had a real effect in the legal system and that it produced some

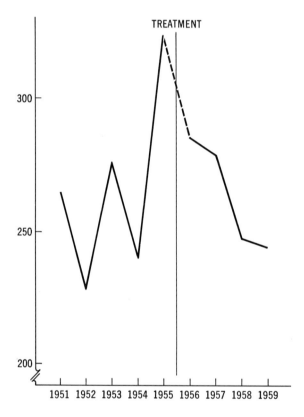

Figure 2a.   Interrupted Time-Series Presentation of Traffic Deaths in Connecticut (Raw Figures).

unanticipated and unintended consequences. No control-state figures were obtained, but the single-state time-series are quite convincing.

Figure 4 provides evidence that the crackdown was put into effect as indicated by a great increase in suspensions of licenses for speeding.

Figure 5 plots the percentage which speeding violations constitute of all traffic violations. This shows a decline, ostensibly due

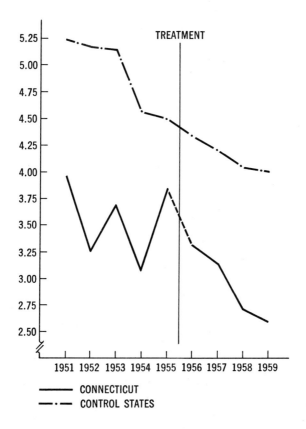

Figure 3.   Multiple Time-Series Comparing Connecticut Fatalities with Those of Four Comparable States.

to greater conformity to speed limits, although it is also likely that policemen and prosecutors were more willing to overlook minor infractions or to charge them as something else.

Figure 6 concerns persons whose licenses were further suspended because they were convicted of driving with a suspended license. As a percentage of all suspensions, this jumps from an almost consistent zero to some 4 to 6 per cent. Our interpretation of this phenomenon is that automobile transportation has become a virtual necessity for many residents of the diffusely settled megalopolitan region that includes Connecticut and that these people are willing to risk very severe punishments in order to continue daily routines that involve driving.

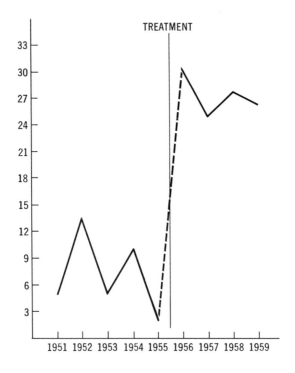

Figure 4.   Suspensions of Licenses for Speeding, as a Percentage of All Suspensions.

Figure 7 shows a reaction of the legal system to the administratively imposed crackdown. Even with fewer speeding violations reaching the courts, the courts were more lenient in their handling of these cases, as expressed by proportions of not-guilty judgments. Such leniency could be the result of more generous handling by judges and prosecutors or of more vigorous defenses by the accused because more is at stake. The two effects shown in Figures 6 and 7 indicate a vitiation of the punitive effects of the crackdown in a society that acknowledges dependence on automobile transportation.

In conclusion, our analysis has shown that the Connecticut crackdown on speeding was a substantial enforcement effort, though its most punitive aspects were mitigated in practice by fewer arrests

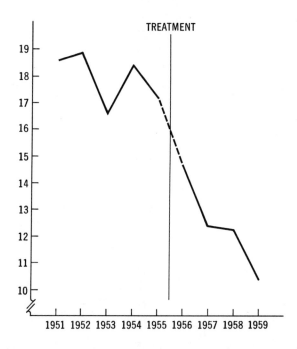

Figure 5.   Speeding Violations, as a Percentage of All Traffic Violations.

and convictions and by a willingness of some people to drive with suspended licenses. As to its effects, we are forced to conclude that they comprised no substantial reduction in traffic fatalities.

More important, we believe, than the specific findings of the study is the methodology here exemplified. While the social scientist cannot as a rule truly experiment on a societal scale, abrupt focused social change is continually going on, especially in the legal realm, and it can be evaluated by the careful researcher despite the lack of classical controls. We hope that familiarity with quasi-experimental techniques such as Time-Series will increase the ambitions as well as the results of sociologists who study societal changes.

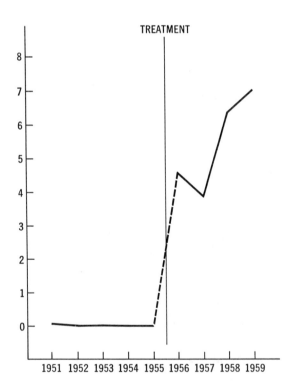

Figure 6.   Arrested while Driving with a Suspended License, as a Percentage of Suspensions.

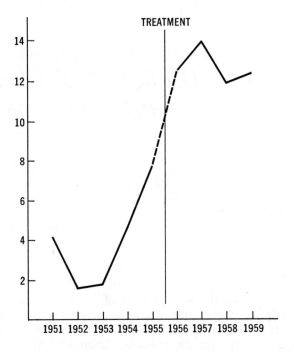

Figure 7.   Percentage of Speeding Violations Judged Not Guilty.

11

The Behavioral Scientist as a Public Informant

RICHARD I. EVANS

More and more the social scientist is called upon by the mass media to convey his "expert" opinion about immediate matters of public concern. In many instances, this situation creates a dilemma for the scientist: Should he allow his private opinion to be expressed even though he is in a sense increasing his perceived credibility by playing the role of a scientist? As the author points out, it is, in most instances, impossible for the social scientist to give definitive "answers" to contemporary social issues because of the lack of agreement among social scientists themselves concerning theory, methodology, and priority of interests.

The present report discusses in detail this dilemma and suggests a possible solution which is tested for its effectiveness in an actual "dilemma" situation on a television program involving a debate with a leader of an extremist political organization. Whether or not one agrees with the position of maintaining an "analytic objective" position, it is of importance that society be aware of the problems faced by the conscientious social psychological investigator when he honestly tries to live up to society's expectations of a scientist in such discussion.

From: *Journal of Social Issues*, 19(2): 107–112, 1963. Reprinted by permission of The Society for the Psychological Study of Social Issues.

With the increasing role of mass communications in our culture today, it becomes clear that the behavioral scientist will be called upon more and more to present his views through media such as television. In very recent history this trend became apparent. For example in 1953, when the nation's first non-commercial educational television station began operations at the University of Houston, the writer was asked to offer the first psychology course through this medium. Since then, open-circuit educational television has presented a multitude of courses, not only in psychology, but in sociology, political science, and history. Through the facilities of the over 60 educational television stations alone, the general population has had at least some degree of contact with more behavioral scientists than ever before in the entire history of education. Added to this, with the post-Sputnik interest in the professor and researcher in general, commercial television has involved increasing numbers of behavioral scientists in one capacity or another, ranging from participating on television discussion panels to serving as technical advisors on scripts for dramatic productions.

One question that this situation increasingly presents is, what role should the behavioral scientist play when he is invited to participate on television programs or other public forums dealing with areas of social controversy? It certainly cannot be denied that as a citizen, the behavioral scientist, like any other citizen has the option of participating and making any contribution which he desires, taking any side on controversial issues with which he feels comfortable out of personal conviction. However, because of his academic or research discipline, he is often perceived differently by the general public than is the lay citizen, since he is often an expert on the very issue that may be under discussion. As an expert, his pronouncements on issues would naturally have high source credibility with many members of the audience. Yet, behavioral scientists can hardly serve as ultimate authorities when there is seldom consensus among them in support of one position or another with respect to most controversial social issues. The general public often fails to realize that on many social issues a continuum of expert opinion exists even as continua of lay opinion are present. Still, in any given instance, the public, giving high source credibility to a given expert, may confuse this expert's opinion with fact. Furthermore, in his efforts to communicate

lucidly in such situations, the behavioral scientist may unwittingly
fail to qualify his opinions adequately, since in the heat of discussion the process of qualifying statements may often be unduly
demanding of even the most objective individual.

As an example of this problem and the alternatives it presents,
the extremist groups in the United States may be considered. Discussing them publicly certainly offers an interesting challenge to
the behavioral scientist. As citizens, many behavioral scientists
may be concerned with Communism, the John Birch Society,
pacifists, or the Ku Klux Klan. Their personal reactions may be
strong, yet theoretical conceptualizations of the behavior of such
groups and their impact on society, although provocative, hardly
have yielded, thus far, a baseline of data which justify objectively
definitive conclusions concerning their ultimate danger to society.
What pronouncements concerning them can they make publicly
as professionals, however? If they take public stands as pro- or
anti- such groups, the question may be raised concerning the kinds
of objective (rather than value-laden) information that they may
present in defense of such stands. If they choose to capitalize on
their identification as professionals as a means of increasing their
personal credibility and persuasiveness, however, emphasizing their
own personal convictions and values might be a questionable
procedure by their own objective standards. Still another alternative for the behavioral scientist, by very virtue of these qualifying
circumstances in his role as public informant, is to simply refuse
to participate in public forums concerning extremist groups.

Thus, he can play the citizen role, stating honestly his own
personal feelings toward the group, and attempt to disclaim his
expertness in such a manner that he is not exploiting his professional label to reinforce his personal influence; he can play the role
of the authority attempting to bring expert judgment to bear on
the issue while maintaining that theory and data are insufficient
to arrive at irrefutable conclusions concerning extremist groups;
or he can simply elect not to participate at all in public discussions
concerning extremist groups.

Among these extremes are many possible variations, of course.
Let us consider one. In the writer's opinion, the role most com-
fortably assumed in such situations by the professional is one of
objective analysis. Not only is this the fundamental framework
of research by the behavioral scientist, but it is essentially the

traditional pattern of classroom instruction. It might be argued that if he plays such a role in the classroom while discussing radical groups, the argument that he should withdraw from public participation because of possible misperceptions by the audience does not hold. Students as target groups of communication are subject to the same perceptions or misperceptions as the general public. The role of objective analyzer, in the best tradition of education, in or out of the classroom, allows the uncommitted individual member of the audience to make his own decisions concerning the extremist group being discussed by virtue of a "new look" at this group, not available through biased appraisals of extremist groups most often made available to him.

However, our models of attitude change hold little promise for the effectiveness of such an analytical approach in influencing the attitudes or cognitions of individuals already strongly committed for or against a radical group. On the other hand, however, none of the other possible roles for the behavioral scientist mentioned earlier can be effective with individuals already holding extreme views toward a radical group either. In fact, some current theories suggest that such strong statements may even defensively strengthen existing attitudes or cognitions.

Consequently, it might be worth exploring the possibility that objective analyses of these groups by behavioral scientists in public discussions, projected particularly to the uncommitted portion of the general population, may be one of the most effective means of challenging them. In other words, if he is willing to communicate such objective analyses of extreme ideological groups, it is the writer's opinion that the behavioral scientist in our culture may very well be able to make an effective "action" contribution as a public informant and do justice to the credibility of the perception of his role as a scientist or educator referred to earlier. It might be further postulated that functioning as an "action person" by expressing strongly his *personal* values concerning such groups in the manner discussed earlier, the behavioral scientist may no longer be able to hide behind his professional cloak of immunity from the same sort of criticism from the general public to which any citizen may be susceptible when he ventures into community conflict.

As a participant-observer in a situation several months ago the writer was able to explore the range of possibilities examined so far, impressionistically at least. This situation occurred in Houston in an incident involving Dr. Fred Schwarz and his Christian Anti-Communism Crusade. Dr. Schwarz and a collaborator, Mr. William Strube, Jr., sought and received permission from a Houston commercial television station to appear on a regularly scheduled midnight discussion program for a period of five nights in succession (Monday through Friday) to tell the story of the Christian Anti-Communism Crusade. Although the station management allowed an initial forty-minute presentation by Schwarz and Strube on each program, it was to be followed by two different citizens of the community each night appearing in open discussion and rebuttal. The citizens who were invited to participate included local university professors representing behavioral science areas, attorneys, journalists, clergymen, and businessmen. These telecasts were allowed to continue until the discussion began to dwindle—often for as long as two and one-half hours. Response to the programs indicated that great numbers of viewers watched, spellbound by this interesting, often testy, series of discussions which took the form of name-calling, intense emotionality, sarcasm, and occasionally honest debate. The writer, who was asked to appear on the last evening of the series along with an articulate member of the clergy, was in a position to explore his own behavior in such a situation.

The program's producer estimated from a station mail response that the constellation of attitudes toward the Christian Anti-Communism Crusade of members of the audience for these telecasts might be described as more supportive than rejecting. It might be also concluded that as is found in investigations of such social attitudes in a population of television viewers most individuals would be indifferent or undecided.

As the behavioral scientist finds himself in this pattern, he may raise the question (from the standpoint of impact) to which of these attitudinal sub-groups—(favorable, unfavorable, middle)—can he most effectively address himself. If he personally is opposed to or supportive of such a movement and addresses himself to the group that shares his personal views, even if he attempts to be analytical, he may be unconsciously seeking good will and commendation from the members of his "attitudinal reference group" with whom, of course, he identifies. This behavior is obviously not compatible with the objective analytical approach which he is attempting to pursue. In fact, neither of these extreme sub-groups (supportive or rejecting) of a movement such as the Christian Anti-Communist Crusade would likely modify or change their existing attitudes on the basis of truly objective, analytical content of a single television program, challenging as it might be. Suppose for a moment, however, that he chose to present this objective, analytical position directed primarily at the uncommitted, theoretically, middle sub-group of the television audience. He would not now be attempting to challenge *existing* attitudes toward the Crusade. He would instead be attempting to engage in a maximum educational effort for a group that is, theoretically at least, most receptive to it.

This is the approach the present writer elected to take in this instance. When he was called on during the course of the television broadcast to make his presentation, he elected to utilize an objective, analytical approach directed toward the middle group of the audience. He simply went to a blackboard and outlined an analysis of the Christian Anti-Communism Crusade in terms of a simple communication theory model (source-goals-message-channel-target). For example, he asked Dr. Schwarz and his colleague to detail who was behind this movement, its goals, and the persuasion techniques in its message, that is, the ideas presented by Schwarz and Strube. Continuing in this vein, he inquired of Schwarz and Strube what they believed the target group of their Crusade was, and so on.

This process of discussing systematically the Crusade within the framework of a simple communication model was essentially a rational discussion in which reversion to emotionality on the part of Schwarz or Strube or for that matter the writer became painfully apparent to the viewer through the sensitive eye of the television camera, according to viewers' reports later. As Schwarz and Strube began to unfold the story of the Christian Anti-Communist Crusade within this communication model, it was very clear that they became more candid at times than they wished—and less able to employ emotional appeals.

Although no systematic evaluation of the impact of these telecasts on viewers was made (because of lack of preparation time), mail response, telephone calls, or informal discussion supplied some support of the thesis presented by the writer at the beginning of this presentation. Such support is gained from the following typical estimates of viewer reaction:

1. Responses from many viewers apparently *supportive* or *indifferent* to the Crusade alike indicated severe criticism of *all* participants including behavioral scientists, who were "discourteous," particularly to Schwarz by employing emotional techniques such as name-calling. Some particularly formidable anti-Crusade presentations may have thus lost considerable impact, superficial though such criticism appears to be, because of the concern with such courtesy in the culture of East Texas.

2. Many viewers apparently hostile to the Crusade were "reinforced" by the formidable anti-Crusade presentations, including those by behavioral scientists, and tended to respond to emotional techniques such as sarcasm or name-calling as a display of "guts" by the participant employing them. Although some of these viewers responded favorably to the analytic technique employed by the present writer, others labeled it as overly conservative.

3. The originally apparently middle or uncommitted sub-group of viewers in some instances openly suggested that they were now seriously considering *support* of the Crusade, and in a few other instances were now becoming *displeased* with the Crusade. The presentation of the present writer was frequently cited by this group as a deterrent to their committing themselves to the Crusade, and frequently seemed to instill a need to explore more carefully its motives.

Obviously, the very nature of the participant-observer role of the speaker in his television interaction with Schwarz and Strube and the lack of hard, evaluative data allows us to use this particular experience as the basis for no more than tentative hypothesis about the relative impact of the "analytical action role" of the behavioral scientist as compared with a qualified or unqualified expression of his own values in this situation. However, the writer does suggest that with the increasing prestige of the behavioral scientist in our society, the professional skill of the behavioral scientist as an objective analyzer of extremist ideological groups— or for that matter any issues of social controversy—may be a powerful contemporary application of the Socratic position of "letting the truth be known."

PART TWO

Experimental Manipulation

12

Models and Helping: Naturalistic Studies in Aiding Behavior

JAMES H. BRYAN and
MARY ANN TEST

It is well known in psychology that under certain conditions people, after observing another's behavior, will themselves behave in a similar fashion. These investigators point out that most studies dealing with adult imitation or conformity involving self-sacrificial behavior have been conducted in university laboratory settings where pressures to conform are unusually high. Will the results generated from laboratory experiments be consistent with those obtained from modeling experiments conducted in real-life situations? This crucial question is the major concern of this report.

A series of experiments was carried out in novel situations outside the laboratory. It is interesting to follow this series of experiments since the questions raised by the first experiment lead to execution of the second and likewise for the third and fourth. These investigators are keenly aware of the methodological difficulties of carrying out experiments in natural settings and set an excellent example in social scientific writing by carefully pointing out other plausible, alternative ways in which their results could be explained. This report also emphasizes a principle especially important in social science: Greater confidence in a particular experimental result

is gained if this result can be consistently demonstrated
across a wide variety of settings, people, and experimental
tasks.

Recently, concern has been evidenced regarding the determinants
and correlates of altruistic behavior, those acts wherein individuals
share or sacrifice a presumed positive reinforcer for no apparent
social or material gain. Studies addressed to these behaviors have
explored both individual differences in the tendency to be altruistic
and the situational determinants of such responses. Gore and
Rotter (1963) found that students at a southern Negro college
were more likely to volunteer for a social protest movement if
they perceived sources of reinforcement as internally rather than
externally guided. Subjects high on internal control were more
likely to volunteer as freedom riders, marchers, or petition signers
than subjects who perceived others as primary agents of reinforcement. Experimental evidence has been generated supporting the
often-made assumption that guilt may serve as a stimulus to altruistic activity. Darlington and Macker (1966) found that subjects
led to believe that they had harmed another through incompetent
performances on the experimental tasks (three paper-and-pencil

From: *Journal of Personality and Social Psychology*, 6(4): 400–407,
1967. Reprinted by permission of the authors and of the American Psychological Association.

NOTE: While Mary Ann Test collaborated with the senior author on
Experiment I, the remaining work is the latter's sole responsibility.
Thanks are due to Cheryl Dellhoussay, Betty Umann, Joe McNair, and
Frank Siri who served as the experimenters and stooges for Experiment I,
and to Edward Nystrom, Alice Anderson, Katherine Moore, and Irene
Paramoure who served as the models, observers, and solicitors in studies II,
III, and IV. Studies II, III, and IV were carried out while the author was
affiliated with Educational Testing Service and were supported by the National Institute of Child Health and Human Development, under Research
Grant 1 PO1 HD1762–01. The authors are especially grateful to the Salvation Army of Trenton, New Jersey, and specifically to George H. Gibb,
whose cooperation made these experiments possible. Thanks are also due
to Perry London, David Rosenhan, Ladd Wheeler, Lawrence Stricker, and
Bruce K. Eckland for the many helpful comments upon various portions of
the manuscript.

tests) were more willing than control subjects to donate blood to a local hospital. Aronfreed and Paskal[1], and Midlarsky and Bryan (1967) found that children exposed to treatment conditions designed to produce empathy were more willing to donate M&M candies than subjects given control conditions, while Handlon and Gross (1959), Ugurel-Semin (1952), Wright (1942), and Midlarsky and Bryan have found sharing to be positively correlated with age among school-age children. Lastly, Berkowitz and Friedman (1967) have demonstrated that adolescents of the working class and the bureaucratic middle class are less affected in their helping behaviors by interpersonal attraction than adolescents of the entrepreneur middle class.

Three hypotheses have emerged regarding the situational determinants of self-sacrificing behaviors. One suggests that individuals behave in an altruistic fashion because of compliance to a norm of reciprocity. That is, individuals are aware of the social debts and credits established between them, and expect that ultimately the mutual exchange of goods and services will balance (Gouldner, 1960). Berkowitz and Daniels (1964) have suggested that individuals might show a generalization of such obligatory feelings and thus aid others who had not previously assisted them.

A second hypothesis was put forth by Berkowitz and his colleagues (Berkowitz, 1966; Berkowitz & Daniels, 1963; Berkowitz, Klanderman & Harris, 1964; Daniels & Berkowitz, 1963), who have postulated the social responsibility norm. They have contended that dependency on others evokes helping responses even under conditions where the possibility of external rewards for the helper are remote. Using supervisor's ratings of an unknown and absent other to produce dependency, and a box-construction task as the dependent variable, considerable support has been generated for the suggestion that dependency increases helping.

A third major determinant of helping may be the presence of helping (or nonhelping) models. While attention to the effects of models has generally been directed toward antisocial behaviors (cf. Bandura & Walters, 1963; Freed, Chandler, Mouton & Blake, 1955; Lefkowitz, Blake & Mouton, 1955), some recent evidence

[1] J. Aronfreed & V. Paskal. Altruism, empathy and the conditioning of positive affect. Unpublished manuscript, 1965.

suggests that observation of self-sacrificing models may lead to subsequent succorant behavior by children. For example, Rosenhan and White (1967) have demonstrated that children are more likely to donate highly valued gift certificates to residents of a fictitious orphanage if they have seen an adult do so. Hartup and Coates[2] found that nursery school children who have been exposed to a self-sacrificing peer were more likely to be altruistic than children not so exposed. Test and Bryan[3] found that female college students were more likely to render aid to another in computing arithmetic problems if they saw other people so doing.

The present series of experiments was designed to test the effects of models in natural settings on subject samples other than college or high school students, and in contexts other than a school room or university setting. The first three experiments reported are concerned with the impact of observing helping models upon subsequent helping behaviors, while the fourth is addressed to the influence of interpersonal attraction upon donation behavior.

EXPERIMENT I: LADY IN DISTRESS: A FLAT TIRE STUDY

Few studies have been concerned with the effects of models upon *adults*, and fewer still with the impact of *prosocial* models upon them (Wheeler, 1966). Those that have been concerned with such behaviors have invariably employed college students as subjects. For example, Rosenbaum and Blake (1955) and Rosenbaum (1956) have found that college students exposed to a model who volunteered, upon the personal request of the experimenter, to participate in an experiment would be more likely to consent than subjects not exposed to such a model or than subjects who observed a model refuse to cooperate. Pressures toward conformity in these experiments were great, however, as the request was made directly by the experimenter and in the presence of a large number of other students.

[2]W. W. Hartup & B. Coates. Imitation of peers as a function of reinforcement from the peer group and rewardingness of the model. Unpublished manuscript, 1966.

[3]M. A. Test & J. H. Bryan. Dependency, models and reciprocity. Unpublished manuscript, 1966.

Test and Bryan found that the observation of helping models significantly increased the subsequent offers of aid by observers. However, in that study, subjects were given the task of solving arithmetic problems and then rating their difficulty, a task ordinarily requiring autonomous efforts. Furthermore, the experiment was conducted within a university setting, a context where independence of thought is often stressed. The effects of the model may have been simply to increase the subjects' faith that assisting others was allowed. While questionnaire data of the study did not support this interpretation, such effects could not be ruled out entirely. Thus, it is possible that the model impact was simply a propriety-defining activity which reduced the inhibitions associated with such helping behavior.

In general, then, investigations of modeling that employ adults as subjects and that demand self-sacrifice on the part of subjects are limited in number, exploit strong pressures toward conformity, and rely upon college students as subjects. The present experiment was designed to assess the impact of models upon subsequent spontaneous offers of help in other than a university setting.

Method

The standard condition consisted of an undergraduate female stationed by a 1964 Ford Mustang (control car) with a flat left-rear tire. An inflated tire was leaned upon the left side of the auto. The girl, the flat tire, and the inflated tire were conspicuous to the passing traffic.

In the model condition, a 1965 Oldsmobile was located approximately ¼ mile from the control car. The car was raised by jack under the left rear bumper, and a girl was watching a male changing the flat tire.

In the no-model condition, the model was absent; thus, only the control car was visible to the passing traffic.

The cars were located in a predominantly residential section in Los Angeles, California. They were placed in such a manner that no intersection separated the model from the control car. No turn-offs were thus available to the passing traffic. Further, opposite flows of traffic were divided by a separator such that the first U turn available to the traffic going in the opposite direction of the control car would be after exposure to the model condition.

The experiment was conducted on two successive Saturdays between the hours of 1:45 and 5:50 P.M. Each treatment condition lasted for the time required for 1000 vehicles to pass the control car. While private automobiles and trucks, motorscooters, and motorcycles were tallied as vehicles, commercial trucks, taxis, and buses were not. Vehicle count was made by a fourth member of the experiment who stood approximately 100 feet from the control car, hidden from the passing motorists. On the first Saturday, the model condition was run first and lasted from 1:45 to 3:15 P.M. In order to exploit changing traffic patterns and to keep the time intervals equal across treatment conditions, the control car was moved several blocks and placed on the opposite side of the street for the no-model condition. The time of the no-model treatment was 4:00 to 5:00 P.M. On the following Saturday, counterbalancing the order and the location of treatment conditions was accomplished. That is, the no-model condition was run initially and the control car was placed in the same location that it had been placed on the previous Saturday during the model condition. The time of the no-model condition was 2:00 to 3:30 P.M. For the model condition, the control car was placed in that locale where it had been previously during the no-model condition. The time of the model condition was 4:30 to 5:30 P.M.

Individuals who had stopped to offer help were told by the young lady that she had already phoned an auto club and that help was imminent. Those who nonetheless insisted on helping her were told the nature of the experiment.

Results

The dependent variable was the number of cars that stopped and from which at least one individual offered help to the stooge by the control car. Of the 4000 passing vehicles, 93 stopped. With the model car absent, 35 vehicles stopped; with the model present, 58 halted. The difference between the conditions was statistically significant ($x^2 = 5.53$, corrected for continuity, $df = 1$, $p < .02$, detailed). Virtually all offers of aid were from men rather than women drivers.

The time of day had little impact in the offering of aid. Fifty vehicles stopped during the early part of the afternoon; none during the later hours. Likewise, difference in help offers were not great between successive Saturdays, as 45 offers of aid were made on the first Saturday, 48 on the second Saturday.

The results of the present study support the hypothesis that helping behaviors can be significantly increased through the observation of others' helpfulness. However, other plausible hypotheses exist which may account for the findings. It is possible to account for the differences in treatment effects by differences in sympathy arousal. That is, in the model condition, the motorist observed a woman who had had some difficulty. Such observations may have elicited sympathy and may have served as a reminder to the driver of his own social responsibilities.

Another explanation of the findings revolves around traffic slowdown. It is possible that the imposition of the model condition served to reduce traffic speed, thus making subsequent stopping to help a less hazardous undertaking. While the time taken for 1000 autos to pass the control car was virtually identical in the model and no-model condition and thus not supportive of such an explanation, the "slowdown" hypothesis cannot be eliminated. Assuming the model effect to be real, one might still argue that it was not a norm of helping that was facilitated by the model, but rather that inhibitions against picking up helpless young ladies were reduced. That is, within the model condition, the passing motorists may have observed a tempted other and thus felt less constrained themselves regarding similar efforts. Indeed, the insistence of some people to help in spite of the imminent arrival of other aiders suggested the operation of motives other than simply helping. Indeed, while the authors did not index the frequency of pick-up attempts, it was clear that a rather large number were evidenced.

Because of the number of alternative explanations, the evidence supporting the hypothesis that the observation of helpers per se will increase subsequent aiding is weak. Experiment II was designed to test further the prediction that the perception of another's altruistic activity would elicit similar behavior on the part of the observer.

EXPERIMENT II: COINS IN THE KETTLE

The investigation was conducted on December 14th between the hours of 10:00 A.M. and 5:00 P.M. The subjects were shoppers at a large department store in Princeton, New Jersey. Observations made on the previous day indicated that the shoppers were overwhelmingly Caucasian females.

A Salvation Army kettle was placed on the sidewalk in front of the main entrance to the store. Two females, both in experimenter's employ, alternatively manned the kettle for periods of 25 minutes. One solicitor was a Negro, the other a Caucasian. Each wore a Salvation Army cape and hat. Although allowed to ring the Salvation Army bell, they were not permitted to make any verbal plea or to maintain eye contact with the passing shoppers, except to thank any contributor for his donation.

The model condition (M) was produced as follows: Once every minute on the minute, a male dressed as a white-collar worker would approach the kettle from within the store and contribute 5 cents. As the model donated, he started a stopwatch and walked from the kettle toward a parking lot as if searching for someone. He then returned to the store. The following 20-second period constituted the duration of the treatment condition.

Following a subsequent lapse of 20 seconds, the next 20-second period defined the no-model condition (NM). Within any one minute, therefore, both M and NM treatments occurred. There were 365 occasions of each treatment.

It should be noted that it was possible that some subjects in the NM condition observed the contribution of the model or a donor affected by the model. If that hypothesis is correct, however, the effects of such incidents would be to reduce rather than enhance the differences between treatments.

Results

The dependent variable was the number of people who independently donated to the Salvation Army. People obviously acquainted, as for example, man and wife, were construed as one potential donating unit. In such conditions, if both members of a couple contributed, they were counted as a single donor.

Since there were no differences in model effects for the Negro or Caucasian solicitor, data obtained from each were combined. The total number of contributors under the NM condition was 43; under the M condition, 69. Assuming that the chance distribution of donations would be equal across the two conditions, a chi-square analysis was performed. The chi-square equaled 6.01 ($p < .01$).[4]

In spite of precautions concerning the elimination of correlated observations within a treatment condition, it was possible for subjects in any one observational period to influence one another. Such influence may have been mediated through acquaintances not eliminated by our procedures or the observations of others as well as the model donating. A more conservative analysis of the data, insuring independent observation, was therefore made. Instead of comparing treatments by analyzing the number of donors, the analysis used, as the dependent variable, the number of observation periods in which there was a contribution, that is, those periods in which more than one donation occurred were scored identically to those in which only a single contribution was received. Occasions of donations equaled 60 in the M treatment, 43 in the NM condition. The chi-square equaled 2.89 ($p < .05$).

The results of Experiment II further support the hypothesis that observation of altruistic activity will increase such behavior among observers. But the matter is not yet entirely clear, for when the observer saw the model donate he saw two things: first, the actual donation, and second, the polite and potentially reinforcing interaction that occurred between the donor and solicitor. Conceivably, the observation of an altruistic model, per se, who was not socially

---

[4]All chi-square analyses were corrected for continuity and all tests of significance were one-tailed.

reinforced for his behavior, would have little or no effect on an observer. The third experiment was designed to examine this possibility.

EXPERIMENT III: COINS IN THE KETTLE II

The experiment was conducted at a Trenton, New Jersey, shopping center from the hours of 10:00 A.M. to 5:00 P.M. Again, the majority of the patrons were Caucasian females. It is likely, however, that these shoppers were of a lower socioeconomic status than those in the Princeton group.

Salvation Army kettles were placed before the main entrance of a large department store (Kettle 1) and a large food center (Kettle 2). The kettles were separated by more than 200 yards. During the first 120 observations (10:00 A.M. to 12:00 P.M.), two male college students, employed by the Salvation Army and wearing its uniform, manned the kettles. The site of the experiment was Kettle 1, except on those occasions where the worker took his "coffee break." At those times, data collection was centered at Kettle 2. An equal number of M and NM conditions were run at each site, although approximately two-thirds of the observational time was spent at Kettle 1. During the remaining 240 observational periods (1:00 P.M. to 5:00 P.M.) the same male worker and his spouse alternately manned Kettle 1. The wife was stationed by the kettle for 136 minutes, the male for 104 minutes. The experiment was conducted only at Kettle 1 during the afternoon period.

Solicitors were told to make no verbal appeals for donations or responses to the model upon his contribution. While they were not informed of the hypothesis underlying the experiment, they may well have deduced it. The model was the same as in Experiment II, and again was dressed as a white-collar worker.

The imposition of the treatment conditions were identical to those described in Experiment I with the following exceptions. Since the kettle was more visible at this site than at the previous one, 30-second rather than 20-second periods were used for each treatment. To simplify the procedures, no waiting periods between treatments occurred. Additionally, after donating, the model would return to the parking lot. There were a total of 360 occasions of each of the M and NM conditions.

Results

The criteria defining a donor were identical to those outlined in Experiment I. Under the M condition, 84 donors were tallied; under the NM treatment, 56. The chi-square value was 4.86 ($p < .025$).

Since it was possible that one donor might have seen a donor other than the model receive social approval from the solicitor, the more conservative comparison of the treatments as outlined in Experiment II was made. That is, treatments were compared by noting the number of observational periods in which any donation occurred. Therefore, those donors who may have been influenced by a contributor receiving the solicitor's thanks were excluded. Of the 360 observational periods under the M condition, there were 75 in which some donation was made. Of the 360 periods, 51 were marked by contributing. Chi-square yielded a value of 5.09 ($p < .011$).

EXPERIMENT IV: ETHNOCENTRISM AND DONATION BEHAVIOR

While Experiment III was conducted to eliminate the solicitor's explicit social approval as a mechanism underlying donation behavior, it is possible that the model's impact was due to the information communicated to the observer regarding the consequence of donations. Work by Bandura, Ross, and Ross (1963), for example, found that children observing a model rewarded for aggression would be more aggressive than children who had observed a model being punished for such behavior. Additionally, considerable data have been gathered with the university laboratory suggesting that interpersonal attraction may greatly influence the helping response. Berkowitz and Friedman (1967), Daniels and Berkowitz (1963), and Goranson and Berkowitz (1966) have suggested that positive affect increases the probability of low payoff helping behavior.

The present experiment was designed to assess the impact of the solicitor's race upon the donation behavior of shoppers. It was assumed that a Negro solicitor would be held in less esteem by Caucasian shoppers than a solicitor of their same race, and that such attitudes would affect contributions. While the applicability of the "consequence to the model" hypothesis in accounting for the model's effect was not tested directly, the study assesses the importance of interpersonal attraction in eliciting charitable behavior.

Method

The experiment was conducted on December 2 and 3 between the hours of 10 A.M. and 6 P.M. at the Trenton area site. The subjects were Caucasian shoppers at a large department store.[5] Three thousand seven hundred and three shoppers were observed; 2,154 females and 1,549 males. In order to reduce the possibility of including the same subject in the experiment on more than one occasion, tallies were made only of exiting shoppers.

Two Salvation Army kettles were placed at two store exits, their location being separated by approximately 75 yards. Two female solicitors, a Negro and a Caucasian, manned the kettles. Both were in their early twenties, wore the uniform of the Salvation Army, and were in the employ of the experimenter. Each was instructed to make no verbal appeals for donations and to avoid eye contact with the shoppers. After a period of 25 minutes, the girls rotated kettle assignments, and during the last 10 minutes of the hour were allowed to take a coffee break. Hence, during a single hour, each solicitor manned both kettles. Each solicitor manned each kettle on seven occasions per day. Thus, each solicitor was observed for a total of 28 observational periods; 14 on each day (seven on each kettle) over a period of two days.

Two observers, each assigned to a particular kettle, tallied the number and sex of the exiting shoppers and contributors during each of the 25-minute periods. In addition, records were kept of the amount of money donated within any period, although it was

[5]As there were very few Negro donors ($N = 7$), analysis was confined to the behavior of Caucasian shoppers.

impossible on this measure to separate those donations made by incoming from outgoing customers.

Results

The dependent variable was the percentage of donors contributing to the kettle within an observational period. That is, observational periods were assigned a percentage donor score. Shoppers within an observational period were treated as a single group, with differences between groups on percentage donor score forming the critical comparisons. The total N of the study was then the 56 observational periods, rather than the 3,703 shoppers. Since the mean group size for the Negro solicitor was 70.32 and for the Caucasian 61.93 (standard deviations equal to 53.33 and 42.98, respectively), it was assumed that the percentage score was relatively stable.

The effects of race, kettle location, and day and their interactions were analyzed by analysis of variance.

As can be seen from Table 1, both the main effect of race and of day were significant. As predicted, the Negro solicitor elicited a statistically significant lower percentage of donors than did the Caucasian. For the Negro solicitor, the average percentage donor score for observational periods was 2.22 ($SD = 2.36$), while for the Caucasian solicitor the average percentage donor score

TABLE 1
ANALYSIS OF VARIANCE OF PERCENTAGE DONOR SCORES

	df	MS	F
Race (A)	1	38.778	4.84*
Day (B)	1	98.315	12.28**
Kettle (C)	1	.018	
A × B	1	1.511	
A × C	1	11.340	
B × C	1	1.031	
A × B × C	1	3.206	
Error	48	8.009	

*p $<$ .05 (2-tailed).
**p $<$ .01 (2-tailed).

was 3.89 (*SD* = 3.60). Additionally, Saturday shoppers were by and large less generous than Friday customers. The average percentage donor score of the group was 1.73 (*SD* = 1.97) for the Saturday shopper, and 4.38 for the Friday shopper (*SD* = 3.52).

A second dependent variable was the amount of money donated during each time period. No significant differences were found for race, day, or kettle location.

The present investigation does support, albeit equivocally, the notion that interpersonal attraction may affect donations even when the solicitors are not the eventual recipients of such contributions. While it is possible that race differences simply fail to remind observers of their social responsibilities, it is also feasible that the subjects wanted to avoid interpersonal contact with a minority group member. If this is true, then it is interesting to note that interpersonal attraction may play an important role even in those situations where personal anonymity is high and escape from unpleasant situations easy.

DISCUSSION

The results of the first three experiments clearly replicate those of Test and Bryan and extend the findings over a variety of subject populations, settings, and tasks. The results hold for college students, motorists, and shoppers; in the university laboratory, city streets, and shopping centers; and when helping is indexed by aiding others solve arithmetic problems, changing flat tires, or donating money to the Salvation Army. The findings then are quite consistent: the presence of helping models significantly increases subsequent altruistic behavior.

That generosity breeds generosity is interesting in light of the recent concern with helping behaviors in emergency contexts. Darley and Latané[6] and Latané and Darley[7] have found that subjects are less inclined to act quickly in emergency situations when in the presence of other potential helpers. Whether faced with a medical emergency (a simulated epileptic seizure) or a

[6]J. Darley & B. Latané. Diffusion of responsibility in emergency situations. Unpublished manuscript, 1966.

[7]B. Latané & J. Darley. Group inhibition of bystander intervention in emergencies. Unpublished manuscript, 1966.

dangerous natural event (simulated fire), the rapidity with which students sought to aid was reduced by the presence of others. These findings have been interpreted in three ways: as reflecting the subjects' willingness to diffuse responsibility (others will aid); as reflecting their diffusion of blame (others didn't aid either); or as reflecting conformity to the nonpanicked stooges. It is clear that the results of the first three experiments in the present series do not follow that which might be predicted by the diffusion concepts. A giving model apparently does not lend credibility to the belief that others than the self will make the necessary sacrifices. The helping other did not strengthen the observer's willingness to diffuse his social obligations, but rather stimulated greater social responsibility. In light of these results, the delayed reaction exhibited by the subjects tested by Darley and Latané might be best attributable to conformity behavior. As they have suggested, subjects faced with a unique and stressful situation may have been either reassured by the presence of calm others or fearful of acting stupidly or cowardly. Additionally, it is possible that diffusion of responsibility is only associated with anxiety-inducing situations. The current data fail to indicate that such diffusion occurs in non-stressful situations which demand fulfillment of social obligations.

While it appears clear that the behavior of the motorists and shoppers was not dictated by a variety of situational and social pressures usually associated with the study of modeling in adults or experiment in academic settings (Orne, 1962), the mechanisms underlying the effects are not obvious. While the presence of the model in the flat-tire study may have reminded the motorists as to the social responsibility norm, a hypothesis does not appear reasonable in accounting for the results in the coins-in-the-kettle series. The bell-ringing Salvation Army worker, with kettle and self placed squarely in the pathway of the oncoming pedestrian, would seem to be reminder enough of one's obligation toward charity. A priori, it would not appear necessary to superimpose upon that scene the donating other for purposes of cognitive cueing (Wheeler, 1966).

One hypothesis to account for the model effect is that the observer is given more information regarding the consequences of such donation behavior. Experiment IV suggested that solicitor status or personal attraction might operate on donation behaviors

even under conditions of personal anonymity and few social con-
straints. It is possible that the model serves to communicate to the
potential donor relevant information concerning the consequences
of his act. That is, the model may demonstrate that an approach
to the solicitor does not involve an unwanted interpersonal interaction (e.g., lectures on religion).

A second hypothesis to account for the data pertains to the
shame-provoking capacities of the model. It is reasonable to
assume that most people feel that they are, by and large, benevolent
and charitable. Furthermore, it is likely that such a self-image is
rarely challenged: first because charitable acts are not frequently
required; second, at least in the street scenes employed in the current series of studies, solicitations are made in the context of many
nongiving others. That is, a multitude of negative models—of
noncharitable others—surround the solicitations in the current
series of studies. Indeed, the contexts are such that most people
are not helping; many more cars pass than stop to offer aid to
the lady in distress; and there are many more people who refuse
to put coins in the kettle than those who do. However, the witnessing of a donor, an individual who not only recognizes his social
responsibility but in fact acts upon it, may produce a greater
challenge to the good self-image of the observer. Acts rather than
thoughts may be required of the observer in order to maintain
the self-image of benevolence and charity. If such is the case, then
the model characteristics most effective in producing prosocial behavior by socialized adults would be those directed toward shame
or guilt production (e.g., donations from the poor), rather than
those reflecting potential reinforcement power (e.g., donations
from the high status).

Whatever the mechanism underlying the model effect, it does
appear quite clear that prosocial behavior can be elicited through
the observation of benign others.

ABSTRACT

Four experiments concerned with helping behavior were conducted. Three were addressed to the effects of altruistic models

upon helping, while one was concerned with the impact of the solicitor's race upon donations. Three investigations employed as a site parking lots of two large department stores in New Jersey, and indexed helping by contributions to the Salvation Army. A fourth experiment indexed helping by offers of aid by passing motorists to a woman with a disabled vehicle. Whether one employed motorists in California or shoppers in New Jersey, the results were quite consistent. The presence of a helping model significantly increased helping behavior. As race of the Salvation Army solicitor did affect the percentage of donors willing to contribute money, it was concluded that interpersonal attraction is a relevant variable affecting donations.

REFERENCES

BANDURA, A., ROSS, D., and ROSS, S.   Vicarious reinforcement and imitative learning. *Journal of Abnormal and Social Psychology*, 1963, 66, 601–607.

BANDURA, A., and WALTERS, R. H.   *Social Learning and Personality Development.* New York: Holt, Rinehart & Winston, 1963.

BERKOWITZ, L.   A laboratory investigation of social class and national differences in helping behavior. *International Journal of Psychology*, 1966, 1, 231–240.

BERKOWITZ, L., and DANIELS, L.   Responsibility and dependency. *Journal of Abnormal and Social Psychology*, 1963, 66, 429–436.

BERKOWITZ, L., and DANIELS, L.   Affecting the salience of the social responsibility norm: Effects of past help on the response to dependency relationships. *Journal of Abnormal and Social Psychology*, 1964, 68, 275–281.

BERKOWITZ, L., and FRIEDMAN, P.   Some social class differences in helping behavior. *Journal of Personality and Social Psychology*, 1967, 5, 217–225.

BERKOWITZ, L., KLANDERMAN, S. B., and HARRIS, R.   Effects of experimenter awareness and sex of subject and experimenter on reactions to dependency relationships. *Sociometry*, 1964, 27, 327–337.

DANIELS, L., and BERKOWITZ, L.   Liking and response to dependency relationships. *Human Relations*, 1963, 16, 141–148.

DARLINGTON, R. B., and MACKER, C. E. Displacement of guilt-produced altruistic behavior. *Journal of Personality and Social Psychology*, 1966, 4, 442–443.

FREED, A., CHANDLER, P., MOUTON, J., and BLAKE, R. Stimulus and background factors in sign violation. *Journal of Personality*, 1955, 23, 499.

GORANSON, R., and BERKOWITZ, L. Reciprocity and responsibility reactions to prior help. *Journal of Personality and Social Psychology*, 1966, 3, 227–232.

GORE, P. M., and ROTTER, J. B. A personality correlate of social action. *Journal of Personality*, 1963, 31, 58–64.

GOULDNER, A. The norm of reciprocity: A preliminary statement. *American Sociological Review*, 1960, 25, 161–178.

HANDLON, B. J., and GROSS, P. The development of sharing behavior. *Journal of Abnormal and Social Psychology*, 1959, 59, 425–428.

LEFKOWITZ, M., BLAKE, R., and MOUTON, J. Status factors in pedestrian violation of traffic signals. *Journal of Abnormal and Social Psychology*, 1955, 51, 704–706.

MIDLARSKY, E., and BRYAN, J. H. Training charity in children. *Journal of Personality and Social Psychology*, 1967, 5, 408–415.

ORNE, M. On the social psychology of the psychological experiment: With particular reference to demand characteristics and their implications. *American Psychologist*, 1962, 17, 776–783.

ROSENBAUM, M. The effect of stimulus and background factors on the volunteering response. *Journal of Abnormal and Social Psychology*, 1956, 53, 118–121.

ROSENBAUM, M., and BLAKE, R. Volunteering as a function of field structure. *Journal of Abnormal and Social Psychology*, 1955, 50, 193–196.

ROSENHAN, D., and WHITE, G. M. Observation and rehearsal as determinants of prosocial behavior. *Journal of Personality and Social Psychology*, 1967, 5, 424–431.

UGUREL-SEMIN, R. Moral behavior and moral judgment of children. *Journal of Abnormal and Social Psychology*, 1952, 47, 463–474.

WHEELER, L. Toward a theory of behavioral contagion. *Psychological Review*, 1966, 73, 179–192.

WRIGHT, B. A. Altruism in children and perceived conduct of others. *Journal of Abnormal and Social Psychology*, 1942, 37, 218–233.

13

Social Status in Jury Deliberations

FRED L. STRODTBECK, RITA JAMES SIMON, and CHARLES HAWKINS

This report reflects an excellent example of an exploratory investigation into an inaccessible aspect of our legal system, the jury. The jury is perhaps one of the most significant small groups in our society. There are many legal and ethical problems involved in the observation of an actual jury in deliberation.

In this study, mock jury deliberations were utilized in such a manner that an experimental situation could be developed. The individuals involved were selected from actual jury pools, therefore making the composition of the mock juries representative of real-life juries. The deliberations of these juries were carefully recorded and a thorough analysis of each group's activities was conducted. From these analyses it was discovered that definite patterns of group structure emerged and that the positions of power that different jurists assumed while deliberating were closely related to their actual, real-life social status. These interesting results are based on data gathered from 49 different mock juries.

From: *Current Studies in Social Psychology*, edited by Ivan D. Steiner and Martin Fishbein. Copyright © 1965 by Holt, Rinehart and Winston, Inc. Reprinted by permission of authors of Holt, Rinehart and Winston, Inc.

Occupational specialization has two distinguishable effects. First, it increases productivity and, second, it provides the basis for a status hierarchy. Perhaps it is less commonplace to think that role differentiation in face-to-face groups arises from a similar economic process and results in similar status differences. For groups to define and achieve their goals, however, they must control the use of their primary-group resource—their common time together. Only one, or at most a few persons, can talk at any given instant and be understood. Who talks and how much he talks is, within limits, determined by the reactions of the group to the speaker. Acts that are perceived as relevant to the solution of the group's problems are generally favorably received and the responsible speaker is encouraged to continue. In the long run participation tends to become differentiated, and a small fraction of the group's members will account for most of the participation.

For the purposes of the present study, which inquires into the relationships between occupation and selected aspects of role differentiation, it is desirable that the focus of the small-group discussion is not too narrowly circumscribed by status prerogatives. For example, a group of officers and enlisted men discussing military problems or a group of doctors and nurses discussing a medical problem would not provide the circumstance we require. A greater presumption of equality is desired.

In the jury situation not only does the widespread norm assume that group members should act toward one another as equals, but the presumption of equality is reinforced by the requirement that the verdict be unanimous. Equal and responsible participation in the deliberation, therefore, is an institutionalized expectation. If evidence indicates that the status differences of the larger community become manifest during the deliberation, then it may be expected that a similar generalization of status will be found in other situations of interaction where hierarchical considerations are more prominent.

It is essential for our study that wide background differences

NOTE: Revised from a version prepared especially for *Readings in Social Psychology* by E. E. Maccoby, T. M. Newcomb, and E. L. Hartley (Eds.), New York: Holt, Rinehart and Winston, 1958. This article reports one phase of experimental jury investigations conducted under the sponsorship of the Ford Foundation.

be present within the juror population. This is assured in metro-politan areas such as Chicago, St. Louis, and Minneapolis where our experimental jury research has been conducted since jurors are selected here by a random process from voting registration lists. The resultant jury-pool population compares closely with the expected population computed from census reports, although the professions and very low education and occupation groups are slightly under-represented.

Occupations are classified in four groups: proprietor, clerical, skilled, and labor. "Proprietor" includes the census category[1] of proprietors, managers and officials as well as professionals such as architects, accountants, and engineers who are not excluded from service. "Clerical" and "skilled" categories correspond to the census categories and "labor" subsumes the census categories of semiskilled workers, nonfarm laborers, and servants. Farm own-ers and laborers are absent from our populations, and retired per-sons have been classified by their occupations prior to retirement. Women are classified by their stated occupations, except that housewives are classified by their husbands' occupations.

Previous studies indicate that power and participation in face-to-face situations are related to status. Caudill[2] observed the daily exchange of information at administrative conferences among the staff of a small psychiatric hospital and found that the relative participation by the director of the service, the residents, the head nurse, the nurses, and the occupational therapist were ordered by their statuses in the hospital, even though the lower status persons ordinarily spend more time with the patients. Torrance[3] used non-military problems but found that pilots, navigators, and gunners recognized a power hierarchy in the contrived situation which paralleled that ordinarily in effect in airship operation. Strodtbeck[4]

[1]Alba M. Edwards, *Bureau of the Census Alphabetical Index of Occupa-tions by Industries and Social-Economic Groups* (Washington, D.C.: De-partment of Commerce, 1937).

[2]William Caudill, *The Psychiatric Hospital as a Small Society* (Cam-bridge, Mass.: Harvard University Press, 1957).

[3]E. P. Torrance, *Some Consequences of Power Differences on Decision Making in Permanent and Temporary Three-Man Groups*, "Research Studies," XXII (Pullman: State College of Washington, 1954), pp. 130–140.

[4]F. L. Strodtbeck, "Husband-Wife Interaction Over Revealed Differences," *Am. Sociol. Rev.*, 1951, XVI, 141–145.

demonstrated that the greater economic and religious power of Navaho in contrast with Mormon women was reflected in their greater power in husband-wife decision making. More pertinent, perhaps, is a study relating to the continuation in jury deliberations of a strong emphasis by women on expressive and integrative acts.[5] The components that had been found descriptive of women's roles in family interaction situations were found to characterize women's roles in jury deliberations.

It is important to stress that while the related studies are consistent insofar as they suggest a parallel between generalized status and status in face-to-face systems, they do not provide a firm basis for generalizing to the situation at hand, at least in terms of the measure of correspondence. In Torrance's experiment the pilots probably dominated to a lesser degree in the experimental situation than they would have when the airship was in operation. While the ordering was preserved, it was undoubtedly attenuated. In the present case, what differences are to be expected? The relation between roles like pilot and gunner or clerical worker and laborer is not equally clear in the interaction differences they imply. There is no compelling reason to believe that clerical workers and laborers will have had sufficient experience together to evolve a stable pecking order. Furthermore, once the jurors have completed their deliberations, they do not expect a continued relationship that would provide an opportunity for external status differences to become manifest. If status differences are present in the jury room, it is almost certain that they arise in part because the varied requirements of the deliberation re-create within the jury the need for the differential experiences associated with status. Whether or not the differences which stem from the external system are great enough to become apparent in a one- to two-hour deliberation is the empirical question we seek to answer.

SOURCE OF DATA

Mock jury deliberations were conducted in which the participants were jurors drawn by lot from the regular jury pools. The

[5]F. L. Strodtbeck and R. D. Mann, "Sex Role Differentiation in Jury Deliberations," *Sociometry*, 1956, XIX, 3–11.

jurors listened to a recorded trial, deliberated, and returned their verdict—all under the customary discipline of bailiffs of the court. The jury deliberations were recorded, fully transcribed, and scored in terms of interaction-process categories.

This paper is based primarily upon 49 deliberations for which interaction process analysis has been carried out. Two civil trials were used as the basis for the deliberations. In the first (29 deliberations) the plaintiff, a secretary, sought compensation for injuries incurred in a two-car collision. In the second (20 deliberations) a young child sought compensation for facial disfigurement incurred in a fire alleged to have been caused by a defective vaporizer. A total of 49 by 12, or 588, different jurors were involved. Data on 14 additional vaporizer cases and 28 recent experimental trials are utilized in other portions of the paper. In total data from 91 juries are used in the examination of different status effects.

PROCEDURES

Selecting a Foreman

After the jury listened to the case, they were told to select their foreman and begin their deliberation. In more than half of the deliberations, the foreman was nominated by one member and then quickly accepted by the remainder of the group. In about a third of the deliberations the man who opened the discussion and sought either to nominate another, or to focus the group's attention on their responsibility in selecting a foreman, was himself selected foreman. However, in all instances the selection of a foreman was quickly and apparently casually accomplished. There was no instance in which mention of any socio-economic criteria was made, but this is not to say that socio-economic criteria were not involved. For example, Table 1 shows that some foremen were selected from all strata, but the incidence was three and a half times as great among proprietors as among laborers. In addition, although the details are not given in the table, tabulations show that only one-fifth as many women were chosen foreman as would be expected by chance.

TABLE 1
OCCUPATIONAL STATUS OF 49 JURY FOREMEN

Occupation	Expected*	Observed	Index
Proprietor	9.73	18	185
Clerical	15.03	15	100
Skilled	9.56	8	84
Labor	14.68	8	54

*Computed under assumption that foremen will be proportional to portion of sample in the given occupation.

Relative Participation

The deliberations were recorded with two microphones to facilitate binaural identification of individual participants. The protocols were fully transcribed, and from the protocol each speaker's contributions were separated into units of discrete action, each of which is roughly the equivalent of a simple declarative sentence. Identification of the speaker was checked with the original observer's notes, and an assistant tabulated the scores with the aid of the recording plus indications of nonverbal gestures made by the original observer.

Since there were 12 persons in the jury, one twelfth of the total acts is the pro-rata percentage for each juror's acts. This provides the base line against which the effects of external status may be appraised. The higher the average participation of an occupational group, the greater their relative share of the common resource of time. It may be seen in Table 2 that in all occupations males talked more than females and the amount of participation was sharply differentiated between higher than expected values for proprietors and clerical workers, and lower than expected values for skilled and unskilled laborers.

While the moderately differing values in Table 2 are averages based upon the scores of more than 500 persons, within any particular deliberation there was a very steep differentiation between the most- and least-verbal jurors. For example, in 82 percent of the juries the top three participators accounted for one-half or more of the total acts, while the remaining acts were distributed among the other nine members. It is to be emphasized that the

TABLE 2
PERCENTAGE RATES OF PARTICIPATION IN JURY DELIBERATION
BY OCCUPATION AND SEX OF JUROR

Sex	Occupation				
	Proprietor	Clerical	Skilled	Laborer	Combined
Male	12.9	10.8	7.9	7.5	9.6
	(N = 81)*	(N = 81)	(N = 80)	(N = 107)	(N = 349)
Female	9.1	7.8	4.8	4.6	6.6
	(N = 31)	(N = 92)	(N = 28)	(N = 62)	(N = 213)
Combined	11.8	9.2	7.1	6.4	8.5
	(N = 112)	(N = 173)	(N = 108)	(N = 169)	(N = 562)†

*Numbers of jurors are shown in parentheses.
†Twenty-six of 588 jurors from the 49 juries used were not satisfactorily classified by occupation and are omitted.

averages of Table 2 describe the relative participation of occupation and sex groups; they do not reflect the wide variation within any one jury.

One source of differences in participation within a jury may be attributed to the election of one member to play the role of foreman. The foreman was responsible for approximately one-fourth of the total acts and as shown in Table 1 was more frequently selected from the higher status groups. When foreman scores were eliminated the average participation values were:

proprietor	8.9
clerical	7.0
skilled	6.3
labor	5.9

The gap between clerical and skilled workers is narrower but the rank order is unchanged.[6]

The latent premise in the study of participation is that high participation indicates greater ability to influence others. Earlier research supports such an interpretation for *ad hoc* problem solving groups and for families. Further evidence is available from

[6]A further check was made on the effects of jury participation when another person of one's own occupation group was also present. For juries in which at least two of each occupational group are present, the values are quite similar to Table 2, and while there is some tendency for higher status persons to talk more when they are alone, or in a marked minority, further corrections have minor effects.

the present research. Jurors were asked before the deliberation what, if anything, they would award the plaintiff. In general the higher the socio-economic status of the juror, the lower the award. The relative magnitude of the awards in terms of an index number with the mean equal 100 is proprietor, 83; clerical, 92; skilled, 97; and laborer, 122. A detailed examination of individual predeliberation decisions with the subsequent group awards in 29 deliberations reveals that the more active jurors shifted their predeliberation position less often than less active jurors in the process of reaching a unanimous group verdict.[7] The relation between participation and influence by status level may be documented by comparing the average predeliberation award (listed according to occupational group) with the jury verdict. The correlations are:

proprietor	.50 ($p < .05$)
clerical	.11
skilled	.29
labor	.02

Members from the same occupational group sometimes initially favored different verdicts, and in this case not all the members of this group achieved their desired outcome. Nonetheless, the correlation between the proprietors' average and the jury verdicts is significant. This result corresponds to the participation values after they have been corrected by eliminating the foreman. Since our content analyses clearly show that foremen were more neutral than other actively participating jurors during the discussion of monetary awards, the corrected participation values are probably a more satisfactory measure of influence in the damage award deliberation.

The meaning of participation levels may be viewed from still another perspective. After the deliberation, the jurors were asked to answer a battery of questions concerning their personal satisfaction with the quality of the deliberation and the tone of interpersonal relations. The level of an individual's satisfaction was positively correlated with the level of his own participation ($r = .52$,

[7]Allen Barton, *Persuasion and Compromise in Damage Awards*, December, 1956, unpublished manuscript.

$p < .05$). The involvement that high participation represented in the jury is not unlike the involvement of higher status people in the affairs of the larger community; both are instruments for group derived satisfactions.

In addition, responses to the post-deliberation question, "Who do you believe contributed most to helping your group reach its decision?" were tabulated by occupation of the target person. The average number of helpfulness votes received by occupation groups (see Table 3) closely parallels the participation by occupation

TABLE 3
AVERAGE VOTES RECEIVED AS HELPFUL JUROR BY OCCUPATION
AND SEX

Sex	Occupation				
	Proprietor	Clerical	Skilled	Laborer	Combined
Male	6.8	4.2	3.9	2.7	4.3
	(N = 113)	(N = 108)	(N = 115)	(N = 143)	(N = 479)
Female	3.2	2.7	2.0	1.5	2.3
	(N = 34)	(N = 116)	(N = 36)	(N = 76)	(N = 262)
Combined	6.0	3.4	3.5	2.3	3.6
	(N = 147)	(N = 224)	(N = 151)	(N = 219)	(N = 741)*

*This number includes 14 additional juries for which interaction process scores are not available.

groups (see Table 2). The correlation between votes received and participation is about .69 when sets of individual values are correlated. Male clerical workers get slightly fewer votes than their participation would appear to warrant and male skilled workers get slightly more, but the overwhelming impression is that the number of such votes received, like participation, influence, and satisfaction, parallels status differentiation in society at large.

Perceived Fitness as Jurors

The Courts Martial reform, which permitted enlisted men to request other enlisted men for their trial panels, was largely nullified by their preference to leave their cases in the hands of officers. How do jurors react? A departure from random selection might have two possible effects. Given a choice, jurors might tend to overselect people in the higher occupations just as they had in distributing their helpfulness ballots. Or, taking the class theory as the basis of our prediction, we might assume that the chooser might select more jurors from his own occupation group. How these counter tendencies might be balanced is a question for which we have no theoretical answer and, therefore, must investigate empirically.

In an effort to probe deeper for evidence of class identifications, the following question was asked of 28 juries:

> The jury pool is made up of people from all walks of life. However, if a member of your family were on trial and you had your choice, which of the following kinds of people would you prefer to make up the majority of the jurors who would hear your case?
>
> _____ business and professional people
> _____ clerical and white collar workers
> _____ skilled workers
> _____ unskilled workers

The expected values, determined by assuming that equal preference will be shown for each status group, have been divided into the observed values, and the resultant ratio was multiplied by 100 to give the index numbers shown in Table 4. All groups, except laborers, would prefer to have a member of their family

TABLE 4
CHOICE OF JUROR IF MEMBER OF RESPONDENT'S FAMILY WERE
ON TRIAL, BASED UPON OCCUPATION STEREOTYPES
(PRO RATA EXPECTED IS 100)*

Respondent's Occupation		Preferred Occupation			
		Proprietor	Clerical	Skilled	Laborer
Proprietor	(N = 63)	241	95	51	13
Clerical	(N = 107)	206	112	71	11
Skilled	(N = 72)	172	55	139	33
Laborer	(N = 76)	126	42	147	84

*These data were collected from jurors in our 28 most recent experimental juries.

tried before a jury the majority of whose members were proprietors. Like other groups, laborers were also upwardly oriented in
their preferences but their first choice was skilled workers, then
proprietors. Clerical and skilled workers chose persons from their
own occupation group as their second choice. All groups except
laborers ranked laborers last. Laborers placed themselves third
and clerks last. It is to be stressed that Table 4 represents the
choice of jurors in terms of occupational stereotypes. It is what
a member of one occupational group perceives in terms of his
generalized conception of his own and other occupational groups.

We also asked jurors to choose "four of your fellow jurors
whom you would best like to have serve on a jury if you were on
trial." This question asks jurors not for generalized conceptions
of other occupational groups but for evaluations of particular
persons. We wished to know if the selections made on the basis
of face-to-face contact were similar or different from stereotype
choices.[8] If a prototype of a social system had grown during
deliberation, jurors might come to regard one another more in
terms of performance in the task at hand than in terms of general
social status. It was also possible for the deliberation to reveal
status-based ideologies that would open latent schisms. The data
suggest that differences were ordinarily not magnified by the deliberation and the jurors came to be convinced that a just job had
been done. The special thrust of the question "if a member of your
family were on trial" could have sensitized jurors to think in terms
of personal interests rather than abstract principles such as competence or justice. Possibly these respondents became so sensitive
to their personal interests that they turned away from those jurors
who had been the arbiters of consensus in their own deliberations.

Table 5 shows a preference for proprietors but at a somewhat
lower level. More detailed effects of the face-to-face experience
in contrast with the response to occupational categories may best
be illustrated by subtracting Table 4 from Table 5. It is to be
noted that while Tables 4 and 5 are based on different populations,

[8]The stereotype-juror preference question was not asked of the juries in
Table 5. The 28 juries of Table 4 are an entirely different set, so that the
possible bias of face-to-face choices by the prior administration of the
stereotype choices is avoided.

TABLE 5
CHOICE OF JUROR IF RESPONDENT WERE ON TRIAL,
BASED UPON DELIBERATION EXPERIENCE
(PRO RATA EXPECTED IS 100)*

Respondent's Occupation		Preferred Occupation			
		Proprietor	Clerical	Skilled	Laborer
Proprietor	(N = 78)	169	110	119	39
Clerical	(N = 129)	145	100	101	75
Skilled	(N = 74)	147	104	84	73
Laborer	(N = 130)	162	100	112	74

*The expected values used to form the index numbers have been determined by assuming that each person distributes his four choices simultaneously under conditions that give an equal chance of each of the 11 fellow jurors' being chosen.

the respondents in both cases are random samples from the population available in successive weeks in the jury pool. When Table 4 is subtracted from Table 5 (see Table 6) a positive value in the matrix represents an increase in index value associated with the face-to-face experience.

The main diagonal shows that "own group" choices were lower at each occupation level, particularly among proprietors and skilled laborers. That is, choices after the deliberation experience are not determined by a narrow "interest group." In addition, all values above the main diagonal are positive. That is, face-to-face experience caused lower status persons to be evaluated more highly! As shown below the main diagonal, proprietors were reduced in the evaluation of clerical and skilled workers and increased in the evaluation of laborers; clerical workers were rated more highly by

TABLE 6
CHANGE IN INDEX VALUE ASSOCIATED WITH
DELIBERATION EXPERIENCE
(VALUE OF TABLE 4 SUBTRACTED FROM TABLE 5)

Respondent's Occupation	Preferred Occupation			
	Proprietor	Clerical	Skilled	Laborer
Proprietor	−72	15	68	26
Clerical	−61	−12	30	64
Skilled	−35	49	−55	40
Laborer	36	58	−35	−10

both skilled workers and laborers; and laborers decreased their former preference for skilled workers. The lower range of index values in the face-to-face situation arose in part from the effects of forcing the distribution of four votes among the 11 jurors who were members of the respondent's particular jury. Notwithstanding this flattening effect, it still appears that the face-to-face experience (1) results in fewer proprietor and skilled worker "own group" choices; and (2) brings the choice gradients into smoother conformity with the observed contribution of each status group to the deliberation.

DISCUSSION

Jury deliberations have been used to examine the intersection of occupational status and sex with the typically small-group measures of participation, influence, satisfaction, and perceived competence. The assumption that there is no relation between these modes of classification can be safely rejected. Men, in contrast with women, and persons of higher status, in contrast with lower status occupations, have higher participation, influence, satisfaction, and perceived competence for the jury task.

The present study does little to explain the cause of this differentiation. Insofar as selection of the foreman may be taken as a guide to more general expectations concerning desirable attributes for the jury task, it appears that the foreman is expected to be a male, preferably a male of higher occupational status. Although we know of no empirical studies, we assume that the business discipline and related experiences of higher status occupations involve both substantive knowledge and interactional skills that may be used during the deliberation. Hence, in the competition for the available deliberation time, higher status males may rise to prominence because their comments are perceived to have greater value. On the other hand, since the cues of status— dress, speech, and casual references to experiences—are easily read, the differentiation may in part be explained by these expectations instead of actual performance.

Jurors who spoke at greater length were perceived by respondents to be the jurors desired if they were on trial. This finding suggests that whatever the criteria used by the groups to regulate the contributions of their members, these criteria were broadly held. The different distribution of speaking time was achieved without serious violation of developing group norms. Further, choices made after face-to-face experience, in contrast with those based on occupational stereotypes, tended to smooth into a gradient which paralleled both activity rates and status. These findings and others reported above constitute a preliminary clarification of the small-group process during a jury deliberation.

While our data do little to illuminate *how* differentiation arises, they show that status gradients emerge clearly in as brief a time as the one- or two-hour discussions under study. Although careful study will be required to determine the degree to which one may generalize from status in the larger social system to a particular interaction context, this demonstration of status continuity should be noted in any theory concerned with describing the process of status affirmation and maintenance.

14

The Influence of Frustrations Imposed by the In-Group on Attitudes Expressed Toward Out-Groups

NEAL E. MILLER and
RICHARD BUGELSKI

One of the most frequent reactions to a frustrating experience is aggression. This experiment demonstrates that aggressive responses may be displaced, that is, directed toward ethnic groups which are clearly not responsible for the frustrating event. This study is an example of how the social psychologist can execute an experimental procedure in an opportune natural setting without the respondents being aware that they are actually serving in an experiment, thus preserving the "naturalistic" nature of the research effort.

From: *Journal of Psychology*, 25: 437–442, 1948. Reprinted by permission of the authors and of The Journal Press. Copyright © 1948 by The Journal Press.

War, race prejudice, and other forms of hostility against members of the out-group usually involve, according to a hypothesis which has been elaborated elsewhere, a certain component of irrational aggression which is brought into play by the mechanism of displacement (1, 2, 4, 5). According to this hypothesis members of an out-group may be not only the target for the direct aggression which they arouse by competition with the members of the in-group, but also may be the scapegoats for strong aggression which is first aroused by friction within the in-group, then suppressed by in-group taboos and conveniently displaced to members of the out-group.

The purpose of the present investigation was to explore the possibility of securing evidence for two of the assumptions involved in this analysis, namely: *(1) that frustration arouses aggression,* and *(2) that the members of the out-group are sufficiently similar as stimulus objects to members of the in-group so that responses (in this case to aggression) will generalize from one to the other.*

PROCEDURE

The subjects were 31 young men between the ages of 18 and 20, working at a camp. It was known that these young men were about to encounter a frustrating situation. As a part of the educational program of the camp they were going to be required to take some long, uninteresting tests most of which were so difficult that everyone would be bound to fail miserably. Furthermore, the tests would be certain to run far overtime so that the young men would miss what they looked forward to as the most interesting event of the otherwise dull week: Bank Night at the local theater, which was awaited with special eagerness on this occasion because one member of the group had won $200.00 the preceding week. To the extent that the young men were motivated to succeed on the tests, the failure which was in store for them on many items would interfere with their goal of giving correct answers. To the extent that they were motivated to attend Bank Night at the local theater—and here both previous behavior and verbal report allowed us to predict strong motivation—an additional strongly motivated goal response would be interfered with by the testing program. Thus the sudden substitution of the regime of testing for the leisure time activities of the young men may be considered a relatively strong frustration.[1]

In order to determine whether this frustration aroused any aggression that was generalized to out-groups who obviously could not have been to blame for the situation, the attitude of the young men toward Japanese[2] and Mexicans was measured, first *before* they knew what was in store for them, and then *after* they had done poorly on the difficult tests and missed the evening's entertainment.

Attitudes toward the foreigners were measured by a simple rating scale in which the subjects checked a list of 10 desirable and 10 undesirable traits as being either present or absent in the average foreigner. A previous study had suggested that a night of sleep-deprivation, non-smoking, and in general non-amusement, caused subjects to give an unduly low rating on similar lists to the experimenters who were directly responsible for these frustrations (6). An item analysis of the check list employed in this previous experiment seemed to indicate that in general certain milder, vaguer words were the best items. Although the number of cases was so small that the item analysis was not very reliable, the best items and ones apparently similar were used in the present list.

The directions for rating an out-group were as follows:

> Below you will find a list of words. Some of these apply in general to people of the nationality written in capital letters at the top of this page. Others do not apply very well to the majority of the people of this nationality. Check the words which *do* apply in general to the people of this nationality. Do not check the other words. When you check a word it does not have to mean that all of the people are exactly like that but only that most of them tend to be.

Below the directions in one, double-spaced column were the words to check. These words are presented below in the order used, but

---

[1]For formal definitions and detailed illustrations of terms such as goal-response, frustration and aggression, see J. Dollard *et al.*, *Frustration and Aggression*, 1939, 3–18.

[2]This experiment was performed several years before Pearl Harbor.

changed from a single column to a paragraph. Those counted as favorable traits in the eventual scoring are accompanied by a + sign; those considered to represent unfavorable traits are designated by a — sign. These designations were, of course, absent from the check lists used by the subjects. The 22 words used, 11 scored as undesirable, were as follows:

Friendly +, selfish —, smart +, awkward —, stingy —, clean +, cheerful +, sly —, honest +, unfair —, brave +, cruel —, polite +, stupid —, dangerous —, patient +, dirty —, dependable +, stubborn —, good-looking +, liars —, peaceful +.

First the men were called together and seated in the main assembly room. Before they were fully aware of the fact that tests were going to be hard and long and cut seriously into their recreation time, the blanks containing the directions and check lists were distributed.[3] The directions were then read to the men and they were told to proceed. Half the blanks were headed by the word "JAPANESE." The men receiving these blanks rated the average Japanese. The other half of the blanks were headed by the word "MEXICAN." The men receiving these blanks rated the average Mexican. After the blanks had been checked they were collected. Then the main testing program, which was the purpose of calling the men together, but was irrelevant to the present experiment save that it frustrated the men, was administered.

After the men had worked for two hours on these tests and missed the chance to catch the truck to the Bank Night at the theater, the spontaneous comments which they made indicated that they were angry at the camp officials who ordered the tests and the experimenters who administered them. Thus the first assumption, that frustration arouses aggression, was verified. In order to investigate the second assumption by determining whether or not any of this aggression was generalized to members of an out-group, the check lists were distributed to the men again. This time

[3]The men were somewhat frustrated even at this time, but incidental observation indicated that they were far more frustrated at the end of the test procedure. Any error introduced by initial frustration would be in such a direction as to work opposite to the findings, rather than to produce spuriously positive results.

the men who had rated Japanese before were asked to rate Mexicans and the men who had rated Mexicans before were asked to rate Japanese. In short, half the men rated Japanese before the frustrating experience of missing Bank Night to take hard tests, and Mexicans afterwards; the other half rated Mexicans before and Japanese afterwards.

RESULTS

The results are presented in Table 1. It can be seen that after the frustrating situation there was a definite decrease in the number of favorable items checked.[4] This decrease was relatively reliable, being of a magnitude to be expected less than three times in 100 by chance alone.

That this decrease was not solely due to an indiscriminate tendency for the men to check fewer items in general after the testing session than before is indicated by the fact that, if anything, slightly more negative items were checked afterwards than before.[5] That

TABLE 1
THE EFFECT OF A FRUSTRATION IMPOSED BY THE IN-GROUP
UPON ATTITUDES EXPRESSED TOWARD OUT-GROUPS

| | Favorable traits | | Unfavorable traits | |
	Before	After	Before	After
Mean	5.71	4.11	2.93	3.26
Sigma	3.03	3.06	2.70	2.76
Sigma mean	.55	.56	.49	.50
After minus before	−1.60		+.33	
Sigma difference	.78		.70	
Critical ratio	2.05		.47	

[4]This was true of both the Mexicans and the Japanese.

[5]The results were probably produced by the joint operation of two factors: (1) a tendency to be less cooperative with the experimenter and hence to check fewer items, and (2) a tendency to give the foreigners a slightly less favorable rating. With respect to the positive items these two tendencies would operate in the same direction and produce a relatively stable difference; with respect to the negative items these two tendencies would be operating in opposite directions and hence tend to cancel each other out, producing a small difference.

these results were the function of the intervening activity, presumed to be frustrating, and were not merely changes produced
by a repetition of the testing situation is indicated by the fact that
a control group given the same check lists separated by an equal
period of time not involving strong frustration showed changes
slightly in the opposite direction: that is, they checked more
favorable items and fewer unfavorable items.

Since the decrease in number of favorable items checked does
not seem to have been the product of either the retesting situation
or a general tendency to check fewer items, it seems plausible to
assume that it represents a real change in the attitudes expressed
as a result of the frustrating situation. To the extent that the less
favorable attitude toward the foreigners may be termed aggression,
the results suggest that the frustrations imposed on the young men
by the experimenters elicited aggression which was generalized
somewhat to the faraway foreigners, who could not possibly have
been to blame for the situation. This is in line with the two assumptions under investigation, namely: (1) that frustration arouses
aggression, and (2) that the members of out-groups are sufficiently
similar as stimulus objects to members of the in-group so that
responses (in this case to aggression) will generalize from members of the in-group to members of the out-group.

Although the results are favorable enough to suggest that further
work of a similar nature might profitably be done to test these
assumptions, they may by no means be considered definite proof
of the assumptions. Before such results could be more convincing,
the following points would have to be more definitely established:
(1) That the scale used is actually a valid measure of aggression.
Objections on this score might be overcome by employing a variety
of better measures of aggression. (2) That the seeming spread of
aggression actually is a generalization of aggression. This might be
established by demonstrating that it follows such laws of generalization as have already been definitely established in experiments on
conditioned responses. One such law is that, other things being
equal, the amount of generalization varies directly as the similarity
of the stimulus patterns involved. Unfortunately the extremely
short notice that was available in preparing material for this experiment prevented the inclusion of refinements which might have
made the results more conclusive.

SUMMARY

Thirty-one young men at a camp were asked to indicate their attitudes toward Japanese and Mexicans before and after a situation which involved the frustration of giving up attending Bank Night at the local theater and taking hard tests instead. After the frustration they attributed a smaller number of desirable traits and a larger number of undesirable traits to these foreigners, who could not possibly have been to blame for the situation. The first difference was statistically reliable, the second was not. This suggests that the foreigners were similar enough as stimulus objects to the experimenters so that the aggression aroused against the former generalized to the latter. Further experiments would be necessary in order definitely to establish this point.

REFERENCES

1. DOLLARD, J., *et al.*   *Frustration and Aggression.* New Haven: Yale Univ. Press, 1939.
2. DOLLARD, J.   *Caste and Class in a Southern Town.* New Haven: Yale Univ. Press, 1937.
3. HOVLAND, C. I., and SEARS, R. R.   Minor studies of aggression: VI. Correlation of lynchings with economic indices. *J. of Psychol.*, 1940, 9, 301–310.
4. MILLER, N. E.   Theory and experiment relating psychoanalytic displacement to stimulus-response generalization. *J. Abn. and Soc. Psychol.*, (in press).
5. MILLER, N. E., *et al.* The frustration-aggression hypothesis, *Psychol. Rev.*, 1941, 48, 337–342.
6. SEARS, R. R., HOVLAND, C. I., and MILLER, N. E.   Minor studies of aggression: I. Measurement of aggressive behavior. *J. of Psychol.*, 1940, 9, 275–295.
7. SEARS, R. R., and SEARS, P. S.   Minor studies of aggression: V. Strength of frustration-reaction as a function of strength of drive. *J. of Psychol.*, 1940, 9, 297–300.

15

New Measure of Effects of Persuasive Communications: A Chemical Indicator of Toothbrushing Behavior

RICHARD I. EVANS, RICHARD M. ROZELLE, THOMAS M. LASATER, THEODORE M. DEMBROSKI, and BEM P. ALLEN

Individuals do not always behave in the manner they claim. This problem has plagued the social psychologist, especially when he is attempting to deal with attitudes that are supposed to predict actual behavior in real-life settings. In most studies of persuasion, for example, the effects of exposure to various persuasive messages are assessed by paper and pencil tests in which people simply report their behavior. For many reasons (e.g., the person feels he will be subject to criticism if he does not report behavior expected of him) there is considerable doubt as to the accuracy of these verbal reports concerning actual behavior. Another related problem deals with reports of the intention to behave. Here also there is doubt. Do individuals actually do what they say they are going to do?

The reason for the predominance of verbal tests as a reflection of actual behavior is that it is rarely feasible to accurately observe and measure an individual's actual behavior. This

From: *Psychological Reports*, 23: 731–736, 1968. Reprinted by permission of the authors and publisher. Copyright © 1968 by Southern Universities Press.

report reflects the development of a measure of actual behavior in a real-life setting that is not dependent on the verbal
reports of subjects, and demonstrates how it will be used in
an extensive, basic research effort in a real-life setting dealing
with many basic problems in the social psychology of persuasion.

The present report describes one aspect of a large-scale study of
attitude change designed to examine the inter-relationship of cognitive, affective, predispositional, and actual behavioral change as
a function of persuasive communications involving differential
emotional arousal. This investigation extends earlier, more limited
work (e.g., Janis & Feshbach, 1953) in real-life settings, with a
greater focus on change of actual behavior. A pilot study was conducted to develop and field test a more generally usable, reliable,
and valid measure of behavioral change.

A recurring question implicit in research on attitudes concerns
the inter-relationship of components. For example, is there necessarily a relationship between changes in cognition as recorded
by paper-and-pencil tests and behavioral change? Many definitions
of the construct attitude have implied such a relationship. For
example, the definitions of attitude by Campbell (1963), Krech,
Crutchfield, and Ballachey (1962), Harding, Kutner, Proshansky,
and Chein (1954), and Allport (1935) have reflected the notion
of disposition to act. Yet some investigators (La Piere, 1934;
Harding, *et al.*, 1954; Festinger, 1964; Fishbein, 1967) have emphasized the lack of an adequate demonstration of a true behavioral component in attitudes as evidenced in studies of attitude
change.

NOTE: This research was supported in the context of Psychology Research
Training Grant No. 5 TI DE 138 from the National Institute of Dental
Research, under the direction of the first author. This paper was presented
at the Southwestern Psychological Association meeting, New Orleans,
Louisiana, April, 1968. Thanks are expressed for the fine cooperation of
the Aldine Independent School District, Houston, Texas, and in particular,
Supt. W. W. Thorne and Nurse Barbara Wallace.
    Special thanks are expressed to Dean Sumter S. Arnim of the University
of Texas Graduate School of Bio-medical Sciences for his advice from a
dental perspective in the adapting of the disclosing tablet (which he
developed) to the special requirements of our investigation.

Implicit in this problem is the need for suitable behavioral measures. Many have suffered from a number of basic drawbacks. Studies such as those of Rokeach and Mezei (1966) have used experimental procedures involving nonrepresentative behavior samplings, which could result in their measurements reflecting only situation specific behavioral changes. Often these and other techniques such as recording X-rays taken (Leventhal & Niles, 1964) and tetanus inoculations (Leventhal, Singer, & Jones, 1965) are essentially measures of an infrequent rather than a common behavior. In studies where there is an attempt to measure behavior over any length of time, they often must rely upon relatively indirect measures which have limitations.

In response to the many problems traditionally involved in developing an adequate measure of behavior for studies of attitude change and as the result of an examination of psychological research possibilities in dentistry (Evans, 1966), the present investigators became interested in a recent development. Arnim (1963) described a technique for assessing cleanliness of a patient's mouth, which involved the use of a disclosing agent (erythrosin) in tablet form which, when chewed, dyes red the bacterial placque present on the teeth. By taking Kodachrome photographs of the stained teeth and measuring the percentage of the surface containing bacteria, Arnim was able to evaluate the differential effectiveness of various techniques of dental hygiene. Arnim also reports successful use of the tablets by patients in their homes as a means of identifying areas of the teeth consistently missed during normal brushing. Since his work indicates that the amount of bacteria disclosed by the tablet can be used as a measure of cleanliness of S's mouth and since cleanliness can be taken as a direct reflection of S's dental hygiene, the writers felt the technique might be a useful behavioral criterion. The present investigation was designed to test the utility of the tablet in a social psychological field study.

For this technique to be an acceptable criterion of behavioral change relating to attitudinal change in a field setting with large populations, the following conditions should be met. The measure should (a) be relatively inexpensive, (b) require a minimum amount of time, and (c) yield a reliable and valid index of cleanliness as a function of practices of dental hygiene.

In view of the first two requirements it was decided to abandon the tedious and time consuming procedure of actually measuring the exact percentage of the surface of the teeth covered by bacterial placque, which Arnim had used, and instead attempt to develop a simpler method that would not require special equipment or training. After some experimentation with various scaling procedures, it was concluded that a five-point rating scale would fulfill requirements adequately. It was also felt that further evidence in support of the validity of the method could be obtained by the reflection of changes in measured cleanliness, which should follow the presentation of several types of persuasive appeals designed to modify practices of dental hygiene. A number of investigators have demonstrated the effectiveness of various emotional appeals to motivate attitudinal and behavioral change (Janis & Feshbach, 1953; Leventhal, *et al.*, 1965; Leventhal & Niles, 1964; Janis, 1967).

METHOD

Three groups of Ss were formed by choosing two eighth grade classes from two junior high schools and one ninth grade class from a senior high school (combined $n = 68$). Since the comparisons to be made were between pre- and posttests within each group, the approximate 1 year age difference between the eighth and ninth grades was not considered critical. The advantage of not risking an "intra-group contamination effect" was deemed experimentally more sound than strictly matching groups. However, there were no apparent differences between groups with respect to socio-economic background.

Three persuasive appeals were designed and presented to the different groups. One stressed the positive consequences of proper dental hygiene, the second stressed the negative consequences of failing to use the proper techniques, and the third made no reference to consequences but simply discussed dentistry and science.

The formal presentation of these persuasive appeals was made within the context of an ostensible program of dental hygiene training. Included in each appeal was a presentation of a set of detailed procedures for care of the teeth. These presentations were made in conjunction with the on-going public health education program of the local school system. In the present brief report, rather than detailing the rationale and operations involved in the manipulation of the independent variable, a description of the standardization of the dependent variable (novel behavioral measure) is stressed.

A single lens reflex 35-mm. camera was utilized to record pre- and posttest color slides, closeups of the mouths of the 68 Ss. Ss were first asked to chew the disclosing wafers, then standard dental retractors were used to expose the stained teeth. The entire procedure took an average of 1½ min. per S.

All 136 slides were randomly assigned an identifying number between 1 and 136. This made identification of a slide with a specific experimental group or as a pre- or posttest picture impossible except by reference to the master list, to which raters did not have access.

The procedure for developing a five-point rating scale of cleanliness of teeth had a number of discrete steps. First, all slides with poorly aligned, chipped or missing teeth, as well as those wearing braces, were eliminated from consideration as a possible standard. This was done in order to prevent compounding of the structure of the teeth with amount of red dye evident upon them.

Three sophomore dental students were then asked to view independently all the remaining slides and note the identifying numbers of all those that were "very dirty" and those that were "very clean." The selections were compared and those chosen by all three raters retained. The two resulting groups of 15 slides each were then ranked by each rater utilizing a paired-comparison procedure. The ranks assigned each slide were averaged and the one receiving the median average rank within each group was selected as representative of that extreme group. The "very clean" anchor was designated as "1" and the "very dirty" as "5."

The next step involved the selection of the midpoint of the scale. The two extreme standards were projected on a screen simultaneously and all the rest of the slides projected one at a time at a point midway between the two standards. The raters, again independently, selected all those slides that seemed to fall midway between the two previously established standards of "very clean" and "very dirty."

The 20 slides chosen by all three raters were then presented in differing orders to three groups of 20 undergraduate students. These students were instructed to decide to which of the two standards each of the slides was most similar. Each slide had to be rated as either 1 or 5 as these were the only permissible responses. The ratings of all 60 raters were then combined and the slide that was rated a "1" by 50% of the raters and as "5" by the remaining raters was chosen as representative of that point midway between "1" and "5" (i.e., "3").

Exactly the same procedure used to determine the "3" point on the scale was used to determine "2" and "4," the only difference being that to establish a standard for "2" the previously selected "1" and "3" were used, and to find "4," "3" and "5" were utilized.

After the selection of the five standards representing the five points of the rating scale, all pre- and posttest slides, except for those which were employed as standards, were rated by reference to these standards. This was done by projecting all five standards on a screen and then presenting each slide to be rated below the standards. Four raters working independently rated each slide by deciding to which of the five standards it was most similar. The final rating for each slide was the average scale value attributed to it. The values of the slides of Ss whose slides were employed as standards were also included in the analysis.

RESULTS AND DISCUSSION

The results indicated that the disclosing tablet measure met the reliability and validity criteria. Interrater reliability coefficients, which were computed on the basis of the final ratings, showed high interrater agreement (.81, .82, .83, .84, .86).[1] In terms of validity, differences between pre- and post-communication ratings

[1]Preliminary analysis of data obtained in our extensive follow-up study indicates that interrater reliabilities, utilizing refined procedures for training raters, are higher than those of our pilot study.

were statistically significant for a group presented with a fear-appeal communication ($t = 3.67$, $p < .001$) and a group presented with a positive communication ($t = 3.71$, $p < .001$), but not for a group presented with a neutral communication. Means, standard deviations and ns are presented in Table 1. The group who received the fear appeal is cleaner on the pre-test measure than are the other two groups. It should be noted that this group was composed of the ninth grade high school Ss and the other groups

TABLE 1
MEAN AND STANDARD DEVIATION VALUES FOR PRE- AND POSTTEST
MEASURES OF TEETH CLEANLINESS FOR EACH APPEAL GROUP

Type of Appeal	n	Pretest		Posttest	
		M	SD	M	SD
Fear	26	2.03	.86	1.44	.56
Positive	19	2.85	.99	1.92	.67
Neutral	23	2.52	1.26	2.45	1.09

were composed of eighth grade junior high school Ss. As mentioned earlier, an effort was made to select Ss who were highly similar in age and background, but these results suggest that there may be behavioral differences with regard to dental hygiene practices between junior and senior high school Ss even though their ages differ by only 1 year. In sum, preliminary results indicate the effectiveness and utility of this procedure in assessing behavioral change. In addition, it is relatively inexpensive and requires a minimum amount of time to utilize. As reported above, reliability and validity data appear to meet the proposed criteria satisfactorily. Consequently, this method is now being explored in an extensive follow-up field research study.

SUMMARY

The purpose of the present investigation was to develop a behavioral measure of attitude change and examine its utility for large-scale field research efforts. Three groups were formed from

68 junior and senior high school students and each was presented
with a different form (positive, fear, neutral) of a communication
within the context of a public school system's on-going dental hygiene program. Cleanliness of their teeth was measured by a
chemical in tablet form called a "disclosing tablet" which, when
chewed, stains red the areas of concentration of bacterial placque
on the teeth. The study involved taking a 35-mm. color slide of
each S's mouth before and two weeks after the experimental communication. Preliminary results lend support to the effectiveness
and utility of this procedure in assessing behavioral change within
a natural setting.

REFERENCES

ALLPORT, G. W. Attitudes. In C. Murchison (Ed.), *A handbook of
social psychology*. Worcester, Mass.: Clark Univer., 1935. Pp.
798–884.

ARNIM, S. S. The use of disclosing agents for measuring tooth cleanliness. *Journal of Periodontology*, 1963, 34, 227–245.

CAMPBELL, D. T. Social attitudes and other acquired behavioral
dispositions. In S. Koch (Ed.), *Psychology: a study of a science.*
Vol. IV. New York: McGraw-Hill, 1963. Pp. 94–172.

EVANS, R. I. Psychologists in dental research: some social psychological parameters. *American Psychologist*, 1966, 21, 167–172.

FESTINGER, L. Behavioral support for opinion change. *Public
Opinion Quarterly*, 1964, 28, 404–417.

FISHBEIN, M. Attitudes and the prediction of behavior. In M. Fishbein (Ed.), *Readings in attitude theory and measurement*. New
York: Wiley, 1967. Pp. 477–492.

HARDING, J., KUTNER, B., PROSHANSKY, H., and CHEIN, I. Prejudice
and ethnic relations. In G. Lindzey (Ed.), *Handbook of social
psychology*. Vol. II. *Special fields and applications*. New York:
Addison Wesley, 1954. Pp. 1021–1061.

JANIS, I. L. Effects of fear arousal on attitude change: recent develop-
ments in theory and experimental research. In L. Berkowitz (Ed.),
Advances in experimental social psychology. Vol. 3. New York:
Academic Press, 1967. Pp. 166–224.

JANIS, I. L., and FESHBACH, S. Effects of fear-arousing communications. *Journal of Abnormal and Social Psychology*, 1953, 48,
78–92.

KRECH, D., CRUTCHFIELD, R. E., and BALLACHEY, E. L.   *Individual in society.* New York: McGraw-Hill, 1962.

LA PIERE, R. T.   Attitudes vs. actions. *Social Forces,* 1934, 13, 230–237.

LEVENTHAL, H., and NILES, P.   A field experiment in fear arousal with data on the validity of questionnaire measures. *Journal of Personality,* 1964, 32, 459–479.

LEVENTHAL, H., SINGER, R. P., and JONES, S.   The effects of fear and specificity of recommendation upon attitudes and behavior. *Journal of Personality and Social Psychology,* 1965, 2, 20–29.

ROKEACH, M., and MEZEI, L.   Race and shared belief as factors in social choice. *Science,* 1966, 151, 167–172.

16

Unintended Communication of Interpersonal Expectations

ROBERT ROSENTHAL

Individuals often communicate their feelings and expectations in subtle ways that are not readily observable to others—even to the trained social observer. In the following report, data are presented which raise crucial questions as to the adequacy of present methods of analysis of the expression of human feelings and expectations. The data reveal the existence of unintended but highly significant communications both in the controlled laboratory setting and everyday, real-life settings.

In spite of his efforts to be objective, the scientist may be more influenced by these unintended communications. What is perhaps most disturbing is that this research raises questions which have yet to be answered in a way acceptable to the special problems of the social psychologist as he carries out investigations in real-life settings.

From: *The American Behavioral Scientist*, 10(8): 24–26, April, 1967. Reprinted by permission of the author and of Sage Publications, Inc.

Ever since Pfungst's (1911, 1965) brilliant series of experiments with Clever Hans, we have known that the expectation of the behavioral scientist could become an unintended determinant of the response of his research subject. Hans, it will be remembered, was that clever horse who could solve problems of mathematics and musical harmony with equal skill and grace, simply by tapping out the answers with his hoof. A committee of eminent experts testified that Hans, whose owner made no profit from his horse's talents, was receiving no cues from his questioners. Of course, Pfungst later showed that this was not so, that tiny head and eye movements were Hans' signals to begin and to end his tapping. When Hans was asked a question, the questioner looked at Hans' hoof, quite naturally so, for that was the way for him to determine whether Hans' answer was correct. Then it was discovered that when Hans approached the correct number of taps, the questioner would inadvertently move his head or eyes upward —just enough that Hans could discriminate the cue, but not enough that even trained animal observers or psychologists could see it.

THE "CLEVER HANS" PHENOMENON

The "Clever Hans" phenomenon has also been demonstrated to occur in more ordinary and more recent experiments, the details of which are found elsewhere (Rosenthal, 1966). Briefly, the expectancy or hypothesis of the experimenter has been shown to be a significant determinant of the results of his research in studies of person perception, verbal conditioning, personality assessment and animal learning. The basic paradigm for such studies has been to divide a sample of experimenters into two equivalent groups and to create in each an expectancy for the data they

NOTE: The research described in this paper has been supported by research grants (G-17685, G-24826, GS-177, GS-714) from the Division of Social Sciences of the National Science Foundation. A greatly expanded version of this paper has been prepared for publication in the *Psychological Bulletin* under the title "Covert Communication in the Psychological Experiment."

would obtain which was opposite in direction to the expectancy induced in the other group of experimenters. Thus, in the animal learning studies, half the experimenters were told that their rats had been specially bred for "maze brightness" or "Skinner box brightness." The remaining experimenters were told that their animals had been specially bred for maze or "Skinner box" dullness. The rats run by experimenters expecting good performance performed significantly better than did the rats run by experimenters expecting poor performance. This was equally true in maze learning and in operant learning experiments.

In the person perception studies, half the experimenters were told that their subjects (humans now) had been selected because they tended to see photos of people as reflecting a great deal of past success, while the remaining experimenters were told that their subjects had been selected for the perception of failure in other people's faces. Subjects were then randomly assigned to their experimenters who subtly communicated their expectancies to their subjects in such a way that subjects expected to be success-perceivers became success-perceivers while subjects expected to be failure-perceivers became failure-perceivers. We can safely say that the communication processes whereby subjects learned of experimenter expectations were subtle ones because for nearly five years we have been analyzing sound films of such experiments and we have yet to find the specific cues that mediate the "Clever Hans" phenomenon to human subjects. This is not for want of careful observation. The films have been observed by dozens of psychologists, graduate students, and undergraduate students. We all wish Pfungst were here to help us now, though there is some experimental evidence that human subjects are not using the same sort of cues that Clever Hans employed.

What we do know of the communication to subjects of the experimenter's expectancy has been learned as much from experiments as from the analysis of sound motion pictures of experimenters interacting with their human subjects. The experiments are briefly summarized below.

In an experiment by Fode (1960) screens were interposed between experimenters and subjects so that the communication of the experimenters' expectancies could occur only through the auditory channel. Under these conditions of restricted communication, the effects of experimenters' expectancies were significantly reduced but by no means eliminated.

Just how important auditory cues may be for the communication of an experimenter's expectation to his research subject has been dramatically demonstrated by John Adair and his students (1966). They first conducted a study which was essentially a replication of the basic experiment on the self-fulfilling effects of experimenters' prophecies or hypotheses. Results showed that, just as in the original studies, experimenters who prophesied the perception of success by their subjects fulfilled their prophecies, as did the experimenters who had prophesied the perception of failure by their subjects.

During the conduct of this replication experiment, Adair's group tape recorded the experimenter's instructions to their subjects. The second experiment was then conducted not by experimenters at all, but by tape recordings of experimenters' voices reading standard instructions to their subjects. When the tape recorded instructions had originally been read by experimenters expecting success perception by their subjects, the tape recordings evoked greater success perceptions from their subjects. When the tape recorded instructions had originally been read by experimenters expecting failure perception by their subjects, the tape recordings evoked greater failure perceptions from their subjects. Self-fulfilling prophecies, it seems, come about as a result of the prophet's voice alone.

Most recently it has been discovered that when an experimenter's instructions to subjects include a recitation of response alternatives it is possible to predict how a subject will respond to the experimental task from a para-linguistic analysis of the experimenter's reading of the response alternatives (Duncan and Rosenthal, 1966). In the photo rating task described earlier, when the experimenter gave greater vocal emphasis to the response alternatives associated with ratings of success, subjects rated photos as being of more successful people. When greater vocal emphasis was given to the response alternatives associated with ratings of failure subjects rated photos as being of less successful people.

Early in the history of the research program on self-fulfilling prophecies in the behavioral sciences it had been thought that a process of operant conditioning might be responsible for their operation. It was thought that perhaps every time the subject gave a response consistent with the experimenter's expectation, the experimenter might look more pleasant, or smile, or glance at the subject approvingly, even without the experimenter's being aware of his own reinforcing responses. The experimenter, in other words, might unwittingly have taught the subject what responses were the desired ones. Several experiments were analyzed to see whether this hypothesis of operant conditioning might apply. If it did apply, we would expect that the subjects' responses gradually became more like those prophesied by the experimenter—that there would be a learning curve for subjects. But no learning curve was found. On the contrary, it turned out that the subjects' very first responses were about as much affected by their experimenters' expectancies as were their very last responses. Since the very first response, by definition, cannot follow any unwitting reinforcement by the experimenter, the mechanism of operant conditioning can be ruled out as necessary to the communication of experimenters' expectancies.

True, there was no learning curve for subjects, but there seemed to be a learning curve for experimenters. Several studies showed that prophesied results became more likely as more subjects were contacted by each experimenter. In fact, there was very little expectancy effect in evidence for just the very first-seen subjects. If the experimenter were indeed learning to increase the unintended influence of his prophecy, who would be the teacher? Most likely, the subject. It seems reasonable to think of a subject's responding in the direction of the experimenter's hypothesis as a reinforcing event. Therefore, whatever the covert communicative behavior of the experimenter that preceded the subject's reinforcement becomes more likely to recur. Subjects, then, may quite unintentionally shape the experimenter's unintended communicative behavior. Not only does the experimenter influence his subjects to respond in the expected manner, but his subjects may well evoke just that unintended behavior that will lead them to respond increasingly as prophesied. Probably neither subject nor experimenter "knows" just exactly what the unintended communication behavior is—and neither do we.

When it was mentioned earlier that the observation of the films of experimenters interacting with their subjects had not solved the modern riddle of Clever Hans, it was not meant that the films had not been worth while. One of the most exciting findings was that it was possible to predict whether an experimenter would subsequently influence his subjects to respond in accordance with his hypothesis from the experimenter's behavior during the first half-minute of his interaction with the subject. Experimenters who were more likable, dominant, personal, relaxed, and important-acting during these initial seconds of the interaction and less given to leg movements, later obtained data significantly biased in the direction of their hypothesis.

Observations were made of the sound films by one group of observers, of the silent films by another group, and of the sound track alone by a third group. Interestingly, during this phase of the experiment, it did not help the observers at all to have access to the sound track. None of the observations made by the group with access only to the sound track was predictive of subsequent effects of the experimenter's expectancy. The group of observers with access only to the silent films did just as well in predicting subsequent biasing as did the observers who had access to the sound films. During this brief pre-instructional phase, then, tone-of-voice variables seemed to be of little consequence.

Observations of the experimenter's behavior during the instruction-reading period showed much the same pattern of variables to be predictive of subsequent biasing of the subject's responses. Only now there were a great many more predictor variables which reached significance, and the correlations became larger. (The largest of the newly significant predictors of subsequent biasing was the variable of professionalness of manner, $r = +.45$, $p < .005$). The details are presented elsewhere (Rosenthal, 1966), but one interesting phenomenon must be mentioned. During the instruction-reading period of the experiment, a number of tone-of-voice variables became significant predictors of the experimenter's subsequent unintended biasing effects. Very often, the direction of the predictive correlation with a variable judged from the sound track alone was in the opposite direction from the correlation with the same variable judged from the films without sound track. One example must do. Experimenters who later biased their subjects' responses more were *seen* as more honest ($r = +.40$, $p < .01$) in the films but were *heard* as less honest ($r = -.30$, $p < .05$).

Current work in the search for the cues mediating the "Clever Hans" phenomenon has turned to a closer examination of the implications for unintended communication processes of such channel discrepancy. Such an examination may have consequences for areas other than the social psychology of the psychological experiment. It is, for example, part of clinical lore, though the evidence is scanty (Ringuette and Kennedy, 1966), that such channel discrepancies may have important consequences for the development of psychopathology (Bateson, *et al.*, 1956).

The clinical and social importance of a better understanding of discrepancies among communication channels has been recently implied in a study of the treatment of alcoholism. Tape recordings were made of nine physicians' voices as they talked about their experiences with alcoholic patients. There was no relationship between the amount of hostility judges perceived in the doctors' speech and the doctor's effectiveness in getting alcoholics to accept treatment. However, when the content was filtered out of the tape recordings, the degree of hostility found in the doctors' tone of voice alone was found to correlate significantly and negatively with their success in influencing alcoholics to accept treatment (Milmoe *et al.*, 1966).

BEYOND THE LABORATORY

The particular patterns of covert communication which have been described as relevant to the experimenter's communication of his expectancy to his subject are no doubt specific to the type of experiment being performed. We are in no position to speak for the generality of any of these findings across different experiments, much less for their generality in the other "real world," that one outside the laboratory. But there are some conclusions to be drawn from the data presented here and from the program of research which has investigated the effects of the experimenter's expectancy.

Perhaps the most compelling and most general conclusion is that human beings can engage in highly effective and influential unprogrammed and unintended communication with one another. If such communication is responsible in the psychological experiment for the fulfillment of the experimenter's expectancy, it might also be responsible for the fulfillment of other expectancies held by humans outside the laboratory. If rats learn better when their experimenter thinks they will, then children may learn better if their teachers think they will.

The experiment, a longitudinal one, has been described elsewhere (Rosenthal and Jacobson, 1966). The procedure was exactly as in the experiments on the effects of the experimenter's expectancy. All the children in an elementary school were given an intelligence test which was disguised as a test which would predict academic "blooming." There were 18 classes, three at each of six grade levels. By the use of a table of random numbers, about 20 per cent of the children in each class were chosen for the experimental condition. The experimental treatment consisted of telling their teachers that they had scored on the predictive achievement test such that they would show unusual intellectual development within the next academic year. At the end of the academic year the children were retested with the same test of intelligence.

For the 18 classes combined, children whose teachers expected them to gain in performance showed a significantly greater gain in I.Q. than did the control children, though the mean relative gain in IQ was small (3.8 points). Teachers' expectancies, it turned out, made little difference in the upper grades. But at the lower levels the effects were dramatic. First graders purported to be bloomers gained 15.4 IQ points more than did the control children and in the second grade, the relative gain was 9.5 IQ points. These effects were especially surprising in view of the large gains in IQ made by the control group, which had to be surpassed by the experimental groups. Thus, first graders in the control group gained 12 IQ points and second graders gained 7 IQ points, somewhat larger than might simply be ascribed to practice effects. More likely, the entire school was affected to some degree by being involved in an experiment with consequent good effects on children's performance.

Experimenters, teachers, probably psychotherapists, and probably "ordinary" people can affect the behavior of those with whom they interact by virtue of their expectations of what that behavior will be. Of course, we must now try to learn how such communication takes place—how teachers communicate their expectations to their pupils. Considering the difficulties we have had in trying to answer that same question for the case of experimenters, whose inputs into the experimenter-subject interaction could be much more easily controlled and observed, we should not expect a quick or easy solution. But that should not deter us from making the effort.

REFERENCES

ADAIR, J. G.   Personal communication, July, 1966.

BATESON, G., et al.   Toward a theory of schizophrenia, *Behavioral Science*, 1, (1956), 251–264.

DUNCAN, S. and ROSENTHAL, R.   Vocal Emphasis in Experimenters' Instruction Reading as Unintended Determinant of Subjects' Responses (Unpublished manuscript, University of Chicago, 1966).

FODE, K. L.   The Effect of Non-visual and Non-verbal Interaction on Experimenter Bias (Unpublished master's thesis, University of North Dakota, 1960).

MILMOE, SUSAN, et al.   The doctor's voice: Postdictor of successful Referral of Alcoholic Patients, *Journal of Abnormal Psychology*, 71 (1966).

PFUNGST, O.   *Clever Hans (The Horse of Mr. von Osten): A Contribution to Experimental, Animal, and Human Psychology*, trans. C. L. Rahn, 1965 ed., (New York: Holt, 1911).

RINGUETTE, E. L. and KENNEDY, TRUDY.   An experimental study of the double-bind hypothesis. *Journal of Abnormal Psychology*, 71 (1966), 136–141.

ROSENTHAL, R.   *Experimenter Effects in Behavioral Research*, New York: Appleton-Century-Crofts, 1966.

ROSENTHAL, R. and JACOBSON, LENORE.   Teachers' expectancies: Determinants of pupils' IQ gains, *Psychological Reports*, 19 (1966), 115–118.

17

Conformity and Character

RICHARD S. CRUTCHFIELD

In many instances the social psychologist, when studying natural setting behavior, must remain as unobtrusive as possible. When an experimental procedure is involved, this requirement is not easily satisfied. It is obviously difficult to expose individuals to an experimental treatment without their becoming aware of it. When, however, individuals expect to be tested as part of the normal situation anyway, and experimental procedure merely involves additional testing, remaining unobtrusive is not so difficult for the researcher.

In this report the social psychologist took advantage of an already programmed intensive testing situation in which individuals who were involved in some leadership capacity were being assessed on various factors related to superior performance in their respective professions. A set-up to measure conformity behavior was introduced as simply another testing procedure.

The entire experiment was thus conducted without any of the individuals involved realizing that they were actually serving in a carefully designed experiment. Valuable information

From: *American Psychologist*, 10: 191–198, 1955. Reprinted by permission of the author and of American Psychological Association.

was obtained which revealed among other things that a surprising number of leaders, who hopefully are individualists, tend to fall prey to group pressure to conform. Ethical problems in the use of such deceptive ways of conducting an experiment are also discussed.

During the Spring of 1953, one hundred men visited the Institute of Personality Assessment and Research at the University of California, Berkeley, to participate in an intensive three-day assessment of those qualities related to superior functioning in their profession.[1]

As one of the procedures on the final day of assessment, the men were seated in groups of five in front of an apparatus consisting of five adjacent electrical panels. Each panel had side wings, forming an open cubicle, so that the person, though sitting side by side with his fellow subjects, was unable to see their panels. The experimenter explained that the apparatus was so wired that information could be sent by each man to all the others by closing any of eleven switches at the bottom of his panel. This information would appear on the other panels in the form of signal lights, among five rows of eleven lights, each row corresponding to one of the five panels. After a warm-up task to acquaint the men with the workings of the apparatus, the actual procedure commenced.

Slides were projected on a wall directly facing the men. Each slide presented a question calling for a judgment by the person. He indicated his choice of one of several multiple-alternative answers by closing the appropriately numbered switch on his panel. Moreover, he responded *in order*, that is, as designated by one of five red lights lettered A, B, C, D, E, on his panel. If he were A,

NOTE: Adapted from the address of the retiring president of the Division of Personality and Social Psychology, American Psychological Association, New York City, September 4, 1954.

[1]The principal study reported here owes much to the collaboration of Dr. Donald W. MacKinnon, director of the Institute of Personality Assessment and Research, and of his staff. Mr. Donald G. Woodworth has contributed especially to the statistical analysis of data.

he responded first, if B, second, and so on. The designations, A, B, C, D, and E, were rotated by the experimenter from time to time, thus permitting each person to give his judgments in all the different serial positions. No further explanation about the purpose of this procedure was offered.

It may help to convey the nature of the men's typical experiences by giving an illustrative description of what happens concretely to one of the men. The first slide calls for a simple judgment of which of two geometrical figures is larger in area. Since his red light C is on, he waits for A and B to respond before making his response. And, as he is able to observe on the panel, his own judgment coincides with the judgments of A and B who preceded him, and of D and E who follow him. After judgments on several further slides in position C, he is then shifted to position D for more slides, then to A.

The slides call for various kinds of judgments—lengths of lines, areas of figures, logical completion of number series, vocabulary items, estimates of the opinions of others, expression of his own attitudes on issues, expression of his personal preferences for line drawings, etc. He is not surprised to observe a perfectly sensible relationship between his judgments and those of the other four men. Where clear-cut perceptual or logical judgments are involved, he finds that his judgments are in perfect agreement with those of the other four. Where matters of opinion are involved, and some differences in opinion to be expected, his judgments and those of the other four men are sometimes in agreement and sometimes not.

Eventually the man finds himself for the first time in position E, where he is to respond last. The next slide shows a standard line and five comparison lines, of which he is to pick the one equal in length to the standard. Among the previous slides he has already encountered this kind of perceptual judgment and has found it easy. On looking at this slide it is immediately clear to him that line number 4 is the correct one. But as he waits his turn to respond, he sees light number 5 in row A go on, indicating that that person has judged line number 5 to be correct. And in fairly quick succession light 5 goes on also in rows B, C, and D.

At this point the man is faced with an obvious conflict between his own clear perception and a unanimous contradictory consensus of the other four men. What does he do? Does he rely on the evidence of his own senses and respond independently? Or does he defer to the judgment of the group, complying with their perceptions rather than his own?

We will postpone for a moment the answer as to what he does, and revert to the description of our apparatus.

We have been describing the situation as if seen from the perspective of one of the men. Actually his understanding of the situation is wrong. He has been deceived. For the apparatus is *not* really wired in the way that he was informed. There actually is no connection among the five panels. Instead, they are all wired in an identical manner to a control panel where the experimenter sits behind the men. It is the experimenter who sends all the information which appears on the panels, and the wiring is in parallel in such a way that whatever signals are sent by the experimenter appear simultaneously and identically on all five panels. Moreover, the designations of serial order of responding—A through E—are identical at all times for the five panels, so that at a given moment, for instance, all five men believe themselves to be A, or at another time, E.

As we have just said, the responses actually made by the five men do not affect in any way the panels of the others. They do get registered individually on one part of the experimenter's control panel. The *latency* of each individual response to one tenth of a second is also recorded by timers on the control panel.

Hence, the situation as we have described it for our one illustrative man is actually the situation simultaneously experienced by all five men. They all commence in position C, and all shift at the same time to position D, and to A, and finally E. They all see the same simulated group judgments.

The entire situation is, in a word, contrived, and contrived so as to expose each individual to a standardized and prearranged series of group judgments. By this means the simulated group judgments can be made to appear sensible and in agreement with the individual, or, at chosen critical points, in conflict with his judgments.

Most of you will recognize at once the basic similarity of our situation to that invented by Asch (2) in his extremely important work of recent years on independence of individual judgment under opposing group pressure. In his method, ten subjects announced aloud and in succession their judgments of the relative length of stimulus lines exposed before the group. The first nine subjects were actually confederates of the experimenter, and gave uniformly false answers at pre-established points, thus placing pressure on the single naive subject.

For extensive research use, for instance in personality assessment, Asch's technique is handicapped by the severely unfavorable ratio of confederates to true subjects. The present technique, utilizing the electrical network described above, avoids this difficulty. There are no confederates required; all five subjects are tested simultaneously in a thoroughly standardized situation. The experimenter exercises highly flexible control of the simulated group judgments, and of the serial order of responding. Stimulus material to be judged can be varied as widely as desired by use of different slides.

Now at last come back to our man, still sitting before his panel, still confronted with the spurious group consensus, still torn between a force toward independent judgment and a force toward conformity to the group. How he is likely to behave in the situation can best be described by summarizing the results for our study of 50 of the 100 men in assessment.

EFFECTS OF CONSENSUS

All of these men were engaged in a profession in which leadership is one of the salient expected qualifications. Their average age was 34 years. Their educational levels were heterogeneous, but most had had some college training.

Fifty of the men were tested in the procedure as described. Another 40 served as *control* subjects; they simply gave individual judgments of the slides without using the apparatus, and hence without knowledge of the judgments of others. The distribution of judgments of these control subjects on each slide was subsequently used as a baseline for evaluating the amount of group pressure influence on the experimental subjects.

Now as to results. When faced with the dilemma posed by this first critical slide, 15 of the 50 men, or 30 per cent, conformed to the obviously false group consensus. The remaining 70 per cent of the men maintained independence of judgment in face of the contradictory group consensus.

The first critical slide was followed by 20 others, all with the subjects responding in position E. The 20 slides involved a broad sampling of judgmental materials, exploring the question of what would happen to other kinds of perceptions, to matters of factual appraisal and of logic, of opinion and attitude, of personal preference—all under the same conditions of group pressure. Interpolated among them were occasional neutral slides, in which the group consensus was simulated as correct or sensible, in order to help maintain the subjects' acceptance of the genuineness of the apparatus and situation.

The results on several more of the critical slides will give a representative picture of what happens under group pressure. First, take another kind of perceptual judgment. A circle and a star are exposed side by side, the circle being about one third larger in area than the star. The false group consensus is on the *star* as the larger, and 46 per cent of the men express agreement with this false judgment.

On a simple logical judgment of completion of a number series, as found in standard mental tests, 30 per cent of the men conform to an obviously illogical group answer, whereas not a single control subject gives an incorrect answer.

As striking as these influence effects are, they are overshadowed by the even higher degree of influence exhibited on another set of items. These pertain to perceptual, factual, and logical judgments which are designed to maximize the *ambiguity* of the stimulus. There are three such examples: (a) two actually equal circles are to be judged for relative size; (b) a pair of words are to be judged as either synonyms or antonyms, though actually entirely unrelated in meaning and unfamiliar to all subjects; (c) a number series is to be completed which is actually insoluble, that is, for which there is no logically correct completion.

To take the third example, which gives the most pronounced influence effect of all 21 critical items, 79 per cent of the men conform to a spurious group consensus upon an arbitrarily chosen and irrational answer.

Influence effects are found, we see, on both well-structured and poorly-structured stimuli, with markedly greater effects on the latter.

Turning from perceptual and factual judgments to opinions and attitudes, it is clearly evident that here, too, the judgments of many of the men are markedly dependent upon a spurious group consensus which violates their own inner convictions. For example, among control subjects virtually no one expresses disagreement with the statement: "I believe we are made better by the trials and hardships of life." But among the experimental subjects exposed to a group consensus toward disagreement, 31 per cent of the men shift to expressing disagreement.

It can be demonstrated that the conformity behavior is not found solely for attitudes on issues like the foregoing, which may be of rather abstract and remote significance for the person. Among the control sample of men, not a single one expresses agreement with the statement: "I doubt whether I would make a good leader," whereas 37 per cent of the men subjected to group pressure toward agreement succumb to it. Here is an issue relating to appraisal of the self and hence likely to be of some importance to the person, especially in light of the fact already mentioned that one of the salient expected qualifications of men in this particular profession is that of leadership.

The set of 21 critical items ranges from factual to attitudinal, from structured to ambiguous, from impersonal to personal. With only two exceptions, all these items yield significant group pressure influence effects in our sample of 50 men. The very existence of the two exceptional items is in itself an important finding, for it demonstrates that the observed influences are not simply evidence of indiscriminate readiness to conform to group pressure regardless of the specific nature of the judgment involved. The character of the two exceptional items is significant, for they are the two most extremely personal and subjective judgments, namely, those in which the individual is asked which one of two simple line drawings *he prefers*. On these slides there is virtually no effective result of group pressure. Not more than one man of the 50 expresses agreement with the spurious group consensus on the nonpreferred drawing. Such personal preferences, being most isolated from the relevance of group standards, thus seem to be most immune to group pressure.

INDIVIDUAL DIFFERENCES

To what extent do the 50 men differ among themselves in their general degree of conformity to group pressure?

A total "conformity score" is readily obtainable for each individual by counting the number of the 21 critical items on which he exhibits influence to the group pressure. The threshold for influence for each item is arbitrarily fixed on the basis of the distribution of judgments by control subjects on that item.

Considering that we are dealing with a fairly homogeneous sample of limited size, the range of individual differences that we obtain is astonishingly large, covering virtually the entire possible scope of our measure. At the lower extreme, several of the men showed conformity on no more than one or two of the critical items. At the upper extreme, one man was influenced on 17 of the 21 items. The rest of the scores are well distributed between these extremes, with a mean score of about eight items and a tendency for greater concentration of scores toward the lower conformity end.

The reliability of the total score, as a measure of generalized conformity in the situation, is obtained by correlating scores on two matched halves of the items. The correlation is found to be .82, which when corrected for combined halves gives a reliability estimate for the entire 21-item scale of .90.

To recapitulate, we find large and reliable differences among the 50 men in the amount of conformity behavior exhibited, and there appears to be considerable generality of this conformity behavior with respect to widely varied judgmental materials. Whether such conformity tendencies also generalize to other quite different behavioral situations is a question for future research.

RELATIONS TO PERSONALITY VARIABLES

Assuming that we are, indeed, measuring conformity tendencies that are fundamental in the person, the question is what traits of character distinguish between those men exhibiting much conformity behavior in our test and those exhibiting little conformity. The assessment setting within which these men were studied provides an unusually fertile opportunity to explore this question, in light of the wide range of personality measurements available.

Correlational study of the conformity scores with these other variables of personality provides some picture of the independent and of the conforming person. As contrasted with the high conformist, the independent man shows more intellectual effectiveness, ego strength, leadership ability, and maturity of social relations, together with a conspicuous absence of inferiority feelings, rigid and excessive self-control, and authoritarian attitudes.

A few correlations will illustrate. The assessment staff rating on "intellectual competence" correlates $-.63$ with conformity score, this being the highest relationship of any found. The *Concept Mastery Test*,[2] a measure of superior mental functioning, correlates $-.51$ with conformity. An "ego strength" scale, independently derived by Barron (3), correlates $-.33$, and a staff rating on "leadership ability," $-.30$ with conformity. Scales of Gough's *California Psychological Inventory* (6), pertaining to such dimensions as "tolerance," "social participation," and "responsibility," range in correlation from $-.30$ to $-.41$ with conformity.

And as for some of the positive correlates, the F scale (1), a measure of authoritarian attitudes, correlates $+.39$ with conformity, and a staff rating on amount of authoritarian behavior manifested in a standard psychodrama situation correlates $+.35$ with conformity.

The general appraisal of each man by the assessment staff in the form of descriptive Q sorts further enriches this picture. Those men exhibiting extreme independence in the situation as contrasted

[2]Used with the kind permission of Dr. Lewis M. Terman.

with those at the high conformity end are described more often in the following terms by the assessment staff, which was entirely ignorant of the actual behavior of the men in the group pressure procedure:

Is an effective leader.
Takes an ascendant role in his relations with others.
Is persuasive; tends to win other people over to his point of view.
Is turned to for advice and reassurance.
Is efficient, capable, able to mobilize resources easily and effectively.
Is active and vigorous.
Is an expressive, ebullient person.
Seeks and enjoys aesthetic and sensuous impressions.
Is natural; free from pretense, unaffected.
Is self-reliant; independent in judgment; able to think for himself.

In sharp contrast to this picture of the independent men is the following description of those high in conformity behavior:

With respect to authority, is submissive, compliant, and overly accepting.
Is conforming; tends to do the things that are prescribed.
Has a narrow range of interests.
Overcontrols his impulses; is inhibited; needlessly delays or denies gratification.
Is unable to make decisions without vacillation or delay.
Becomes confused, disorganized, and unadaptive under stress.
Lacks insight into his own motives and behavior.
Is suggestible; overly responsive to other people's evaluations rather than his own.

Further evidence is found in some of the specific items of personality inventories on which the answers of the high and low conformers are significantly different. Here are some illustrative items more frequently answered "True" by the independent subjects than by the conforming subjects:

Sometimes I rather enjoy going against the rules and doing things I'm not supposed to.
I like to fool around with new ideas, even if they turn out later to be a total waste of time.

A person needs to "show off" a little now and then.

At times I have been so entertained by the cleverness of a crook that I have hoped he would get by with it.

It is unusual for me to express strong approval or disapproval of the actions of others.

I am often so annoyed when someone tries to get ahead of me in a line of people that I speak to him about it.

Compared to your own self-respect, the respect of others means very little.

This pattern of expressed attitudes seems to reflect freedom from compulsion about rules, adventurousness (perhaps tinged with exhibitionism), self-assertiveness, and self-respect.

Turning to the opposite side of the picture, here are some illustrative items more frequently answered "True" by the extreme conformists, which reflect a rather rigid, externally sanctioned, and inconsistent moralistic attitude.

I am in favor of very strict enforcement of all laws, no matter what the consequences.

It is all right to get around the law if you don't actually break it.

Most people are honest chiefly through fear of being caught.

Another set of items reveals a desire for clarity, symmetry, certainty, or, in presently popular phraseology, "an intolerance of ambiguity."

I don't like to work on a problem unless there is a possibility of coming out with a clear-cut and unambiguous answer.

Once I have made up my mind I seldom change it.

Perfect balance is the essence of all good composition.

Other items express conventionality of values:

I always follow the rule: business before pleasure.

The trouble with many people is that they don't take things seriously enough.

I am very careful about my manner of dress.

Anxiety is revealed in numerous items:

I am afraid when I look down from a high place.

I am often bothered by useless thoughts which keep running through my head.

> I often think, "I wish I were a child again."
> I often feel as though I have done something wrong or
> wicked.

And finally, there are various expressions of disturbed, dejected, and distrustful attitudes toward other people:

> When I meet a stranger I often think that he is better than
> I am.
> Sometimes I am sure that other people can tell what I am
> thinking.
> I wish that I could get over worrying about things I have
> said that may have injured other people's feelings.
> I commonly wonder what hidden reason another person
> may have for doing something nice for me.
> People pretend to care more about one another than they
> really do.

Although there is an unmistakable neurotic tone to many of the foregoing statements, one must be chary of inferring that those high on conformity are measurably more neurotic than the others. There does not in fact appear to be any significant correlation of the conformity scores with obvious standard measures of neuroticism as found, for instance, in scales of the Minnesota Multiphasic Personality Inventory. A similar negative finding has been reported by Barron (4) in his study of the personality correlates of independence of judgment in Asch's subjects.

In another area—attitudes concerning parents and children—differences between those high and low on conformity are especially interesting. The extreme conformists describe their parents in highly idealized terms, unrelieved by any semblance of criticism. The independents, on the other hand, offer a more balanced picture of praise and criticism.

Most of the men in the sample are fathers, and it is instructive to see that in their view of child-rearing practices, the conformers are distinctly more "restrictive" in their attitudes, and the independents distinctively more "permissive" (5).

Finally, there appears to be a marked difference in the early home background of the conformists and independents. The high conformers in this sample come almost without exception from stable homes; the independents much more frequently report broken homes and unstable home environments.

Previous theoretical and empirical studies seem to converge, though imperfectly, on a picture of the overconformist as having less ego strength, less ability to tolerate own impulses and to tolerate ambiguity, less ability to accept responsibility, less self-insight, less spontaneity and productive originality, and as having more prejudiced and authoritarian attitudes, more idealization of parents, and greater emphasis on external and socially approved values.

All of these elements gain at least some substantiation in the present study of conformity behavior, as objectively measured in our test situation. The decisive influence of intelligence in resisting conformity pressures is perhaps given even fuller weight in the present findings.

CONFORMITY BEHAVIOR IN DIFFERENT POPULATIONS

Two further studies have been made. The first was with 59 college undergraduates, mostly sophomores. Forty were females, 19 males. An additional 40 students served as control subjects.

Using the same procedures and the same items for judgment, the conformity results for this student sample were highly similar to those already reported for the adult men. Here again extensive group pressure effects are found on almost all items. And here again there are wide individual differences, covering virtually the entire score range.

The male students on the average exhibit just about the same level of conformity as do the adult men. The female students, on the other hand, exhibit significantly *higher* amounts of conformity than the male groups. This greater conformity among females is evident across the entire range of items tested. Interpretation of this sex difference in conformity will require further research.

But before male egos swell overly, let me hasten to report the results of a third study, just completed. Fifty women, all college alumnae in their early forties, were tested in the same group pressure procedure, again as part of a larger assessment setting, and under the auspices of the Mary Conover Mellon Foundation.[3] As

[3]The assessment was under the direction of Dr. R. Nevitt Sanford.

in the previous populations, virtually the entire range of individual differences in conformity is exhibited by these women. Some of them show no effect at all; others are influenced on almost all items. But the average conformity score for these 50 women is significantly *lower* than that found in the previous populations.

Thus we find our sample of adult women to be more independent in judgment than our adult men. The interpretation is difficult. The two groups differ in many particulars, other than sex. The women are highly selected for educational and socio-economic status, are persons active in their community affairs, and would be characterized as relatively stable in personality and free of psychopathology. The adult men in our professional group are less advantageously selected in all these respects. Differences in intellectual level alone might be sufficient to account for the observed differences in conformity scores.

PSYCHOLOGICAL PROCESSES

Turn now to questions concerning the nature of the psychological processes involved in these expressions of conformity to group pressure. How, for instance, is the situation perceived by the individual? The most striking thing is that almost never do the individuals under this pressure of a false group consensus come to suspect the deception practiced upon them. Of the total of 159 persons already tested in the apparatus, and questioned immediately afterwards, only a small handful expressed doubt of the genuineness of the situation. Of these not more than two or three really seem to have developed this suspicion while in the actual situation.

Yet all the subjects are acutely aware of the sometimes gross discrepancies between their own inner judgments and those expressed by the rest of the group. How do they account for these discrepancies?

Intensive individual questioning of the subjects immediately following the procedure elicits evidence of two quite different tendencies. First, for many persons the discrepancies tend to be resolved through self-blame. They express doubt of their own accuracy of perception or judgment, confessing that they had probably misread or misperceived the slides. Second, for many other persons the main tendency is to blame the rest of the group, expressing doubt that they had perceived or read the slides correctly. This is not a neat dichotomy, of course. Most persons express something of a mixture of these explanations, which is not surprising in view of the fact that some slides may tend to favor one interpretation of the difficulty and other slides the opposite interpretation.

As might be predicted, there is a substantial relationship between conformity score and tendency to self-blame; or, putting it the other way, those who remain relatively independent of the group pressure are more likely to blame the discrepancies on poor judgments by the rest of the group.

But this is by no means a perfect relationship. There are many persons who, though retrospectively expressing doubt of the correctness of the group's judgment, did in fact conform heavily while in the situation. And what is even more striking is that a substantial number of the subjects—between 25 and 30 per cent—freely admit on later questioning that there were times when they responded the way the group did *even when they thought this not the proper answer*. It seems evident, therefore, that along with various forms of cognitive rationalization of the discrepancies, there occurred a considerable amount of what might be called deliberate conforming, that is, choosing to express outward agreement with the group consensus even when believing the group to be wrong.

Another noteworthy effect was the sense of increased psychological distance induced between the person himself and the rest of the group. He felt himself to be queer or different, or felt the group to be quite unlike what he had thought. With this went an arousal of considerable anxiety in most subjects; for some, manifest anxiety was acute.

The existence of these tensions within and between the subjects became dramatically manifest when, shortly after the end of the procedure, the experimenter confessed the deception he had practiced and explained the real situation. There were obvious and audible signs of relaxation and relief, and a shift from an atmosphere of constraint to one of animated discussion.

The Ethical Issue

This is an appropriate point to comment on ethics. No persons when questioned after explanation of the deception expressed feelings that they had been ethically mistreated in the experiment. The most common reaction was a positive one of having engaged in an unusual and significant experience, together with much joking about having been taken in.

Undeniably there are serious ethical issues involved in the experimental use of such deception techniques, especially inasmuch as they appear to penetrate rather deeply into the person. My view is that such deception methods ethically require that great care be taken immediately afterwards to explain the situation fully to the subject.

These remarks on ethics of the method are especially pertinent as we move from study of those judgmental materials which are noncontroversial to those which are controversial. In the studies of college students and of mature women, many new critical items were introduced and subjected to the pressure. They were intended to explore more deeply the conformity tendencies in matters of opinion and attitude. And they were so chosen as to pertain to socially important and controversial issues involving civil liberties, political philosophy, crime and punishment, ethical values, and the like.

Here are two salient examples. An expression of agreement or disagreement was called for on the following statement: "Free speech being a privilege rather than a right, it is proper for a society to suspend free speech whenever it feels itself threatened." Among control subjects, only 19 per cent express agreement. But among the experimental subjects confronted with a unanimous group consensus agreeing with the statement, 58 per cent express agreement.

Another item was phrased as follows: "Which one of the following do you feel is the most important problem facing our country today?" And these five alternatives were offered:

Economic recession
Educational facilities
Subversive activities

Mental health
Crime and corruption

Among control subjects, only 12 per cent chose "Subversive activities" as the most important. But when exposed to a spurious group consensus which unanimously selected "Subversive activities" as the most important, 48 per cent of the experimental subjects expressed this same choice.

I think that no one would wish to deny that here we have evidence of the operation of powerful conformity influences in the expression of opinion on matters of critical social controversy.

REINFORCEMENT OF CONFORMITY

There is one final point upon which I should like to touch briefly. That is the question of whether there are circumstances under which the power of the group to influence the judgments of the individual may be even more greatly reinforced, and if so, how far such power may extend.

One method has been tried as part of the study of college students. With half of the subjects, a further instruction was introduced by the experimenter. They were told that in order to see how well they were doing during the procedure, the experimenter would inform the group immediately after the judgments on each slide what the correct answer was. This was to be done, of course, only for those slides for which there was a correct answer, namely, perceptual judgments, logical solutions, vocabulary, etc. No announcement would be made after slides having to do with opinions and attitudes.

The experimenter here again deceived the subjects, for the answers he announced as correct were deliberately chosen so as to agree with the false group consensus. In short, the external authority of the experimenter was later added on as reinforcement to the group consensus.

The effect of this so-called "correction" method is striking. As the series of judgments goes on, these individuals express greater and greater conformity to the group pressure on slides which are of the same character as those for which earlier in the series the false group consensus was thus reinforced by the false announcement by the experimenter.

But the more critical issue is whether this enhanced power of the group generalizes also to judgments of an entirely unrelated sort—namely, matters of opinion and attitude—rather than of fact. In other words, will the group, through having the rightness of its judgment supported by the experimenter on matters of perception, logic, and the like, thereby come to be regarded by the individual as more right, or more to be complied with, on entirely extraneous matters such as social issues?

The answer is absolutely clear. The enhanced power of the group does *not* carry over to increase the effective influence on expression of opinions and attitudes. The subjects exposed to this "correction" method do not exhibit greater conformity to group pressure on opinions and attitudes than that found in other subjects.

This crucial finding throws some light on the nature of the psychological processes involved in the conformity situation. For it seems to imply that conformity behavior under such group pressure, rather than being sheerly an indiscriminate and irrational tendency to defer to the authority of the group, has in it important rational elements. There is something of a reasonable differentiation made by the individual in his manner of reliance upon the group. He may be led to accept the superiority of the group judgment on matters where there is an objective frame of reference against which the group can be checked. But he does not, thereby, automatically accept the authority of the group on matters of a less objective sort.

CONCLUSION

The social psychologist is concerned with the character of conformity, the personologist with conformity of character. Between them they raise many research questions: The comparative incidence of conformity tendencies in various populations; the influence of group structure and the individual's role in the group on

the nature and amount of conformity behavior; the effects of reward or punishment for conforming on habits of conformity; the
genesis and change of conformity behavior in the individual personality; the determinants of extreme *anti*conformity tendencies.

Contributing to such questions we have what appears to be a
powerful new research technique, enabling the study of conformity
behavior within a setting which effectively simulates genuine group
interaction, yet preserves the essential requirements of objective
measurement.

REFERENCES

1. ADORNO, T. W., FRENKEL-BRUNSWIK, ELSE, LEVINSON, D., and
   SANFORD, R. N. *The Authoritarian Personality.* New York:
   Harper, 1950.
2. ASCH, S. E. *Social Psychology.* New York: Prentice-Hall, 1952.
3. BARRON, F. An ego-strength scale which predicts response to
   psychotherapy. *J. Consult. Psychol.*, 1953, 17, 327–333.
4. BARRON, F. Some personality correlates of independence of judgment. *J. Pers.*, 1953, 21, 287–297.
5. BLOCK, J. Personality characteristics associated with fathers' attitudes toward child-rearing. *Child Developm.*, 1955, 26, 41–48.
6. GOUGH, H. G. *A preliminary guide for the use and interpretation
   of the California Psychological Inventory.* Privately distributed
   by the Institute of Personality Assessment and Research, Univer.
   of California, Berkeley, 1954. (Mimeo.)

18

Video Tape Recording in Social Psychological Research: An Illustrative Study in Pedodontia

BEM P. ALLEN and
RICHARD I. EVANS

An ever-present concern of the social scientist conducting research in real-life settings is that of a reliable and objective method of recording ongoing events. Human observers tend to select out various aspects of the situation and not include others in their data recording. To this extent, the observation is "biased" to conform to various expectancies, motivations, and skills of the observer. In fact the mere presence of the scientist-observer may cause the individuals being observed to behave in a way different from what is normal for them. Thus, even if the observer is a highly skilled recorder of behavior, he may unwittingly be exposed to a non-typical or biased sample of behavior.

The present report offers one innovative solution to this problem by demonstrating the use of video tape recording in a natural setting experiment. For this report the experimental results are of secondary importance: The real value of this piece of research is that it demonstrates the feasibility of the video tape recording techniques for unobtrusive and objective recording of human behavior.

From: *Psychological Reports*, 23: 1115–1119, 1968. Reprinted by permission of the authors and publisher. Copyright © 1968 by Southern Universities Press.

Barker (1965), Sanford (1965), Evans (1966, 1967), McGuire (1967), and Evans and Leppmann (1968), among others, have recently emphasized the increasing importance in social psychology of observation in the field or in real-life settings. For example, Sanford has reminded research psychologists that an understanding of behavior as it occurs in the complex natural setting should be the ultimate goal of psychology. He urges psychologists to relate their research to the natural setting by gaining research ideas from observation in the field rather than from their journals. Evans's work, based on his observations of the dental setting, calls attention to it as a possible natural setting for research. Barker has presented a procedure for implementation of such research. Barker's technique involves verbatim recordings by a human observer which are later coded for analysis. Since such methods may invite observer bias, a more objective method of recording might be desirable. Electronic media of communication may supply this desired objectivity.

The one such medium which has not yet been extensively used is television. The purpose of the present investigation, then, was to illustrate the utility of televised recordings in a field situation, using the dental setting as an illustration of this capability.

The video tape recorder was employed in an investigation ostensibly designed to explore the question of whether or not the mother's presence in the dental setting while her child is receiving treatment affects her child's behavior during treatment. The possible effects of the mother's presence were considered in terms of the level of cooperativeness exhibited by her child in response to commands given by a dentist.

PROCEDURE

Twenty-two mothers and their children, who ranged in age from 3 to 7 years (median age, 6), were employed as Ss. The mothers and children met E in a waiting room at The University of Texas

NOTE: This paper is based in part on a thesis completed to fulfill partially the requirements for the M.A. degree in psychology at the University of Houston under the direction of co-author Evans. It was presented at the Southwestern Psychological Association meetings, New Orleans, Louisiana,

Dental Branch. Prior to the meeting, the mothers had been informed by phone that they were to bring their children back to the
dental school for a follow-up of previous treatment (prophylaxis
or cleaning of the teeth was to be performed on the children without charge).

After an introduction, E explained how to fill out a Semantic
Differential questionnaire (Osgood, Suci, & Tannenbaum, 1957)
reflecting 20 concepts related to dentistry. Each concept was to be
rated on seven 7-point scales, the extremes of which were labeled
with bipolar adjectives. For half the mother-child pairs, the mothers
were requested to fill out the Semantic Differential form in an
outside room, while the children were escorted into a treatment
area for the first half of a 16-minute prophylaxis session. In the
case of the remaining mother-child pairs, the mother and child
together were escorted to the treatment area for the first half of
the session, with the mothers being informed that they could complete the questionnaire later. Thus, for all the child Ss, the mothers
were present for only one-half of the entire 16-min. session.
However, as a control, this situation was counterbalanced. For half
the children, the mother was present during the first half of the
session and for the remaining children, the mother was present
during the second half of the session.

Mothers and children were escorted to a television studio which
had been furnished in such a manner that it clearly appeared to be
a temporary dental office. One end of the studio, which contained
a door relabeled, "temporary dental office," was partitioned by
the use of black, paper, stage props (20 ft. long and 8 ft. high on
the long side and 8 ft. by 8 ft. on the short side, where the same
proportions of studio wall completed the rectangular office). The
office was lighted brightly enough for video tape recording. It contained a standard dental chair, a dental machine, and a stand
containing all other materials necessary for prophylaxis. A chair for
the mother was placed in front of the dental chair.

The television camera was placed behind the paper wall at about

April, 1968. The investigation was supported in part under Research Training Grant No. 5 TI DE 138, National Institute of Dental Research, co-
author Evans, Director. The authors express appreciation to the University
of Texas Dental Branch for the use of its facilities in this investigation and
to Dr. Richard E. Jennings of its faculty for his invaluable assistance
throughout.

the midpoint of the 20-ft. section. The camera lens was inserted into a tin can, which in turn was fitted into a 4-ft. by 4-ft. plaster board mounted behind the 20-ft. section. The tin can, the outer edge and interior of which were painted a flat black, was inserted at the middle of the plaster board and about 4-ft. from the floor. The body of the tin can extended behind the partition rather than into the temporary dental office so that, when the floor lights were properly positioned, the lens of the camera was invisible from within the office.

A post-D.D.S. graduate student in pedodontia at The University of Texas Dental Branch performed the prophylaxis. He was fitted with a commercially available television listener ear plug so that he could receive commands from E. The wiring for the ear plug was concealed in the dentist's clothing and extended from his trouser leg to a control room at the back of the studio. E operated the tape recorder located in the control room. The camera itself needed only to be focused. A microphone for E to relate commands to the dentist was also connected to the video tape recorder so that the commands constituted the audio portion of the tape.

After E had introduced the child S and the mother to the dentist, if she was to be present for the first half-session, he retired to the control room. The dentist then asked the child a series of standardized "dummy" questions, which consumed about 3-min. After this brief time lapse, E began to relay a series of eight commands, delivered at 1-min. intervals, to the dentist.[1] At this moment the video tape recorder was started and the prophylaxis session also began. The commands were requests for cooperation on the part of the child S and were immediately repeated by the dentist to the child. Thus, the command, and the child's reaction immediately following it, were recorded.

After each first half-session E returned to the temporary office to escort the mother to the waiting area if she had been present, or E went directly to the waiting area and asked the mother to accompany him to the temporary office for the second half-session. In

[1](1) "O.K., what do you say we get started! Sit up tall and open wide, please." (2) "Hold your chin up high." (3) "Open wide, please." (4) "Sit up straight, please." (5) "Please put your head back real far." (6) "Sit real tall." (7) "Hold your chin higher, please." (8) "Open wide, please."

the former case the mother was told she must return to the waiting area to complete the Semantic Differential; in the latter case E told the mother that her presence in the dental office might be helpful to the dentist. After each complete session, E dismissed the mother and child after explaining the nature of the present investigation, so that any eventual concern over possible deceptiveness would be averted.

After the completion of each day's experimental session (from 2 to 6 S pairs were run per day for five days), the tapes were viewed by two judges, one male and one female. The judges rated each minute of each half-session for each child on a three-point scale. The extremes of this scale were labeled "cooperative" and "uncooperative," and the judges were told that the middle category was for "uncertain" responses. The half-sessions for each child were rated separately as a control. The judges were not aware of when the mother was or was not present while the video tapes they were rating were recorded.

RESULTS AND DISCUSSION

The analysis of the data was completed in two phases. First, the responses of the child Ss were analyzed for the possibility of the influence of the mother's presence on cooperativeness: the level of cooperativeness of each child S with the mother present was compared with the level of his cooperativeness in his mother's absence.

A Wilcoxon matched-pairs, signed-ranks test (Siegel) did not yield a statistically significant difference (.05 level of confidence or beyond) in cooperativeness between half-sessions when the mother was present and half-sessions when she was absent. As discussed in more detail elsewhere (Allen) no statistically significant relationship was found between children's level of cooperativeness and their mothers' attitudes toward dentistry.

The lack of a significant difference between the mother-present and the mother-absent situations in the present results confirmed the results of Law and Lewis but partially contradicted the results of more recent investigations by Frankl (1961), and Frankl, Shiere, and Fogels (1962). The latter studies found that the presence of the mother "improved" the behavior of the child for children between the ages of 42 to 49 months but had no influence on the behavior of children in the age range 50 to 66 months. However, an investigation more precisely paralleling the present one apparently has not been completed at this time.

In terms of the primary aims of the present investigation, examination of the video tape recorder as a tool in such research demonstrated this recorder has several advantages over other methods of behavior sampling in the field. For example, unlike film, video tapes do not require development, which thus gives it the advantage of immediate playback. This characteristic is particularly useful when immediate feedback from an experimental session is desirable. Coupling the immediate playback capability of video tape recording with its erasure (record over) properties, the video tape recorder is more economical than film. That is, the researcher may use the same tape over and over, thus saving the time and expense normally required for film development or coding of verbatim records. In the present investigation, for example, only one tape was available, but since the tape held a whole day's run, it was possible to record the day's sessions and replay them for the raters all within one day, so that on the next day E simply recorded over the previous day's session. If a permanent record is required, however, video tapes can be stored for long periods without appreciably lowered quality. In addition, with recent modification, the video tape recorder is virtually as easy to operate as an audio recorder. The tape it produces can be edited with astonishing speed and accuracy, as the instant replays of television sports illustrate. This characteristic and the fact that video tapes are easily replayed means that a researcher can explore all or any part of an experimental session with whatever degree of thoroughness he desires. Also, technological progress appears rapidly to be eliminating the drawbacks of the video tape recorder as a means of behavior sampling. The initial cost of equipment, for example, is becoming appreciably lower.

The question of concealment can be solved quite easily, as it was in the present investigation. Only a few children and their mothers suspected "something unusual was going on," and most were quite surprised to learn that they had been on television. The silent operation of the camera and the glare of the lights, which further blurred the already barely discriminable aperture in the partition, along with the fact that Ss did not expect to be televised, probably accounted for the successful concealment of the camera.

For those investigations where behavior recordings are to be made in a natural setting, the presence of a human observer is undesirable, immediate replay is desired, and ease of editing responses is helpful, the video tape recorder appears to be a very promising means of behavior recording.

SUMMARY

The present paper examines the capability of the video tape recorder as a behavior sampling instrument within the context of an investigation ostensibly designed to determine possibly positive or aversive effects of the absence or presence of mothers on children's behavior in a dental treatment situation. The behavior of 22 children was video tape recorded as a dentist cleaned their teeth. The mothers of all children were present for one half and absent for the other half of these teeth cleaning sessions. There were no significant behavioral differences as determined from judges' ratings of video tapes of the children's behavior while mothers were absent and present. A description of the means by which the video tape recorder may be used as an instrument for such behavior sampling is presented. The advantages of this recorder over more conventional means of behavioral recording or observation are also discussed.

REFERENCES

ALLEN, B. P.   The mother's influences on the child's behavior in a dental treatment situation: an exploration of social psychological research capability in a field setting. Unpublished master's thesis, Univer. of Houston, 1966.

BARKER, R. G.   Explorations in ecological psychology. *American Psychologist*, 1965, 20, 1–15.

EVANS, R. I.   A new interdisciplinary dimension in graduate psychological research training: dentistry. *American Psychologist*, 1966,
21, 167–172.

EVANS, R. I.   Social and behavioral sciences research 1962–1966.
Journal of the American Dental Association, 1967, 74, 1500–
1511.

EVANS, R. I., and LEPPMANN, P. K.   *Resistance to Innovation in
Higher Education*. San Francisco: Jossey-Bass, 1968.

FRANKL, S. H.   Evaluation of the effects of separation of the mother
and preschool child in the dental office. *Journal of Dental Research*, 1961, 40, 673.

FRANKL, S. H., SHIERE, R., and FOGELS, H. P.   Should the parent
remain with the child in the dental operatory? *Journal of Dentistry
for Children*, 1962, 29 (2nd quarter): 150–163.

LAW, D. B., and LEWIS, T. M.   Investigation of certain autonomic
responses of children to a specific dental stress. *Journal of the
American Dental Association*, 1958, 57, 769–777.

MCGUIRE, W. J.   Theory-oriented research in natural settings: the
best of both worlds for social psychology. In M. Sherif (Chm.),
Problems of interdisciplinary relationships in the social sciences,
symposium presented at Pennsylvania State Univer., May, 1967.

OSGOOD, C. E., SUCI, G. J., and TANNENBAUM, P. H.   *The Measurement of Meaning*. Urbana: University of Illinois Press, 1957.

SANFORD, N.   Will psychologists study human problems? *American
Psychologist*, 1965, 20, 192–202.

SIEGEL, S.   *Nonparametric statistics for the behavioral sciences*. New
York: McGraw-Hill, 1956.

19

Reference Groups, Membership Groups, and Attitude Change

ALBERTA E. SIEGEL and
SIDNEY SIEGEL

This classic study represents an excellent example of what might be termed a "natural" experiment. These social psychologists took advantage of an administrative procedure in a college setting that resembled an experiment which might have been designed and conducted under the more artificial conditions of the laboratory.

All of the students lived for one year under conditions in which they had the same reference group (occupants of "Fraternity Row" houses) and membership group (occupants of freshman dormitory). By a process of random selection, at the end of the first year, some of the students were permitted to live in the desired location, others were not. Thus, during their second year of college, for some of the students reference and membership groups were the same (occupants of Row houses); for others, the membership group (occupants of other housing) was different from their reference group (occupants of Row houses). The effects of these different experiences upon basic attitudes are examined.

From: *Journal of Abnormal and Social Psychology*, 55: 360–364, 1957. Reprinted by permission of the authors and the American Psychological Association.

In social psychological theory, it has long been recognized that an individual's *membership groups* have an important influence on the values and attitudes he holds. More recently, attention has also been given to the influence of his *reference groups*: the groups in which he aspires to attain or maintain membership. In a given area, membership groups and reference groups may or may not be identical. They are identical when the person aspires to *maintain* membership in the group of which he is a part; they are disparate when the group in which the individual aspires to *attain* membership is one in which he is not a member. It has been widely asserted that both membership and reference groups affect the attitudes held by the individual (Sherif and Sherif, 1953).

The present study is an examination of the attitude changes which occur over time when reference groups and membership groups are identical and when they are disparate. The study takes advantage of a field experiment which occurred in the social context of the lives of the subjects, concerning events considered vital by them. The subjects were not aware that their membership and reference groups were of research interest; in fact, they did not know that the relevant information about these was available to the investigators.

The field experiment permitted a test of the general hypothesis that both the amount and the direction of a person's attitude change over time depend on the attitude norms of his membership group (whether or not that group is chosen by him) and on the attitude norms of his reference group.

This hypothesis is tested with subjects who shared a common reference group at the time of the initial assessment of attitudes. They were then randomly assigned to alternative membership groups, some being assigned to the chosen group and others to a nonchosen group. Attitudes were reassessed after a year of experience in these alternative membership groups with divergent attitude norms. During the course of the year, some subjects came

NOTE: This study was supported by grants from the Committee for the Study of American Values at Stanford University and from the Stanford Value Theory Project. We wish to acknowledge with gratitude the assistance given by Davis W. Thompkins, Marilyn Sanchez-Corea, and Coleen Baker in the execution of this study, and the generous administrative cooperation of Elva Fay Brown, Dean of Women at Stanford University, and her staff.

to take the imposed (initially nonpreferred) membership group as their reference group. Attitude change after the year was examined in terms of the membership group and reference group identifications of the subjects at that time.

THE FIELD EXPERIMENT

The Ss of this study were women students at a large private co-educational university. The study was initiated shortly before the end of their freshman year, when they all lived in the same large freshman dormitory to which they had been assigned upon entering the university. At this university, all women move to new housing for their sophomore year. Several types of housing are available to them: a large dormitory, a medium-sized dormitory, several very small houses which share common dining facilities, and a number of former sorority houses which have been operated by the university since sororities were banished from the campus. These latter are located among the fraternity houses on Fraternity Row, and are therefore known as "Row houses." Although the Row houses are lower in physical comfort than most of the other residences for women, students consider them higher in social status. This observation was confirmed by a poll of students (Siegel, 1954, p. 205), in which over 90 per cent of the respondents stated that Row houses for women were higher in social status than non-Row houses, the remaining few disclaiming any information concerning status differences among women's residences.

In the Spring of each year, a "drawing" is held for housing for the subsequent year. All freshmen must participate in this drawing, and any other student who wishes to change her residence may participate. It is conducted by the office of the Dean of Women, in cooperation with women student leaders. Any participant's ballot is understood to be secret. The woman uses the ballot to rank the houses in the order of her preference. After submitting this ballot, she draws a number from the hopper. The rank of that number determines the likelihood that her preference will be satisfied.

In research reported earlier (Siegel, 1954), a random sample was drawn from the population of freshman women at this university, several tests were administered to the Ss in that sample, and (unknown to the Ss) their housing preferences for the forthcoming sophomore year were observed by the investigator. The Ss were characterized as "high status oriented" if they listed a Row house as their first choice, and were characterized as "low status oriented" if they listed a non-Row house as their first choice. The hypothesis under test, drawn from reference group theory and from theoretical formulations concerning authoritarianism, was that high status orientation is a correlate of authoritarianism. The hypothesis was confirmed: freshman women who listed a Row house as their first choice for residence scored significantly higher on the average in authoritarianism, as measured by the E-F scale (Adorno *et al.*, 1950; Gough, 1951) than did women who listed a non-Row house as their first choice. The present study is a continuation of the one described, and uses as its Ss only those members of the original sample who were "high status oriented," i.e., preferred to live in a Row house for the sophomore year. In the initial study (Siegel, 1954) of the 95 Ss whose housing choices were listed, 39 were "high status oriented," i.e., demonstrated that the Row was their reference group by giving a Row house as their first choice in the drawing. Of this group, 28 were available to serve as Ss for the follow-up or "change" study which is the topic of the present paper. These women form a homogeneous subsample in that at the conclusion of their freshman year they shared a common membership group (the freshman dormitory) and a common reference group (the Row). These Ss, however, had divergent experiences during their sophomore year: nine were Row residents during that year (having drawn sufficiently low numbers in the housing drawing to enable them to be assigned to the group of their choice) and the other 19 lived in non-Row houses during that year (having drawn numbers too high to enable them to be assigned to the housing group of their choice).

E-F scores were obtained from each of the 28 Ss in the course of a large-scale testing program administered to most of the women students at the university. Anonymity was guaranteed to the Ss, but a coding procedure permitted the investigators to identify each respondent and thereby to isolate the Ss and compare each S's second E-F score with her first.

To prevent the Ss from knowing that they were participating in a follow-up study, several procedures were utilized: (1) many persons who had not served in the earlier study were included in the second sample, (2) the testing was introduced as being part of a nation-wide study to establish norms, (3) the test administrators were different persons from those who had administered the initial tests, (4) Ss who informed the test administrator that they had already taken the "Public Opinion Questionnaire" (E-F scale) were casually told that this did not disqualify them from participating in the current study.

The Ss had no hint that the research was in any way related to their housing arrangements. Testing was conducted in classrooms as well as in residences, and all procedures and instructions were specifically designed to avoid any arousal of the salience of the housing groups in the frame of reference of the research.

The annual housing drawing was conducted three weeks after the sophomore-year testing, and, as usual, each woman's housing ballot was understood to be secret. In this drawing, each S had the opportunity to change her membership group, although a residence move is not required at the end of the sophomore year as it is at the end of the freshman year. If an S participated in this drawing, the house which she listed as her first choice on the ballot was identified by the investigators as her reference group. If she did not, it was evidence that the house in which she was currently a member was the one in which she chose to continue to live, i.e., was her reference group. With the information on each S's residence choice at the end of her freshman year, her assigned residence for her sophomore year, and her residence choice at the end of her sophomore year, it was possible to classify the subjects in three categories:

A. Women ($n = 9$) who had gained assignment to live on the Row during their sophomore year and who did not attempt to draw out of the Row at the end of that year.

B. Women ($n = 11$) who had not gained assignment to a Row

house for the sophomore year and who drew for a Row
house again after living in a non-Row house during the
sophomore year; and

C. Women ($n = 8$) who had not gained assignment to a Row
house for the sophomore year, and who chose to remain in
a non-Row house after living in one during the sophomore
year.

For all three groups of Ss, as we have pointed out, membership
group (freshman dormitory) and reference group (Row house)
were common at the end of the freshman year. For Group A,
membership and reference groups were identical throughout the
sophomore year. For Group B, membership and reference groups
were disparate throughout the sophomore year. For Group C,
membership and reference groups were initially disparate during
the sophomore year but became identical because of a change in
reference groups.

As will be demonstrated, the Row and the non-Row social
groups differ in attitude norms, with Row residents being generally
more authoritarian than non-Row residents. From social psychological theory concerning the influence of group norms on individuals' attitudes, it would be predicted that the different group identifications during the sophomore year of the three groups of Ss
would result in differential attitude change. Those who gained ad-
mittance to a Row house for the sophomore year (Group A)
would be expected to show the least change in authoritarianism,
for they spent that year in a social context which reinforced their
initial attitudes. Group C Ss would be expected to show the greatest change in authoritarianism, a change associated not only with
their membership in a group (the non-Row group) which is typically low in authoritarianism, but also with their shift in reference
groups, from Row to non-Row, i.e., from a group normatively
higher in authoritarianism to a group normatively lower. The
extent of attitude change in the Ss in Group B would be expected
to be intermediate, due to the conflicting influences of the imposed
membership group (non-Row) and of the unchanged reference
group (Row). The research hypothesis, then, is that between the
time of the freshman-year testing and the sophomore-year testing,

the extent of change in authoritarianism will be least in Group A, greater in Group B, and greatest in Group C. That is, in extent of attitude change, Group A < Group B < Group C.

RESULTS

Group Norms

From the data collected in the large-scale testing program, it was possible to determine the group norms for authoritarian attitudes among the Row and the non-Row women at the university. The E-F scale was administered to all available Row residents ($n = 303$) and to a random sample of residents of non-Row houses ($n = 101$). These Ss were sophomores, juniors, and seniors. The mean E-F score of the Row women was 90, while the mean E-F score of the non-Row was 81. The E-F scores of the two groups were demonstrated to differ at the $p < .001$ level ($x^2 = 11.1$) by the median test (Siegel, 1956, pp. 111–116), a nonparametric test, the data for which are shown in Table 1.

TABLE 1
FREQUENCIES OF E-F SCORES ABOVE AND BELOW COMMON MEDIAN
FOR ROW AND NON-ROW RESIDENTS

	Residents of Non-Row Houses	Residents of Row Houses	Total
Above Median	36	166	202
Below Median	65	137	202
Total	101	303	404

Attitude Change

The central hypothesis of this study is that attitude change will occur differentially in Groups A, B, and C, and that it will occur in the direction which would be predicted from knowledge of the group norms among Row and non-Row residents in general. The 28 Ss of this study had a mean E-F score of 102 at the end of their freshman year. The data reported above concerning authoritarianism norms for all women residing on campus would lead to the prediction that in general the Ss would show a reduction in authoritarianism during the sophomore year but that this reduction would be differential in the three groups; from the knowledge that Row residents generally are higher in authoritarianism than non-Row residents, the prediction based on social group theory would be that Group A would show the smallest reduction in authoritarianism scores, Group B would show a larger reduction, and Group C would show the largest reduction. The data which permit a test of this hypothesis are given in Table 2. The Jonckheere test (Jonckheere, 1954), a non-parametric k-sample test which tests the null hypothesis that the three groups are from the same population against the alternative hypothesis that they are from different populations which are ordered in a specified way, was used with these data. By that test, the hypothesis is confirmed at the $p < .025$ level.

DISCUSSION

Substantively, the present study provides experimental verification of certain assertions in social group theory, demonstrating that attitude change over time is related to the group identification of the person—both his membership group identification and his reference group identification. The hypothesis that extent of attitude change would be different in the three subgroups of Ss, depending on their respective membership group and reference group identifications, is confirmed at the $p < .025$ level; in extent of change in authoritarianism, Group A < Group B < Group C, as predicted.

Another way of looking at the data may serve to highlight the influence of membership groups and reference groups. At the end of the freshman year, the Ss in Groups A, B, and C shared the same membership group and the same reference group. During the sophomore year, the Ss in Group A shared one membership group while those in Groups B and C together shared another. From membership group theory, it would be predicted that the extent of attitude change would be greater among the latter Ss. This hypothesis is supported by the data (in Table 2): by the

TABLE 2
FRESHMAN YEAR AND SOPHOMORE YEAR E-F SCORES OF SUBJECTS

Group	E-F Score		Difference
	End of Freshman Year	End of Sophomore Year	
	108	125	−17
	70	78	−8
	106	107	−1
	92	92	0
A	80	78	2
	104	102	2
	143	138	5
	110	92	18
	114	80	34
	76	117	−41
	105	107	−2
	88	82	6
	109	97	12
	98	83	15
B	112	94	18
	101	82	19
	114	93	21
	104	81	23
	116	91	25
	101	74	27
	121	126	−5
	87	79	8
	105	95	10
	97	81	16
C	96	78	18
	108	73	35
	114	77	37
	88	49	39

Mann-Whitney test (Siegel, 1956, pp. 116–127), the change scores of these two sets of Ss (Group A versus Group B and C together) differ in the predicted direction at the $p < .025$ level. This finding illustrates the influence of *membership* groups on attitude change. On the other hand, at the conclusion of the sophomore year, the Ss in Groups A and B shared a common reference group while those in Group C had come to share another. From reference group theory, it would be predicted that attitude change would be more extensive among the subjects who had changed reference groups (Group C) than among those who had not. This hypothesis is also supported by the data (in Table 2): by the Mann-Whitney test, the change scores of these two sets of Ss (Groups A and B together versus Group C) differ in the predicted direction at the $p < .05$ level. This finding illustrates the influence of *reference* groups on attitude change. Any inference from this mode of analysis—as contrasted with the main analysis of the data by the Jonckheere test—must be qualified because of the non-independence of the data on which the two Mann-Whitney tests are made, but it is mentioned here to clarify the role which membership and reference groups play in influencing attitude change.

The findings may also contribute to our understanding of proc-esses affecting attitude change. The imposition of a membership group does have some effect on an individual's attitudes, even when the imposed group is not accepted by the individual as his refer-ence group. This relationship is shown in the case of Group B. If the person comes to accept the imposed group as his reference group, as was the case with the Ss in Group C, then the change in his attitudes toward the level of the group norm is even more pronounced.

Methodologically, the study has certain features which may de-serve brief mention. First, the study demonstrates that it is possible to define the concept of reference group operationally. The act of voting by secret ballot for the group in which one would like to live constitutes clear behavioral specification of one's reference group, and it is an act whose conceptual meaning can be so di-rectly inferred that there is no problem of reliability of judgment in its categorization by the investigator. Second, the study demon-strates that a field study can be conducted which contains the critical feature of an experiment that is usually lacking in natural-istic situations: randomization. The determination of whether or not a woman student would be assigned to the living group of her choice was based on a random event: the size of the number she drew from the hopper. This fact satisfied the requirement that the treatment condition be randomized, and permitted sharper inferences than can usually be drawn from field studies. Third, the test behavior on which the conclusions of this study were based occurred in a context in which the salience of membership and reference groups was *not* aroused and in which no external sanctions from the relevant groups were operative. This feature of the design permitted the interpretation that the E-F scores represented the Ss' internalized attitudes (Sherif and Sherif, 1953, p. 218). Finally, the use of a paper-and-pencil measure of attitude and thus of attitude change, rather than the use of some more behavioral measure, is a deficiency of the present study. Moreover, the measure which was used suffers from a well-known circularity, based on the occurrence of pseudo-low scores (Adorno *et al.*, 1950, p. 771; Siegel, 1953, pp. 221–222).

SUMMARY

In the social context of the lives of the subjects, and in a natural social experiment which provided randomization of the relevant condition effects, the influence of both membership and reference groups on attitude change was assessed. All subjects shared a common reference group at the start of the period of the study. When divergent membership groups with disparate attitude norms were socially imposed on the basis of a random event, attitude change in the subjects over time was a function of the normative attitudes of both imposed membership groups and the individuals' reference groups. The greatest attitude change occurred in subjects who came to take the imposed, initially non-preferred, membership group as their reference group.

REFERENCES

ADORNO, T. W., FRENKEL-BRUNSWIK, ELSE, LEVINSON, D. J., and SANFORD, R. N. *The Authoritarian Personality*. New York: Harper & Row, 1950.

GOUGH, H. G.   Studies of social intolerance: I. Some psychological and sociological correlates of anti-Semitism. *J. Soc. Psychol.*, 1951, 33, 237–246.

JONCKHEERE, A. R.   A distribution-free k-sample test against ordered alternatives. *Biometrika*, 1954, 41, 133–145.

SHERIF, M., and SHERIF, CAROLYN W.   *Groups in Harmony and Tension.* New York: Harper & Row, 1953.

SIEGEL, S.   Certain determinants and correlates of authoritarianism. *Genet. Psychol. (Monograph)* 1954, 49, 187–229.

SIEGEL, S.   *Nonparametric Statistics: For the Behavioral Sciences.* New York: McGraw-Hill, 1956.

APPENDIX I

ADDITIONAL REPORTS INVOLVING SOCIAL
PSYCHOLOGICAL ANALYSES OF PROBLEMS IN
REAL-LIFE SETTINGS

ABELSON, R. P., and J. C. MILLER. Negative persuasion via personal insult. *Journal of Experimental and Social Psychology*, 1967, 3(4):321–333.

ABU-LUGHOD, I. The mass media and Egyptian village life. *Social Forces*, 1963, 42 (1):97–104.

AGGER, R., et al. Political cynicism: measurement and meaning. *Journal of Politics*, 1961, 23:477–506.

AIKEN, M., and N. J. DEMERATH III. The politics of tokenism in Mississippi's delta. *Trans-action*, 1967, 4(5):26–34.

ALEXANDER, C. N., JR. A method for processing sociometric data. *Sociometry*, 1963, 26(2):268–269.

ALLPORT, G. W., and L. J. POSTMAN. The basic psychology of rumor. *Transactions of the New York Academy of Sciences*, 1945, Series II, 8:61–81. (In Proshansky and Seidenberg: *Basic Studies in Social Psychology*, pp. 47–58.)

ANDERSON, J. G., and D. SAFAR. The influence of differential community perceptions on the provision of equal educational opportunities. *Sociology of Education*, 1967, 40(3):219–250.

ANDERSON, L. R., and A. R. BASS. Some effects of victory or defeat upon perception of political candidates. *Journal of Social Psychology*, 1967, 73(2):227–240.

ANDERSON, R. E. Status structures in coalition bargaining games. *Sociometry*, 1967, 30(4):393–403.

ARONSON, E., and V. COPE. My enemy's enemy is my friend. *Journal of Personality and Social Psychology*, 1968, 8(1, Pt. 1):8–12.

ARONSON, S. H., and C. C. SHERWOOD. Researcher versus practitioner: problems in social action research. *Social Work*, 1967, 12(4):89–96.

AYAL, E. B. Value systems and economic development in Japan and Thailand. *Journal of Social Issues*, 1963, 19(1):35–51.

BACON, M .K., I. L. CHILD and H. BARRY III. A cross-cultural study of the correlates of crime. *Journal of Abnormal and Social Psychology*, 1963, 66:291–300.

BARCLAY, A. G., and D. R. CUSUMANO. Testing masculinity in boys without fathers. *Trans-action*, 1967, 5(2):33–35.

BARKER, R. G., and P. V. GRUMP. *Big School, Small School.* Stanford: Stanford University Press, 1964.

BARKER, R. G., H. F. WRIGHT. *Midwest and Its Children.* New York: Harper and Row, 1955.

BARKER, R. G., H. F. WRIGHT, L. S. BARKER and M. F. SCHOGGEN. *Specimen Records of American and English Children.* Lawrence, Kansas: University of Kansas Press, 1961.

BAY, C. Political and apolitical students: Facts in search of theory. *Journal of Social Issues*, 1967, 23(3):76–91.

BECKER, H. S. Whose side are we on? *Social Problems*, 1967, 14(3):239–247.

BEECHER, H. K. Surgery as placebo. *Journal of the American Medical Association*, 1961, 176:1102–1107.

BERGER, A. A. Authority in the comics. *Trans-action*, 1966, 4(2):22–26.

BERGER, B. M. Hippie morality—more old than new. *Trans-action*, 1967, 5(2):19–23, 26–27.

BERKOWITZ, L., and N. WALKER. Laws and moral judgments. *Sociometry*, 1967, 30(4):410–422.

BERLINER, J. S. Russia's bureaucrats—why they're reactionary. *Trans-action*, 1967, 5(2):53–58.

BETTELHEIM, B. Individual and mass behavior in extreme situations. *Journal of Abnormal and Social Psychology*, 1943, 38:417–452. As adapted for Swanson, G. E., Newcomb, T. M., and Hartley, E. L. (Eds.), *Readings in Social Psychology* (rev. ed.). New York: Holt, Rinehart, and Winston, 1952.

BLUMBERG, A. S. Lawyers with convictions. *Trans-action*, 1967, 4(8):18–24.

BLUMBERG, H. H. Accounting for a nonviolent mass demonstration. *Sociological Inquiry*, 1968, 38(Winter):43–50.

BOULDING, E. The study of conflict and community in the International system: Summary and challenges to research. *Journal of Social Issues*, 1967, 23(1):144–158.

BOULDING, K. The role of the war industry in international conflict. *Journal of Social Issues*, 1967, 23 (1):47–61.

BRADBURN, N. Interpersonal relations within formal organizations in Turkey. *Journal of Social Issues*, 1963, 19(1):61–67.

BRONFENBRENNER, U. The mirror image in Soviet-American relations. *Journal of Social Issues*, 1961, 17(3):45–56.

BROWN, D. R. Student stress and the institutional environment. *Journal of Social Issues*, 1967, 23(3):92–107.

BRYAN, J. H. Apprenticeships in prostitution. *Social Problems*, 1964, 12(3):287–297.

BRYAN, J. H. Occupational ideologies and individual attitudes of call girls. *Social Problems*, 1966, 13(4):441–449.

CAMILLERI, S. F., and J. BERGER. Decision making and social influence: a model and an experimental test. *Sociometry*, 1967, 30(4): 365–378.

CANTRIL, H. The invasion from Mars. In Maccoby, E. E., Newcomb, T. M., and Hartley, E. L. (Eds.), *Readings in Social Psychology*, pp. 291–300. New York: Holt, Rinehart, and Winston, 1958.

CARTER, L. F., R. J. HILL and S. D. MCLEMORE. Social conformity and attitude change within non-laboratory groups. *Sociometry*, 1967, 30(1):1–13.

CARTWRIGHT, D. Some principles of mass persuasion. *Human Relations*, 1949, 2:253–267.

CHAPANIS, A. Words, words, words. *Human Factors*, 1965, 7(1): 1–17.

CHRISTIE, R. The prevalence of Machiavellian orientations. Paper presented at the annual meeting of the American Psychological Association, Los Angeles, September 7, 1964.

CICOUREL, A. V. Fertility, family planning, and the social organization of the family: some methodological issues. *Journal of Social Issues*, 1967, 23(4):57–81.

CLARK, K. B., and M. P. CLARK. Racial identification and preference in Negro children. In Newcomb, T. M. and Hartley, E. L. (Eds.), *Readings in Social Psychology*. New York: Henry Holt & Co., 1947.

CONWAY, J. A. Problem solving in small groups as a function of "open" and "closed" individual belief systems. *Organization Behavior and Human Performance*, 1967, 2(4):394–405.

COOK, S. W. Desegregation: A psychological analysis. *American Psychologist*, 1957, 12:1–13. In Vinacke, et al., *Dimensions of Social Psychology*, 503–514. Chicago: Scott, Foresman and Co., 1964.

CORROZI, J. F., and R. L. ROSNOW. Consonant and dissonant communications as positive and negative reinforcements in opinion change. *Journal of Personality and Social Psychology*, 1968, 8(1, Part 1):27–30.

CORTIS, L. E. A comparative study in the attitudes of Bantu and European workers. *Psychology in Africa*, 1962, 9:148–167.

CROTTY, W. J. Democratic consensual norms and the college student. *Sociology of Education*, 1967, 40(3):200–218.

DAVIS, F. Why all of us may be hippies someday. *Trans-action*, 1967, 5(2):10–18.

DEUTSCH, K. Changing images of international conflict. *Journal of Social Issues*, 1967, 23(1):91–107.

DEUTSCH, M., and M. E. COLLINS. The effect of public policy in housing projects upon interracial attitudes. Adapted from Deutsch, M. and Collins, M. E. *Interracial Housing: A Psychological Evaluation of a Social Experiment*. Minneapolis: University of Minnesota Press, 1951.

DRABECK, T. E., and E. L. QUARANTELLI. Scapegoats, villains, and disasters. *Trans-action*, 1967, 4(4):12–17.

DYNES, R., and E. L. QUARANTELLI. What looting in civil disturbances really means. *Trans-action*, 1968, 5(6):9–14.

ENNIS, P. H. Crime, victims, and the police. *Trans-action*, 1967, 4(7):36–44.

EVANS, C. Sleeping and dreaming—a new, "functional" theory. *Trans-action*, 1967, 5(2):40–45.

EVANS, R. I. Changes in attitude toward innovation. In Evans, R. I., *Resistance to Innovation in Higher Education*. San Francisco: Jossey-Bass, 1968, pp. 99–123.

EVANS, R. I. A new social psychological dimension in juvenile delinquency prevention: Television. (Carbon MS.) Houston: University of Houston, 1963.

EVANS, R. I. Predicting consumer behavior. *Forum*, Jan. 1957, 23–26.

EVANS, R. I. Prejudice: A threat to the leadership role. *Personnel Administration*, 1962, 25(1):17–23.

EVANS, R. I. A psychology professor on the Carson show. *Television Quarterly*, 1967, 6(1):54–59.

EVANS, R. I. Social psychology on television: Experimental programming. *American Psychologist*, 1957, 12(8):531–532.

EVANS, R. I. Stereotypes can cloud human relations. *Hydrocarbon Processing and Petroleum Refiner*, 1961, 40(11):326–329.

EVANS, R. I., and J. D. HILDRETH. Psychologists view a *Candid Camera* seminar. *American Psychologist*, 1964, 19(3):210–211.

EVANS, R. I., and P. K. LEPPMANN. Views from nine universities. In Evans and Leppman, *Resistance to Innovation in Higher Education*. San Francisco: Jossey-Bass, 1968, pp. 124–151.

FARLEY, J. U., and H. J. LEAVITT. Population control and the private sector. *Journal of Social Issues*, 1967, 23(4):135–143.

FEATHER, N. T.   Evaluation of religious and neutral arguments in religious and atheist student groups. *Australian Journal of Psychology*, 1967, 19:3–12.

FLACKS, R.   The liberated generation: an exploration of the roots of student protest. *Journal of Social Issues*, 1967, 23(3):52–75.

FRANK, L. K.   Society as the patient. *American Journal of Sociology*, 1936, 42:335–344.

FRENKEL-BRUNSWICK, E., D. J. LEVINSON, and R. N. SANFORD.   The antidemocratic personality. In Newcomb, T. M., and Hartley, E. L. (Eds.), *Readings in Social Psychology*, New York: Henry Holt & Co., 1947. Pp. 636–646.

FRENKEL-BRUNSWICK, E., D. J. LEVINSON, and R. N. SANFORD.   The authoritarian personality. In Newcomb, T. M., and Hartley, E. L. (Eds.), *Readings in Social Psychology*, New York: Henry Holt & Co., 1947.

FRIED, M., and J. LEVIN.   Some social functions of the urban slum. In Frieden, B. J., and Morris, R. (Eds.), *Urban Planning and Social Policy*. New York: Basic Books, 1968. Pp. 60–83.

GAGNON, J. H., and W. SIMON.   Pornography—raging menace or paper tiger? *Trans-action*, 1967, 4(8):41–47.

GANS, H. J.   Why was Kennedy killed? *Trans-action*, 1968, 5(8):5–6.

GERARD, H. B., and N. MILLER.   Group dynamics. *Annual Review of Psychology*, 1967, 18:287–332.

GLADSTONE, R., and C. G. GUPTA.   A cross-cultural study of the behavioral aspects of religion. *Journal of Social Psychology*, 1963, 60(2):195–201.

GLASSE, R. M., and S. LINDENBAUM.   How New Guinea natives reacted to a total eclipse. *Trans-action*, 1967, 5(2):46–52.

GOFF, R. M.   Psychology and intercultural interaction. *Journal of Social Psychology*, 1962, 58(2):235–240.

GOFFMAN, E.   *Asylums*. Garden City, New York: Doubleday, 1961.

GOFFMAN, E.   Embarrassment and social organization. In Goffman, E. *Interaction Ritual: Essays on Face-to-Face Behavior*. Garden City: Doubleday, 1967. Pp. 97–112.

GOFFMAN, E.   Where the action is. In Goffman, E. *Interaction Ritual: Essays on Face-to-Face Behavior*. Garden City: Doubleday, 1967. Pp. 194–214.

GOLDBERG, P.   Are women prejudiced against women? *Trans-action*, 1968, 5(5):28–30.

GRAVES, T. D.   Acculturation, access, and alcohol in a tri-ethnic community. *American Anthropologist*, 1967, 69(3–4):306–321.

GREENSTEIN, F. I.   The best-known American. *Trans-action*, 1966, 4(1):12–17.

GREENWALD, A. G., and J. S. SAKUMURA.   Attitude and selective learning: Where are the phenomena of yesteryear? *Journal of Personality and Social Psychology*, 1967 7(4):387–397.

GREENWALD, H. J., and D. B. OPPENHEIM.   Reported magnitude of self-misidentification among Negro children: Artifact? *Journal of Personality and Social Psychology*, 1968, 8(1):49–52.

GRUNER, C. R.   Effect of humor on speaker ethos and audience information gain. *Journal of Communication*, 1967, 17(3):228–233.

GULLAHORN, J. T., and J. GULLAHORN.   An extension of the U-curve hypothesis. *Journal of Social Issues*, 1963, 19(3):33–47.

GUSFIELD, J. R.   Moral passage: The symbolic process in public designations of deviance. *Social Problems*, 1967, 15(2):175–188.

GUTTENTAG, M.   The relationship of unemployment to crime and delinquency. *Journal of Social Issues*, 1968, 24(1):105–114.

HADDEN, J. K.   A Protestant paradox—divided they merge. *Trans-action*, 1967, 4(8):63–69.

HAGEN, E. E.   How economic growth begins: A theory of social change. *Journal of Social Issues*, 19(1):20–34.

HARDYCK, J. A., and M. BRADEN.   Prophecy fails again. *Journal of Abnormal and Social Psychology*, 1962, 65:136–141.

HAZARD, W. R.   Anxiety and preference for television fantasy. *Journalism Quarterly*, 1967, 44(3):461–469.

HENRY, W. E.   The business executive: The psychodynamics of a social role. *American Journal of Sociology*, 1949, 54:286–291.

HIMMELSTRAND, U., and F. O. OKEDIJI.   Social structure and motivational tuning in social and economic development. *Journal of Social Issues*, 1968, 24(2):25–41.

HIRSCHMAN, A. O.   Underdevelopment, obstacles to the perception of change, and leadership. *Daedalus*, Summer 1968. Proceedings of the American Academy of Arts and Sciences, 97(3):925–937.

HORTON, J.   Time and the cool people. *Trans-action*, 1967, 4(5):5–12.

HOWARD, J. R.   The making of a Black Muslim. *Trans-action*, 1966, 4(2):15–21.

HUDSON, B. B.   Problems and methods of cross-cultural research. *Journal of Social Issues*, 1959, 15(3):5–19.

HUNT, M. F. JR., and G. R. MILLER.   Open- and closed-mindedness, belief-discrepant communication behavior, and tolerance for cognitive inconsistency. *Journal of Personality and Social Psychology*, 1968, 8(1):35–37.

IACONO, G. An affiliative society facing innovations. *Journal of Social Issues*, 1968, 24(2):125–130.

JACOBSON, H. K. Changing dimensions of the colonial problem. *Journal of Social Issues*, 1967, 23(1):79–88.

JAHODA, G. Traditional healers and other institutes concerned with mental illness in Ghana. *International Journal of Social Psychiatry*, 1961, 7(4):235–268.

JANIS, I. L., and D. KATZ. The reduction of intergroup hostility: Research problems and hypotheses. *Journal of Conflict Resolution*, 1959, 3:85–100.

JOHNSON, N. J., R. WYER, and N. GILBERT. Quality education and integration: An exploratory study. *Phylon*, 1967, 28(3):221–229.

JOSHI, V. Attitude towards reception of technology. *Journal of Social Psychology*, 1962, 58(1):3–7.

JULIAN, J. W., and S. B. KATZ. Internal versus external control and the value of reinforcement. *Journal of Personality and Social Psychology*, 1968, 8(1):89–94.

JUNGHARE, Y. N., and P. ROY. The relation of health-practice innovations to social background characteristics and attitudes. *Rural Sociology*, 1963, 28(4):394–400.

KAHL, J. A. Modern values and fertility ideals in Brazil and Mexico. *Journal of Social Issues*, 1967, 23(4):99–114.

KAHN, M. Students for McCarthy—what unites them. *Trans-action*, 1968, 5(8):30.

KAVANAUGH, J. J. Religious hang-ups. *Psychology Today*, 1967, 1(3):16–23.

KELLEY, H. H., J. C. CONDRY, JR., A. E. DAHLKE, and A. H. HILL. Collective behavior in a simulated panic situation. *Journal of Experimental Social Psychology*, 1965, 1:20–54.

KELLY, G. A. The language of hypothesis: Man's psychological instrument. *Journal of Individual Psychology*, 1964, 20:137–152.

KELLY, G. A. The strategy of psychological research. (Mimeo MS.) Ohio State University, 11–18–64.

KENISTON, K. How Community Mental Health stamped out the riots, 1968–1978. *Trans-action*, 1968, 5(8):20–29.

KIESLER, C. A. Conformity and commitment. *Trans-action*, 1967, 4(7):32–35.

KILLIAN, L. M. The significance of multiple-group membership in disaster. *American Journal of Sociology*, 1952, 57:309–314.

KING, M. L., JR.   The role of the behavioral scientist in the civil rights movement. *Journal of Social Issues*, 1968, 24(1):1–12.

KIRAY, M. B.   Values, social stratification and development. *Journal of Social Issues*, 1968, 24(2):87–100.

KLOSS, H.   Bilingualism and nationalism. *Journal of Social Issues*, 1967, 23(2):39–47.

KNOFF, W. F.   Role: A concept linking society and personality. *American Journal of Psychiatry*, 1961, 117:1010–1015.

KNOX, R. E., and J. A. INKSTER.   Postdecision dissonance at post time. *Journal of Personality and Social Psychology*, 1968, 8(4): 319–323.

KOGAN, L. A.   The Jewish conception of Negroes in the North: An historical approach. *Phylon*, 1967, 28(4):376–386.

KUNKEL, J. H.   Psychological factors in the analysis of economic development. *Journal of Social Issues*, 1963, 19(1):68–87.

LACHMAN, R., M. TATSUOKA, and W. J. BONK.   Human behavior during the tsunami of May, 1960. *Science*, 1961, 133:1405–1409.

LADNER, J.   What "black power" means to Negroes in Mississippi. *Trans-action*, 1967, 5(1):7–15.

LAMBERT, W. E.   A social psychology of bilingualism. *Journal of Social Issues*, 1967, 23(2):91–109.

LAMMERS, C. J.   Stratification in a small group. *Human Relations*, 1967, 20(3):283–299.

LEVENTHAL, H., and P. NILES.   A field experiment on fear arousal with data on the validity of questionnaire measures. *Journal of Personality*, 1964, 32:459–479.

LEVENTHAL, H., and J. C. WATTS.   Sources of resistance to fear-arousing communications. *Journal of Personality*, 1966, 34:155–175.

LINCOLN, C. E.   Extremist attitudes in the Black Muslim movement. *Journal of Social Issues*, 1963, 19(2):75–85.

LOPATA, H. Z., and J. R. NOEL.   The dance studio—style without sex. *Trans-action*, 1967, 4(3):10–17.

LYMAN, S. M., and M. B. SCOTT.   Territoriality: A neglected sociological dimension. *Social Problems*, 1967, 15(2):236–249.

MACLEOD, R. B.   The Arab Middle East: Some social psychological problems. *Journal of Social Issues*, 1959, 15(3):69–75.

MARRIS, P.   Individual achievement and family ties: Some international comparisons. *Journal of Marriage and Family*, 1967, 29(4):763–771.

MARTIN, W. C.   Shepherds vs. flocks: Ministers and Negro militancy. *Atlantic Monthly*, 1967, 220(6):53–59.

MARTINEZ, T. M. Why employment agency counselors lower their clients' self-esteem. *Trans-action*, 1968, 5(4):20–25.

MARX, G. T. The white Negro and the Negro white. *Phylon*, 1967, 28(2):168–177.

McCOMBS, M. Editorial endorsements: A study of influence. *Journalism Quarterly*, 1967, 44(3):545–548.

McGREW, J. M. How "open" are multiple-dwelling units? *Journal of Social Psychology*, 1967, 72:223–226.

McGUCKIN, H. E., JR. The persuasive force of similarity in cognitive style between advocate and audience. *Speech Monograph*, 1967, 34(2):145–151.

McNAMARA, J. The bilingual's linguistic performance—a psychological overview. *Journal of Social Issues*, 1967, 23(2):58–77.

McQUEEN, A. J. Education and marginality of African youth. *Journal of Social Issues*, 1968, 24(2):179–194.

McWHORTER, G. A., and R. L. CRAIN. Subcommunity gladiatorial competition: Civil rights leadership as a competitive process. *Social Forces*, 1967, 46(1):8–21.

MENZEL, H., and E. KATZ. Social relations and innovation in the medical profession: The epidemiology of a new drug. *Public Opinion Quarterly*, 1955–56, 19:337–352.

MILLER, G. A. Some psychological perspectives on the year 2000. *Daedalus*, Summer 1967. Proceedings of the American Academy of Arts and Sciences, 96(3):883–896.

NAESS, A. A systematization of Gandhian ethics of conflict resolution. *Journal of Conflict Resolution*, 1958, 2:140–155.

NELSON, H. A. The Defenders: A case study of an informal police organization. *Social Problems*, 1967, 15(2):127–147.

NORBECK, E. The interpretation of data: Puberty rites. *American Anthropologist*, 1962, 64:463–485.

PAN LU, L., H. C. CHEN, and L. P. CHOW. An experimental study of the effect of group meetings on the acceptance of family planning in Taiwan. *Journal of Social Issues*, 1967, 23(4):171–177.

PAREEK, U. A motivational paradigm of development. *Journal of Social Issues*, 1968, 24(2):115–122.

PARMENTER, T. Breakdown of law and order. *Trans-action*, 1967, 4(9):13–22.

PELTO, P. J. The differences between "tight" and "loose" societies. *Trans-action*, 1968, 5(5):37–40.

PETTIGREW, T. F. Complexity and change in American racial patterns: a social psychological view. *Daedalus*, Fall 1965. Proceedings of the American Academy of Arts and Sciences, 94(4):974–1008.

PETTIGREW, T. F.　Social psychology and desegregation research. *American Psychologist*, 1961, 16:105–112.

PHOLMAN, E.　A psychologist's introduction to the birth planning literature. *Journal of Social Issues*, 1967, 23(4):13–27.

PIERCE-JONES, J., J. B. REID, and F. J. KING.　Adolescent racial and ethnic group differences in social attitudes and adjustment. *Psychological Reports*, 1959, 5(3):549–552.

PILISUK, M., and P. SKOLNICK.　Inducing trust: A test of the Osgood proposal. *Journal of Personality and Social Psychology*, 1968, 8(2):121–133.

PINARD, M.　Poverty and political movements. *Social Problems*, 1967, 15(2):251–263.

PLATH, D. W.　A case of ostracism—and its unusual aftermath. *Trans-action*, 1968, 5(3):31–36.

POLSKY, N.　Poolrooms: End of the male sanctuary. *Trans-action*, 1967, 4(4):32–40.

QUARTON, G. C.　Deliberate efforts to control human behavior and modify personality. *Daedalus*, Summer 1967. Proceedings of the American Academy of Arts and Sciences, 96(3):837–853.

RAINWATER, L.　Fear and the house-as-haven in the lower class. In Frieden, B. J., and R. Morris, (Eds.), *Urban Planning and Social Policy*. New York: Basic Books, 1968. Pp. 84–95.

RAINWATER, L.　Open letter on white justice and the riots. *Trans-action*, 1967, 4(9):22–23.

RAMIREZ, M.　Identification with Mexican family values and authoritarianism in Mexican-Americans. *Journal of Social Psychology*, 1967, 73(1):3–11.

REISS, A. J., JR.　Police brutality—answers to key questions. *Trans-action*, 1968, 5(8):10–19.

REISS, I. L.　How and why America's sex standards are changing. *Trans-action*, 1968, 5(4):26–32.

RETTING, S. and P. N. SINGH.　The risk hypothesis in judgments of unethical behavior: A cross-cultural replication. *Manas*, 1962, 9:3–23.

ROHTER, I. S.　The righteous rightists. *Trans-action*, 1967, 4(6):27–35.

ROKEACH, M.　The problem of identity. In Rokeach, M. *The Three Christs of Ypsilanti: A Psychological Study*. New York: Alfred A. Knopf, 1964. Pp. 19–36.

ROKEACH, M.　A theory of organization and change within value-attitude systems. *Journal of Social Issues*, 1968, 24(1):13–33.

ROSEN, B. C.   Socialization and achievement motivation in Brazil. *American Sociological Review*, 1962, 27(5):612–624.

ROSENBLATT, A.   Negroes in baseball: The failure of success. *Transaction*, 1967, 4(9):51–53.

ROSENBLATT, P. C.   Functions of games: An examination of individual difference hypotheses derived from a cross-cultural study. *Journal of Social Psychology*, 1962, 58(1):17–22.

ROSENBLATT, P. C.   Marital residence and the functions of romantic love. *Ethnology*, 1967, 6(4):471–480.

ROSENTHAL, B. G., D. MILLER, and F. TERYENYI.   The measurement of social interaction among Negro and white children in a housing community. *Journal of Social Psychology*, 1967, 71:27–37.

ROSENTHAL, R.   *Pygmalion in the Classroom.* New York: Holt, Rinehart and Winston, 1968.

ROSENTHAL, R., and L. JACOBSON.   Teachers' expectancies: Determinants of pupils' IQ gains. *Psychological Reports*, 1966, 19:115–118.

RUESCH, J.   Technological civilization and human affairs. *Journal of Nervous and Mental Disease*, 1967, 145(3):193–205.

SAENGER, G.   Changing prejudice through contact. In Saenger, G. *The Social Psychology of Prejudice.* New York: Harper and Row, 1953. Pp. 213–231.

SAMPSON, E. E.   Student activism and the decade of protest. *Journal of Social Issues*, 1967, 23(3):1–33.

SANFORD, N.   Institutionally induced personality change: A case study. In Sanford, N., *Self and Society: Social Change and Individual Development.* New York: Atherton Press, 1966. Pp. 52–69.

SANFORD, N.   The study of human problems. In Sanford, N., *Self and Society: Social Change and Individual Development.* New York: Atherton Press, 1966. Pp. 3–22.

SCHAAR, J. H.   Can society be sick? In Schaar, J. H., *Escape from Authority: The Perspectives of Erich Fromm.* New York: Harper and Row, 1961. Pp. 159–168.

SCHMUCK, R., and M. CHESLER.   On super-patriotism: A definition and analysis. *Journal of Social Issues*, 1963, 19(2):31–50.

SCHWARZWELLER, H. K., and J. F. SEGGAR.   Kinship involvement: A factor in the adjustment of rural migrants. *Journal of Marriage and Family*, 1967, 29(4):662–671.

Sechrest, L., and Wallace, J., *Psychology and Human Problems.*
SECHREST, L., and J. WALLACE.   Ecological factors in adjustment. In Columbus, Ohio: Charles E. Merrill, 1967. Pp. 480–535.

SEGALMAN, R.   The Protestant ethic and social welfare. *Journal of Social Issues*, 1968, 24(1):125–141.

SHERIF, M.   Superordinate goals in the reduction of intergroup conflicts. *American Journal of Sociology*, 1958, 63:349–356.

SHERIF, M., O. J. HARVEY, J. B. WHITE, N. R. HOOD, and C. W. SHERIF.   Main conclusions. In Sherif, et al, *Intergroup Conflict and Cooperation: The Robbers' Cave Experiment*. Norman: University of Oklahoma, Institute of Group Relations, 1961. Pp. 205–212.

SHERIF, M. and W. SHERIF.   *Explorations into Conformity and Deviation of Adolescents*. New York: Harper and Row, 1964.

SIEGMAN, A. W.   A cross-cultural investigation of the relationship between ethnic prejudice, authoritarian ideology, and personality. *Journal of Social Psychology*, 1961, 63(3):654–655.

SIEGMAN, A. W.   A cross-cultural investigation of the relationship between introversion, extraversion, social attitudes, and antisocial behavior. *British Journal of Social and Clinical Psychology*, 1963, 2:196–208.

SILBERMAN, C. E.   Up from apathy: The Woodlawn experiment. In Frieden, B. J., and Morris, R. (Eds.), *Urban Planning and Social Policy*. New York: Basic Books, 1968. Pp. 183–197.

SIMMON, G., and G. TROUT.   Hippies in college—from teeny-boppers to drug freaks. *Trans-action*, 1967, 5(2):27–30, 32.

SIMON, W., and J. H. GAGNON.   Femininity in the lesbian community. *Social Problems*, 1967, 15(2):212–221.

SINGER, D.   Reading, writing, and race relations. Trans-action, 1967, 4(7):27–31.

SKEDGELL, R. A.   How computers pick an election winner. *Transaction*, 1966, 4(1):42–46.

SMITH, M. B.   A map for the analysis of personality and politics. *Journal of Social Issues*, 1968, 24(3):15–28.

SMITH, M. B.   The personal setting of public opinions: A study of attitudes toward Russia. *Public Opinion Quarterly*, 1947, 11:507–523.

STARK, R., and C. Y. GLOCK.   Will ethics be the death of Christianity? *Trans-action*, 1968, 5(7):7–14.

STEFFLRE, V.   The reflection of similarity judgments in language and behavior. *Psychonomic Bulletin*, 1967, 1(2):18.

STENDAHL, K.   Religion, mysticism, and the institutional church. *Daedalus*, Summer 1967. Proceedings of the American Academy of Arts and Sciences, 96(3):854–859.

STOODLEY, B. H.   Normative family orientations of Chinese college students in Hong Kong. *Journal of Marriage and Family*, 1967, 29(4):773–782.

SUDNOW, D. Dead on arrival. *Trans-action*, 1967, 5(1):36–43.

SZASZ, T. The psychiatrist as double agent. *Trans-action*, 1967, 4(10):16–24.

TAFT, R. Adjustment and assimilation of immigrants: A problem in social psychology. *Psychological Reports*, 1962, 10(1):90.

TAGIURI, R., J. S. BRUNER, and R. R. BLAKE. On the relation between feelings and perception of feelings among members of small groups. In Maccoby, E. E., Newcomb, T. M., and Hartley, E. L. (Eds.), *Readings in Social Psychology*. New York: Henry Holt, 1958. Pp. 110–116.

THUNE, J. M. Racial attitudes of older adults. *Gerontologist*, 1967, 7(3):172–182.

VALLIER, I. Challenge to Catholicism in Latin America. *Trans-action*, 1967, 4(7):17–26, 60.

VROOM, V. H. Projection, negation, and the self-concept. *Human Relations*, 1959, 12:335–344.

WALTERS, P. A., JR. Student apathy. In Blaine, G. B., Jr., and McArthur, C. C. (Eds.), *Emotional Problems of the Student*. Garden City: Anchor Books, 1966. Pp. 170–191.

WATSON, J. S. Why is a smile? *Trans-action*, 1967, 4(6):36–39.

WEYRAUCH, W. O. Law in isolation—the penthouse astronauts. *Trans-action*, 1968, 5(7):39–46.

WHITING, J. W. M. Sorcery, sin, and the superego: A cross-cultural study of some mechanisms of social control. In Whiting, J. W. M., and Jones, M. R. (Eds.), *Nebraska Symposium on Motivation*. Lincoln: University of Nebraska Press, 1959. Pp. 174–195.

WILDAVSKY, A. The empty-head blues: Black rebellion and white reaction. *Public Interest*, 1968, 11:3–16.

WILLEMS, E. P. An ecological orientation in psychology. *Merrill-Palmer Quarterly of Behavior and Development*, 1965, 11(4): 317–343.

WILLEMS, E. P. Toward an explicit rationale for naturalistic research methods. (Mimeo MS.) Rice University, 1966.

WILLIAMS, W. Cleveland's crisis ghetto. *Trans-action*, 1967, 4(9): 33–42.

WOLF, E. P., and C. N. LEBEAUX. On the destruction of poor neighborhoods by urban renewal. *Social Problems*, 1967, 15(1):3–8.

YOSHIDA, M., M. MORIYAMA, and C. TAMAI. Structure of authority in the Japanese mind. *Japanese Journal of Psychology*, 1962, 32:353–366.

APPENDIX II

RECOMMENDED REFERENCES DEALING WITH
RESEARCH METHODOLOGY RELATING TO SOCIAL
PSYCHOLOGICAL ANALYSES OF PROBLEMS IN
REAL-LIFE SETTINGS

BARKER, R. G.   On the nature of the environment. *Journal of Social Issues*, 1963, 19(4):17–38.

CAMPBELL, D. T., and J. C. STANLEY.   *Experimental and Quasi-Experimental Designs for Research*. Chicago: Rand McNally, 1963.

KATZ, D., and L. FESTINGER.   *Research Methods in the Behavioral Sciences*. New York: Dryden Press, 1953.

LAZARSFELD, P. F., and M. ROSENBERG.   *The Language of Social Research*. New York: The Free Press, 1955.

SCOTT, W. A., and M. WERTHEIMER.   *Introduction to Psychological Research*. New York: John Wiley and Sons, 1962.

SELLTIG, C., M. JAHODA, M. DEUTSCH, and S. W. COOK.   *Research Methods in Social Relations* (rev. ed.). New York: Holt, Rinehart and Winston, 1961.

SHERIF, M. (Ed.)   *Problems of Interdisciplinary Relationships in the Social Sciences*. Chicago: Aldine, 1968.

WEBB, E. J., D. T. CAMPBELL, R. D. SCHWARTZ, and L. SECHREST.   *Unobtrusive Measures: Nonreactive Research in the Social Sciences*. Chicago: Rand McNally, 1966.

28639

Evans, Richard I
AUTHOR

Social psychology in life
TITLE